"*During the dark, early months of WWII, it was only the tiny American force that held off the Japanese Empire and enabled our fleets to replace their losses and repair their wounds. The spirit and courage of the Submarine Force shall never be forgotten.*" —Admiral Chester W. Nimitz, Commander-in-Chief, U.S. Navy Pacific Fleet

"Brings the drama and heroism to the reader's doorstep . . . Only submariners understood the fear, hardships, and rewards of serving in such a specialized branch of the wartime Navy. Whitlock's powerful book ensures that readers will now comprehend some of that."

—John Wukovits, author of *One Square Mile of Hell*

"A lively account of wartime U.S. Pacific submarines that expresses the claustrophobia of fighting boats undergoing depth charges and the other dangers of the deep in the war against Japanese shipping. The highlights of heroic war patrols are interwoven with personal submariners' stories, particularly Ron Smith's progress through boot camp, torpedo school, and sub school, climaxing with exciting war patrols aboard the fleet boat USS *Seal*. All in all, a rousing good read." —William Tuohy, author of *The Bravest Man*

"A tale of incomparable courage. The depth of [the authors'] scholarly research is evident in the fast-paced narrative, relating vignettes of the mundane, the heroic, and the harrowing in the U.S. Navy of World War II. Together, these outstanding authors have provided an eloquent voice to the 'Silent Service.'" —Michael E. Haskew, editor, *WW II History* magazine

"An authoritative and adventurous account of the submarines and submariners of the Pacific War. It will inform a new generation of both victors and vanquished of the courage and bravery of these singular seamen. But, it is also a very human story that makes for compelling reading."

—Dirk A. Ballendorf, Professor of History and Micronesian Studies, University of Guam

THE
Depths of Courage

AMERICAN SUBMARINERS AT WAR
WITH JAPAN, 1941–1945

Flint Whitlock and Ron Smith

Foreword by Vice Admiral Albert Konetzni (USN, Ret.)

BERKLEY CALIBER, NEW YORK

THE BERKLEY PUBLISHING GROUP
Published by the Penguin Group
Penguin Group (USA) Inc.
375 Hudson Street, New York, New York 10014, USA
Penguin Group (Canada), 90 Eglinton Avenue East, Suite 700, Toronto, Ontario M4P 2Y3, Canada
(a division of Pearson Penguin Canada Inc.)
Penguin Books Ltd., 80 Strand, London WC2R, 0RL, England
Penguin Group Ireland, 25 St. Stephen's Green, Dublin 2, Ireland (a division of Penguin Books Ltd.)
Penguin Group (Australia), 250 Camberwell Road, Camberwell, Victoria 3124, Australia
(a division of Pearson Australia Group Pty. Ltd.)
Penguin Books India Pvt. Ltd., 11 Community Centre, Panchsheel Park, New Delhi—110 017, India
Penguin Group (NZ), 67 Apollo Drive, Rosedale, North Shore 0632, New Zealand (a division of
Pearson New Zealand Ltd.)
Penguin Books (South Africa) (Pty.) Ltd., 24 Sturdee Avenue, Rosebank, Johannesburg 2196,
South Africa

Penguin Books Ltd., Registered Offices: 80 Strand, London WC2R 0RL, England

The publisher does not have any control over and does not assume any responsibility for author or
third-party websites or their content.

PRINTING HISTORY
Berkley Caliber hardcover edition / November 2007
Berkley Caliber trade paperback edition / November 2008

Berkley Caliber trade paperback ISBN: 978-0-425-22370-3

The Library of Congress has catalogued the Berkley Caliber hardcover edition as follows:

Whitlock, Flint.
    The depths of courage: American submariners at war with Japan, 1941–1945 / Flint Whitlock and
Ron Smith.
        p. cm.
    Includes bibliographical references and index.
    ISBN 978-0-425-21743-6
    1. United States. Navy—Submarine forces—History—World War, 1939–1945. 2. World War,
1939–1945—Naval operations, American. 3. World War, 1939–1945—Naval operations—
Submarine. 4. World War, 1939–1945—Campaigns—Pacific Area. I. Smith, Ron. II. Title.

    D783.W45 2007
    940.54'510973—dc22

                                                                                2006100881

PRINTED IN THE UNITED STATES OF AMERICA

10 9 8 7 6 5 4 3 2

THE NAVY HYMN

Eternal Father, strong to save,
Whose arm hath bound the restless wave,
Who bidd'st the mighty ocean deep
Its own appointed limits keep;
Oh, hear us when we cry to Thee,
For those in peril on the sea!

Oh Father, King of earth and sea,
We dedicate this ship to thee.
In faith we send her on her way;
In faith to Thee we humbly pray:
Oh, hear from heaven our sailor's cry
And watch and guard her from on high!

During the dark, early months of World War II, it was only the tiny American submarine force that held off the Japanese Empire and enabled our fleets to replace their losses and repair their wounds. The spirit and courage of the Submarine Force shall never be forgotten.

—Admiral Chester W. Nimitz
Commander in Chief, Pacific

This book is respectfully dedicated to the memory of the 3,453 men of the United States Navy Submarine Force who lost their lives during World War II and to the fifty-two American submarines that failed to return:

U.S.S. *Albacore* (SS–219)	85 men lost
U.S.S. *Amberjack* (SS-219)	73 men lost
U.S.S. *Argonaut* (SS-166)	105 men lost
U.S.S. *Barbel* (SS-316)	81 men lost
U.S.S. *Bonefish* (SS-223)	85 men lost
U.S.S. *Bullhead* (SS-332)	84 men lost
U.S.S. *Capelin* (SS-289)	76 men lost
U.S.S. *Cisco* (SS-290)	76 men lost
U.S.S. *Corvina* (SS-226)	82 men lost
U.S.S. *Darter* (SS-227)	0 men lost
U.S.S. *Dorado* (SS-248)	77 men lost
U.S.S. *Escolar* (SS-294)	82 men lost
U.S.S. *Flier* (SS-250)	78 men lost
U.S.S. *Golet* (SS-361)	82 men lost
U.S.S. *Grampus* (SS-207)	71 men lost
U.S.S. *Grayback* (SS-208)	80 men lost
U.S.S. *Grayling* (SS-209)	75 men lost
U.S.S. *Grenadier* (SS-210)	0 men lost (4 died in POW camp)
U.S.S. *Growler* (SS-215)	86 men lost
U.S.S. *Grunion* (SS-216)	70 men lost
U.S.S. *Gudgeon* (SS-211)	78 men lost
U.S.S. *Harder* (SS-257)	78 men lost
U.S.S. *Herring* (SS-233)	83 men lost
U.S.S. *Kete* (SS-369)	87 men lost
U.S.S. *Lagarto* (SS-371)	88 men lost
U.S.S. *Perch* (SS-176)	0 men lost (6 died in POW camp)

U.S.S. *Pickerel* (SS-177)	74 men lost
U.S.S. *Pompano* (SS-181)	77 men lost
U.S.S. *Robalo* (SS-273)	81 men lost
U.S.S. *Runner* (SS-275)	78 men lost
U.S.S. *Scamp* (SS-277)	83 men lost
U.S.S. *Scorpion* (SS-278)	77 men lost
U.S.S. *Sculpin* (SS-191)	62 men lost
U.S.S. *Sealion* (SS-195)	5 men lost
U.S.S. *Seawolf* (SS-197)	79 men lost
U.S.S. *Shark I* (SS-174)	59 men lost
U.S.S. *Shark II* (SS-314)	87 men lost
U.S.S. *Snook* (SS-279)	82 men lost
U.S.S. *Swordfish* (SS-193)	89 men lost
U.S.S. *Tang* (SS-306)	78 men lost
U.S.S. *Trigger* (SS-237)	89 men lost
U.S.S. *Triton* (SS-201)	74 men lost
U.S.S. *Trout* (SS-202)	81 men lost
U.S.S. *Tullibee* (SS-284)	80 men lost
U.S.S. *Wahoo* (SS-238)	79 men lost
U.S.S. *R-12* (SS-89)	46 men lost
U.S.S. *S-26* (SS-131)	26 men lost
U.S.S. *S-27* (SS-132)	0 men lost
U.S.S. *S-28* (SS-133)	49 men lost
U.S.S. *S-36* (SS-141)	0 men lost
U.S.S. *S-39* (SS-144)	0 men lost
U.S.S. *S-44* (SS-155)	56 men lost

CONTENTS

FOREWORD

THEY were iron men who took iron ships to sea and left an unparalleled record of courage and duty, faithfully performed. Less than 2 percent of U.S. sailors served in submarines, yet submarines would sink 55 percent of all Japanese ships lost in World War II—more than the U.S. Navy's surface ships, its carrier planes, and the Army's Air Force combined! Yet, for its many vital achievements, the submarine force paid a terrible price in the war. Fifty-two boats and more than 3,400 submariners—one out of every five—failed to return.

I've had the great fortune over the years to serve as a career submariner. During and after my thirty-eight years of service, I've had, and continue to have, the distinct privilege of knowing these iron men, these submarine veterans of World War II.

Vice Admiral Charles "Uncle Charlie" Lockwood, a commander of the U.S. Submarine Force during the war in the Pacific—an assignment I had some fifty years later—wrote of these men with which he served, "They were no supermen, nor were they endowed with any supernatural qualities of heroism. They were merely top-notch American lads, well trained, well treated, well armed, and provided with superb ships."

The submarine veterans of World War II have provided their successors in the submarine force powerful traditions that continue to serve the submarine force well.

First of these is the tradition that demands "forceful backup" of each crew member—a tradition that makes it known that each and every crew member regardless of seniority is critical to the safe operation of the ship.

Second is the tradition that submariners take care of one another. Life in submarines is one without physical or psychological privacy. Our veterans have instilled in us all a realization that this lack of privacy demands complete mutual respect of others. These veterans taught us the true meaning of *mentoring* before it became an overly used word in leadership and management books.

Finally, these veterans provided the catalyst for "continuous improvement" of the submarine force. During the war, they solved major problems in tactics, weaponry, and selection of leaders at all levels. It was this "continuous improvement" that resulted in major post-world-war developments in the use of passive sonar ranging, nuclear energy, and cold-war tactics against the Soviet Union.

Sadly, today our nation faces many of the same problems our submarine force faced prior to and early in World War II. Tragically, we Americans don't understand history. The strong traditions our veterans provided us have made our submarines a dominant force for national defense. Our ability to take the fight to potential enemies and stay for months without resupply are strong arguments for a robust submarine force. The missions that our submarines carry out in peacetime, the onset of conflict, and during hot war are not transferable to other forces.

With this said, our nation has built less than a submarine a year over the last decade and a half. Fourteen different studies have recommended a force level of at least fifty-five submarines, yet we are cascading to a force of thirty ships. Meanwhile, a potential competitor, China, states, "After the First World War, the dominant vessel was the battleship. In the Second World War, it was the aircraft carrier. If another global war breaks out, the most powerful weapon will be the submarine." China will have commissioned at least sixteen new attack submarines in the last two years.

"Uncle Charlie" Lockwood of World War II said, "May God grant there will be no World War III; but, if there is, whether it be fought with the weapons we know or with weapons at whose type we can only guess, submarines and submariners will be in the thick of the combat, fighting with skill, determination, and matchless daring for all of us and for our United States of America."

Americans must learn from history! *The Depths of Courage* is a history book that comes to life as it intertwines the individual stories of young Americans with the phenomenal history of our submarines in World War II. Most of the men mentioned in the text are long gone—on "Eternal Patrol." Many of those who survived the war are now deceased and resting in "Safe Harbor."

With the above said, *The Depths of Courage* has had a profound effect on me. It pushed me to rededicate myself to ensuring that our great nation understands that today we are rapidly moving toward an inadequate submarine force, a force that only meets 60 percent of global missions, a force so small that within ten years, we will not have the ability to design and build submarines properly because we are allowing critical skills and knowledge to atrophy under an anemic build rate.

May you enjoy this true adventure book! I pray that when you complete it, you will feel as I do that we as a nation need to rededicate our efforts to maintain an adequately sized submarine force. Our World War II submarine veterans deserve no less.

God Bless and Keep Charging!

—Al Konetzni, Vice Admiral, U.S. Navy (Ret.)
Commander Submarine Force, U.S. Pacific Fleet (1998–2001)

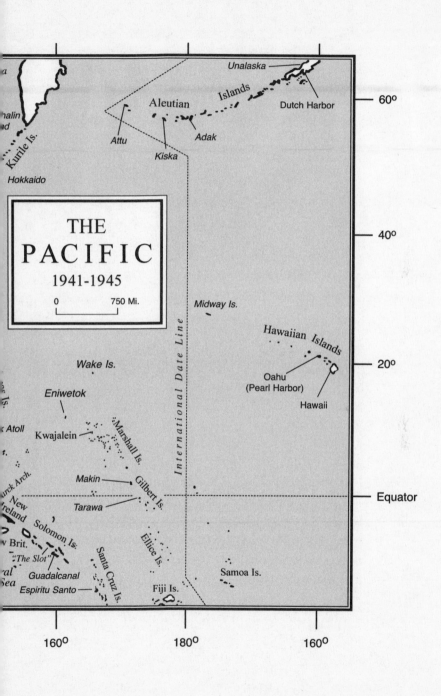

THE
PACIFIC
1941-1945

0   750 Mi.

Unalaska

Aleutian   Islands
Dutch Harbor

60°

Attu   Adak

Kiska

Kurile Is.

Hokkaido

40°

International Date Line

Midway Is.

Hawaiian   Islands

20°

Oahu
(Pearl Harbor)

Hawaii

Wake Is.

Eniwetok

Kwajalein   Marshall Is.

Atoll

Makin   Gilbert Is.

Tarawa

Equator

New
Ireland   Solomon Is.

Brit.

Ellice Is.

"The Slot"

Guadalcanal   Santa Cruz Is.

Espiritu Santo   Fiji Is.

Samoa Is.

Sea

160°   180°   160°

INTRODUCTION

WRITERS of fairy tales begin their fantasies with "Once upon a time . . ." Tellers of sea stories begin, "This is no bullshit."

This is a book by and about a special breed of World War II sailors known as submariners. The stories woven throughout the book may seem far-fetched, startling, amazing, funny, gruesome, tragic—even fantastic— yet all are true. "This is no bullshit," as the sailors would say.

With the resurgence of interest in World War II, new generations are discovering what it took for the United States and its allies to be victorious in history's most devastating conflict. Victory required incredible amounts of money, manpower, industrial might, visionary leadership, sacrifice of the highest order, a tremendous national will to win, and a fathomless depth of personal courage to ultimately triumph over the Axis powers—Japan, Germany, and Italy.

There was no "safe" or "easy" branch of service, no place for cowards to hide. Each branch had its own special dangers, governed by the luck of the draw. A soldier, sailor, Marine, or airman was just as likely to be killed in his first engagement with the enemy as in his last. A Marine or infantryman in a foxhole faced no more or fewer hazards than a crewman on a bomber or a battleship. The truck driver hauling supplies to the front line was no more immune from enemy fire than was a doctor or nurse working to save a wounded patient in an emergency operating ward within range of German or Japanese artillery.

Of all the American fighting men of World War II, though, perhaps none stood less of a chance of returning home alive than the submariners, for the U.S. Navy's Submarine Force suffered an inordinately high killed-in-action rate.

And no other branch of service required a higher level of intelligence and fortitude (not to mention the ability to overcome the fear of being in a small, suffocatingly hot enclosed space deep underwater) than the U.S. Navy's Submarine Force.

As an experiment, to appreciate what conditions in a submarine undergoing a depth charging might have been like, have a friend seal you inside a large metal diesel-fuel drum—with most of the fuel, but not the smell, removed; place it on a barbecue grill to simulate the heat generated inside, beat on the sides of the drum with a baseball bat for a few hours to simulate a depth-charge attack, rock the drum back and forth until motion sickness sets in, and then roll the drum into a swimming pool and wait until it sinks to the bottom. We guarantee that you will have a greater respect for the life of the submariner.

The Submarine Force, in the authors' opinion, has received less attention and praise for its contributions to victory than it deserves. The reasons for this oversight are unclear, but it is *not* because the submarines' contributions to victory were insignificant. Quite the opposite, as the following startling submarine facts and figures will demonstrate:

At the beginning of World War II, the United States had only 111 submarines in commission, with another 73 in one stage of construction or another; 51 of those new submarines were either already on, or available for, duty in the Pacific. By the end of the war, the United States would have a total of only 252 submarines—far fewer than the more than 1,100 deployed by Germany and the more than 600 built by Japan. Yet, what submarines they were! The "Fleet" submarines that came into service in 1943 were the most sophisticated and complex war machines of their day. Each multimillion-dollar submarine was manned by the equivalent of less than half an infantry rifle company and was commanded by the Navy's equivalent of an Army major or lieutenant colonel. Yet each submarine could carry some twelve tons of explosive warheads—ten tons more than the bomb load of a typical B-24 "heavy" bomber. The submarines had tremendous range—approximately 10,000 miles—and could stay on patrol for forty-five to sixty days.

Submarines carried out a wide variety of tasks—everything from their primary mission of sinking enemy ships to performing reconnaissance missions, delivering commandos onto enemy-held islands, rescuing downed Allied fliers, even saving the Philippines gold treasury!

By the end of the war, it is estimated that 54.6 percent of the total number of Japanese naval and merchant ships lost were sunk by submarines. This loss rate crippled Japan's ability to resupply and reinforce her outlying garrisons, and led to the steady march of the Americans toward the Home Islands and Japan's ultimate downfall.

As the smallest segment of the Navy's fleet, the Submarine Force nevertheless suffered the highest percentage of casualties; it is estimated that over 3,400 men, or 22 percent of the force, died while on war patrols. And unlike the Army, Air Corps, Marines, and surface Navy, there were very few wounded or captured submariners who lived to tell their sea stories.

As interesting and revealing as these statistics are, however, this book is not about numbers. It is about the steadfast courage of the men who volunteered—and the submariners were all volunteers—to go down to the sea in these most hazardous of vessels. It is about a branch of service, ineffective at first, which overcame tremendous obstacles to carry out its mission.

Most of all, it is an unabashed, heartfelt, loving tribute to the selfless devotion of those 3,400 submariners who set out on their war patrols and never returned to receive the thanks of a grateful, victorious nation or enjoy the blessings of postwar peace and liberty.

WITH the clarity of hindsight born of six decades, the victory over Japan may seem today as inevitable. It was not so then, when the Japanese were regarded by many as unbeatable. The ultimate American triumph would not come swiftly, nor be purchased cheaply or without considerable heartache.

During the early months of the conflict, the American Submarine Force was virtually the only branch of service capable of taking the war to the Japanese enemy. The submarines and their brave, outnumbered crews were a thin gray line that stood between hope and disaster. Most importantly, the submarines bought time for America to rebuild, rearm, and recruit the massive numbers of men who eventually reclaimed the Pacific.

Yet the Submarine Force faced enormous problems of its own—obsolescent equipment, a lack of radar, overly cautious skippers, an incoherent tactical and strategic doctrine, and perhaps worst of all: unreliable weapons.

Several years would elapse before American submarines would be able to overcome the myriad obstacles placed in their path. This is the story of that struggle—and the heroic, persistent efforts of America's smallest fighting force to sweep the sea clean of Japanese shipping and bring about the inevitable triumph.

—Flint Whitlock and Ron Smith

CHAPTER 1

BLACK SUNDAY

IT was, by almost every measure, the worst of times.

As the Mitsubishi A6M "Zero" fighters and Nakajima B3N "Kate" torpedo bombers and Aichi D3A "Val" dive-bombers of Vice Admiral Chuichi Nagumo's task force banked triumphantly away from the flaming, smoking, exploding wreckage that was once the United States Navy's Pacific Fleet at Pearl Harbor, Hawaii, and headed back to their carriers, the casual observer could be forgiven for assuming that America had lost the war before war could even be officially declared.

All the evidence graphically spoke of a devastating, humiliating defeat for the United States. There, in the shallow blue Hawaiian waters that were turning black with spilled fuel oil and red with the blood of dead and dying sailors, one of the world's mightiest naval armadas lay crippled.

Back on the mainland on that seventh day of December 1941, Americans were just receiving the first incomplete, mind-numbing, gut-wrenching reports of the disaster in Hawaii. The first distress signal had already gone out even while the bombs were falling: AIR RAID ON PEARL HARBOR X THIS IS NOT DRILL.*

Although the full extent of disaster was still undisclosed, one thing was unmistakable: the Pacific Fleet, commanded by Admiral Husband

---

* The original wording. Whether the sender meant to say "This is not a drill" or "This is no drill" remains unknown. The meaning, however, is abundantly clear. (Camp, 7)

E. Kimmel, had suffered a terrific blow, like a heavyweight fighter who had just been sucker-punched and was lying flat on his back.

Within thirty minutes of the start of the attack, all eight American battleships moored tightly along the east side of Ford Island in the center of Pearl Harbor had either been sunk or severely damaged, along with three light cruisers and three destroyers. Dozens of other craft were also sunk or damaged.[1]

On that fateful day, Bill Trimmer, who had joined the Navy from Pine Top, Virginia, in August 1940 and would later serve in the submarines *S-37* and *Redfish* (SS-395), was a twenty-three-year-old electrician third class aboard the battleship *Pennsylvania*. He recalled that *Pennsylvania*, lying in dry dock south of Ford Island for overhaul, had been drawing its electrical power from shore. At about 0750 hours on the morning of 7 December, he went below to the electrical shop on the third deck for muster at his duty station.

"I had just gotten in the shop," he said, "when the PA system came on sounding 'General quarters, air defense, and this is no drill!' A lot of background noise of planes roaring and bombs exploding could be heard."

Trimmer took off running for his battle station on the fifth deck in the forward distribution room, where he donned headphones that connected him to the battleship's various electrical departments.

About ten minutes into the attack, as he recalled, "a bomb blew our power lines in two. All the lights went out and all the machinery stopped running. It was pitch-dark until we turned on our battle lanterns—large, battery-powered lights. Our emergency lights then came on, taking their power from batteries. They were very dim, but better than the battle lanterns.

"I could hear all kinds of reports coming over the headphones, such as, 'There goes the *Cassin*, the *Downs*, the *Oklahoma*, the *California*, and the *West Virginia*.' I'm reporting all this to our chief, a man named Moorehouse. There was a little humor down there when one of the men asked Chief Moorehouse, in all sincerity, if he thought this would make the papers back in the States. The Chief said, 'I guess so.'

"It was about this time that I felt the ship shudder and a loud boom come from starboard aft. We had been hit with a 500-pound bomb that

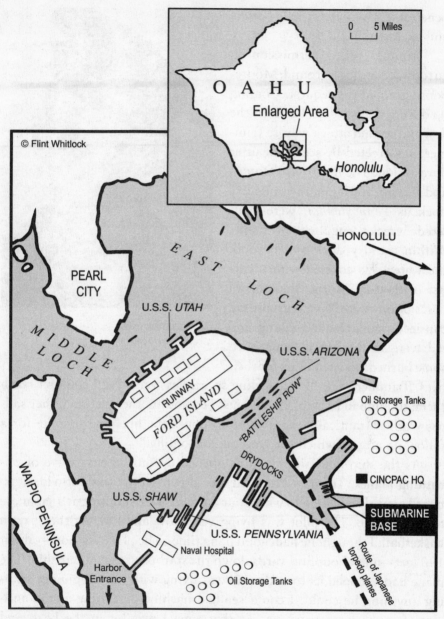

© Flint Whitlock

OAHU
Enlarged Area
Honolulu

0   5 Miles

HONOLULU

PEARL CITY

EAST LOCH

MIDDLE LOCH

U.S.S. *UTAH*

U.S.S. *ARIZONA*

Oil Storage Tanks

RUNWAY

FORD ISLAND

"BATTLESHIP ROW"

DRYDOCKS

CINCPAC HQ

WAIPIO PENINSULA

U.S.S. *SHAW*

U.S.S. *PENNSYLVANIA*

SUBMARINE BASE

Naval Hospital

Harbor Entrance

Oil Storage Tanks

Route of Japanese torpedo planes

Pearl Harbor, Ohau, Hawaii, 7 December 1942.

penetrated two-and-a-half decks and exploded."

Trimmer asked permission to go topside for a look around; Moorehouse granted the request. Coming up during the brief lull between the first and second attack waves, Trimmer was greeted by scenes of utter devastation. The destroyers *Downs* and *Cassin,* resting in the same dry dock as *Pennsylvania*, were shattered wrecks engulfed in flame. Within the dry dock and beyond, the water was covered with a carpet of floating debris. Ships of all description were burning, listing, capsized, sunk. Sailors young and old were in the water, some hurt,

Bill Trimmer, 1942.
(Courtesy Bill Trimmer)

some burned, all swimming for their lives. Trimmer said, "I was feeling so helpless knowing I couldn't reach them; to jump in to help, I would just become another victim. Other sailors worked frantically everywhere to douse the fires and prepare for a follow-up attack, which was not long in coming."

As the ship's antiaircraft guns opened up on the next wave of on-rushing planes, Trimmer "flopped face down on the six-foot-wide starboard catwalk, looking to where our gunners were shooting at a Japanese torpedo plane. The pilot was flying very slow and low. As they say in basketball, I thought he had 'good hang time.' The plane was low—about 100 feet—and about fifty yards down the starboard side of our ship. The plane had dropped its torpedo and was flying with its rear gunner strafing anything he could. I could see his machine gun firing at the antiaircraft guns just above me. At that time I was hit in the head and shoulder with fragments and thought I was going to die."

Trimmer's wounds were not as serious as he feared, and he scrambled to the aft of the ship, where he encountered scenes of horror. "I saw one kid that had been hit laying there, and I pulled him up under

Number Three turret and went to help others. I left the boat deck to go down to the afterdeck, where they were bringing out the dead and wounded. I helped with this and won't ever write about it because it was so gruesome. I also tried to help fight the fire caused by the bomb. I didn't have a mask and the fumes were heavy, so I couldn't do much."[2]

By the time the attack ended an hour and a half later, 2,403 soldiers and sailors were dead or missing, and 1,178 more lay wounded. Over a hundred civilians in Honolulu had been killed or wounded. Scores of Army and Navy aircraft had been destroyed—most of them on the ground. By comparison, Japan's losses were almost insignificant: six fighters and fourteen dive-bombers, five midget and one large submarine. Rarely had any military victory been so lopsided or defeat so complete.[3]

Once the first telegrams and radio confirmations flashed back to Washington, D.C., there was collective shock that nearly paralyzed the highest levels of the American government. Some no doubt thought it was another hoax, like Orson Welles's 1938 radio drama about Martians invading the earth. But this was not science fiction.

Disbelief even at the highest levels was rampant. Harry Hopkins, President Franklin Delano Roosevelt's chief adviser, told him that the initial reports were probably a mistake; the Japanese would never dare attack Pearl Harbor. The Japanese knew that America had been trying hard to stay neutral, to keep out of the war; such an attack would immediately thrust the United States into the conflict. These reports must be wrong, Hopkins assured FDR, probably just test messages sent in error.

Hopkins's skepticism was soon replaced by cold reality when official Washington learned that Pearl Harbor wasn't the only place bombed that Sunday; American installations in the Philippines and on Wake Island were also being subjected to the savagery of surprise attack. In one stroke, the halcyon days of peacetime, isolationist America were over.[4]

As bad as the attack on Pearl Harbor had been, it could have been considerably worse. According to William O'Neill in *A Democracy at*

The U.S.S *Shaw* explodes in one of the most enduring images of the
Japanese attack on Pearl Harbor, 7 December 1941.
(Courtesy National Archives)

War, "Nagumo had denied his air commander permission to launch a
second strike, thus sparing the shipyards, dry docks, machine shops, and
especially tank farms, upon which everything depended."[5] If these facilities had been destroyed, the Pacific Fleet would have had no choice but
to withdraw to its bases on the mainland.

Fortunately for the Americans, half the Pacific Fleet—including all
of its aircraft carriers—was at sea when the enemy struck. Also either at
sea or unharmed in their berths along the eastern shore of Pearl Harbor
were the submarines—the small, slim, precious submarines.

Of the twenty-two American submarines of the Pacific Fleet normally based at Pearl, only five were actually in port on that infamous
day; the others were either at sea or back in the States. Lieutenant Commander Elton W. Grenfell, U.S. Naval Academy class of 1926 and skipper of *Gudgeon* (SS-211), was engaged in training exercises near Maui;
John R. Pierce's *Argonaut* (SS-166) and *Trout* (SS-202), under Frank
"Mike" Fenno, were conducting mock war patrols in the vicinity of

Midway Island; while William L. Anderson and his *Thresher* (SS-200) were returning to Pearl from Midway. John W. Murphy's *Tambor* (SS-198) and *Triton* (SS-201), under Willis A. Lent, were patrolling even farther west, near Wake Island. *Pollack* (SS-180), *Pompano* (SS-181), and *Plunger* (SS-170) were en route to Hawaii from San Francisco. The last two Hawaii-based boats, William Brockman's *Nautilus* (SS-168) and John L. DeTar's *Tuna* (SS-203), were undergoing maintenance at Mare Island Naval Yard, near San Francisco.

That left just five subs—the aging *Cachalot* (SS-170), *Cuttlefish* (SS-171), *Dolphin* (SS-169), *Narwhal* (SS-167), and *Tautog* (SS-199) at Pearl—and most of these were undergoing maintenance and were not seaworthy. None of them had their full crews aboard on Sunday, 7 December; most of the men were either ashore, at church, at breakfast, or just sleeping late when the first wave of Japanese planes roared overhead. But once the alarm was given, those skeleton crews sprang into action.

Under the direction of her duty officer, William Sieglaff, *Tautog* managed to muster enough crew to man the three-inch gun mounted on her deck, along with a .50-caliber machine gun. *Tautog*, *Narwhal*, and a nearby destroyer opened up on a low-flying torpedo plane and splashed it; all three craft were given credit for downing the intruder. For a solid hour, every ship, boat, and gun that could be brought into action against the attackers was fully engaged. Once the raid was over, men from the sub base pitched in to rescue trapped crews on stricken vessels and to provide aid and comfort to the wounded.[6]

After the attacks had ended, the crew of *Pennsylvania* was taken ashore and detailed as a repelling party in the event the Japanese tried to land troops on Oahu. Sixty-two of Bill Trimmer's shipmates had lost their lives, and he recalled looking out across the harbor and being sickened by the sight of "boats towing or dragging bodies to shore with lines tied to their arms, legs, or anything they could find."[7]

For the rest of the day and well into the night, trigger-happy American gunners fired at anything that moved. *Thresher*, returning to Pearl from Midway, was attacked by an American destroyer and driven off as the sub approached the Hawaiian Islands; luckily, the boat suffered no damage or casualties. *Thresher* finally pulled into port, her captain and crew mad as hell.[8]

* * *

THE Hawaii-based Pacific Fleet was not the only American naval presence in the vast ocean. Anchored 4,600 nautical miles west of Hawaii in the Philippines was the U.S. Asiatic Fleet, commanded by Admiral Thomas C. Hart, whose mission it was to guard the Western Pacific and keep an eye on the Japanese.

It was a stretch even to call the Asiatic Fleet a "fleet"; it consisted of only a single heavy cruiser, one light cruiser, thirteen World War I–era destroyers, various other smaller craft, plus six older, S-class subs, and twenty-three newer models. Fortunately, on 8 December (still 7 December, Hawaii time), many of the surface warships had been dispersed far to the south, beyond the range of Japan's Formosa-based aircraft. Minutes after learning of the Pearl Harbor attack, Hart warned all his subordinate commands: "Japan has started hostilities. Govern yourselves accordingly."[9]

Early on 8 December, the Japanese hit the Asiatic Fleet. By this time, fully aware of the disaster at Pearl, Hart's command was on alert, and antiaircraft batteries were ready and waiting. A swarm of aircraft bearing the red "meatball" insignia on their wings and fuselages swooped down upon American warships at the Cavite and Mariveles Naval Bases. Unfortunately for the Yanks, there seemed to be more targets than weapons to shoot at them, and the frenzied gunners fired blindly, hitting little.

On Luzon, more than half of the 160 U.S. warplanes stationed at Clark Field near Manila, and others at Olongapo Naval Station, were plastered by the raiders and rendered useless. To make matters worse, tens of thousands of Japanese marines and infantrymen were storming ashore at various points throughout the Philippines.

Also on that first day of the war, the American outpost on Wake Island came under attack; it eventually would be wiped out. In China, Japanese prime minister and minister of war Hideki Tojo's troops overran the American garrisons at Tientsin and Shanghai; the crew of the American gunboat *Wake*, also at Shanghai, surrendered.

ON the smoke-shrouded afternoon of 7 December, Admiral Harold R. Stark, the chief of naval operations in Washington, D.C., took it upon himself to abrogate the 1936 London Naval Treaty, an international

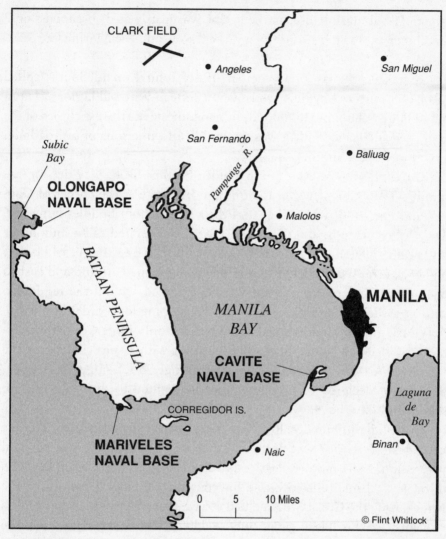

Manila area.

agreement that spelled out restrictions in the use of submarines. Without waiting for a formal declaration of war from Congress, Stark sent an unequivocal, no-nonsense directive to all American naval facilities in the Pacific: "Execute unrestricted air and submarine warfare against Japan."[10]

It was, however, a directive far easier to issue than to execute, for the

American submarine force in the Pacific was nearly as disorganized on 7 December as was the surface Navy, the Army, and the Marine Corps.

On that seventh day of December 1941, John Ronald Smith (called "Ron" or "Smitty" by his friends) was a sixteen-year-old junior at Hammond High School in Hammond, Indiana, in the northwest corner of the state, near Chicago. Smitty was the middle of three sons of railroadman Ernest and Pearl Smith.

On that Sunday, Ron Smith's older brother, Bob, was driving the family's 1936 Chrysler over to Sohl's, a drugstore at the corner of Conkey and Harrison, where they and their high school buddies hung out. They never made it; shortly before 1 P.M., the excited radio announcer on WBBM interrupted the latest music with the news that Pearl Harbor had been attacked. Bob and Ron immediately turned around and rushed back home. There they and their father huddled around the big Philco console radio for the remainder of the day, hoping for more information. Very little news was forthcoming; about the only thing known for certain was that the United States had been hit with a sneak attack by the Japanese. As they listened to the frustratingly brief snippets of news, Ron Smith declared to his father that he wanted to drop out of high school and join the Navy.

Ernie Smith reminded Ron that Navy requirements said that recruits needed to be at least seventeen, and then could enlist only with parental permission. Ron's mother, Pearl, had passed away in 1938, when Ron was thirteen, so Ernie resisted giving his consent. He himself had joined the Navy during the Great War, and had served aboard the battleship *Utah*[*] as a member of the "black gang," whose duty it was to shovel coal into the fire-breathing, steam-generating furnaces and keep the mighty engines running. Especially chilling were the elder Smith's stories of the *Utah* being attacked by German U-boats. "Whenever there was a U-boat attack," Smitty

---

[*] The *Utah* was commissioned in 1911, saw action in the Atlantic during World War I, and in 1932 was converted into a highly sophisticated target ship against which aircraft, surface ships, and even submarines practiced their gunnery and bombardment skills. The Japanese sank her on 7 December 1941, and her rusting remains—today a memorial—are still visible on the west side of Ford Island. (www.xmission.com)

recalled his father saying, "they closed the huge steel doors to the fire room, sealing the men in and keeping them at their station, shoveling coal."

While he naturally worried about his son's safety—and the safety of millions of other sons who were at that moment across the land similarly lining up at recruiting offices—Ernie Smith was also immensely proud that his son wanted to follow in his Navy footsteps. He promised to give his consent if Ron finished his junior year and held a full-time job for at least three months.

Yet, the distant sea called to Smitty, and he could barely wait for next year. He said, "The group I ran around with wanted to be old enough to go to Canada and join the British military. A lot of guys did. The United States had really been in the war for almost two years before Pearl Harbor; our destroyers were escorting convoys going across the Atlantic with Lend-Lease goods going to Britain and Russia."*

In the late 1930s and early 1940s, the dangers posed by Nazi Germany, Fascist Italy, and Imperial Japan had been made clear by the Roosevelt administration, the news media, and by Hollywood. "We were pretty well indoctrinated," recalled Smitty, "and we knew it. We realized what Adolf Hitler was doing and what the Japanese were doing and, as we matured, we realized that we Americans were the only ones in the world who could stop them. So when the Japanese attacked Pearl Harbor, it was like opening a floodgate of emotion—we were ready to fight. Everybody rushed down to enlist as soon as they could; we were eager to get at the enemy. Our attitude was 'Let's get all this bureaucratic stuff like boot camp out of the way and let's get at 'em.' "[11]

By 10 December, Japanese troops had landed on Tarawa and Makin Islands in the Gilberts group, and were swarming across northern Malaya. Even Bangkok, Thailand, had fallen to the invaders. Guam's 427-man American garrison surrendered to 5,400 of the enemy, and the British battleships *Prince of Wales* and *Repulse,* part of a task force steaming

---

* Lend-Lease was a program devised by President Roosevelt that enabled the U.S. to supply Great Britain and the Soviet Union with war matériel (such as tanks, trucks, and ships) during a period when the United States was "officially" neutral. The Lend-Lease Act was passed by Congress on March 11, 1941. (Haskew, 30, 101–103)

The Smith family in 1934. Left to right: Ernie, Ron, Rex, Pearl, Bob.
(Courtesy Ron Smith)

from Singapore to Malaya, were spotted by eighty-four Japanese torpedo planes, attacked, and sunk.[12]

That same day, 10 December, the Philippines again came under aerial attack, with the prime target being Cavite Naval Station. Aerial bombs fell in clusters, straddling a submarine tender and blasting two sister submarines that were being overhauled—*Seadragon* (SS-194) and *Sealion* (SS-195)—damaging the first and destroying the latter.

In *Silent Victory*, naval historian Clay Blair Jr. describes the chaos and carnage at the submarine base: "Cavite was a burning shambles. Five hundred were dead and many more wounded. In addition to the loss of *Sealion* [on which five men were killed] the submarine force had lost all Cavite submarine repair facilities, the torpedo overhaul shop, and a total of 233 Mark XIV torpedoes . . . The low-frequency radio tower for transmitting to submerged submarines was also destroyed . . . All the submarine force could salvage from Cavite were about 150 torpedoes and some spare parts . . . These were transferred to tunnels on Corregidor."

Unlike at Pearl Harbor, the Japanese would return to plaster Cavite for several more days, but, by 11 December, twenty-two of the submarines had left port to seek out and attack enemy shipping presumed to be headed to the Philippines with reinforcements.[13]

DESPITE news reports that tried to find a silver lining within the roiling black clouds of defeat and humiliation, and the radio commentator Gabriel Heatter, who began his nightly broadcast with the cheery introduction "There's good news tonight," there was actually very little good news to report during the early months of the war. America and her allies were losing in dramatic fashion everywhere in the Pacific.

On 18 December 1941, the Japanese landed on Hong Kong Island, brutally murdering British soldiers who had surrendered; on the twentieth, they captured the Philippine island of Mindanao. Four days later, General Douglas MacArthur abandoned his threatened headquarters in Manila for the fortified island of Corregidor.

Perhaps no defeat more symbolized the futility of American resistance and the superiority of Japanese strategy, however, than the debacle of Bataan, in the Philippines.

On 22 December 1941, 43,000 Imperial Japanese Army troops under Lieutenant General Masaharu Homma began piling onto the shore at Lingayen Gulf, on the main Philippine island of Luzon, and fighting their way southward toward the capital of Manila, being resisted doggedly every step of the way by desperate American and Filipino troops under MacArthur's command. But it was clear that the Americans and Filipinos would not be able to resist forever, nor throw the invaders back into the sea.[14]

The cancer of defeat in the face of Japanese aggression was spreading. On Christmas day, the British garrison at Hong Kong threw down their arms and threw up their hands. Five days later, the British also gave up much of Malaya.[15]

New Year's Day saw Emperor Hirohito's men attack the island of Labuan. The next day, Japanese troops strutted into Manila like they owned the place—which they now did. American and Filipino forces were forced to evacuate Manila and the advancing Japanese inflicted terrible suffering on the Filipinos. Author and ex-Marine William Manchester says, "Time has blurred the jagged contours of the Greater East Asia Co-Prosperity Sphere, but it should be remembered that the Nipponese were a savage foe, at least as merciless and sadistic as the Spaniards. In Manila they slew nearly 100,000 civilians; hospital patients were strapped to their beds and set afire, babies' eyeballs were gouged out and smeared on walls like jelly."[16]

By 10 January 1942, British forces, under severe pressure, had to abandon Malaya's Kuala Lumpur and Port Sweetenham; the important naval and air bases at Rabaul, New Britain Island, also fell to the conquerors. At the end of the month Dutch Borneo's oil-rich island of Tarakan was taken over by the Japanese. U.S. and Philippine forces were squeezed into the Bataan Peninsula, from which the only escape—if escape were even possible—was by sea. Army Chief of Staff George C. Marshall promised MacArthur that help was on the way, but in truth, no help was coming because no help was yet available.

As the Japanese continued to pressure MacArthur's men, they were also gobbling up scores of islands in the Pacific and threatening to devour Australia.[17]

TRY as they might, the pitifully few American submarines trying to cover millions of square miles of ocean and wage "unrestricted warfare" were not able to make much of a dent in the thousands of enemy warships, troop transports, tankers, or cargo freighters full of munitions, guns, and vehicles heading out from Japanese and Japanese-controlled ports. It was as though the little Dutch boy had been asked to plug with his finger a gaping hole the size of the Panama Canal.

Obviously, with the thousands of enemy ships out there, many more American submarines would be needed to reduce their numbers. But there was also something even more potentially serious than a lack of numbers: the American torpedoes were defective.

More and more reports of malfunctioning torpedoes poured in to the Bureau of Ordnance, dumped on admirals' desks like so much rotten fish. At first, the Navy's top brass refused to believe the evidence that was piling up, preferring to blame the problem on the inefficiency of the boats' captains and their crews.

Admiral Ralph Waldo Christie.
(Courtesy National Archives)

Several high-ranking officers, including Admiral Ralph Waldo Christie, Commander, U.S. Submarine Force, Southwest Pacific (ComSubSoWesPac), who should have been the submariners' most stalwart advocate, rejected the idea that the problem was in the torpedo; he, like the others, preferred to point the finger at the men.

A major factor in Christie's reluctance to blame the torpedoes was that, in the 1920s and 1930s, he had been heavily involved in the development of the modern torpedo, especially its top secret magnetic detonator; so exalted was he that, around the hallowed halls of the Navy Department, he was known as "Mr. Torpedo."[18]

BuOrd—the Navy's Bureau of Ordnance—was particularly sensitive to criticism—and unsympathetic to reports that the torpedoes might be at fault. Maybe the skippers and crews were just bad shots, BuOrd responded. Maybe they were simply avoiding a fight or being scared away. Maybe they were looking in the wrong place for enemy ships. Maybe they needed more training.*

The submarine commanders were incensed when their training, marksmanship, courage, and devotion to duty were called into question. No, they shot back, the torpedoes were *malfunctioning*. BuOrd and the sub skippers went round and round—and with good reason. Junior officers in the Submarine Service, writes Theodore Roscoe, "staked their lives on torpedo performance [and] were up in arms against the doctrinaire and

---

* BuOrd was held in low esteem by many submariners, who often referred to it as "The Gun Club," owing to the clannishness of its officers. Clay Blair says, "It performed like most military bureaucracies: slowly, cautiously, unimaginatively, and, at times, stupidly." (Blair, 10)

bureaucratic inertia that refused to recognize or properly diagnose the difficulty and thereby impeded the cure. Massive military organizations . . .
resist change. They may move at a glacial pace where the speed of an
avalanche is imperative."[19]

Whatever the problem, it needed to be identified and corrected—and
fast—before the Japanese gained total mastery of the seas.

THE torpedo problem was, of course, top secret—mustn't let the enemy
know what your weaknesses are, lest he exploit them. Thus the papers
were full of vague, hopeful stories, when they mentioned submarines at
all, of how the little boats were taking on Japan's navy and doing tremendous damage.

But not all the news could be presented with a positive spin. Ever
since the "unprovoked and dastardly attack" on Pearl Harbor, as President Roosevelt had phrased it in his request to Congress for a formal
declaration of war, Ron Smith and his classmates had been following in
great detail the progress of the war, reading in the *Hammond Times*
about German U-boats sinking ship after ship in the Atlantic; about
far-flung Pacific outposts falling one after the other; about heroic defenders, such as those on Wake Island, going down fighting; about the
savage Japanese soldiers who regarded surrender as beneath contempt
and thus slaughtered their American, British, Australian, Filipino, and
Dutch prisoners of war—including scores of female nurses and their
helpless, wounded patients—with impunity. The murder of helpless, un-
armed enemy troops was expressly forbidden by *bushido*, the warriors'
code, but many Japanese, with a warped sense of honor, perverted the
code and either permitted or committed atrocities—much as Muslim
extremists would do a half century later.

While Ron Smith waited to prove his moxie to his father, the war
marched on without him. Like racehorses in the gate, straining to hear
the starter's bell, Ron and his buddies were champing at the bit to get
into uniform and begin to settle the score.

ON Monday, 8 December, once the United States Congress voted 470–1
to declare war on Japan, young men (and women, too) from across the
country were already flocking to recruiting centers, queuing up in lines

that sometimes stretched for blocks, all eager to join the military and do their part to fight for their country.

Although the attack on Pearl Harbor came as a surprise to most Americans, the United States' involvement in another world war was seen by many as inevitable. While almost everyone in America had been nervously eyeing for nearly a decade the worrisome developments in Europe—the rise of an obscure rabble-rouser named Adolf Hitler to the post of chancellor of Germany in 1933; Italian dictator Benito Mussolini's invasion of Ethiopia in 1935; the aid provided by Italy and Germany to assist Francisco Franco in a Fascist takeover of Spain; Germany's reoccupation of the Rhineland; Hitler's bullying of Czechoslovakia to give up the Sudetenland; and Germany's annexation of Austria—fewer Americans had been casting a worried eye at events taking place in the Far East, the exotic, inscrutable Orient.

This ignoring of the situation in Asia seems surprising, even in hindsight, for the signs of Japan's aggression and growing anger at the West were unmistakable and had been going on for far longer than the events in Europe. Dai Nippon's seemingly "unprovoked" decision to go to war stemmed from years of perceived (and real) slights and insults.

Especially galling to Japan was the sense of being snubbed by the other victorious nations following the end of the First World War. After all, during the Great War, as it was then known, Japan had helped the Allies by ousting the German kaiser's troops from a number of Pacific islands. As a reward for her help, Japan was given a mandate to govern the Marshall Islands, the Carolines, the Ladrones, and the Palaus. But with these rewards also came restrictions to Japan's growing strength.

Simultaneously, Japan's postwar economy was booming as never before. However, she lacked the natural resources needed to sustain her march toward becoming a world industrial power—resources such as coal, oil, iron ore, bauxite, rubber, lead, nickel, and other commodities. Japan's neighbors, on the other hand, were awash in these resources. Why not just invade those countries and take what we need, argued Japan's ultraconservative military leaders, who chafed under the liberal policies of the ruling democratic government. After all, the militarists said, it is the Japanese people who are racially and culturally superior, the Japanese people whose emperor is a god, the Japanese people who are divinely destined to rule the world.

The militarists were incensed when their government signed the 1922 Washington Naval Arms Limitation Treaty (later replaced by the London Naval Treaties of 1930 and 1936), which restricted the size of navies and prohibited Japan from establishing new military bases in the Pacific. Matters were not helped when anti-Japanese sentiment in the United States led to a halt in 1924 of Japanese immigration. Rebuffed and insulted by the West, primarily the United States, Japan's militarists looked elsewhere to realize their expansionist goals. They did not have far to look.

In 1926, China was in a state of turmoil. The Chinese Nationalists, under Chiang Kai-shek, and the Communists, led by Mao Tse-tung, had joined forces to defeat the warlords in the northern provinces, but then, in 1928, the two sides had a falling-out and launched a civil war. The unrest gave the militarists in Japan the opportunity they needed to exploit the situation. After manufacturing an "incident" in 1931, a large Japanese army thrust into the Chinese portion of southern and central Manchuria. With lightning speed, the invaders gained control of much of the province, renamed it Manchukuo, and placed it under a puppet government.

This act drove the United States to impose trade restrictions on Japan—restrictions that served only to further infuriate the militarists and inflame anti-American feelings within Japan—and perhaps even aided in driving Japan into the Fascist camp. In late 1936, Japan and Germany signed an anti-Comintern pact that pledged each other to oppose communism; the next year Italy also joined the pact and the three nations became known as the "Rome-Berlin-Tokyo Axis" or, simply, the Axis powers.

To Japan, America seemed to be nothing more than a paper tiger—all bluster and no bite. On one hand, the United States seemed determined to involve herself in what Japan considered to be her internal affairs, yet, on the other, remained aloof and on the world sidelines, refusing to join the League of Nations (which her president, Woodrow Wilson, had fought passionately to create)—an organization that might have helped settle international disputes.

In the end, of course, America's neutral stance and unwillingness to play a leadership role in the growing crises around the globe simply invited more aggression. On 17 December 1937, for example, a United States Navy gunboat, U.S.S. *Panay*, and a British gunboat, H.M.S. *Ladybird*, were both attacked by Japanese aircraft on China's Yangtse River, near Nanking. The *Panay* was one of five American vessels that had been patrolling the Yangtse since the 1920s, protecting from bandits American shipping that used the river, through international agreement, as a highway of commerce. *Panay* was carrying the last of the American embassy personnel who had been evacuated from Nanking in the face of the advancing Japanese forces, and was also escorting three Standard Oil tankers upriver. Japanese warplanes swooped in and, for more than two hours, bombed and strafed the ship and groups of survivors clinging to floating bits of wreckage. Three American sailors were killed while forty-three crew members and five civilians were wounded. President Roosevelt was furious and the cabinet discussed various forms of response and retaliation. Few Americans wanted to attack Japan, however, and so the incident was downplayed by the government and in the press. The lack of action on the part of the United States only served to embolden Japan.

By now Japan controlled a huge portion of eastern China and, in early 1939, invaded China's Hainan Island and took the Spratly Islands, which would make ideal air and naval bases for Dai Nippon's planned expansion into Southeast Asia. Japan's militarists, while keeping the weak "boy king" Hirohito on the throne as a figurehead, deposed the elected government and took control of the nation. Now they would set their own course and pursue their own policies, regardless of what the rest of the world thought.

The ultra-right-wing army officer Hideki Tojo, who had been minister of war briefly in 1938, was reappointed to that post in July 1941, and resumed his belligerent stance, including a hard line against the United States. That same month Japan invaded southern Indochina, and the United States imposed a total halt of all exports—including precious steel and oil—to Japan, an act that probably did more than anything else to ensure that war would come.

On 16 October 1941, Tojo became prime minister. He and his cronies decided that the only course of action left to Japan was to kick the Americans, British, Dutch, and other colonialists out of the Pacific. Once these adversaries were evicted, Tojo figured that Japan could help herself to the East's mineral riches with impunity, build up her defenses to the point of impregnability, and await the inevitable attempt by the Americans to invade the Home Islands. To provide a sort of early warning network, Dai Nippon's warlords planned to invade and establish formidable military bases on those Pacific islands they did not already control. With total mastery of the sea-lanes, Japan could then ferry unlimited quantities of men, matériel, food, ammunition, and other supplies to these island outposts, making them impervious to conquest.

But first, the two thorns in their side—the American naval bases in Hawaii and the Philippines—would need to be neutralized. The last days of peace between Japan and America were at hand.[20]

AMERICA, too, had spent years planning on what to do in the event of war with Japan. Surmising that American policies might ultimately provoke Japan into firing the first shot, the United States War Department developed a plan after World War I called "Orange," which presupposed several factors: (1) that there would be sufficient warning before any Japanese attack; (2) that war would be declared by Japan in advance of the outbreak of hostilities; and (3) that American air forces based in the Pacific would be able to track Japanese naval movements and provide accurate information prior to any strikes. All of these assumptions proved to be incorrect.

Although ravaged by a decade of economic depression and high unemployment, the United States was still the world's most powerful industrialized nation. As William O'Neill points out, "the U.S. [in 1938] created 28.7 percent of the world's manufacturing output, compared to Germany's 13.2 percent and Japan's 3.8 percent. Beyond that, Americans were a proud people who subscribed to a common culture based on work, family, respect for institutions, and faith in self and nation. It was these intangibles that the Axis powers neglected to take into account when declaring war on the United States. Aware of the nation's industrial strength, they discounted it, regarding Americans as soft, enfeebled by ethnic and racial divisions, an excessive love of material goods, and a contempt for martial values. Rarely has prejudice had a more fateful outcome."[21]

In his epic work, *At Dawn We Slept,* Gordon Prange writes, "Many Japanese believed the United States was a hollow shell, its people divided politically, softened by luxurious living and decadent morals, no match for the tough, disciplined men of Japan. But [Admiral Isoruku] Yamamoto knew that the good-natured giant could be pushed just so far and that Pearl Harbor would be the end of the line."[22]

Yet never was a giant so ill prepared for all-out conflict. Despite nearly ten years of observing the world sliding toward war, the United States, at the time of Germany's invasion of Poland in 1939, had fewer than 400,000 men under arms. The U.S. Army was only the world's fifteenth largest land force, behind such countries as Spain and India.[23]

America had no aircraft then capable of outperforming the Japanese Zero, and no ground forces large enough, near enough, or well trained enough to wrestle a single Pacific island from the tenacious enemy. And, although a massive wave of patriotic fervor swept over the country in the wake of Pearl Harbor, American morale could not have been lower during the next several months—months of alarming radio commentary and newspaper headlines that reported one Japanese victory after another sweeping across the Pacific and ever closer to America's West Coast.

CHAPTER 2

THE FRUITS OF WAR

THE last three weeks of 1941 and the first three months of 1942 were marked by nothing but a series of heady Japanese triumphs and devastating Allied losses—"golden days for the conquering soldiers of Dai Nippon," as William Manchester puts it.

Japan's sudden and relatively easy victories were also worrying to the quiet, bespectacled Emperor Hirohito, who expressed his misgivings to an aide: "The fruits of war are tumbling into our mouth almost too quickly." The emperor, however, did nothing to spit out the fruit or, as Manchester says, dissuade his "elated generals and admirals [who] had no such misgivings. They knew they had broken the myth of white supremacy. They had surpassed the Allies on every level. Their strategy was superior, the tactics more skillful, their navy and air force larger and more efficient, their infantry better prepared and more experienced. In amphibious operations . . . their landings of whole armies on surf beaches were of a magnitude only dreamt of in the West."[1]

WITH much of the American Navy in tatters, with American airpower reduced to nearly nothing, and with American ground forces dying, retreating, or surrendering in droves throughout the Pacific, there seemed to be little hope for a major counteroffensive against the Japanese anytime soon.

The United States had but one force left in the Pacific capable of taking the fight to the enemy—the Submarine Force. Small though that force was—an army of ants trying to stop a stampeding herd of elephants—

brave and sometimes foolhardy attempts were made by the submariners to interrupt Japan's drive to dominate the Pacific.

During the remaining three weeks of December 1941, thirty-nine American submarines sailing from Pearl Harbor, Fremantle, and the Philippines conducted their first war patrols; fourteen went on their second; and one—Adrian Hurst's *Permit* (SS-178)—went on its third. The results of the patrols were not just disappointing—they were downright appalling.

There *were* a few successes, however. Three Manila-based submarines did manage to draw blood. On 16 December, Chester C. Smith's *Swordfish* (SS-193) sank a transport, while another enemy freighter was sent to the bottom by Wreford G. Chapple's *S-38* (SS-143) on 22 December; a third freighter was destroyed by Kenneth C. Hurd's *Seal* (SS-183) the following day.

During those final three weeks of December 1941 at least eleven other subs sighted targets, fired their torpedoes, but had no confirmed hits.[2] On 14 December 1941, Frederick B. Warder's *Seawolf* (SS-197), normally based at Manila, slipped unnoticed into the harbor at Aparri, on the east coast of Luzon, where a small Japanese force had landed the day before. Seeing a seaplane tender at anchor, Warder fired a spread of four Mark XIV torpedoes armed with the new magnetic detonators—but there were no explosions. Somehow the torpedoes had either missed their targets entirely or their detonators failed to detonate. On his way out of the harbor, Warder fired four more torpedoes, but again, nothing. As Clay Blair notes, "Warder was furious. He had penetrated a harbor, fired eight precious torpedoes, achieved zero results."[3]

Sadly, most of the other American submarines had no better luck; their skippers' patrol reports read like a laundry list of missed opportunities and heartbreaking failures. Near Formosa, Bill Wright's *Sturgeon*, based in Fremantle, Australia, made a surface attack against a sitting-duck cargo ship; all four torpedoes either missed or misfired. From Manila, Ted Aylward's *Searaven* (SS-196) attacked two freighters, also near Formosa, without inflicting damage, while David Hurt, in *Perch* (SS-176), with a good-size convoy in his sights, could not verify that any torpedoes struck home. *Snapper* (SS-185), under Hamilton "Ham" Stone, took on a cargo ship; it escaped unscathed. *Pickerel* (SS-177), with Barton

E. Bacon Jr. at the helm, shot five torpedoes worth $10,000 apiece at a patrol boat; none hit it. Roland F. Pryce's *Spearfish* (SS-190) attacked an enemy submarine with four torpedoes, again without result.

Skipjack (SS-184), commanded by Charles L. Freeman, had a similar disappointing patrol. Spotting the choicest of targets—a big, fat Japanese aircraft carrier—Freeman closed in for the kill, fired three torpedoes, and got that sick feeling in his gut when none of them exploded. On Christmas day, Freeman tried again, this time at point-blank range against a heavy cruiser; as with the carrier, the target lived to fight another day. On New Year's Eve 1941, *Tarpon* (SS-175), under Lewis Wallace, went after a light cruiser, but there was no New Year's celebration because no hits were scored.

After firing at least seventy torpedoes—$700,000 worth—Freeman and Wallace reported that in December they had sunk twenty-one enemy ships for a total of 120,400 tons. However, postwar records, compiled once access was gained to Japanese naval records, showed that only six ships, totaling 29,500 tons, were actually sunk. Not an auspicious beginning.[4]

EVEN at this early stage of the war, and despite the many problems being encountered, legends of the submarine service were being created. One of the most unusual was that of the "red submarine." When the Japanese struck Cavite Naval Base in the Philippines on 8 December, William E. "Pete" Ferrall's *Seadragon* was undergoing an overhaul, including a complete repainting. There was no time to finish the paint job, so *Seadragon* set sail with just her red-lead undercoating showing.

The radio propagandist Tokyo Rose got wind of this unusual-color boat and soon was broadcasting to her listeners that America had a fleet of "Red Pirates" that were plundering Japanese shipping lanes; she promised that these criminal pirates would be executed when caught. Learning of the broadcast, Ferrall's men had a good laugh.*[5]

---

* Ensign Sam Hunter of *Seadragon* was killed during the Japanese attack on Cavite, perhaps the first casualty in the submarine force. *Seadragon*'s CO refused to repair the battle damage to her conning tower; he wanted it left as is so that all crew members would be forever reminded of the debt she owed to "a treacherous enemy." (Lockwood, 35)

Although badly outnumbered, America's antiquarian submarines were doing their best to make the Japanese warlords think twice before believing they had free rein in the Pacific. On 2 January 1942, Lieutenant Commander Edward C. Stephen of *Grayback*, sailing from Pearl Harbor, sank the 2,180-ton monster submarine *I-18* in the Solomons. On 24 January, as Japanese troops were preparing to land at Balikpapan, on Borneo's southeast coast, a task force of four American destroyers and seven submarines, including William L. Wright's Fremantle-based *Sturgeon* (SS-187), attacked and disrupted the amphibious operation, sinking four of the sixteen transports. Although the invasion was not halted, the damage done marked the first American naval "victory" of the war. It was small, it was insignificant, but it represented the tiniest glimmer of hope.[6]

HOPE would have been greater had the torpedoes been reliable. America's submarines were armed with the latest Mark XIV steam-powered torpedoes equipped with Mark VI influence exploders. The failure of many torpedoes to detonate upon contact or within proximity of their targets was not the only problem; other torpedoes, for mysterious reasons, exploded prematurely, either just seconds after being launched or partway to the target.

Tyrell D. Jacobs, commander of the Manila-based *Sargo* (SS-188), experienced *both* vexations on one patrol. Encountering a large convoy near the major Japanese port at Cam Ranh Bay in French Indochina (later Vietnam) on 14 December 1941, Jacobs launched a torpedo; it exploded eighteen seconds after leaving the firing tube and nearly wrecked the sub. On the twenty-fourth, Jacobs fired five torpedoes at three heavily laden transport ships north of Borneo without recording any hits. Three days later, *Sargo* went after two more freighters and a tanker; again, zero hits.

A total of thirteen torpedoes that had cost American taxpayers $130,000 had been fired on *Sargo*'s first war patrol, and not one of them had so much as knocked the paint off an enemy vessel. *Sargo* might as well have been firing spit wads for all the good they were doing. Jacobs had a well-trained crew, so he knew the chances for "operator error" were slight; it *had* to be the "tin fish" themselves. He analyzed the data, did the math, and concluded that the Mark XIVs were running ten feet deeper than their settings indicated and passing too far beneath the enemy hulls to set off the magnetic exploders. Jacobs compensated by instructing his torpedomen to set the depth shallower, but he knew he was only guessing at a solution.

A few days later, Jacobs spotted a slow-moving tanker, had one torpedo set to run at a depth of just ten feet, and fired. The gunnery officer, after calculating range and torpedo speed, stood by in the control room with his stopwatch, marking off the seconds until the torpedo, if it was working correctly, would detonate. At the moment he should have heard an explosion, there was only silence. Jacobs upped the periscope to see the tanker continuing on its merry way, oblivious to the fact that it had just escaped destruction.

Angry and frustrated, Jacobs reported the problem of the malfunctioning torpedoes to higher command; the torpedo problem soon would become a scandal of major proportions within the Navy.[7]

It did the American war effort little good for submarine commanders to risk their boats and crews' lives by traveling thousands of miles into enemy-controlled waters to locate a target, fire their torpedoes, and then watch in helpless frustration as the intended targets sailed away unharmed. But that is exactly what was happening, and on a large scale.

The number of ships sunk by American submarines in January 1942 was woefully insignificant. Of the six boats that sailed from Pearl Harbor that month, only three of them reported hitting anything—just four enemy vessels worth 23,200 tons. *Pollack*, commanded by Stan Mosely, sank a merchantman near Tokyo Bay on 5 January, and David C. White's *Plunger* lived up to its name, sending a cargo ship plunging beneath the waves near Kii Suido on 18 January. Grenfell's *Gudgeon* sank the enemy submarine *I-173*, on 27 January in empire waters.[8] Eight additional American subs departing their Australia and Java bases did little better, sinking but six ships during the entire month, for a total of only 23,000 tons.[9]

The scarcity of sinkings was due not only to the unreliability of the torpedoes but also to their scarcity. Admiral Thomas Withers, Commander of Submarines, Pacific, or ComSubPac, criticized boat commanders who "wasted" torpedoes on targets. If a commander shot a second fish at a target that had been hit by the first one, Withers would dash off a withering note condemning the "profligate expenditure" of precious munitions. And, in January 1942, the torpedoes *were* precious—only 101 were in reserve at Pearl Harbor. Clay Blair notes, "According to prewar production schedules, [Withers] was to receive 192 more by July—about 36 a month. However, his quota had been recently cut to 24 a month. At the rate his boats were expending torpedoes, he would need more than 500 to reach July. There was no way the production rate could be drastically increased to meet this demand. Unless his skippers were more conservative, Pearl Harbor would soon run out of torpedoes."[10]

The submarine force, then, faced two equally important problems— a physical shortage of torpedoes and torpedoes that, when they *were* fired, rarely sank anything.

THERE are three main reasons why torpedoes might not sink their intended targets.

First, getting the torpedoes' firing platform—the submarine—into firing position without being spotted and attacked by the enemy is not always easy. Second, the range is important; the closer the submarine is to the target, the more likely the chance of a hit. Conversely, the farther away, the less likely it is that the torpedo will strike home. Finally, a stationary target, obviously, is much easier to hit than a moving one. If the target is zigzagging or employing some other type of evasive maneuver, the chance of hitting it is even more remote.

In many instances, the submarine captain would fire a "spread" of torpedoes—usually three torpedoes fired within a few seconds of one another—in the hope that at least one of them would hit. And hitting a target presenting its broad flank to the submarine—and thus making for a larger target area—is preferable to trying to put a torpedo "down the throat" (a head-on shot at a target coming toward the submarine) or "up the skirt" (shooting at the rear of a ship as it is steaming away).

Setting the correct information into the torpedo's guidance system is also critical. For best results, a torpedo should explode just beneath the centerline of a ship; the detonation will usually be enough to "break her back" and cause immediate sinking. If set to run too deeply, the torpedo will glide completely beneath the target's hull; if set too shallow, it will strike just below the waterline and not cause enough damage to ensure a sinking.

What must *never* happen is that, after maneuvering carefully into a good firing position, taking steady aim, dialing the correct information into the torpedo, and firing at the proper moment, the torpedo itself malfunctions. Unfortunately, malfunctioning torpedoes were all too often a curse that plagued American submariners, especially during the first half of the war.[11]

During the First World War, only one manufacturing facility made torpedoes for the United States Navy—the Alexandria Torpedo Station of Alexandria, Virginia. The armistice of 1918 had led to the closure of that station for, after all, the Great War was supposed to have been the "war to end all wars." The Washington and London Naval Treaties also put a damper on torpedo development, for the nations of the world fully believed that it was possible to outlaw war and the tools of war. As history proved, their idealism could not have been more misplaced.

In the 1930s, with obvious signs that civilization was marching in lockstep toward a new world conflict, the U.S. Naval Torpedo Station at Newport, Rhode Island, which had been established in 1869 as the Navy's experimental station for torpedoes and torpedo equipment, explosives, and electrical equipment, went into the full-time manufacture of the underwater missiles; political wrangling delayed the reopening of the Alexandria facility until July 1941. In addition to these two, five more facilities—in Forest Park, Illinois; St. Louis, Missouri; Keyport, Washington; the Pontiac Division of General Motors in Michigan; and the International Harvester Corporation—received contracts to build torpedoes, not only for submarines but also for destroyers and aircraft. By the end of the war, over 57,000 torpedoes would be built. But the end of the war was a long way off. The torpedoes were needed *now*.[12]

Even if there had been no torpedo shortage, the fact that the tin fish were so unreliable did not boost anyone's confidence. Who in their right mind would want to sail into enemy-controlled waters and risk their boats and the lives of their crews with so little assurance that their torpedoes, once fired, would actually work?

And no matter how many submarine skippers sent in reports detailing the torpedo-detonation problem, there was no indication that anyone at ComSubPac or BuOrd or anywhere else was the slightest bit interested in acknowledging that a problem existed or that they wanted promptly to fix it. Just as maddeningly, the problem was intermittent; sometimes the torpedoes worked fine and sometimes they didn't. How could anyone isolate a problem if the problems weren't consistent?

The situation allowed innumerable enemy ships to escape destruction, and doubtless contributed to the prolongation of the war in the Pacific and the loss of many American lives.

BECAUSE of their ability to escape enemy detection, submarines were drafted for a number of special missions. Duane Whitlock, who had joined the Navy in 1935, was one of several dozen cryptanalysts working in a tunnel on Corregidor breaking highly secret, coded Japanese messages. The enemy, moving down the Bataan Peninsula, was coming ever closer to the island and the invasion of Corregidor seemed imminent. Whitlock said that persons with access to such sensitive crypto information were not to be allowed to fall into enemy hands, and so it was decided to remove these specialists by submarine.[13]

At the end of January 1942, Ferrall's red *Seadragon* received orders to return to the Philippines and begin evacuating the code-breaking teams* on Corregidor. Slipping past the Japanese destroyer screen that was set up to guard the entrance of Lingayen Gulf, *Seadragon* docked at Mariveles Naval Base and began taking on passengers.

Withdrawing to open water, Ferrall happened upon a convoy and

* In the 1930s, the Japanese had obtained an "Enigma" encoding device from the Germans and created facsimile machines called the "Alphabet Typewriter Model 97" to send and decode their own diplomatic and military messages. The U.S. installed a team of code-breakers within the tunnels of Corregidor which, after a few years of intense work, broke Japan's "Red" and "Purple" diplomatic codes and the JN-25 Imperial Navy code. (home.earthlink.net/~nbrass1/3enigma)

fired two torpedoes—sometimes referred to as "pickles"—but missed. The following day, 2 February, he found a five-ship convoy, attacked, and sank the 6,441-ton transport *Tamagawa Maru*, which was full of troops, trucks, artillery pieces, ammunition, and other equipment intended to kill Americans. Ferrall then returned to Mariveles and whisked away more code breakers, taking them temporarily to Surabaya on the Indonesian island of Java, where they could practice their indispensable skill in safety.[14]

Each month, more and more code breakers and analysts were evacuated by submarine; around the middle of March, there was just a handful of men left. One night, as artillery boomed in the far distance, Duane Whitlock noticed the section's two officers stripping and cleaning their weapons. "What's the matter—are you expecting a war tonight?" he joshingly asked one of the officers, Rufus Taylor. Taylor stopped cleaning and fixed Whitlock with a hard stare. "The C.O. and I have decided that we're going to shoot every one of you and then ourselves the minute the Japanese set foot on this island," said Taylor. Whitlock's blood ran cold; he knew Taylor was not kidding.

As the weeks went by, the Japanese continued to bomb and shell Corregidor, and the island's defenders had run out of antiaircraft ammunition. A submarine, *Permit*, now captained by Wreford G. "Moon" Chapple, was bringing an emergency load of three-inch shells to the island when it came across a broken-down PT boat about 200 miles south of Manila. This was one of four PT boats that had evacuated MacArthur and his staff and family from the Philippines on 11 March but had developed engine troubles; the general and his entourage were taken to Mindanao by the other boats, but this particular PT boat and crew had been left stranded. Chapple piled the PT boat crew into *Permit* and continued to Mariveles.

One night Whitlock and fourteen other men were taken by launch from Corregidor to Mariveles, but *Permit* was too full. In addition to the crew of the PT boat, there were fifteen code breakers needing evacuation, plus Army nurses and officers. Someone made the decision to order the PT boat crew off; Whitlock and the other fourteen took their place. There were now 111 persons crammed into *Permit*. "We found out later that the PT boat crew became part of the defense of Bataan and were taken prisoner and some of them died," Whitlock said. "It's always been a pain in my heart to think that those poor guys were taken off the submarine so we could get in."

Permit sailed under cover of darkness and made it to open water, where she avoided two Japanese task forces totaling over 200 ships. At one point *Permit* plunged to the bottom to escape a heavy depth charging by three destroyers. The journey to Australia took twenty-three days, and Whitlock and the other code breakers continued their vital mission safely in Melbourne.[15]

ONE American submarine played a crucial and unusual role just prior to Corregidor's fall. The island's antiaircraft gunners had done a remarkable job of keeping Japanese aircraft at bay, shooting down thirteen medium bombers on the first day, but the necessary ammunition had run out.[16] Mike Fenno's *Trout* was entrusted with the dangerous job of transporting from Pearl Harbor to Corregidor 3,500 rounds of high-altitude antiaircraft rounds. She managed to slip past enemy ships that were blockading the entrance to Manila Bay and deliver the goods.

Realizing that *Trout* would require ballast in order to make the return trip, Francis B. Sayre, the U.S. high commissioner to the Philippines, had a brilliant idea. To prevent the nation's precious treasury of gold and silver from falling into enemy hands, Sayre had the treasury taken to the United States by submarine for safekeeping.

Over several tense days in early February, the treasury was emptied and the fortune carried on small boats to Corregidor, where it was loaded into *Trout*. By the time *Trout* was ready to depart, she was filled with 319 gold bars, weighing six and a half tons, and 630 bags of silver coins. Together, the ballast was worth nearly $10 million; the paper money was burned after the serial numbers were recorded. The gold and silver were then brought back without incident to Fort Knox, Kentucky, and were returned to the Philippines after the war.*[17]

---

* *Trout* was not as fortunate as the gold; on her eleventh war patrol, under the command of Albert H. Clark, while attacking enemy transports on 29 February 1944 southeast of Okinawa, she and all hands were lost. (Roscoe, 79–80; www.corregidor.org/chs/trident/uss-trout; www.history.navy.mil/faqs/faq82-1.htm)

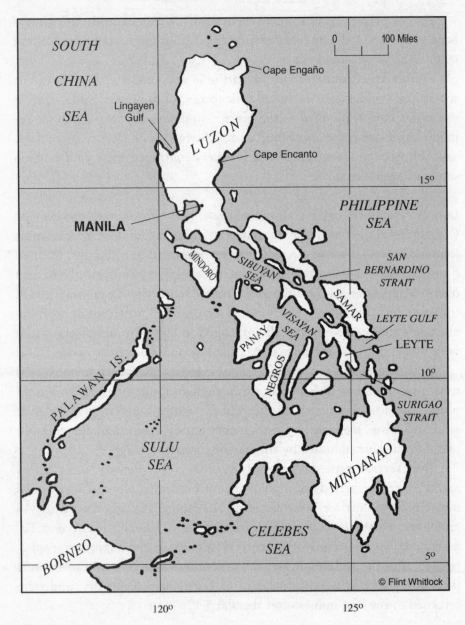

Philippine Islands.

February 1942 would prove to be another bleak month for the United States. American submarine skippers, no matter how brave and brazen, could not by themselves hold back the Japanese onslaught. That month, after Chet Smith's *Swordfish* had rescued Philippine president Manuel Quezon from Luzon, and MacArthur was ordered by President Roosevelt to transfer his headquarters from Manila to Australia, the Philippines were considered as good as lost.

With the invading Japanese army seemingly attacking from every direction on the island nation, the American and Filipino defenders were slowly pushed out of their strongholds and toward the peninsula of Bataan, which hung like an appendix into Manila Bay. For weeks Tojo's men hammered away at the "battling bastards of Bataan," who, despite their gutsy, heroic stand, knew they were doomed.[18]

DESTROYERS are the sworn enemy of submarines. Small, agile, and armed with deck guns and deadly depth charges, destroyers are perfect for warding off underwater attacks. But a submarine commander with sufficient guts could take one on, as did Lieutenant Commander James C. Dempsey, in the venerable *S-37*, on 8 February 1942 in the waters near Makassar City.

Finding himself on the surface in the path of a large, night-running convoy, Dempsey studied the menu of tempting targets. Seeing that the bigger ships were screened by destroyers, he decided to attempt to bump off some of the "tin cans," as destroyers are irreverently known, before attacking their wards. Dempsey launched a series of torpedoes at the convoy and watched in awe as the third destroyer in line, the 1,900-ton *Natsushio*, went up in an orange ball of flame.

The rest of the destroyers went crazy, like junkyard dogs dashing madly about in search of an intruder, and alarm sirens screamed into the night as the tin cans sought vengeance for the loss of one of their own. *S-37* slipped beneath the waves to wait out the inevitable depth-charge bombardment.

In five attacks over the next seventeen days, Dempsey kept up his one-sub war against Japanese destroyers but could not repeat his success of the eighth. By the end of the war, however, American subs

Sailors unload the Philippines' national gold reserves that *Trout* has brought to Pearl Harbor, March 1942.
(*Courtesy National Archives*)

would be credited with sinking a total of thirty-nine Nipponese destroyers.[19]

THE Japanese maintained their unrelenting pressure throughout the region. On 15 February 1942, the British bastion at Singapore, long be-

THE FRUITS OF WAR 39

lieved to be impregnable, surrendered; 62,000 British, Australian, and Indian troops went into captivity. It was a devastating blow, but worse was to come.[20]

In an attempt to rally flagging American spirits in the face of a barrage of bad war news, President Roosevelt declared in his "fireside chat" national radio address on 23 February, "We Americans have been compelled to yield ground, but we *will* regain it. We and other United Nations are committed to the destruction of the militarism of Japan and Germany. We are daily increasing our strength. Soon *we*, and not our enemies, will have the offensive; and *we*, not they, will win the final battles; and *we*, not they, will make the final peace."[21]

For the time being, however, defiant words were about the only weapon the Allies had; their armies continued to give ground throughout Japan's self-proclaimed "Greater East Asia Co-Prosperity Sphere." On 24 February, British Prime Minister Winston S. Churchill warned King George VI that Burma, Ceylon, and parts of India and Australia might soon "fall into enemy hands." The following day, General Sir Archibald Wavell, commander of British forces in the Far East, was forced to begin his withdrawal from Java; 100,000 American, Dutch, British, and Australian troops became prisoners of the Japanese.

The rout continued. On the night of 28 February–1 March 1942— the same night that Java capitulated—a combined Allied naval task force was defeated during the Battle of the Sunda Strait in the Java Sea, and both the American cruiser *Houston*, the flagship of the Asiatic Fleet, and the Australian cruiser *Perth* were sunk.[22]

The American sub *Perch*, based in Fremantle, became the fifth submarine to be lost since 7 December (in addition to *Sealion*, *S-26* (SS-131), *S-36* (SS-141), and *Shark I* (SS-174)). On just her second patrol, David A. Hurt's *Perch*, in a brave but futile attempt to prevent the Japanese from taking over Java, was patrolling northeast of the Kangean Islands when she was attacked by two cruisers and three destroyers on 1 March. The unmerciful depth charging badly damaged the sub. Unable to resubmerge as a result of severe leaks, *Perch* floated helplessly on the surface. On 3 March, after sighting two destroyers—the *Sazanami* and *Ushio*—heading toward the boat with murderous intent, Hurt ordered

Perch to be abandoned, and the crew climbed into life rafts that were soon picked up by the advancing enemy.*[23]

IT was bad enough that the torpedoes were suspect; having submarines attacked by friendly forces was another issue. After picking up thirty-one Navy officers and men from the submarine base at Soerabaja, Java, on 25 February 1942, *Sargo* was returning to its Fremantle base. On 4 March, the sub was spotted by a Lockheed Hudson bomber of the Royal Australian Air Force's 14th Squadron and mistaken as Japanese. Traveling on the surface, *Sargo*'s lookouts on the bridge saw the twin-engine plane boring in on them on what looked like a low-level bombing run and flashed a recognition signal at the aircraft. The bomber's crew gave no indication that they had seen the signal and closed in for the kill. Hitting the dive alarm, the men on the bridge scrambled below. *Sargo* had just submerged to forty feet when a pair of bombs exploded nearby and lifted the stern out of the water, dipping the sub forward and sending her plunging downward like a roller-coaster car on its first vertical drop.

Inside, all hands were either hanging on for dear life or doing whatever they could to put the brakes on and level her out. After all corrective actions had been taken and failed, and *Sargo* was at 300 feet and still falling, Jacobs ordered the crew to try the last-ditch maneuver—blowing all the ballast tanks, plus safety and bow buoyancy, and ordering the crew to the stern.

The trick worked, but now there was a new problem—*Sargo* was rocketing toward the surface! She broached spectacularly, as though she were trying to get airborne, then plunged again, the Hudson bomber dropping more ordnance on her as she surfaced. These bombs exploded very near her starboard beam, shattering lights, gauge faces, and the optics in both periscopes, as well as knocking out the sub's electrical system. In addition, the concussion damaged the seals around several doors and hatches, causing *Sargo* to take on water fiercely.

---

* The prisoners were then taken to the POW compound at Makassar Celebs, Dutch West Indies, where they were held until being liberated on 13 September 1945. Six men died while in the prison camp. (www.csp.navy.mil/ww2boats/perch)

The sub's electricians somehow managed to get emergency power restored, and Jacobs discovered that if he kept the sub at a certain depth, the water pressure would squeeze the warped doors and hatches just enough that the leaks were temporarily sealed off. He remained at this depth all day, surfacing only that night after the Hudson had flown home. Jacobs contacted Fremantle to report the incident and was told the bomber crew would be waiting at the dock to apologize.

Sure enough, when *Sargo* docked, a very sheep-faced bomber crew was there to ask forgiveness. It took the submarine crew a few minutes to consider the matter, but they accepted the apology and there were handshakes all around. The bomber pilot was later exonerated by a board of inquiry, but the incident so rattled Jacobs that he asked to be relieved. It took until 8 June 1942 before *Sargo* was repaired and ready to go out on another patrol, this one under a new skipper, Richard V. Gregory, class of 1932, the submarine force's youngest commander.[24]

THE remainder of March 1942 held no prospect of victory for the hard-pressed Allies. Even the British king confided to his diary, "I cannot help feeling depressed at the future outlook."

Things were far different in the enemy's camp. The Imperial Japanese Army, leaping from one victory to another and spreading like a bloody stain across the map of the southwestern Pacific, landed next in New Guinea; on the Solomon Island of Buka; and in the Andaman Islands in the Bay of Bengal. Nothing and no one seemed capable of stopping them.

By this time, General MacArthur and his family had already escaped by motor torpedo boat from Luzon, reached Mindanao, and then flew on to Brisbane, Australia, with the ringing promise "I shall return." It seemed to the embattled defenders of Bataan, and the Filipino people at large, like an empty promise.[25]

APRIL started out as badly as March had ended. On 8 April 1942, the Japanese renewed their assault against Lieutenant General Jonathan M. Wainwright's 12,000 American and 64,000 Filipino troops bottled up on the steadily shrinking Bataan Peninsula, and forced their surrender;

2,000 defenders managed to escape across the water to the small island fortress of Corregidor, which guarded the entrance to Manila Bay; they were compelled to give up on 6 May 1942. What the surrendered soldiers were subjected to during the subsequent "Bataan Death March" has gone down in the annals of history as one of the most heinous crimes ever committed by the army of a "civilized" nation against helpless prisoners of war.[26]

In the four months since Pearl Harbor, the United States had been fighting a losing battle in the Pacific. But, on 18 April 1942, Army Air Corps Lieutenant Colonel James H. Doolittle and his sixteen B-25 bombers lifted off from the crowded deck of U.S.S. *Hornet* and gave Americans their first reason to cheer. Flying across 650 miles of open ocean, the "Doolittle Raiders" headed for Tokyo and dropped their ordnance on the city before continuing on and crash-landing in China and Siberia.[27]

Bill Anderson's *Thresher* played a key supporting role in this drama, swimming close to Japan and reporting the weather conditions over the target back to *Hornet*.*[28]

As far as bombing raids went, the Doolittle raid was a tiny pinprick, but it loomed large in the collective mind of the American people. It showed everyone at home and abroad that America could do what the emperor's warlords regarded as impossible—take punishment *and* dish it out. It was also the first sign of hope that the United States was about to go on the offensive.

CORRECTLY surmising that the Japanese would, in addition to their forays across the Central and South Pacific, attempt to control the seas to the north, CinCPac in early 1942 sent two submarines to Dutch Harbor,

---

* On her next patrol, in June–July 1942, *Thresher* was caught like a sport fish in the waters between Kwajalein and Wotje Atolls. On 6 July, after torpedoing and sinking a 4,836-ton torpedo-boat tender, *Thresher* went deep to avoid an enemy depth-bomb attack. A clanking and scraping noise on her hull told Anderson that the Japanese were trying to snag her with a large grappling hook—and they succeeded! Like the shark for which she was named, *Thresher* fought for her life, twisting and turning until the hook came free, and she sped off into deeper water, with some thirty depth charges exploding in her wake. (*Thresher* war patrol report; en.wikipedia.org/wiki/USS_Thresher)

in Alaska's Aleutian Island chain, to stand guard. Selected for the job were *S-18* and *S-23*, a job that proved to be a tremendous test of endurance more than anything else. Numbing cold, snow, ice, ferocious seas, and gale-force winds plagued the submarines and their crews during the early months of 1942.[29]

In March and April 1942, the Alaskan submarine force was augmented by the arrival of eight more aging S-boats. But still there was no sign of the enemy. The Japanese, however, *were* coming.

IN April 1942, as the school year was coming to an end and he turned seventeen, Smitty took a job as a railroad section hand for the Indiana Harbor Belt railroad—a job that was tough and demanding and sometimes dangerous. But he wanted to prove to his father that he could handle anything the Navy—or the enemy—could throw at him.

As he spiked new sections of rail into their creosoted ties and waved to the engineers as their huge Baldwin locomotives chuffed by, Ron Smith was worried. The war, too, was passing him by. He ached for the chance to enlist in the Navy and see action.

What he wanted most in life was to become a naval aviator. He had taken every cent he earned working on the railroad and spent it on weekend flying lessons at the little Lansing airport, across the state line in Illinois. It took almost sixteen hours of work to pay for one hour of flight instruction, but to Smitty it was worth it. He was a fast learner, and after just a few lessons, he had soloed and earned his pilot's license. Many young Americans had gone to Canada at the outbreak of hostilities in 1939 to join either the Canadian or British Royal Air Force and get into combat as quickly as possible. Others headed overseas to join the Eagle Squadron, a volunteer group of 6,700 American pilots flying in conjunction with the RAF.

Near the end of July 1942, after working the requisite three months, he asked his father again to sign the Navy's parental permission forms. This time his dad said yes, and Smitty rushed down to Hammond's Navy recruiting office in the gray-granite federal courthouse building on State Street. He was conditionally accepted, depending on the outcome of his physical. Packing a small suitcase, Smitty said farewell to his father and brothers, had a tearful parting with his girlfriend, Shirley Leach (while he tried to stay brave and manly), and returned to the recruiting office, where he and a handful of other eager, wannabe sailors boarded a bus that took them to the federal courthouse in Chicago and then on to Great Lakes Naval Training Center, north of Chicago, for their induction physical. If he passed, he would immediately begin "boot camp"—the Navy's version of basic training.

Along with several hundred other young men in the cavernous armory, Smitty was handed a sheaf of official Navy forms, stripped down to his skivvies, and paraded from one station to another. Here the eager enlistees were subjected to a battery of tests. Their eyes, ears, lungs, and hearts were scrupulously examined by serious Navy doctors in white coats. They were pinched and prodded; told to read a chart of random letters first with one eye, then the other; checked for color-blindness; had their mouths explored; dropped their drawers to be inspected for sexual diseases; and told to turn and cough while a cold finger tried to detect any sign of hernia. Their scalps were scrutinized under ultraviolet light for ringworm, and they were asked if they had ever had any of a long list of ailments (Smitty fibbed when it came to the question about scarlet fever; he had had a mild case of it at a younger age).

He hoped—no, prayed—that he would pass. How could he look his buddies or Shirley in the eye if he were declared unfit for service? The thought horrified him. Dreams of becoming a naval aviator—and the $225 monthly pay aviators received—filled his head; he could vividly picture himself being launched from a carrier deck in a Hellcat fighter or TBD Avenger dive-bomber and see himself and his squadron flying high in the thin clouds, scanning the slate-gray ocean below for any sign of enemy warships. Then the clouds would part, his squadron leader would spot a great armada down below, and the group would swoop down on them like hawks on a pack of field mice. The Jap gunners on board the ships, of course, would do everything in their power to beat off the attack, but those "yellow bastards" wouldn't stand a chance against real Americans.

Ensign Ron Smith, his teeth clenched, would see the tracers from the antiaircraft guns rushing up to meet him, trying to blow him out of the sky, but somehow he would make it through, raking the decks with his machine guns, watching the enemy sailors fall, and dropping a bomb down the stack of a battleship—the perfect payback for what the sneaky little Nips did to the *Arizona*. Then he'd pull up, up, and away, his aircraft riddled with holes, his fuel tank leaking, a little smoke trailing from a wounded engine. He would wave to his squadron leader and signal that everything was okay—that he could make it back to the carrier without any problems. He would land hard, with flames beginning to devour the fuselage, but he'd scramble out of the cockpit, miraculously unhurt. Soon he'd have thirty days' leave and he'd go back to Hammond and show his envious 4-F buddies and Shirley the medal he got for sinking the Jap battlewagon and she would look up at him with love and admiration in her eyes and they would—

"Okay, move it along, Mac," the medical corpsman was saying to him, puncturing his beautiful hero's reverie and sending him to the next station for the last round of tests.

Smitty and the others who had passed were informed that they would begin four weeks of boot camp the following day, and were assigned to a barracks and a hammock and issued several sets of uniforms, none of which fit. The process of turning boys into warriors was about to begin.

JOHN Ronald Smith thought his football practices at Hammond High under the demanding eye of Coach Huffines had been tough, but boot camp made the Wildcats' football drills seem like a church picnic at Wicker Park.

First came a vitriol-filled welcome by uncompromising drill instructors telling the new recruits that they were the most worthless pieces of shit on which these veterans had ever laid eyes. The instructors' general theme was that the United States Navy was indeed in big trouble if these scrawny, pimple-faced mama's boys in their baggy, sorry-looking dungarees were the best the recruiters could scrape from the bottom of the barrel. This cheery greeting was followed by a trip, at double time, to the base barbershop, where the recruits received their skintight haircuts in about thirty seconds each, followed by a day filled with healthful outdoor exercise—hours of incessant running, endlessly repeated push-ups and pull-ups and deep-knee bends, all the while being verbally assaulted at eardrum-busting volume.

In the days to come, in order to break the monotony of the running and calisthenics, there were hours of marching and close-order drill—a body of men moving as if they were a single entity with a hundred legs in a steady, even cadence with everyone in step, the column rights, column lefts, left flanks, right flanks, the about turns. In reality, the first few days of close-order drill looked more like a Keystone Kops routine than a precise military movement, with the tightly packed groups continually out of step, getting in one another's way, turning in the wrong direction, and colliding with other columns.

Then there was learning how to organize a locker the Navy way, and instruction in the Navy way to wear the uniform. There were ongoing inspections of one's uniforms, one's haircut, one's personal hygiene. There was the polishing of one's shoes and belt buckle until they dazzled the eye, and the swabbing of the barracks' floors until they were cleaner than a hospital operating room—but never quite clean enough to please the instructors. There was swimming in the big pool while wearing all one's clothing and equipment. There was eating in the mess hall, and the admonition to "take all you want but eat all you take."

Even the classroom work, where the boots were schooled in the various parts of a ship using Navy terminology and nomenclature that had not changed for centuries (fore, aft, port, starboard, stern, hull, bulkhead, overhead, deck, topside, ladder, porthole, etc.); how to tie dozens of knots; how to disassemble and reassemble rifles and machine guns; and how to recognize the difference between the various Navy ranks and ratings and insignias so they didn't inadvertently salute a chief petty officer and fail to salute a commodore, was mentally challenging in the extreme. The reason for all the pressure, all the harassment, was easy to understand: the Navy wanted to see who might crack under the strain of battle, and to weed them out in advance, lest they jeopardize their ship and shipmates. Smitty vowed to himself that he would not crack.

Smitty attended classes in Morse code and learned how to signal with semaphore flags. He qualified on the rifle range. He became a strong swimmer. He mastered the art of sleeping in a hammock (some didn't, and paid for their inability with broken arms and cracked skulls when they pitched onto the hard floors).

Everyone called their six weeks at boot camp "hell on earth." There

Ron "Smitty" Smith, photographed in 1943.
(Courtesy Ron Smith)

were no breaks, no leaves of absence, no visits to, or by, family and girlfriends, no phone calls to anyone. It was instruction and training morning, noon, and night. Smitty watched as other young boots in his class, some bigger and older than he and more muscular, quit—"washed out"—because they just couldn't take the physical punishment, the mental strain, the unending harassment. But Smitty gutted it out. When pushed to his limit, when he felt his weary body could not perform one more pull-up or one more sit-up or run one more yard, he somehow dug down into a reservoir of strength and toughness he didn't know he had and endured just a little bit longer. He did it all because of his burning desire to become a naval aviator. And because he knew he couldn't go home a failure. He had to prove himself to his father, to his girlfriend, to his country, to the Navy, to himself.

He had to get into the war and do his part to avenge Pearl Harbor, Cavite, Bataan, Corregidor, Guam, Wake.[30]

CHAPTER 3

A TOUGH ROW TO HOE

THE winds of change began to blow, and the refreshing April breeze brought in fifty-two-year-old Rear Admiral Charles Andrews Lockwood Jr. to take command of the demoralized Asiatic submarine force, replacing both Captain John Wilkes, who had been evacuated from the Philippines to take charge of submarine forces in Fremantle, Australia, and Rear Admiral William R. "Speck" Purnell, head of U.S. naval forces in Western Australia. Previously the American naval attaché in London from February 1941 to March 1942, Lockwood was exactly the shot in the arm the submariners needed.

Born on 6 May 1890 in Midland, Virginia, but raised in Missouri, Lockwood graduated in 1912 from the Naval Academy and had commanded the American submarine *A-2* (SS-3) in 1914. After World War I, he extensively tested German submarines to study their capabilities and shortcomings. From 1926 to 1928, he skippered U.S.S. *V-3*, later named *Bonita* (SS-165).[1]

Brimming with confidence and good cheer, Lockwood made an inspection tour of his new command and informed Richard Edwards, Admiral King's most-trusted adviser, of his observations:

The boys here have had a tough row to hoe in the last four months. Why they didn't get more enemy ships is a highly controversial point, but my reading of all war diaries [patrol reports] thus far submitted has convinced me that among the causes are: (a) bad choice of stations, in

Admiral Charles Lockwood (center) chats with officers aboard a submarine.
(Courtesy National Archives)

that most likely invasion points were not covered soon enough or heavily
enough, (b) bad torpedo performance, in that they evidently ran much
too deep and had numerous prematures . . . (c) buck fever—firing
with [enemy] ship swinging when he [the submarine commander]
thought it was on a steady course; set up for one target and firing at a
totally different one, (d) lack of or misunderstanding of aggressiveness;
many evaded destroyers in the belief that they should save torpedoes
for convoy following; one said he thought a sub should never "pick a
fight with a destroyer."[2]

Points A, C, and D were organizational, training, and personnel issues
that could be solved in a reasonably short time frame; point B, the issue
of the malfunctioning torpedoes, was out of the purview of Commander,
Submarines, Southwest Pacific. Lockwood noted that one submarine
commander succinctly stated the problem: "It's a helluva thing to go all

the way to the China Coast to find out your damned torpedoes won't work."[3]

James Wiggins "Red" Coe, formerly commander of S-39 and now the new skipper of *Skipjack*, sent off a similar blistering complaint about the tin fish to Lockwood. "To make a round trip of 8,500 miles into enemy waters," Coe began, "to gain attack position undetected within 800 yards of enemy ships only to find that the torpedoes run deep and over half the time will fail to explode, seems to me to be an undesirable manner of gaining information [about the torpedoes' faults]."[4]

Although Coe and the obsolescent *Skipjack* had proven their mettle by sinking three ships off the coast of Indochina, Coe knew he could have done even better had the Mark XIVs been more reliable. Lockwood concurred, and Coe's report joined the many others that the admiral sent off to the Bureau of Ordnance. Despite mounting evidence to the contrary, BuOrd continued to insist that there was nothing wrong with the tin fish; the problem, as always, was "poor training and marksmanship on the part of commanders and crews."

BuOrd's reply enraged Lockwood, who became more determined than ever to get to the bottom of the situation—even if he had to conduct torpedo tests on his own.[5]

DURING April and May 1942, American submarines suddenly began enjoying an unusual, inexplicable run of good luck against Japanese shipping. On 26 April, Lieutenant Commander Joe Willingham and his *Tautog* dueled with a large Japanese submarine, *RO-30*, and killed her with a torpedo fired from an aft tube.[6]

Near the end of April, after being upbraided by Admiral Robert H. English, Commander of Submarines, Pacific, or ComSubPac, for the profligate (and unsuccessful) expenditure of eight scarce torpedoes against one freighter on his first war patrol, Henry C. Bruton, commanding *Greenling* (SS-213), sank the 3,200-ton transport *Kinjosan Maru* with a single pickle. Robert H. Rice, in *Drum* (SS-228), sank the biggest enemy warship to date, the 9,000-ton seaplane carrier *Mizuho*; he then went on to sink three more ships over the next three weeks. On 17 May, Creed Cardwell Burlingame, commanding *Silversides* (SS-236), took down a 4,000-ton freighter in empire waters.

No one knew, however, when the Mark XIV torpedoes were going to function perfectly and when they were not, and the launching of the fish was always accompanied by wishes, hopes, prayers, and a lot of crossed fingers. "By guess and by golly" was a hell of a way to run a navy.[7]

LESS than a month after April's Doolittle raid, Japan struck back at the Allies by attempting an invasion of New Guinea.

What the Japanese were planning to do at this time was establish a major air base at Port Moresby, which would threaten northeastern Australia, open that nation up for invasion, gain total control of the Coral Sea area, and permit further expansion eastward into the islands of the South Pacific. To accomplish this mission, Vice Admiral Shigemi Inoue, under Admiral Yamamoto's direction, had assembled a strong naval armada at Truk in the Carolines, while transports full of infantrymen and Imperial marines had been gathered at Rabaul and at Buin on Bougainville Island. The Imperial Japanese Navy convoy full of soldiers determined to kick the Australians out of Port Moresby was intercepted by two American task forces; this action quickly escalated into what became known as the Battle of the Coral Sea. The timely interception came about as a result of the work of the American code breakers. Originally scheduled for March 1942, Operation MO, as it was called, was postponed until May because of the threatening presence of the two American carrier task forces discovered in the New Hebrides, some 600 miles southeast of Guadalcanal.

There were, in fact, *two* Japanese invasion forces, both under the operational command of Inoue. The main Operation MO Striking Force, under Takeo Takagi, would invade Port Moresby itself, while the second, under Kiyohide Shima, would land at Tulagi Island in the Southern Solomons and act as a blocking force against any American incursion. The MO Striking Force consisted of the 5th Carrier Division, commanded by Chuichi Hara, with two heavy carriers, the *Shokaku* and *Zuikaku*, the light carrier *Shoho*, and numerous destroyers, troop transports, and other support vessels.

Opposing them on the American side were Task Forces 11 and 17. Task Force 11, commanded by Rear Admiral Aubrey Fitch, was built

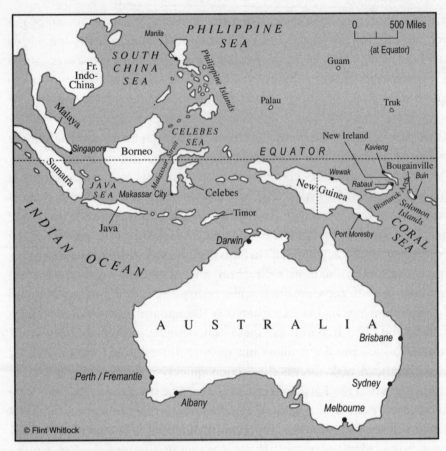

Australia and Southwest Pacific area.

around the carrier *Lexington* and consisted of sixty-nine planes, two heavy cruisers, and six destroyers. Task Force 17, commanded by Rear Admiral Frank J. Fletcher, was centered around the carrier *Yorktown*. Fletcher had sixty-seven aircraft, three heavy cruisers, six destroyers, and two fleet oilers.

The Battle of the Coral Sea was remarkable for a number of reasons. Most famously, it was the first of six major sea battles in the Pacific that was fought solely by aircraft; the surface ships never sighted one another. More importantly, it was also the first major victory over the hitherto undefeated Imperial Japanese Navy by the battered and bandaged naval forces of the United States, and marked the first of several turning points in the Pacific conflict.[8]

ONE of the problems facing the person interested in exploring the history of sea battles (and air combat, for that matter) is that once one navigates to the exact latitude and longitude of the site of the battle, there are no visible traces left of the conflict. There are no outlines of trenches, no half-demolished fortifications, no plaques, signs, memorials, or markers—nothing to indicate that a history-changing event once took place at this spot. A memorial wreath thrown into the water soon floats away. Only in a few places, such as at Pearl Harbor, can one perceive the dim outlines of the sunken casualties of the conflict.

So it is at the site of the Battle of the Coral Sea—merely an empty stretch of blue water, with the barest suggestion of islands on the far horizon. It requires a great leap of imagination to picture what transpired. The only things that tell anyone about the battle that once took place here are the survivors' accounts, the still photographs, and the motion-picture film on which its images were recorded.

The Battle of the Coral Sea became a slugging match between two heavyweights bent on the utter destruction of the other. On 4 May 1942, with Task Force 17 steaming for the Solomons, *Yorktown*'s planes took off and struck Japanese naval elements around Tulagi, sinking a destroyer and a minelayer and damaging the big, 32,000-ton carrier *Shokaku*. Fletcher's ships then joined with Fitch's, and the combined armada headed toward New Guinea.

On the morning of 7 May 1942, American aircraft spotted the enemy ships, near Misima Island, and swarmed on the light carrier *Shoho*, causing enormous damage and sending it to the bottom. Hara's 5th Carrier Division got its planes quickly into the air and struck back with surprising fury, sinking the American destroyer *Sims* and the oiler *Neosho*. But these were just the preliminary bouts. The main engagement took place on 8 May, when both sides launched every one of their planes in an all-out effort to disable the other's ships. The American carriers took a pounding. Badly damaged, *Yorktown* managed to stay afloat, but the 33,000-ton *Lexington*, her fuel lines ruptured, detonated like a huge gasoline bomb with the loss of 200 lives. That night, after the survivors had been evacuated, an American destroyer sent the listing, burning, fatally wounded "Lady Lex," to the bottom.

The final tally showed that each side had lost a carrier; sixty-six American planes had been downed vs. sixty Japanese; and two American destroyers were sunk compared to one Japanese.

The widely scattered American submarine force, with only four boats, played no major role in the Battle of the Coral Sea. Four S-boats—S-38, S-42, S-44, and S-47—fired torpedoes, but, aside from Oliver Kirk's S-42, failed to hit anything; Kirk managed to sink the 4,400-ton minelayer *Okinoshima*.[9]

The carriers *Shokaku*—streaming smoke and code-named "Wounded Bear"—and *Zuikaku* retreated toward Truk. American code breakers had picked up their signals, and four U.S. submarines—*Gar, Grampus, Greenling*, and *Tautog*—were sent to intercept them. Despite the subs' best efforts, the two flattops made it back to Truk without being spotted. Another enemy craft was not so lucky; near Truk *Tautog* sank the submarine *I-28*. *Shokaku* managed to slip out of Truk on 11 or 12 May and return to Japan without being hit, even though seven or eight U.S. subs had spotted her along her journey and gave chase; *Zuikaku* also escaped unscathed to friendly waters.[10]

WHILE the Japanese claimed to have won the Battle of the Coral Sea, the battle in actuality was an American victory, for, in a larger sense, the engagement caused the Japanese to postpone their invasion of Port Moresby and ultimately call off their planned invasion of Australia.

Convinced he had won a great battle by sinking one American carrier and crippling another, Yamamoto next set his sights on Midway Island, located a mere 1,500 miles west of Hawaii. Once he had invaded and secured Midway, Yamamoto firmly believed, he could then concentrate on invading Hawaii. Then, with Midway and Hawaii in the bag, the Japanese invasion of the American West Coast would proceed. [11]

Barely had both sides caught their breath following the Coral Sea clash when they met again on 4 June 1942 in the pivotal Battle of Midway. Having been alerted by decoded intercepts of secret Japanese messages, Admiral Chester William Nimitz,* commander in chief of the Pacific Fleet ("CinCPac") and a former submariner himself, learned of the Japanese plans to strike Midway and another thrust at the Aleutians. Nimitz notified naval units in the Alaskan island chain, then set about gathering his forces to deal with the expected main enemy drive against Midway. He recalled the carriers *Hornet* and *Enterprise* from the South Pacific and ordered the battered *Yorktown* out of the battle zone and back to Pearl Harbor for emergency repairs.

In late May, the Japanese sent Carrier Division 4—with the light carriers *Ryujo* and *Junyo*, plus *Zuiho*—to Alaska's Aleutian Island chain. The Alaska-based American submarines, along with a flotilla of six cruisers and eleven destroyers, proved incapable of stopping the Japanese attacks; Dutch Harbor was bombed on 3 and 4 June, and Imperial Japanese infantrymen waded ashore unopposed on barren, windswept Attu and Kiska Islands. In the foul weather, the American submarines could find no targets, and one of the S-boats, *S-27*, ran aground on Amchitka Island and was scuttled; the cold, miserable sailors were found days later by a Navy search plane and rescued. [12]

But it was Yamamoto's designs on Midway that posed the greatest threat to the Americans—at least for the moment. Positioning his ships and submarines to head off the enemy's drive on that atoll, Nimitz assembled an impressive armada of three carriers, eight cruisers, fourteen destroyers, and twenty-five submarines—the latter given the mission of scouting the enemy fleet and then attacking it. It was the kind of assignment for which the submarine commanders and their crews had been hungering. Used up to now primarily in a random, "freelance" role against Japanese shipping, the submarines were expected to play a crucial part in the upcoming battle. Now, it was hoped, their firepower could be concentrated in order to inflict the greatest damage and casualties on the enemy fleet.

---

* Admiral Nimitz's son, Chester Jr., served aboard *Sturgeon*. The sons of other high-ranking officers were also in the Silent Service; Edward Dean Spruance, son of Admiral Raymond Spruance, was on board *Tambor* and later *Lionfish*. Admiral Husband E. Kimmel, who had commanded the U.S. fleet at Pearl Harbor at the time of the attack, had two sons in submarines: Manning and Thomas. (Blair, 104, 660–661)

At the beginning of May, Admiral Robert H. English had replaced Admiral Thomas Withers as ComSubPac; English now set about readying his undersea force for the coming showdown at Midway. No stranger to submarines, English had been a submariner since 1914 and had commanded subs during World War I. But, as time would tell, English would prove to be inadequate for the job.

English organized the twenty-five submarines at Midway into three task forces: 7.1, 7.2, and 7.3. Task Force 7.1 was the largest, with twelve venerable boats: *Cachalot, Cuttlefish, Dolphin, Flying Fish, Gato, Grayling, Grenadier, Grouper, Gudgeon, Nautilus, Tambor,* and *Trout.* This force, with the exception of *Cuttlefish,* was ordered to group itself about 150 miles to the west of Midway in the formation of a large letter C and act as a mobile line of floating fortresses; *Cuttlefish* would position herself about 550 miles farther west of this picket line and act as an early warning sentinel.

Submarine Task Force 7.2, consisting of *Narwhal, Plunger,* and *Trigger,* would lie north of a line roughly halfway between Midway and the Hawaiian Islands in the event the Japanese tried to launch a secondary or diversionary attack on Oahu. Task Force 7.3, made up of *Finback, Growler, Pike,* and *Tarpon,* would remain on station 300 miles directly north of Oahu to be a last line of defense near Hawaii. Six other fleet submarines, returning from long-distance patrols farther to the west, were expected to arrive in time to keep an eye on the enemy's movements, and also to attack any enemy ships if they retreated from Midway.[13]

ON 3 June 1942 the bulk of Yamamoto's three-prong armada was approaching Midway. Under his command were the Striking Force and Main Body—a powerful assemblage of cruisers, destroyers, four aircraft carriers that had participated in the raid on Pearl Harbor—*Akagi, Hiryu, Kaga,* and *Soryu*—plus several battleships.

Included in the dreadnought lineup was Yamamoto's flagship, the mighty battleship *Yamato,* which, along with its twin sister, *Musashi,* were the world's largest warships. *Yamato* had a displacement of 71,659 tons; a weather deck 863 feet in length; three monstrous turrets each sprouting three 18.1-inch main guns; thirty-one tubs of antiaircraft

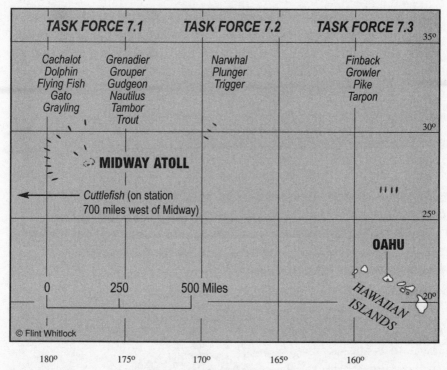

TASK FORCE 7.1	TASK FORCE 7.2	TASK FORCE 7.3
Cachalot Grenadier	Narwhal	Finback
Dolphin Grouper	Plunger	Growler
Flying Fish Gudgeon	Trigger	Pike
Gato Nautilus		Tarpon
Grayling Tambor		
Trout		

MIDWAY ATOLL

← Cuttlefish (on station 700 miles west of Midway)

OAHU

0   250   500 Miles

© Flint Whitlock

HAWAIIAN ISLANDS

35°
30°
25°
20°

180°   175°   170°   165°   160°

Submarine Force disposition at Battle of Midway, dawn, 4 June 1942.
(Based on map in Roscoe, p.125)

machine guns, a bristling array of 5-inch and 6.1-inch guns; twelve engine and boiler rooms; and an armored hull nearly a foot and a half thick. *Musashi* was similarly equipped.[14]

Yamamoto's strategy was simple. After the Striking Force had pummeled Midway's defenders into insensibility, the Main Body would further reduce the target and allow a third arm, the Occupation Force, steaming from the Marianas and loaded with 3,500 invasion troops, to land and finish the job. All of this was to be preceded by a screen of submarines. Yamamoto, it seemed, had thought of everything.

At 0700 hours on 4 June, Martin P. Hottel's *Cuttlefish*, playing the role of Paul Revere, radioed CinCPac that the first ship of the Occupation Force had been spotted. Then an amphibious PBY plane found the Striking Force 150 miles northwest of Midway and reported that scores of enemy planes were on their way. Bells rang, hatches clanged, all hands

Aerial view of Midway Atoll. Eastern Island is in the foreground, Sand Island in distance. *(Courtesy National Archives)*

The monster Japanese battleship *Yamato*, probably photographed in 1941–1942. *(Courtesy of Tobei Shiraishi and National Archives)*

Yamoto's twin sister, the dreaded *Musashi*. Photographed leaving Brunai, possibly on her way to the Battle of Leyte Gulf. *(Courtesy National Archives)*

were ordered to general quarters, and bomb-laden carrier- and land-based aircraft revved up their engines and took to the sky as the heart of Nimitz's fleet, Admiral Raymond Spruance's *Enterprise–Hornet* force, swung into action. The submarines of Task Force 7.1 were alerted and ordered to seek out and destroy the Japanese carriers.

As the subs plied the waters in search of the enemy flattops, nearly a hundred Japanese dive-bombers and torpedo planes, escorted by some fifty Zeros, cruised confidently toward Nimitz's fleet. Outnumbered Marine aviators bravely dashed into the Japanese formation and downed a number of bombers before the Zeros counterattacked in a wild aerial melee in which fifteen U.S. fighters were lost and another seven were damaged. The remainder of Yamamoto's bomber group continued on to the target and saturated Midway with bombs, being careful not to destroy runways they planned to use later.

"One of the war's decisive battles," notes naval historian Theodore Roscoe, "Midway developed as an air show. Planes did most of the attacking, aircraft carriers were the major targets, and there were no blows traded between surface craft . . .

"Far at sea the [land-based] American B-26s and Navy torpedo planes were diving on the Japanese carriers. Swarms of Zeros took to the air to defend Nippon's flat-tops. All but three of these American planes were swept away. Then the 27 Marine dive bombers and 15 [B-17] Flying Fortresses arrived on the scene. Zigzagging, throwing skyward umbrellas of anti-aircraft fire, the Jap carriers raced through evasion maneuvers while the Zeros battled the attackers. Eight Marine bombers were shot down. The remainder, riddled, barely made it back to Midway. The Flying Forts emptied their bomb-racks but not a Japanese carrier was hit."[15]

It appeared that Midway, just like the Philippines, Buna, Wake, Guam, Singapore, and the Solomons—along with Nimitz's Pacific Fleet—was doomed. But Fate, as so often happens in war, intervened. However, Confusion momentarily stepped in to counter Fate.

While on their way to Midway, the Japanese carriers changed course. The first wave of aircraft from *Hornet* and *Yorktown* had already been launched and were searching the last reported location of the Japanese fleet. As a consequence, *Hornet*'s fighters failed to find the enemy, and the

Midway Island under Japanese aerial attack, June 1942.
(Courtesy National Archives)

frustrated pilots, their planes sputtering and out of fuel, were forced to ditch in the sea. The dive bombers from *Hornet*, too, were unable to locate the targets, and only reached Midway on fumes. The fifteen *Hornet*-based planes of Torpedo Squadron 8 did manage to spot the enemy fleet but was driven off by a flight of Zeros and a blizzard of AA fire; all the torpedo planes were shot down without a single missile striking home.

"The Japanese were jubilant," writes Clay Blair Jr. "The striking force seemed invincible. They had beaten off everything the Americans had thrown at them—land-based and carrier-based torpedo planes, high-level bombers. Now they prepared to launch a strike against the American carriers and bring to a conclusion what was certain to be the greatest Japanese naval victory in all history."[16] The only problem for the Japanese was, the American carriers had yet to reveal themselves.

After the initial wave of aircraft had lifted off, the Japanese carriers parked on their decks dozens of planes armed with aerial torpedoes ready to be used against American ships. With no American ships apparently in the vicinity, the armament crews were ordered to replace the torpedoes with bombs for further attacks on the island's defenses and installations. Then *Hornet* and *Yorktown* were sighted by Yamamoto's scout planes and the electrifying news radioed back to the carriers. The order to replace the torpedoes with bombs was countermanded and the crews scrambled to switch back to torpedoes. The resulting delay gave the Yank pilots the window of opportunity they needed.

At 1024 hours, dive-bombers from *Enterprise* and *Yorktown*, flying through a ferocious storm of antiaircraft fire, descended upon *Kaga*, *Akagi*, and *Soryu*. For several tense moments it appeared as if *Enterprise*'s planes would suffer the same fate as *Hornet*'s Torpedo Squadron 8, with American planes, looking like large, flaming meteorites, falling everywhere. But still more came on, heedless of the deadly hailstorm, dropping bombs onto flight decks and thrusting torpedoes into the hulls of enemy carriers. A bomb struck and *Kaga* exploded in a huge ball of fire—catapulting aircraft and sailors into the sea—and stopping her dead in the water. In a frenzy of bravery, and despite heavy losses, the American pilots turned their attention to *Akagi* and *Soryu*; soon these carriers were aflame and exploding. *Hiryu*, a few miles to the north and untouched during this assault, sent her dive-bombers after the American carriers.

Some 200 miles away, a dozen fighters rose up from *Yorktown*'s flight deck to meet thirty-six of *Hiryu*'s planes heading their way. A tremendous battle in the clouds ensued and all the enemy bombers were shot down, but not before the Japanese managed to hit *Yorktown* with three bombs. While *Yorktown*'s crews valiantly tried to extinguish her fires, the carrier was swarmed upon by torpedo planes, which holed her port side. Listing badly, and with fires raging and magazines in danger of exploding, the *Yorktown*'s skipper, Captain Elliott Buckmaster, ordered the ship abandoned.

At approximately the same time that *Yorktown* was being attacked, dive-bombers from her and *Enterprise* found *Hiryu* and turned the Japanese carrier into a floating inferno.[17]

With Yamamoto's fleet concentrated in a relatively small area, one could be forgiven for thinking that Admiral English's submarine force must have had a field day, picking off ships like shooting-gallery ducks.

The U.S.S *Yorktown* lists badly after absorbing enemy punishment during the Battle of Midway, 4 June 1942.
(Courtesy National Archives)

Such was not the case. In fact, of the twenty-five subs on station around Midway, and between Midway and Hawaii, only one became directly involved in the action. On that afternoon of 4 June, with the ocean to the west of Midway shrouded by the smoke from burning carriers, the American submarine *Nautilus*, as part of Task Group 7.1, arrived with hopes of making a contribution to the battle. *Nautilus*, along with *Argonaut* and *Narwhal*, was one of America's oldest, slowest, and largest (at nearly 400 feet long and displacing 2,700 tons) active submarines. Commissioned in 1930, *Nautilus* was now under the leadership of Lieutenant Commander William H. Brockman, renowned as an excellent underwater warrior.

Earlier that morning Brockman had maneuvered *Nautilus* for an attack on a battleship (probably *Kirishima*) and three cruisers, but had been spotted and strafed by a Japanese plane; Brockman submerged in the nick of time, but the aerial assault alerted the foe that a submarine was lurking nearby. An enemy cruiser (*Nagara*) and two destroyers then picked up *Nautilus*'s trail and made several depth-charge attacks. Once the unfriendly greeting ceased, Brockman came up to periscope depth and surveyed the watery landscape. He noted, "The picture presented on raising the periscope was one never experienced in peacetime practices. Ships were on all sides moving across the field at high speed and circling away to avoid the submarine's position. Ranges were above 3,000 yards. The cruiser had passed over and was now astern. The battleship was on our port bow and firing her whole broadside battery at the periscope." Brockman noted that he then launched two torpedoes at *Kirishima* at 4,500 yards, but scored no hits.

Enemy destroyers, pinging* on their sub contact, came roaring back and laid down a deluge of depth charges; *Nautilus* went deep to avoid the explosions. A half hour later, with the sea having again grown quiet, Brockman surfaced to survey the scene. Black smoke on the far horizon indicated a fierce battle (U.S. Marine aircraft had struck the fleet), so he steamed over for a look-see.

Around 0900, Brockman saw a Japanese carrier (*Chikuma*) on fire and lying dead in the water. Before he could attack, he noticed another carrier making waves about 16,000 yards away and decided to go after it instead. Determining from silhouettes of enemy ships pasted on the bulkhead of the conning tower that it was either the *Soryu* or a *Soryu*-class carrier, Brockman was in the process of setting up his tubes for firing when the cruiser *Nagara* and destroyer *Arashi* appeared on the scene and diverted his attention from the flattop. With these sub-killers practically on top of him, Brockman dove. While he was down, the rest of the fleet *Nautilus* had been stalking, subjected to heavy aerial assault, tried to make a run for it. The carriers *Akagi* and *Kaga* were soon both on fire and having difficulty making speed.

At last, at around 1400 hours, the burning *Kaga* came to a halt and Brockman closed in for the kill. His torpedomen fired a spread of four fish at the helpless ship; the first one failed to leave the firing tube, the next two missed, and the fourth, a dud, banged into the carrier's hull and broke in half. Inexplicably, Brockman reported that the carrier had suffered grave damage, and that "red flames appeared along the ship from bow to amidships . . . Many men were seen going over the side."

---

* Sonar, a submarine-finding device, made a distinctive "pinging" noise when its electronic signals hit the sub's hull and bounced back, giving the hunter the direction and range of its target.

Firing a torpedo at an enemy carrier is akin to whacking a beehive with a stick, for it invariably stirs up an angry response. Two Japanese destroyers went in search of *Kaga*'s attacker and Brockman crash-dived *Nautilus* to 300 feet, subjecting her to oceanic pressures that increase by 14.7 pounds per square inch for every 32.8 feet of descent. The old boat groaned and wheezed at that depth, and her rivets threatened to pop, but she was safe. For two hours salvos of depth charges continued to explode near her, but serious damage was averted.[18]

Although there were nine U.S. submarines patrolling near Midway, none but *Nautilus* mounted any kind of attack against the enemy; in several instances the Japanese saw and fired on the prowling American subs, keeping them at bay. Additionally, a series of misadventures plagued the submarine force at Midway; *Tambor*, under John W. Murphy Jr., found what its officers thought was a large concentration of unidentified ships about 100 miles west of Midway on the night of 4–5 June and radioed in a vague, incomplete report. Mistakenly believing these unidentified ships were the Occupation Force on its way to Midway, Admiral Spruance repositioned his carrier and submarine forces, but no invasion was in the offing; *Tambor* had merely seen four cruisers and two destroyers screening Yamamoto's retreat.[19] Then Eliot Olsen's *Grayling* had the misfortune of being bombed by friendly B-17s that mistook her for a Japanese craft. Luckily, she was not seriously damaged. Another sub, the newly commissioned *Trigger*, captained by Jack H. Lewis, had an ignominious encounter with a coral reef near Midway, running aground on 6 June and causing extensive—and expensive—damage.*

However, thanks to the breaking of the Japanese codes and the heroic sacrifice of American pilots and sailors on the carriers, the Battle of Midway ended as a great American victory and a major turning point of the war. No one yet knew it, of course, but the high tide of Japan's objective to dominate the Pacific had been reached at Midway and was about to recede. Because of the reversal, the Japanese now had to forget about

---

* *Trigger* would be hit by enemy aircraft and warships on 28 March 1945 and sunk at Nansei Shoto, Ryukyu Islands. (www.history.navy.mil/faqs/faq82-1.htm)

invading Midway, Hawaii, or the West Coast and worry instead about defending their Home Islands.

The contribution of American submarines to this mid-Pacific victory, however, was insignificant. As Clay Blair notes, "The submariners . . . had nothing of their own to celebrate. Only two or three got off a torpedo, and none hit anything."[20]

As far as the enemy's submarines were concerned, they were almost as ineffective as English's force. Only the *I-168* scored a hit, but it was a big one. On 6 June, *I-168*'s torpedoes sank the wounded *Yorktown*, which was being towed back to Pearl Harbor, as well as her escorting destroyer, *Hammann*.[21]

WITH Yamamoto's Midway invasion fleet in retreat, the Japanese thrust against the Aleutians gained new importance. The enemy reinforced his foothold in American waters, sending the heavy carrier *Zuikaku* from Japan to the Alaskan chain. Despite the many targets, the S-boats, along with seven newer subs (*Finback, Gato, Growler, Grunion, Trigger, Triton,* and *Tuna*) dispatched to Alaska by Admiral English after the Battle of Midway, failed to produce the expected results. Howard W. Gilmore, commanding *Growler* (SS-215), did manage to score, sinking one destroyer and damaging two others off Kiska Island. A few days later, *Triton*, under Charles C. Kirkpatrick, sank another destroyer.

But the enemy had landed on American soil in the Aleutians and was establishing a base from which to mount future operations. It would take a major combined land-air-sea operation to oust him, an operation that would not take place for more than a year.[22]

In the meantime, however, the threat farther south would need to be dealt with—and quickly.

CHAPTER 4

HELL ON EARTH

WITH Midway no longer in imminent danger, the time had come for the Americans to begin the long slow march to reclaim the Pacific. Arrows on planning maps in Nimitz's headquarters pointed the way through the heart of Japan's strongly held outposts—faraway outposts with strange-sounding names that would nevertheless soon be known by every American schoolchild: the Solomons, Guadalcanal, "The Slot," Tarawa, Betio, Kwajalein, Saipan, New Georgia, Bougainville, Rabaul, Kavieng, the Admiralties, Madang, Wewak, Buna, the Kokoda Trail, Cape Glouchester, Truk, Tinian, Guam, Hollandia, Biak, Peleliu, Palau, Iwo Jima, the Philippines, Okinawa, and more. But first, an area called the Bismarcks Barrier needed to be breached.

As Samuel Morison notes, "Too long had the Bismarcks Barrier and its eastern bastions confined the activities of Admiral [William 'Bull'] Halsey's South Pacific Force to the lower Solomon Islands. Too long had that Barrier and its southern bastions prevented General MacArthur from commencing his return to the Philippines. But the operations to break the Barrier's outer bastions and penetrate its weirlike center were difficult and complicated . . . They extended over a period of twenty-one months, from 1 August 1942 to 1 May 1944."[1]

As a preamble to this ambitious offensive, dubbed Operation Cactus, the first American offensive of the war, Admiral Nimitz directed Admiral English to send his Hawaii-based subs to scout the Japanese staging base at Truk and do as much damage as possible to enemy shipping. The submarine commanders were glad to oblige, hoping that they, their crews, and their boats would finally prove their worth.

But before he could place his faith in the ability of his submarines to get the job done and lead the Navy's charge toward Japan, Admiral Charles Lockwood decided to conduct his own torpedo tests at Frenchman's Bay, Albany, Australia. Lockwood's headquarters bought 500 feet of fishing nets and, on 20 and 21 June 1942, replaced the warheads of *Skipjack*'s remaining torpedoes with exercise heads of the same weight. "Red" Coe and the *Skipjack* crew fired them into the netting at a range of 850 yards. The tests determined that the Mark XIVs were indeed the problem, running an average of eleven feet deeper than their setting.

Lockwood reported his findings to Washington, but BuOrd refused to accept the results of Lockwood's tests, telling the admiral that his methodology was flawed and no reliable conclusions could be drawn from his experiments. Furious, Lockwood repeated the tests on 18 July, this time using John L. Burnsides' *Saury* (SS-189). Again, the average error was eleven feet. And, again, BuOrd rejected Lockwood's conclusions; the battle between the submariners and BuOrd raged on, and Japanese ships continued to elude destruction.

Lockwood decided on a career-risking move, going over BuOrd's head and taking his frustrations and findings directly to Admiral Ernest King, the chief of naval operations. King was sympathetic and ordered the Bureau of Ordnance to conduct trials. Tests at Newport, Rhode Island, confirmed that the tin fish were, indeed, running too deeply. Steps were at last taken to remedy the problem.

The remedy, however, would be long in coming, and Nimitz's drive to liberate the South Pacific could not wait for improved torpedoes. From July to September 1942, eleven submarines participated in the operation, but had little to show for their efforts, plagued mainly by unusually strong antisubmarine defenses around Truk and, most importantly, the boats' faulty torpedoes, the unreliability of which had become a tremendous, if secret, scandal. Throughout the Pacific, the noise of American torpedoes churning past or bouncing off Japanese hulls was a tocsin, the alarming sound of potential defeat.[2]

Correcting the deep-running problem uncovered a new one—the

warhead's defective magnetic exploder. During the months it took to solve this new wrinkle, more American submarine crews and commanders continued to sail into harm's way only to be frustrated, and more Japanese ships sailed away from their doom.[3]

IN September 1942, the "Silent Service" broke its silence. Admiral English, under pressure to report some good news by his hitherto relatively unsuccessful underwater force, authorized a heavily censored press conference to extol the remarkable first patrol of the *Guardfish* (SS-217), commanded by Thomas Klakring.

Klakring claimed that *Guardfish*, while off the northeast coast of Honshu, had sunk six ships weighing in at a total of 50,000 tons—four of them in a single day, an unprecedented feat; Klakring got the Navy Cross for the patrol.

The news conference also spawned a legend, albeit a false one. Klakring's exec, Herman Kossler, said that through the periscope he spotted a passenger train traveling along the coast. Seeing a notation on the sub's chart that a racetrack was nearby, someone in the conning tower put two and two together and concluded that the people on the train were going to the horse races. At the news conference, Klakring mentioned, in a spoofing manner, that the officers had a close-up view of the races and began betting on the horses. Kossler said, "I could have killed him for saying that—but what the hell! We'd had a great patrol. He was entitled to spin a sea story if he wanted to. It was a good story— good for morale back home."

The story went out on all the newswires, gaining new layers of imaginative but fictitious details with each retelling. *Guardfish* finally became renowned across the country as the submarine that had sailed into Tokyo Bay and gotten close enough for its officers to wager on the ponies. Later, a "Klakring Day" was held at the Pimlico racetrack, and the skipper was even made an honorary member of the New York State Racing Commission![4]

WHILE Ron Smith waited to get into flight school and a cockpit, it was time for a major ground assault in the Pacific, time for the United States to begin repossessing the islands occupied by the Japanese, time to break through the Bismarcks Barrier. Allied planners had devised three main objectives in the South Pacific. The first was to liberate the all-important Philippines. The second was to cut Japan's lines of communications with her far-flung island strongholds. The third—and most immediate objective—was to capture those island strongholds and turn them into bases from which the American war machine could grind down Japan's ability to resist, thus opening the way for an eventual invasion of Japan itself.

To begin to accomplish these goals, it was determined that Rabaul first needed to be knocked out. Rabaul, a port city on the northeast tip of New Britain Island and the home of a large Japanese air base, was the most powerful and important of all the Japanese bases in the region. "Rabaul had a commodious harbor," Morison writes, "safe from Allied air attack until the outer bastions of the [Bismarcks] Barrier were surmounted. There the bombardment missions, cruiser strikes and 'Tokyo Expresses' that so long bedeviled American efforts in the Solomons were assembled. Rabaul's five airfields supported a pool of air power, reinforceable at will from Japan, whence bombers and fighters flew east and south to attack Allied shipping and ground forces."[5]

But getting to Rabaul first required stepping onto the malarial, green hell of Guadalcanal and neighboring Tulagi, 900 miles directly east of Port Moresby, in an operation known as "Watchtower."

By breaking the Japanese codes, the Americans learned that the Japanese were planning to land at Guadalcanal and Tulagi on 4 July 1942, build an airfield, and establish a base of operations that would allow them to bomb U.S. installations in New Caldonia and New Hebrides, and threaten New Zealand and eastern Australia. The Americans decided to forestall the enemy's plans.

Operation Watchtower, as originally conceived, would be an all-Navy show under the command of Vice Admiral Robert Lee Ghormley, Naval Academy class of 1906, whose headquarters were on the island of Nouméa, northeast of Brisbane, Australia. When MacArthur got wind of the plan, he objected vehemently to the Army being left out; all the glory would go to the Navy and Marine Corps. To calm his ruffled feathers, Army Chief of Staff George C. Marshall and Admiral Ernest J. King, chief of naval operations, came up with an emollient: Ghormley would proceed with his invasions of Guadalcanal and Tulagi; the 1st Marine Division, under Major General Alexander Vandegrift, together with the soldiers of Major General Alexander M. Patch's Americal Division, would hit the beaches of Guadalcanal. MacArthur would be given command of future joint operations in the Solomons.

On 7 August 1942, three months before American troops would land in North Africa and begin the Mediterranean phase of the European campaign, American troops began piling onto the shore of Guadalcanal.[6]

What awaited them far surpassed their worst nightmares.

WHILE Smitty and his classmates continued to sweat into their boots at boot camp, the fight for Malaya raged on, with Australian and Japanese troops battling each other with unusual savagery, and with no quarter asked and none given.[7]

But it was the battle for Guadalcanal that burned its way into head-

U.S. Marines come ashore at Guadalcanal, 7 August 1942.
(Courtesy National Archives)

lines and history books. The Japanese had moved swiftly to occupy Guadalcanal and Tulagi. Just as swiftly, Ghormley had assembled every ship
and every infantry unit on which he could lay his hands and had them
rushed to the area. Included in the group were three carriers: *Wasp*
(which had just arrived from duty in the Mediterranean), *Enterprise*,
and *Saratoga*. The enemy had an airfield on Guadalcanal and was dug in
well enough to cause any American invasion serious problems.

Before the operation began, it was learned that Japan's huge naval
base at Truk, about a thousand miles north of Guadalcanal in the
eastern Caroline Islands, was the assembly area for many of the convoys making the run to the Solomons. American naval commanders
decided to set up a roadblock to hinder Japan's efforts to shuttle men
and matériel into the Solomons. The responsibility for conducting this
blockade fell to five subs: *Drum, Grayling, Greenling, Grenadier,* and
Gudgeon.

Into the waters around Truk the submarine force slipped, and it was
not long before the hunters began to score. On 3 August, Grenfell's *Gudgeon* sank the 4,800-ton passenger-cargo vessel *Naniwa Maru*; two days
later, Hank Bruton's *Greenling* earned her first trophy, the troop-filled,
12,752-ton *Brasil Maru; Greenling* sank another troop carrier, the *Palao
Maru,* the next day. The other three subs, *Drum, Grayling,* and *Grenadier,** also got in on the action, attacking and probably damaging several
large ships. Truk was turning into a happy hunting ground for American
submariners. More importantly, they were throwing a very large monkey wrench into Dai Nippon's plans to reinforce Guadalcanal and Tulagi. Still, the erratic performance of their torpedoes greatly concerned
the submarine commanders.[8]

Picture the Solomon Islands as a long, thin bottle tipped downward
to the right at a thirty-five-degree angle. At the base of the bottle, closest
to New Guinea, is an island named Bougainville. At the opening of the
bottle at the far end are Malaita and Guadalcanal Islands. San Cristobel
Island is the cork. Just inside the opening are a cluster of smaller islands:

---

* *Grayling* would be lost near the Philippines on 9 September 1943; *Grenadier* would be
sunk by Japanese aircraft off Penang on 22 April 1943. (www.history.navy.mil/faqs/
faq82-1.htm)

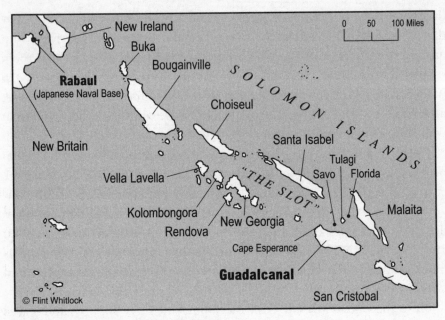

Solomon Islands and Guadalcanal area.

Tulagi, Florida, Savo, and others, all lush tropical paradises with white sand beaches and swaying palm trees. The space between the top wall of the neck of the bottle and the lower wall was dubbed "The Slot," and it was down this long, narrow channel that the Japanese were pouring men, supplies, and warships, all primed and ready to blow the American Navy out of the water.

The Battle of Guadalcanal began in earnest on 7 August 1942, when 19,000 Marines hit the beaches and encountered a huge surprise: almost no resistance. The airfield on Guadalcanal, which had been defended mostly by construction workers, was overrun and taken by late afternoon; Tulagi, although more heavily defended, was declared secured the following day. The victory seemed almost too easy—and it was.

From their bases at Rabaul and Bougainville, the Japanese retaliated with heavy air attacks against American ground troops and ships, while a large flotilla of cruisers and destroyers proceeded to inflict heavy damage on U.S. Navy vessels in what was called the Battle of Savo Island, which began on 9 August. Although American pilots gained the upper hand in the air, downing thirty-three Japanese planes to a dozen of their own, the American Navy took a pounding.

Roaring down The Slot at night, ships of Japan's Eighth Fleet—the "Tokyo Express"—moved almost undetected to Savo Island until it was too late. Gunbursts and explosions lit up the darkness and everything was thrown into confusion. American commanders failed to fire on enemy ships, thinking they were friendly while simultaneously opening up on friendly ships, thinking they were the enemy. Within a half hour, the combined American-Australian fleet was nearly destroyed. Four heavy cruisers—a mixture of Yank and Aussie—were sunk, and a heavy cruiser and a destroyer severely damaged. So distraught was Captain Howard Bode, commanding *Chicago*, that he committed suicide after his damaged cruiser was towed into port. Just as they had done at Pearl Harbor, the Japanese failed to follow up on their surprise victory and sailed away, confident that the job was finished.

The job *was* very nearly finished. Almost 1,300 American sailors and airmen were dead and over 700 were wounded in the Battle of Savo Island; no Japanese vessels were lost during the engagement that Clay Blair calls "the worst defeat ever inflicted on the United States Navy at sea."[9]

THE only submarines available to the Americans in the Solomons at the time were eleven obsolescent "Sugar" (from the military's phonetic alphabet for the letter *S*) boats stationed at Canberra, and these were on their last legs. At 225 feet in length, the S-boats were eighty-three feet shorter than the newer "Fleet" submarines; had two rather than four diesel engines; could carry only half the number of torpedoes; had half the crew members; had a top speed of only eight knots; and could stay out on patrol for only half the time of a Fleet boat. Only one S-boat, John R. "Dinty" Moore's *S-44* (SS-155, commissioned in February 1925), had an air-conditioning system. The men aboard the other Sugar boats complained bitterly about the heat, the lousy food, the electrical and mechanical problems, the inadequate sonar gear, and the millions of cockroaches that infested them.[10]

But the S-boats made up for their shortcomings by having exceptionally fine officers and men filled with an aggressive spirit. During World War II, there were few submarine patrols that could be classified as "routine," and the second war patrol of the ancient *S-38* (SS-143, commissioned in 1923) was certainly anything but ordinary. On 8 August, Henry G. Munson, skipper of the *S-38*, came in tight on a sizable enemy convoy of six transports and their destroyer escorts. Munson submerged, slid beneath a destroyer, and fired two torpedoes into a large transport, the 5,628-ton *Meiyo Maru*, sending her and her cargo of reinforcements to the bottom. The Imperial Japanese Navy, shaken by the episode, turned the convoy around and departed the area. Temporarily at least, Munson and *S-38* bought the Marines on Guadalcanal a little more time to strengthen their defenses. By the end of the war, Hank Munson would be the fifth-highest-rated submarine skipper in terms of tonnage sunk.[11]

Another old sub also scored. While hunting near Kavieng, New Ireland, on 10 August, Dinty Moore in *S-44* sighted a convoy of four heavy cruisers less than a thousand yards away and put four torpedoes into the trailing cruiser, the 7,100-ton *Kako,* at close range, then submerged as the stricken ship was going down. Suddenly, *S-44* was shaken like a snake as *Kako*'s escorting destroyers slammed her with scores of depth charges; *S-44* barely escaped with her life.[12]

Not all the Sugar boats had successful runs. Due to a navigational error, at midnight on 13–14 August Frank Brown's *S-39* ran aground on a reef near Rossel Island in the Louisiade Archipelago and was in danger of being battered to pieces by the pounding surf. Despite trying everything in the book (and a few things that weren't) to refloat her, nothing worked. Brown radioed for help; an Aussie ship, the HMAS *Katoomba,* appeared and *S-39*'s men were transferred to her. *Katoomba* then proceeded to destroy the Yank sub with gunfire to prevent her from falling into enemy hands. It was a sad but necessary end for a proud old gal.[13]

ARGONAUT and *Nautilus* soon found themselves in a new role—that of troop carriers. On 8 August 1942, two companies of Marines—211 handpicked men commanded by Colonel Evans F. Carlson and known as Carlson's Raiders—crammed themselves into the two subs and headed for Makin Island. Their mission was to create a diversion and siphon off enemy units that could be used to resist the 1st Marine Division, which had just landed on Guadalcanal. The mission was a pipe dream.

In the predawn darkness of 17 August, as the seasick Marines who had been cooped up inside the sweltering subs for nine days went ashore, virtually nothing happened as planned. According to Clay Blair, the precisely rehearsed raid turned into a fiasco: "Seas swamped the [rubber] boats, drowning most of the outboard motors. The few boats that ran towed the others as best they could, abandoning their carefully conceived landing pattern. In the darkness, Colonel Carlson lost sight of his 'flag boat' and had to go ashore in someone else's. Somehow, the Japanese had been forewarned or were exceptionally alert, perhaps because of the U.S. attack on Guadalcanal. There were snipers hiding in trees. Cascading through the surf, the Raiders got ashore in helter-skelter formation, in front of the Japanese rather than behind as planned."

Brockman's accompanying *Nautilus*, the only American sub to have scored a hit at Midway, opened up with her deck guns on Japanese ships in the harbor, seven miles away, and sank two—a transport and a patrol boat—on pure luck. Japanese strength on Makin Island, however, was more than the Raiders could overcome, and the decision was made to call off the attack and retreat to the subs under cover of darkness on 17–18 August; it would be more than a year before the Marines would land again on Makin. The withdrawal, too, was a fiasco. The sea was still rough and flipped many of the rubber rafts; fewer than half of the nineteen rafts were able to reach the submarines. The next morning, *Nautilus* and *Argonaut* moved in as close to the beach as possible, hoping to pick up stragglers; a few more men were found, but then Japanese fire and enemy aircraft got dangerously close and the subs had to pull away from shore and submerge.

That night, after waiting underwater all day, the two submarines again approached the shore, guided by a signal light from Colonel Carlson himself. The remaining men, all but thirty presumed to have been killed during the skirmish, returned to the boats.* The ward rooms on

---

* Nine Marines, still alive, were captured and beheaded by the Japanese. (Blair, 292)

Carlson's Raiders aboard the giant submarine *Argonaut* following the 17 August
1942 raid on Makin Island.
(Courtesy National Archives)

both subs were turned into hospital operating rooms in an attempt to
save the lives of the wounded.[14]

The Navy's public-relations office proclaimed Carlson's submarine-
mounted raid "the greatest commando raid carried out in the Pacific
during World War II." Reports told of the Raiders destroying an enemy
radio station, two planes, a supply dump, and 900 barrels of gasoline,
while wiping out the small Japanese garrison.[15]

More objective observers, however, said after the war that the raid
did not achieve its purpose of diverting any Japanese assets away from
Guadalcanal. Yet the reports from the field, inflated though they may
have been, gave Americans heart at a time when heart was most needed.
Colonel Carlson and Major James Roosevelt, one of the president's four
sons and one of the officers who took part in the expedition, became
household names and national heroes.[16]

A major effort was mounted that the Japanese regarded as their all-or-
nothing counteroffensive to drive the Americans off Guadalcanal and
Tulagi. Assembling an armada of one light and two heavy aircraft carri-

ers, eight battleships, and numerous other cruisers, destroyers, and supporting vessels, the Japanese were prepared to ram their naval might
down the throat of the Americans, who had only three carriers, one
battleship, four cruisers, and ten destroyers in the area. The clash would
become known as the Battle of the Eastern Solomons.

The battle was joined on 24 August 1942. In the opening hours,
Ghormley's force sank the light carrier *Ryujo,* plus a cruiser, a destroyer,
and a transport ship carrying several thousand soldiers moving to reinforce Japanese positions on Guadalcanal; ninety enemy aircraft were also
shot down. The Americans also suffered; *Enterprise* sustained severe
damage from dive-bombers, and a few days later, *Saratoga* was torpedoed by a Japanese sub but remained afloat. Despite the damage, the
Yanks had stymied the enemy—at least for the moment.[17]

EVEN as August 1942 melted into September, like a carload of pheasant
hunters assigned to shoot all the birds in Nebraska, there were still too

Marine Colonel Evans Carlson (left) and President Roosevelt's son James, a
major in the Marine Corps, share a laugh with the *Argonaut*'s skipper,
John R. Pierce, following the Makin Island raid.
(*Courtesy National Archives*)

few American submarines in the Pacific and too much ocean to cover. Morale's ballast tanks were open and optimism was sinking.

A shake-up in the naval command structure "down under" didn't help matters any. Vice Admiral Herbert F. Leary, the Navy's top commander in Melbourne and second only to MacArthur, was transferred out. Replacing him was the difficult, hypercritical Vice Admiral Arthur Schuyler "Chips" Carpender. Carpender had a long-standing antagonistic relationship with Charles Lockwood, Commander of Submarines, Southwest Pacific. Their poor relationship deteriorated further when Carpender transferred half of Lockwood's assets—Squadron Two—from Australia's southwest coast to Brisbane, on the east. Lockwood was now down to just eight boats based in the west, but was still expected to patrol a huge area. Lockwood, with his headquarters in Perth, put in a request to transfer to Brisbane to better command Squadron Two, but Carpender not only vetoed the request but placed a junior admiral, Ralph Christie, in command of Squadron Two. Lockwood was livid.

Adding to Lockwood's displeasure was the fact that Christie, as the "father" of the suspect magnetic torpedo exploder, still refused to listen to any complaints about it from the submarine commanders. Although the problem of deep-running was being corrected, the exploders still detonated prematurely or failed entirely when they reached their intended targets. Enemy ships, although aligning themselves in the center of American periscopes on many occasions, continued to lead a charmed life. Not one S-boat during August and September claimed a hit. Believing the Sugar boats were over the hill, CinCPac ordered them back to less hostile waters to be replaced by the newer Fleet boats. Still, the results did not improve; many said Christie was at fault for stationing the submarines in areas that were not conducive to kills—areas bristling with antisubmarine defenses that kept the boats beyond the maximum ranges of their faulty fish.

Part of the blame also attached to Admiral King in Washington, who put a higher priority on the enemy's "hard" targets, such as the well-protected aircraft carriers, battleships, and cruisers, than he did on the softer, easier, but no less important destroyers, transports, cargo ships, and tankers. But how does one tell the Navy's highest-ranking admiral that he was wrong, or should at least consider another course of action?

No one did, and the emperor's ships continued to escape destruction.[18]

THE Japanese knew the same thing the Americans did—that Guadalcanal and the Solomons were strategically vital. If the Japanese could defeat the Americans there, Japan would prevent the United States from building up the amount of men and supplies in Australia necessary for MacArthur to move north and recapture lost territory, especially the Philippines. Cut off from aid, Australia itself would also be strangled to death.

Conversely, the Japanese realized that if they lost the Solomons, there would be little to stop the Americans from driving closer and closer to Japan. It was, therefore, a matter of utmost urgency for the Japanese to do everything in their power to prevent an American victory—just as the Americans were committed to doing everything possible to ensure that *they* would be victorious. Thus the Battle of the Solomons, after Midway, became the most important contest of the Pacific Theater.[19]

The green hell of Guadalcanal consumed men as though they were snacks favored by primordial plants, poisonous snakes, and insects the size of a man's fist. The heat and humidity and the steady, drenching downpours caused uniforms to disintegrate and skin rashes to blossom like mushrooms. Diseases of all sorts lurked in the miasmic jungle, as deadly as a Nambu machine gun or a round from a knee mortar. It took hours of arm-numbing work to hack a few yards of trail through the thick, tangled underbrush—a trail that would be overgrown again a day later, as though the machete work had never been done. Rest was impossible; birds and mammals made shrieking noises that sounded just like men being gored, tortured, disemboweled, emasculated. Blood-bloated, malaria-carrying mosquitoes feasted on human flesh, and the stifling, fetid air was corrupted with the intermingled odors of rotting vegetation and the rotting meat of uncountable corpses.

Despite Guadalcanal's many frightful features, U.S. ground forces continued to make progress—albeit slowly and at a high cost—and were squeezing the enemy into an ever-shrinking perimeter. On New Guinea, too, American units reached Port Moresby and took the unrelenting pressure off the Australians, who were doing their best to prevent the Japanese from gaining control of all of New Guinea.[20]

Guadalcanal was a bloody affair, as the entire history of the Pacific "island-hopping" campaign would prove to be. By the time the Americans realized that the fanatical Japanese troops would fight to the bitter end, 1,600 of the 60,000 U.S. soldiers and Marines on "the Canal" would be killed during the seven-month-long slugfest, with another 4,245 wounded.

The Japanese had it worse; nearly 15,000 of 36,000 Imperial soldiers were either killed or listed as missing; another 9,000 died of tropical diseases. About a thousand Japanese were taken prisoner; the remainder were evacuated in a daring rescue operation and lived to fight another day on other islands—islands that were just as inhospitable as Guadalcanal.[21]

In the middle of September, though, the Japanese struck back hard. The carrier *Wasp* was sunk by enemy submarines in the New Hebrides, and the battleship *North Carolina* was severely damaged. That left the U.S. Pacific Fleet with but one undamaged carrier (*Hornet*) and one

Japanese dead litter the sand of Guadalcanal after a suicidal banzai charge.
(*Courtesy National Archives*)

operational battleship (*Washington*). The war of attrition on the high seas seemed to be swinging in Japan's favor.

The need for submarines with torpedoes that worked—and for trained submariners—was becoming acute.[22]

CHAPTER 5

DAMN THESE TORPEDOES!

THE four weeks of Navy boot camp seemed more like four years, but Ron Smith saw his body transformed into a hard, lean fighting machine. Gradually, the grueling physical work got easier. So did the classroom instruction. He was catching on. He was proving he could do the work; he was proving he could become a *sailor*. The instructors started to ease up on him. He just hoped he would see action before the war ended.

At last, near the end of August 1942, Smitty's boot camp came to a merciful close and he saw his final grades: near the very top of the class. Following the final review, the boys in their sharp-looking blue uniforms were now officially, if not chronologically, men, each with the rank of apprentice seaman. Each graduate received a nine-day leave to say good-bye to families and friends. And then Ron and all the other "boots" from his class were gone, to be replaced at Great Lakes, and at other Army, Navy, and Marine training camps, by tens of thousands of other flabby, nervous young men—war's endless assembly line churning out an endless number of warriors.

Smitty spent his last nine days at home hanging around with his high school buddies and especially with his girlfriend, Shirley. He recalled with a chuckle, "There was a lot of smooching but no sex. I remember one session we had at Wicker Park. My whites were covered with grass stains and lipstick from all the 'wrestling' on the ground."

Soon it was time for parting once more. At the end of August 1942, Smitty said his good-byes for perhaps the last time, packed his seabag, and had his father drive him to Chicago's Union Station to catch the train for San Diego and a new life filled with wonder and danger.

The train ride from Chicago to San Diego was long, boring, and uncomfortable. For many of the young sailors, however, it was their first time away from home, their first time on their own, and the beginning of an exciting adventure. They crossed the flat prairies of Iowa and Nebraska, gazing at endless expanses of farms where the wheat and corn had grown tall and was nearly ready for harvest. They passed large ranches in western Kansas and eastern Colorado where cows grazed placidly and paid little heed to the speeding train. They saw the majestic Rockies rising like a snowcapped backdrop to the west of Denver, then changed trains and continued south along the line of mountains into dry and dusty New Mexico. The weeklong trip impressed many of them with America's vastness, her strength, her riches; no Japanese or German army could ever conquer this rich and immense land, they thought.

From Albuquerque the train took them farther west, toward the ocean, through desolate country that never changed. The food they ate aboard the train—ham, peas, potatoes—was as unchanging as the scenery. Occasionally, when the engine stopped to take on water or coal, the sailors were allowed to get off to stretch their legs and grab a smoke.

At one stop near the Army's Desert Training Center, close to where California, Nevada, and Arizona come together, and where the temperature was well over a hundred degrees, the sailors watched in amazement as a dust-covered tank rumbled up beneath the railroad water tower and dispensed a great gushing stream onto—and into—the tank. Smitty thought the tankers, in their olive-drab leather football helmets and OD coveralls, "looked like cooked lobsters when they took off their helmets to stand under the spout and let the water drench them. God only knew what the temperature was *inside* those tanks." He was glad he had joined the Navy and not the Army.

The journey finally ended late on 11 September when the train pulled into the Santa Fe railroad depot in downtown San Diego. Bleary-eyed from a lack of sleep during their five-day trip, and restless from being cooped up all that time, the sailors wandered around the mission-style station, checked out the attractive females (who mostly ignored them), and waited to claim their bags from the baggage car. They went outside under the palm trees for a smoke and breathed in the cool damp air that smelled like the ocean. Somewhere unseen to the west, in all that darkness, the dragons of the Japanese Empire, although wounded, still breathed fire, and soon these novice sailors would be required to enter the darkness and slay them. Smitty looked around at his train mates and wondered which ones would not return. He never stopped to consider that they might be doing the same with him.

Shortly before midnight a petty officer showed up to gather the brood and herd them onto several gray-painted Navy buses that would take them to the United States Destroyer Base, on the south side of town. At the gate of the base a Marine guard came on board to check everyone's orders and ID cards. Satisfied that they were all authorized to be there, the Marine then permitted the bus to continue.

As the bus wound its way toward the receiving station, the sailors—those who hadn't fallen asleep, anyway—gazed out the windows at their new home. The architecture was pure military; that is to say, dull, drab, utilitarian. The driver turned a corner and, visible in the distance, was the bay, moonlight reflecting off the waves. Suddenly a gigantic black object loomed over the left side of the bus. It looked monstrous. The men jumped out of their seats to get a better look.

"I'll be a son of a bitch," one of them exclaimed. "It's a submarine!" Smitty was amazed; he had no idea that the United States even *had* submarines—he thought only the German navy possessed such underwater craft. But what was it doing out of water? he wondered. The huge shape disappeared behind them and somebody asked the bus driver if they had seen what they thought they had seen.

"Yeah," he answered. "It's an S-boat on the marine railway for some work."

It being too late to be issued proper bedding, the new arrivals slept that night on bare springs in the receiving station; they were so dog-tired they didn't care. The next morning they walked leisurely to the mess hall; they didn't have to march together as a unit as had been required in boot camp. After breakfast—a sumptuous buffet that was a welcome relief from the monotonous diet of ham, peas, and potatoes they had been served on the train—the sailors were formed into ranks outside the receiving station and broken down into smaller groups. They learned that they were at the San Diego Destroyer Base, where various Navy schools were located. Most submariners were trained at the Submarine School in New London, Connecticut, but a fair number were also receiving instruction at San Diego.

A loudspeaker shouted, "Now hear this. Fleet Torpedo School, assemble at the north end of the street in front of this building." The voice began booming out the names of sailors, along with their serial numbers. When it got to the Ss, the voice called Smitty's name: "Smith, John R., 3009553." He hoisted his sea pack to his shoulder and headed off to where other soon-to-be-students of the Fleet Torpedo School were congregating. He thought there must have been some mistake; the Navy needed pilots, and he wanted to be a pilot. If he couldn't be a pilot, he'd settle for being a gunner—anything to be up in the air. His mind flashed back to the tank at the Desert Warfare Center; he definitely did not want to be encased inside some iron coffin like a submarine.

When the loudspeaker had finished sending sailors to their assigned school groups, some thirty men were assembled in Smitty's contingent. A squat, chubby, red-faced chief petty officer stood holding a clipboard and a cigar. Smitty thought that if this CPO had had a white beard, he could have doubled for Santa Claus.

The CPO went through the drill of reading off the names in his group once more. In a quieter, almost fatherly voice, he said, "My name is Evans. I'm a chief torpedoman. I'll be your instructor for the next six weeks. It is a privilege in this man's Navy to be selected for a fleet school. It shows you're smarter than most. I expect you to pay attention. We have to cover in six *weeks* what the peacetime Navy took six *months* to cover.

"I've been in this Navy fifteen years," Evans went on. "It took me four years to make third class. Some of you, the top three, will get third class when you graduate. Ten more will get seaman first class, and the rest of you will be promoted from apprentice seaman to seaman second— if you pass the course. I don't pass men unless they make it, so it's up to you."

A medic, or, as they are known in the Navy, a pharmacist's mate, appeared and walked over to the group. "Oh, yeah," Chief Evans said, "I forgot—short-arm inspection."

"Okay," said the pharmacist's mate, "drop your drawers." After the startled sailors had lowered their trousers and skivvies around their ankles, the PM went down the ranks with his flashlight, briefly checking each man's genitals for signs of venereal disease. The PM finished and the embarrassed sailors pulled up their pants; Smitty couldn't help shaking his head in wonder at the incongruity of thirty young men standing on a street in broad daylight with their private parts exposed. He would soon learn that all enlisted sailors had to undergo this indignity each time they transferred to a new command or returned from leave.

Chief Evans led his charges to the Torpedo School area. The quarters were small huts just big enough to house sixteen men. The wooden walls only went halfway up; the upper half of the walls were screens that could be covered with horizontal shutters in case the weather turned bad. Bunk beds filled the buildings. There was one "head" (latrine) and shower building to serve two huts.

As Smitty and the other sailors assigned to the same hut entered to claim their bunks, they were bemused to find half the building occupied by Marines. When Smitty expressed his surprise at Marines being assigned to Torpedo School, one of the Marines—or jarheads, as Smitty indelicately called them—spoke up: "We're here to learn about the Mark XIII aerial torpedo. Marine aircraft use them, too."

At the word *aircraft*, Smitty's ears perked up, and the question "What is a pilot like me doing at torpedo school?" again flew through his brain. He resolved to talk with Chief Evans and get this matter sorted out.

The next morning, at "zero-dark-thirty," well before the sun was up, the apprentice seamen and their Marine counterparts were outside, going through calisthenics. Couldn't let all that fitness gained at Great Lakes go to waste, Smitty thought. Once the workout was finished, the sweaty group was marched to breakfast, then back to the huts for shaving, showers, and a change into crisp, clean dungarees before heading over to the large Quonset hut that served as the school. Chief Evans's classroom instruction began on the dot at 0800 hours, followed at noon by lunch; classes resumed at 1300 hours (1 P.M.) and ran until 1700 hours (5 P.M.). Half the time was spent on lectures about the theory and practice of torpedoes, the other half with hands-on classes where a working model

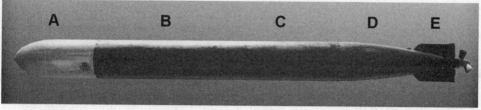

(Author photo)

Schematic view of a typical torpedo.
A: Warhead
B: Air Flask (fuel & water)
C: Midship Section (combustion flask igniter)
D: Afterbody (oil tank, turbines, depth engine, gyro steering engine,
immersion mechanism, starting lever, depth index)
E: Tail (exhaust manifold)

of a torpedo could be studied, examined, dissected, and put back together again.

Smitty was fascinated with the torpedo model; he had built many balsa-wood airplane models in his younger days, so he was good with his hands and mechanically inclined. The students learned how to dial in the prelaunch settings that determined the torpedo's speed and depth. Smitty was intrigued to learn that the torpedo was "steam-powered"; that is, when it was launched from a torpedo tube by a blast of compressed air, a container of alcohol inside the torpedo was ignited, forming a "torch." A spray of water was then forced through this torch and converted into steam, which in turn powered a turbine and propelled the torpedo to its destiny.[1]

From the beginning of hostilities until September 1943, when the new Mark XVIII electric torpedo was made available to the U.S. Submarine Force, American submarines (as well as PT boats, destroyers, cruisers, and TBF torpedo planes) employed three types of torpedoes: the older Mark X (for the older S-boats), the Mark XV for surface craft, and the Mark XIV (for the newer fleet boats). All three types of torpedoes had a diameter of twenty-one inches. The Mark X's warhead held nearly 500 pounds of explosive and detonated when it made contact with a hard surface—such as the hull of an enemy ship. The Mark X weighed 2,215 pounds and had an effective range of 3,500 yards (nearly ten miles) at a speed of thirty-six knots.

The Mark XIV and XV, by contrast, weighed 3,000 pounds, and could be set to travel at either fast or slow speeds. At slow speed, a setting that was seldom used, the Mark XIVs and XVs could travel 9,000 yards at thirty-one and a half knots; the fast setting allowed the missile to traverse up to 4,500 yards at a speed of forty-six knots. The faster a torpedo traveled, the more steam it would consume, thus accounting for the shorter range. The slower setting enabled the torpedo to travel farther, but accuracy suffered. The Mark XIV and XV warhead, at the beginning of the war, held 507 pounds of TNT; later it contained 668 pounds of a special explosive known as Torpex. It could cause enormous damage to an enemy ship.[2]

Depending on the type of detonator—magnetic or contact—the torpedo was safe until launched. The contact detonator was as the name suggests: it did not explode until the torpedo made contact with the hull of a ship, thus slamming the firing pin into the explosive. The magnetic exploder was more complicated, thereby leading to more problems. A sensor in the nose detected the magnetic field of a ship when it passed close to the steel hull and was supposed to detonate the explosive charge. A ship, however, could be "de-gaussed"—that is, have its hull demagnetized, making it much harder for the magnetic exploder to work properly. For both types of detonators, a mechanism inside the nose prevented the arming of the warhead until the fish had traveled approximately 300 yards.[3]

The Mark XIV had one major problem, however.

Its top secret Mark VI exploder, which was designed to work as either a contact or magnetic exploder, often worked as neither—a fact kept hidden from the torpedo school students, but painfully obvious to the submarine crews that had to use them.

"We trained extensively on the exploder mechanism, with emphasis on the Mark XIV's magnetic exploder," Smitty reported. "We knew nothing about the unreliability of the exploder, nor did anyone else at that time."[4]

Smitty and his classmates would soon learn—the hard way.

UNLIKE the students at the Submarine School in New London, Smitty did not have to pass certain tests, such as the "pressure-tank test." Reynold Dittrich, from St. Paul, Minnesota, who would later serve on the *Aspro* (SS-309), recalled that the pressure tank was a way of weeding out those unfit for submarine service. Dittrich said, "The first thing they did with you was they put you in the pressure tank—it was just a big cylinder on the ground—to see if you could take pressure at a hundred feet. You sat on a bench in there and they put fifty-some pounds of air pressure on you. There must have been five or six guys on each side, maybe ten or twelve guys total in there. The Navy needed to see if you can breathe properly. It's painful. The heat gets terrific. It's so hot in there, the water's just pouring off of you. It's a physical thing. You're breathing through your nose and your mouth and keeping the pressure equal in both ears. Some guys wanted out. So they let the air down and let them out, and then they start all over again. Most of these guys had trouble with their sinuses, stuff like that. They couldn't handle that pressure. A lot of guys failed that right there. If you're lucky like me, the pressure didn't bother you, other than sweating so bad."[5]

DESPITE the fact that submarines were about as far as one could get from flying, Smitty was beginning to enjoy torpedo school. He decided not to ask Chief Evans about a transfer to flight school. Instead of spending nine months in naval aviation school, the six-week torpedo school meant he would probably see action sooner rather than later. Plus, as a submariner, he would make a lot of money—almost as much as an ensign on flight status. And it was hard to find a specialty, other than pilot or paratrooper, that carried with it as much mystique, glamour, and awe-producing distinction as a submariner! Anyone could be a swabbie or a grunt, but submariners were a unique breed of men—smarter, braver, and, well, *special* in an ineffable way.[6]

Not everyone could stand the claustrophobic confines of a submarine, or had the courage to face a horrible underwater death. Psychological problems brought on by the long, tense war patrols *were* an ugly reality—and a closely guarded secret—of the submarine service. Clay Blair notes that a war patrol could be "nearly overwhelming. The safety of the ship and crew depended almost entirely on the judgment and acuity of the captain, and one mistake could be the last. It required cool nerves and limitless stamina to bear it, week in and week out, with sleep constantly interrupted by reports from the bridge, periscope, sonar, and radio watches." Gordon B. Rainer, skipper of *Dolphin*, during a patrol to the Marshall Islands that left Pearl Harbor on Christmas Eve 1941, suffered a nervous breakdown and had to be relieved.

Ted Aylward was relieved after he developed physical symptoms brought on by the psychological stress of commanding *Searaven*. Then there was the case of Lieutenant Commander Morton C. Mumma Jr., captain of *Sailfish* (SS-192, formerly *Squalus*). After being battered by an especially vicious depth-charge attack shortly after the outbreak of war, Mumma went to pieces emotionally and ordered his executive officer, Richard Voge, to lock him in his cabin; Mumma was relieved of command. Other officers and untold numbers of enlisted men also succumbed to the intense strain.[7]

Although he knew nothing of these and other cases, Apprentice Seaman John Ronald Smith was convinced that he was tough enough to handle the strain. He cocked his hat at a smarter angle and walked a little taller, basking in the glow of being regarded as a member of an exclusive fraternity—one of the Navy's elite. He could hardly wait until he qualified to wear the dolphin insignia on the right sleeve of his uniform.

THE Navy paid in cash on the fifth and twentieth of each month. At fifty-four dollars a month for an apprentice seaman in Torpedo School, half a month's pay came to twenty-seven dollars—a king's ransom for an eighteen-year-old in 1942. Smitty and two of his friends, Bud Shineman (rhymes with cinnamon), from Louisville, Kentucky, and Jim Feldman, from Wheaton, Illinois, decided to spend some of their newfound wealth in the bars and other places of amusement in San Diego when their first weekend liberty from the school came along.

As they donned fresh uniforms for their foray into town, Smitty and Feldman and Shineman reminded one another to keep a civil tongue in their mouths once they left the base and reentered the "real" world. Such restraint would not be easy. Their language, ever since the beginning of boot camp, had become, to say the least, "salty." Profanities and obscenities foul enough to burn the ears off a Methodist naturally gushed from their mouths like water from a hydrant. As Smitty related, "Sailors had to be very careful in conversation with civilians; words could slip from habit."

Friday-afternoon classes ended for the week at 1700 hours and anyone foolish enough to be standing in front of the Thirty-second Street gate of the U.S. Destroyer Base San Diego after that time risked being trampled to death by the hordes of sailors pouring from the facility and rushing for streetcars, buses, and taxis. Unable to find a mode of transportation that wasn't already packed with naval personnel, the trio decided to walk toward town; maybe when the first wave of weekend revelers had subsided, they could find a place on a passing trolley in which to squeeze. It wasn't long before a streetcar, drooping with humanity but with enough room to fit three extra bodies, came along. They hopped on board and rode into downtown "Dago," as the city was known by anyone disdainful of words containing more than two syllables.

Shineman, Feldman, and Smith got off in the center of town and noticed that Dago looked just like a larger, civilianized version of the naval base. San Diego, like many American cities in 1942, was a military town. Besides the 1,029 land acres that belonged to the destroyer base, there was Fort Rosecrans, whose casemated, sixteen-inch naval guns at Port Loma protected San Diego Bay. The newly opened Marine base known as Camp Pendleton sprawled across 130,000 acres north of the city, and 45,000 civilian workers crowded into the Consolidated Aircraft Corporation facility at the nearby municipal airport, where they churned out scores of B-24 "Liberator" bombers each week.

"The city was teeming with soldiers, sailors, and Marines," Smitty recalled, "thousands of them, bumping and jostling to get into a bar or just walk down the street. Bars, tattoo parlors, and souvenir shops ringed all four sides of San Diego's downtown Plaza Square, a park filled with palm trees. Each bar around the park had a jukebox that was trying to be louder than its neighbor's."

Feldman suggested that they grab a beer, so the teenagers went into the nearest establishment for some suds, marveling at the fact that no one even checked their IDs to see if they were old enough to drink. The crowd in the bar was loud, boisterous, and almost exclusively male. It

Submarine tender U.S.S. *Holland* in San Diego Harbor, photographed 1935, with six submarines tied up beside her.
(Courtesy Naval Historical Foundation)

didn't take long for a fight between drunks—San Diego's normal weekend sporting activity—to break out. "Let's get out of here," Smitty said to his friends, and they did.

As the Shore Patrol and Military Police arrived on the scene and descended in nightstick-wielding fury upon the brawlers, the trio plunked themselves down on a bench in the park, pondering the wisdom of coming downtown on a Friday night; none of them wanted to end his Navy career by being maimed or stabbed or shot by a fellow serviceman while on liberty. The night was getting damp and chilly and the three were glad they had brought their dark blue peacoats with them. They discussed their next move.

"Let's go rent a room so we'll have a place to stay," Feldman offered, and the other two agreed. The three sailors knew without even checking that the elegant Grant Hotel on Broadway and the Westgate were too pricey for them. Just from looking at the façades they could tell that the rooms probably cost ten or twenty dollars a night—and were the special province of captains of industry, movie stars, corporate executives on important wartime business, even young naval officers on their wedding nights. So they left Plaza Square and headed up a side street until they found a house with a "Tourist Rooms" sign out front.

The elderly lady who owned the house carefully eyed the applicants before making them promise not to get drunk and mess up the place. They promised they would behave and paid her the three-dollar weekend rate. The room had two double beds with the bathroom down the hall. It was quiet and pleasant, and it took the edge off the bloody, drunken fight they had just witnessed. Listening to their growling stomachs, the trio decided to venture back downtown and find a place to eat.

"This is great," Shineman said, shoveling in the tasty civilian fare at a nearby diner.

"I never realized how much I missed my mom's cooking," said Feldman, also feeding his face with gusto.

The remark caused Smitty to think about his mom, whom he had lost to breast cancer when he was only thirteen. His dad wasn't much of a chef, and the long procession of housekeepers who came in to make meals also left a lot to be desired. And, while the Navy was reputed to have the best food of all the armed services, it also would win no blue ribbons for culinary excellence. "You want to go get another beer?" Smitty asked.

"Not after that last deal," Shineman replied. "Your life's not worth a plugged nickel in this town."

The trio settled into a nice, quiet movie theater for their evening's entertainment. After the film—a typical 1942 wartime drama designed to boost home-front morale and stimulate enlistments—the three sailors found a peaceable bar for one last beer or two before heading back to the rooming house and turning in. Here they chatted about their pre-Navy lives, their girls back home, and what they planned to do once the war was over. The conversation was getting comradely and mellow when three drunken Marines practically burst into the place.

The Marines, fresh from boot camp at Pendleton and loaded with booze and testosterone, were looking to pick a fight, and Smitty, Feldman, and Shineman appeared to be the perfect victims.

Smitty and Feldman tried to ignore the belligerent jarheads, but skinny Bud Shineman rose to take the bait. After a verbal exchange, the two thinking sailors whisked Shineman off his feet and headed out the door. The trio jogged away from the bar toward the rooming house with the Marines staggering after them.

The sailors reached the porch of the home about the same time the Marines did, and a fistfight broke out on the narrow steps. Shineman, like Horatio at the bridge or Samson against the Philistine army, held off the attackers while Smitty and Feldman looked on with bemused admiration. The smallest of the three sailors, Shineman seemed to be well acquainted with the fine art of self-defense. The staircase was too narrow for more than one Marine at a time, so as each Marine reached the top of the stairs, Shineman would send him flying with a vicious punch out of all proportion to his size. After the sailor sent the bullies tumbling down the steps for about the third time, the Marines gave up and stumbled off into the night, grumbling and nursing sore jaws.

Smitty and Feldman had a new respect for Shineman. They also learned that size is not everything in a fight. And they looked forward to the day when they would be beating up on Japs, not their fellow Americans.

By the end of the fifth week, Smitty knew the torpedo like he knew the back of his hand, and was sure he would be graduated as one of the top three students in his class. Chief Evans had even privately told him that he had the second-highest grades in class, and so he looked forward eagerly to being automatically promoted to torpedoman third class and receive the extra pay such a promotion would bring.

So imagine his chagrin when Lieutenant J. D. Somes, the officer in charge of the Fleet Torpedo School, called him and Chief Evans into his office and told Smitty he had some bad news for him. Telling Smitty he was too young to be promoted to torpedoman third class, Somes gave him seaman first class.

Smitty, stunned, could not speak. He glanced over at Chief Evans, who was glowering at the officer with a look that could kill. "His face was so red, he looked like he could explode," Smitty said. "If it were not for military discipline, the lieutenant would have been lying flat on the floor."

Without allowing either Smitty or Evans to say a word in response, Lieutenant Somes ended the meeting and the two enlisted men walked out into the California sunshine, where Evans vented his spleen toward the officer in a profanity-laced tirade. When he had calmed down, and the two of them began heading back to the school area, Evans said, "You know, son, it's not going to make up for losing the promotion they promised you, but I'm going to give you your choice of duty. That's in my authority, so what'll it be—submarines, PT boats, or destroyers? Give it some thought and let me know tomorrow."

Knowing that Evans was a proud submariner himself, and knowing that the chief had not included flight school as one of the options, Smitty promised to think it over.

Sleep did not come easily that night as Smitty mulled over the choices. He wanted to do something that would really make a contribution to the war effort. If he was to die, he wanted it to be only after doing something that would bring the greatest return for his country. He also knew that getting into the Submarine Service was tough—only the top 10 percent of the volunteers would actually be accepted. But he badly wanted to wear that silver dolphin insignia and so, the following morning, he told Chief Evans that he had chosen submarines; Evans beamed and shook his hand. Now all Smitty had to do was pass the rigorous physical.

IN November 1942, Ron Smith and 106 other torpedo school graduates from the various other classes were herded into the base hospital to take their physicals for submarine duty. The dentist looked into Smitty's mouth and passed him. Then every inch of his wiry, five-foot-eight, 150-pound body was inspected by Navy doctors, who also found nothing to disqualify him. He was sent to another station where he had to stand on one leg, and then the other, for two minutes with his eyes closed—a task much harder than it sounds. Then he had to hold his breath for two minutes—and thought his lungs were going to explode. The final test was an interview by a psychiatrist.

The lieutenant commander was sitting in an office behind a wooden desk and invited Smitty to take a seat. He then began probing him with questions, the first being, "So, young man, you want to die?"

Smitty thought it was a dumb question. "No, sir, I don't want to die."

"Then why do you want to go into submarines? Everyone knows how dangerous they are. You even get fifty percent more pay because it's hazardous duty."

"It may be more dangerous, sir, but that doesn't mean you're going to die."

The psychiatrist grinned, then asked, "Would you kill someone?"

"Sure, if he was trying to kill *me*," responded Smitty, wondering just what kind of game this shrink was playing with him. Was he trying to trap him into saying something that would show he wasn't mentally fit for submarine duty?

"I want to ask you some questions," the doctor said next, in a detached, professional way. He picked up a sheet of paper and began reading. "If you were swimming with your wife and mother and they both started drowning, which one would you try to save first?"

Smitty smiled. "That's easy. I don't have a wife and my mother is dead."

The answer seemed to catch the doctor momentarily off guard, but his blank look was quickly replaced by a hearty belly laugh. The psychiatrist shook Smitty's hand and ushered him out of the room; evidently he had given the correct answer.

By the end of the day, only nine of the 107 volunteers had passed the tests and were accepted to Submarine School; Smitty's friend Bud Shineman made it but Jim Feldman did not. "Nobody ever knew why they failed," Smith said.[8]

CHAPTER 6

SCHOOL DAYS

THE nine young men were placed on orders to attend the Submarine School that had been established right there in San Diego.

"The 'real' Navy Submarine School was in New London, Connecticut," Smitty said, "but we weren't going there. The demand for new men was too great at this time, so an improvised Sub School was set up at the San Diego Destroyer Base."

It wasn't much of a school. There were no textbooks; each student had to make his own workbook. Their instructor was a chief off *Cachalot,* an old "V"-boat. For the first two weeks, the chief showed them pictures and described the various hydraulic, electrical, low-pressure and high-pressure air lines, and other systems and principles that operated the current, state-of-the-art submarines. The students had to draw and write everything in their workbooks. "After two weeks of classroom work, the chief took us down to the docks where *Cachalot,* which was our school boat, was moored," Smitty said.

Over the course of the next few weeks, Smitty got to know his eight fellow classmates well. Besides Shineman, there was tall, good-natured Bill Partin from Oregon; handsome, blond Bill Quillian from Washington state; Montanan Jim Biggars, whose dark complexion and surly look belied his sunny, easygoing personality; Jim Koster, who brought a relaxed Texas demeanor with him from Houston; Hank Brown, a Los Angelino; Bob Kaminsky from Chicago; and San Franciscan Jim Caddes, who seemed the most cynical and worldly

U.S.S. *Cachalot*, photographed 9 July 1934 at Portsmouth, NH.
(Courtesy Naval Historical Foundation)

Fledgling submariners learning the basics at Submarine School,
New London, Connecticut, 1943.
(Courtesy National Archives)

of the group. Smitty hung out with them all but most enjoyed Bill Partin's company.

The students were schooled in the theory of submarines. The concept behind the submarine was simple yet ingenious: create a hollow, watertight chamber capable of withstanding thousands of pounds of water pressure that could intentionally be sunk by filling large ballast tanks with seawater to create "negative buoyancy." The chamber could then be raised by using compressed air to force the water out of the ballast tanks. Diesel engines would be used to rotate the propellers when the craft was on the surface and battery-powered electric motors would take over from the diesels when submerged. There was nothing to generate oxygen to keep the crew alive; the ambient air brought into the submarine while the hatches were open during surface running supplied enough oxygen to last eighty men for nearly a day.

To enable the commander of the submarine to visually survey the sea around him without being obvious and giving his position away, the submarine was fitted with optical devices known as periscopes that could be raised and lowered at will while the bulk of the vessel remained hidden below water. The sub could communicate with the outside world through the use of radio.

Of course, a vessel that merely submerged and surfaced would be good only for reconnaissance work; to turn the submarine into a man-of-war required the addition of armament. Tubes fore and aft would launch torpedoes, and deck-mounted guns and machine guns would be used for offensive and defense actions while surfaced.[1]

Everyone in the U.S. Navy believed American subs to be the best in the world. Mike Geletka, a sailor aboard *Harder* (SS-257), remarked, "I've been on English boats and Dutch boats and German boats—I was on the U-505* when they brought it back in '46; the German U-boats were a hunk of junk. The U.S. got a late start in submarine design but we advanced a lot further than they did. I don't care what anybody says, our boats were Cadillacs compared to the others—the

---

* After the war, Geletka came into possession of the U-505's depth gauge from a buddy named Sears and presented it to the Museum of Science and Industry in Chicago, where the U-505 is on display. He personally installed it in the U-505. (Geletka interview)

others were like Model Ts. We got three meals a day, we had our own bunks and our own showers; we had double hulls. We had no room on board, but we had more than the others had. Ours were just better boats all around. Whoever designed that *Gato*-class did a great job. Then came the *Balao* and then the *Tench*-class, the thick-skins, that were even better."[2]

The World War II "Fleet" submarine of the *Gato* (which was built from 1941 to 1943) or *Balao*-class (built from 1943 to 1945) was as technologically advanced for her time as any weapon of war ever invented. The standard *Gato*-class Fleet submarine was 312 feet long, had a beam of twenty-eight feet, a surfaced keel depth of sixteen feet, displaced more than 1,500 tons, and carried twenty-four torpedoes. She could travel thousands of miles without refueling or docking to take on food or supplies.

The submarine was also a prime psychological weapon. It could, at the first sign of an enemy ship or convoy, glide beneath the surface and carry out her deadly attacks at periscope depth or, when sighted and

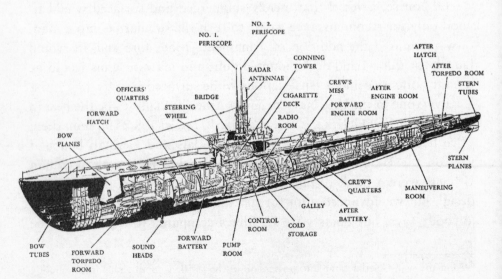

Cutaway view of Fleet-type submarine (*Balao* class).
(From Roscoe, Submarine Operations in World War II. *Reproduced by permission of publisher)*

attacked, dive deeply to escape the effects of bombs and depth charges. She could then resurface at another location to resume her assault—or simply disappear from the area as silently and stealthily as she had come.

Like a nervous native rowing a raft on a river full of crocodiles, the fear of being attacked was always there, always lurking just beneath the surface. There were Japanese captains out there who *had* spotted the slim cyclopean periscopes peering their way, who *had* heard the ominous *clank* of malfunctioning torpedoes bouncing off their hulls, who *had* wondered how long their luck would hold out. For sailors on board enemy vessels, the mere thought that a submarine might be lurking unseen nearby and preparing, at any moment and without warning, to send them to Davy Jones's locker was nerve-racking in the extreme.

The bow of a Fleet submarine contained the forward torpedo room with its four or six torpedo tubes (and, when armed for a combat patrol, sixteen torpedoes), fourteen hinged bunks suspended by chains from the walls, or bulkheads, and an overhead hatch leading to the forward escape trunk, or compartment; during combat operations the bunks were swung out of the way to maximize working space.

Submarine battery.
(Whitlock photo)

Near the center of the boat was "officers' country"—the cramped living quarters and dining area for the ensigns, lieutenants, and commander. The ward room served many functions, including mess hall, meeting room, recreation hall (for cards, cribbage, chess, and checkers). There was also a pantry and the "staterooms" for the officers and chief petty officer.

Directly beneath officers' country and the control room was the largest space on board: the forward battery compartment and pump room. In this compartment stood 126 huge lead-acid batteries, each weighing more than a ton. It was the batteries that enabled the submarine to operate underwater. In the adjacent pump room were the air compressors, hydraulic pumps, air-conditioning compressors, and trim and bilge pumps.

When submerged, the submarine ran solely on battery power—but considerably slower than when running on the surface. Underwater, she had a maximum speed of nine knots, but because prolonged travel at that speed would deplete her batteries within thirty minutes, submerged speed normally did not exceed three knots. A submarine could travel roughly a hundred miles submerged.

Directly aft of the officers' quarters and below the conning tower and bridge was the control room. As its name suggests, this was the location from which the submarine was controlled by the captain when submerged. The right, or starboard, side was called the "dry" side of the control room, for here the electrical and air controls were located. The left, or port, side was known as the "wet" side because it contained the controls for the hydraulic as well as the trim and drain systems.

Here, too, was located the diving station from which, through the use of large control wheels, the boat could be submerged or surfaced. Two large "steering wheels" faced the port bulkhead and were operated by two planesmen. These wheels controlled the "elephant ears," or bow and stern planes, which determined the angle at which the submarine dove or surfaced. Immediately behind the bow planesman's bench was the ladder to the bridge and conning tower.

Located on the bulkhead in this compartment were two panels known as the "Christmas tree," for the red and green indicator lights on these panels showed at a glance if any hatches were open or closed. If a hatch was open, an indicator light glowed red; if it was closed, the light was green. To safely submerge, all indicator lights needed to be green.

The control room also contained the auxiliary steering station, general announcing equipment, and interior communications switchboard. In the center of the room stood two tablelike objects: a plotting table or dead-reckoning tracer that mechanically plotted the boat's latitudinal and longitudinal position, and the master gyrocompass that floated on gimbals and was the essential tool for navigation. Located above the gyrocompass were the fathometer, which measured the depth below the

View of complex array of switches, gauges, dials, and machinery in a submarine control room (U.S.S. *Pampanito*). The black-panel box at upper right is the "Christmas tree." The ladder leading to the conning tower is visible at left. *(Whitlock photo)*

keel, and the bathythermometer, which gave a reading of the outside water temperature—vital for locating cold layers of ocean water that partially negated the enemy's underwater submarine-finding equipment known as sonar.

Aft of the control room was the incredibly cramped radio room, stacked from deck to overhead with radio equipment. One man—preferably of small stature—could just barely squeeze into the chair and desk thoughtfully provided for him.

To the aft of the radio room was a relatively spacious room: the galley and crew's mess hall. It was said that to compensate the submarine crews for their dangerous work and less-than-ideal living conditions, the Navy provided them with the best food of any branch of service. Because of the limited space, the crew ate in shifts of twenty-four men, while cooks and bakers worked around the clock to feed them. Most boats had two cooks and one baker. The cooks worked a full day every other day, and the baker worked every night, baking bread and rolls and pastries.

Two cooks aboard U.S.S. *Batfish* share cramped galley
working space as they prepare a meal for the crew.
(Courtesy National Archives)

The galley also doubled as a recreation center. Here men could relax, read, play cards or board games, and write letters home.

Below the galley deck was a large freezer and refrigerator for cold-food storage. Since storage space was at a premium, every available space, opening, shelf, and cubbyhole on a submarine was crammed with crates, cartons, boxes, barrels, and bags of foodstuffs. A submarine leaving port more resembled a seaborne grocery warehouse than it did a warship. The enlisted crew normally had use of two toilet compartments, or heads; one of them was totally filled with crates of food, and could only be used once all the food taking up space in that head was consumed.[3]

One of the most complicated pieces of apparatus on board a sub was

Crewmen aboard U.S.S. *Batfish* squeeze into the tight galley mess area.
(Courtesy National Archives)

The toilet (U.S.S. *Cobia*).
(Whitlock photo)

the commode. Smitty recalled, "When using the head, there were certain vital steps that had to be taken in the correct sequence or you—or the guy after you—would wind up covered with shit."[4]

A brass plaque mounted on the inside of the hatch spelled out exactly how the toilet was to be operated:

Before using, see that Bowl Flapper Valve A is closed, Gate Valve C in discharge line is open, Valve C in water supply line is open. Then open Valve E next to bowl to admit necessary water. Close Valves D and E. After using, pull Lever A, release Lever A. Open Valve C in air supply line. Rock Air Valve Lever F outboard to charge measuring tank to 10 pounds above sea pressure. Open Plug Cock B and rock Air Valve Lever F inboard to blow overboard. Close Valves B and C. For pump expulsion, open Plug B. Pump waste receiver empty. Close Plug Cock B. Close Valve C. If on first inspection, the expulsion chamber is found flooded, discharge the contents overboard before using the toilet."[5]

Below the deck were the magazines, where ammunition for the deck gun and machine guns was kept; special hatches enabled men in the magazine to hand the ammunition up to the top deck and then to the gunners.

To the rear of the galley was the main crew's berthing area, called the "after battery." Thirty-six bunks, stacked three high, gave the men a place to sleep, but because there were not enough bunks for each man, the men had to "hot-bunk," i.e., use a bunk that had been vacated by a man who was on duty.

Directly behind the bulkhead of the berthing area were two large, stainless-steel evaporator units that turned seawater into about 1,000 gallons of distilled water per day. The first priority for this purified water was to keep the lead-acid batteries filled. The second priority was for drinking and cooking. The lowest priority was for showering (there were two shower stalls on board); on long patrols, the men were allowed to shower—maybe—once every two weeks; on many patrols, however, it was not uncommon for men to go a month or more without showering.

Next came two engine rooms. The H.O.R. (Hooven, Owens, Rentschler) engines—often called "whores" by the crewmen who had to maintain them—had proven to be supremely unreliable, so the new Fleet boats were equipped with four, ten-cylinder, 1,600-horsepower Fairbanks-Morse or General Motors opposed-piston diesel engines, each the length of an automobile, that gave a sub a maximum surface speed of twenty-one knots (about twenty-four miles per hour). The diesels simultaneously charged the storage batteries and powered the lights, food refrigeration, air-conditioning, radar, communications equipment, etc. Most older subs that were kept on active duty were retrofitted with the new engines.

The men who worked in the engine rooms—usually refereed to as the "black gang"—had it the worst of anyone on board. Not only did they have to endure the constant, deafening roar of the diesel engines for hours on end when the submarine was operating on the surface, but they also had to endure the parboiling temperatures given off by the engines; 130-degree heat was common in the engine compartments. But the rest

A submarine crewman reads a book in his bunk just
inches above one of the torpedoes.
(Courtesy National Archives)

of the sub was little better; in most other parts of the boat the temperature remained at or above 100 degrees Fahrenheit when the diesels were
running. It is no wonder that most of the submariners worked only in
sandals and skivvies while on patrol. And it is not hard to imagine the
reeking odor on board a submarine created by the unwashed bodies of
eighty sweating, unbathed men.

Frank Toon, who served aboard *Blenny* (SS-324), recalled that submariners quickly lost their sense of smell once in the boat. "You never really
noticed any smells after you got aboard. Diesel fumes, body odor, cigs, et
cetera—all blended in to make our environment. You got used to it and
never noticed it. Other people would notice it—those who didn't live on
subs. I remember an incident in the ship's service store in the late forties.

There were a half dozen of us who had walked up to get things we needed—toothpaste, foo-foo [deodorant or cologne], et cetera. At the time we were in line there were a couple of women (not sub wives!) who were also in line at the cashier. Although we were all clean, the women could smell us, and made no bones about it with a remark loud enough for all us to hear—about stinking sub sailors! As this was the sub base ship's service, and they were here shopping as only a courtesy, my boss, a quartermaster chief, really let fly at them! *Whooooeeeeee*—they

Frank Toon.
(Courtesy Frank Toon)

couldn't get out of there fast enough. So much for smells. Guess it would have been pretty raunchy to anyone not used to it!"[6]

Just forward of the final section of the submarine—the after torpedo room, with its four tubes, eight torpedoes, and twelve bunks—was the maneuvering room. When the captain issued an order from the bridge, conning tower, or control room to change course or speed, it was conveyed to the maneuvering room, where large brass levers were thrown manually to comply with the order. Here, too, the command to dive or surface was relayed, and the switch to the appropriate propulsive power—diesel or battery—was thrown. Large, twin propellers outside and directly below the aft torpedo room provided the thrust needed.

Abovedecks, the submarine sported a bridge, conning tower, periscope, periscope shears, radar equipment, and armament—usually either a three- or five-inch deck-mounted gun and two twenty-millimeter machine guns.

Because the submarine by itself is little more than a reconnaissance vehicle, inflicting damage on the enemy's ships and coastal installations required something better than the type of spar-mounted explosive charge that had wrecked both the hunter and the hunted during the Civil War. It needed self-propelled projectiles that could blow up enemy vessels without endangering itself. It needed torpedoes.

View of bridge (U.S.S. *Pampanito*).
(Whitlock photo)

The standard American submarine torpedo during the First World War was the Mark VII, which had a diameter of eighteen inches. The Mark VII, with its 326-pound warhead, had a maximum range of 5,000 yards and a top speed of thirty-five knots. But the Mark VII was an inferior fish; its small warhead was insufficient to blast a hole in the thick armor that protected the hulls of most warships of the day. Because torpedo-firing surface ships were using twenty-one-inch Mark X torpedoes, it made sense to build new submarines capable of firing this bigger weapon.

By the time the S-boats came into service in 1920, they were armed with the Mark Xs, which now carried 497 pounds of explosive and had a maximum effective range of 3,500 yards at thirty-six knots.

Other nations, too, were working on improving their armament. The Japanese, for example, were busily developing monster torpedoes such as the twenty-four-inch, Type 93 "Long Lance" oxygen-powered torpedo with a 1,720-pound warhead, which was primarily designed to be launched from destroyers. Many weaponry experts have rated this giant pickle the most effective torpedo up to that time. Japanese submarines were fitted with a slightly smaller version—the twenty-one-inch, Type 95 wakeless, oxygen-propelled torpedo that carried an 893-pound warhead (later increased to 1,213 pounds) and had a range of five miles at forty-nine knots. The speed and size of these two types ensured that any target in its path would be demolished.[7]

All nations in the torpedo-designing contest had abandoned the straight-running fish, which required that the submarine be pointed directly at its target or intercept point, and replaced them with torpedoes that had manual gyros that could be set and enable the torpedo to follow the "dialed-in" setting.

Another innovation, exclusive to the U.S. Navy, was an electromechanical torpedo data computer (TDC). The Bureau of Ordnance at the Torpedo Station at Newport, Rhode Island, was also working to produce the next generation of twenty-one-inch torpedoes that would have a larger warhead, higher speed, and a magnetic proximity exploder that would set it off whenever it came close to a target, rather than be required to actually strike the hull.

The U.S. Navy's TDC was leagues ahead of anything employed by any other nation at that time, and was a precursor to the highly sophisticated computerized target-tracking and firing systems in use today. Whereas other navies had basically done nothing more than mechanized the functions of the "Is-Was" manual computer (a type of circular slide rule used to compute firing angles), the American Navy copied from the complex electromechanical computers that battleships used to direct the aiming and firing of the main guns. The TDC, located in the conning tower, was able to keep track of the submarine's and target's position, course, and speed, and calculate the torpedo's track to hit the target. The TDC also transmitted the constantly updated information directly to the torpedoes.

But, of course, everything hinged on the torpedo actually exploding once it reached its target—something that had been less than a certainty since the war began.

In the early months of World War II, the Germans had used magnetic exploders but found them unreliable; U-boat commanders were ordered to deactivate them. The kill rate of their torpedoes suddenly shot back up. The U.S. Navy's BuOrd, however, kept its collective head in the sand, insisting (as it had with the deep-running problem) that there were no shortcomings with the Mark VI magnetic exploder that more and better training of the submarine crews couldn't fix.

The main problem, however, was not the crews but BuOrd. The organization refused to recognize two vital facts: one, that the earth's magnetic field varies in various parts of the world, and two, that a steel-hulled ship could be demagnetized to make it less vulnerable to being sunk or damaged by a torpedo armed with a magnetic exploder. And so, pickles that came close to enemy hulls, and even actually struck them, did little more than scrape off a few barnacles, cause enemy captains an extra measure of worry, and give American submariners sleepless nights.[8]

HIGHLY sophisticated submarines require highly trained specialists to operate them, and submariners soon became known as the elite of the elite. The submarine historian Norman Polmar noted, "Unlike aviators, who were awarded wings after graduating from flight school, a New London graduate went to sea and qualified in a boat before being awarded his coveted dolphin insignia"—silver for enlisted men and gold for officers.[9]

The officers and enlisted men aboard a submarine were assigned to specific tasks. Among the officers, one was the chief engineer, another the torpedo and gunnery officer, and a third the communications officer, while the lowest-ranking officers served as their assistants. The executive officer was also the navigator. The commander, obviously, was responsible for the overall operation of the boat and its crew, was personally in charge of combat operations, and oversaw the activities of everyone else.

There was an easy familiarity between submarine officers and enlisted men virtually unknown in the other services and other segments of the Navy. There were very few signs of formality or military courtesy within the intimate confines of a sub. Rank was forgotten; there was no saluting, and the use of the term *sir* was kept to a minimum.

Carl Vozniak, an electrician's mate first class aboard *Finback* (SS-230), remarked, "You never say 'yes, sir' or 'no, sir' to any of the officers.

The only officers you ever say 'yes, sir' or 'no, sir' to are the old man [commanding officer] and the officer of the day. All the others you just call by their last names. Not even 'mister'; just 'Jones'—'Hey, Jones.' "[10]

While the officers had their own space aboard a sub, it could by no stretch of the imagination be called "spacious," or "luxurious" or "private." Indeed, to go from one end of the sub to the other it was necessary to pass through the officers' living quarters, known as "officers' country." Only the commander had his own private cabin—which was only slightly larger than a phone booth. From his less-than-normal-size bunk, the skipper could view a wall-mounted compass and depth gauge so he could immediately discern the boat's attitude whenever he was in his cabin. He also had a communications system that enabled him to speak with persons in any other part of the boat without leaving his stateroom. If "rank has its privilege" in other branches of service, such privileges were conspicuously absent aboard a submarine.

No matter how brave a man might be, the claustrophobic, artificially lit interior of a submarine could be unnerving in the extreme. Although a submarine was the length of a football field, it was barely wider than a school bus. There was precious little wasted space. Lines, hoses, and pipes ran the length of the boat, and hardly an inch of wall space wasn't covered by a bank of switches, gauges, circuit boxes, indicator lights, storage lockers, or bookshelves for hundreds of manuals. Every room, galley, head, and passageway was only as large as absolutely necessary for human beings to live, sleep, eat, move, communicate, and defecate. Due to the preciousness of fresh water, shaving, showering, and the washing of clothing were verboten, and officers and men alike usually stripped down to their skivvies during the long, hot patrols. On some patrols, men worked in the buff.

In short, every American submarine was a formidable, highly technical fighting machine with a singular purpose: to hunt down enemy ships and destroy them. And Smitty was excited for the opportunity to be a part of it all.

CHAPTER 7

THE END OF
THE BEGINNING

AT San Diego the Submarine School students learned every inch, inside and out, of the "C"-class *Cachalot*. *Cachalot* and her sister submarine, *Cuttlefish*, had been designed in the late 1920s, built in Portsmouth, and commissioned in the early 1930s. These two boats were larger and more advanced than the World War I "S" boats, but obsolete when compared to the new Fleet subs. *Cachalot* departed from the usual method of riveting hull plates together by becoming the first American submarine with welded inner hull frames in the torpedo rooms; the rest of the boat's seams were riveted.[1] Cachalot (as well as *Cuttlefish*) also held the distinction of having survived the Japanese raid on Pearl Harbor and had participated in three war patrols during the early months of the war.

The first few days on *Cachalot* all Ron Smith and his classmates did was scrape old paint and remove the tarlike waterproofing substance that covered the pressure hull, replacing it with a new coating. At the conclusion of this hard, unpleasant task, the students were ready to go on a short test dive. They and the eighty-man crew piled aboard and the diesel engines roared to life, vibrating the craft and blotting out all other sound. The temperature, especially in the engine room, rose to a level normally found only in the Sahara or Death Valley, and communication within the engine room could only be carried out with hand signals.

Smitty recalled that the crew, or "ship's company," was not especially friendly to the novice submariners. "As soon as the boat got under way," he said, "the crew pushed the nine of us around, constantly yelling at us to get the hell out of the way as they scurried about performing their various assignments. My head was spinning from looking at all the gauges and dials and valves, hundreds of them, mostly in the control room, but also in other places throughout the boat. You could not tell fore from aft unless someone told you."[2]

Slowly the students began to get their bearings and tried their best to just observe and stay out of the way. Before long, *Cachalot* cleared San Diego Bay and headed into water deep enough for the test dive, the purpose of which was to make certain that no leaks or other problems would be encountered underwater. Uppermost in the minds of the students was the fate of *Squalus,* a submarine that had foundered when someone failed to close her main induction valves during a test dive off Portsmouth, New Hampshire, in March 1939. Twenty-six of her fifty-nine-man crewmen drowned; the remainder were miraculously rescued from 242 feet of water.[3]

Also playing in the deep recesses of the students' consciousness were tales of the sinking of O-9 (U.S.S. *0-9*), an old submarine (launched in 1918) whose hull had collapsed while in waters seventeen miles off Portsmouth on 20 June 1941, killing all thirty-three men aboard.*

Smitty, along with Shineman, Quillian, and Partin, was in the crew's mess area when he nearly jumped out of his skin. He said, "The diving alarm, which sounded like the *aaaaooogaa* of a Model-A Ford, only ten times louder, went off twice, followed by a voice on the loudspeaker, shouting 'Dive! Dive!' " The roaring in their ears suddenly stopped when the diesel engines went silent as the boat switched to battery power, and the bow tipped sharply downward. With the abrupt plunge, anything not secured—books, manuals, china, coffee mugs, etc.—went flying off shelves and tables.

Smitty asked a black mess steward, "How long does it take to dive?"

The mess steward glanced at the depth gauge mounted to the

---

* *Squalus,* named after a type of dogfish, was refloated, refitted, and, as noted earlier, renamed *Sailfish*. The remains of O-9 were spotted in 1991, and have been left in place as a silent memorial to her lost crew. (Blair, 118; www.rontini.com)

bulkhead. "We already done it," he said, indicating that they had leveled off at 150 feet. "Jus' don't forget to pop yo' ears." The four novices clamped their nostrils shut and blew, equalizing the pressure.

"There was nothing to it," Smith recalled of his first dive. "Everything was quiet and serene." The only sound that could be heard was the soft whirring of the electric motors as they turned the two large screws propelling *Cachalot* forward.

After a while, the diving alarm blared three times and *Cachalot* surfaced; the hatches were opened to allow a flood of cool fresh air into the hot stuffy vessel. There had been no untoward incidents, no emergencies. The nine students smiled at one another. They had just survived their first dive in a submarine.

SUBMARINE School alternated between trips on *Cachalot* and classroom work. The six weeks went by rapidly and the nine students had their government-issue dress blue uniforms tailored to be skintight on the butt and thighs but flaring to wide bells at the cuffs. They wore their white hats so far back on their heads that they were forever in danger of slipping off. They may have been just students, but they *looked* like sailors.

Smitty and the others were granted no liberty during their school, which ran six days a week from Monday through Saturday. Their only time off was on Sundays, when they could go to church and perhaps to a movie on base; no one was allowed to go into San Diego.

On a Friday evening at the end of the fifth week, Bill Partin's girlfriend, Mary, came down from Portland and the two of them were married at the Destroyer Base chapel; Smitty and his classmates were all in the wedding party. The tall, dark-haired groom looked very handsome in his dark blue uniform. "Mary was just what everyone expected," Smitty said, "a real girl-next-door type. The whole gang liked her and everyone decided that eight 'best men' would stand by Bill on his wedding day."

No one on that happy evening could have imagined the fate that awaited Bill.[4]

THE war continued on its deadly pace, not waiting for the Submarine School students to graduate. Half a world away, the Russians and Germans were battling each other for a prize known as Stalingrad; the battle would last nearly two years and result in over 160,000 German deaths; another 90,000 would surrender. And although American B-17s and B-24s were pounding German cities from the air, American ground forces had yet to see action against the German or Italian enemy.[5]

In the Pacific, malfunctioning torpedoes continued to plague the submarine fleet. One instance when the maddeningly unreliable fish actually worked brought tragedy. On 27 September 1942, another ship, the 7,000-ton freighter *Lisbon Maru*, was outbound from Hong Kong with, in addition to 778 Japanese troops on board, a hold filled with some 1,816 British POWs—mostly members of the Middlesex Regiment (appropriately carrying the moniker "The Diehards") who had been captured in China in December 1941.

At dawn on 1 October 1942, Rob Roy McGregor's *Grouper* (SS-214), on her second war patrol, spotted the *Lisbon Maru* in the waters south of Shanghai, and seeing no markings that would indicate that the transport held POWs, moved in for an attack near the island of Qingbang, Dongji Islands, in the eastern Zhoushan Archipelago. *Grouper*'s first three torpedoes missed, but the fourth one struck home, stopping

Lisbon Maru.
(*Courtesy National Archives*)

the freighter dead in the water. The Japanese crewmen fired back in *Grouper*'s direction with their deck gun. The sub responded with two more torpedoes; one missed but the second hit. An enemy aircraft appeared overhead and dropped depth bombs on *Grouper*, which dove to escape the ordnance. McGregor left the area, thinking his job was done.

As the *Lisbon Maru* was lying disabled and sinking slowly by the stern, the Japanese crewmen were rushing to lower the lifeboats for their own use while other crewmen were battening down the hatches to prevent the escape of the POWs; the prisoners would be left to drown or suffocate in the stifling hold. A nearby destroyer was radioed for help; the *Kure* steamed over and took aboard more than 700 Japanese sailors and soldiers while the British remained trapped in darkness belowdecks. But the regiment's commander, Lieutenant Colonel H.W.M. Stewart, was having none of it.

Discovering a hatchway in the hold, two British officers opened it and were headed to the bridge to demand that the ship's captain release the prisoners when Japanese guards opened fire into the hold, killing one man outright and mortally wounding an officer. Stewart then gave the order for his men to overpower the guards and abandon ship. The men swarmed out of the hold, disarmed the guards, and jumped overboard, all the while being fired at by men on the *Kure* and three other ships standing alongside. The British escapees, braving the bullets, began swimming for the Sing Pan Islands, about three miles away.

Some of the POWs, too weak to swim such a distance, instead reached for ropes being dangled over the sides of the Japanese vessels, only to be kicked back into the water by the enemy sailors; scores of POWs drowned.

Some swimmers rode the currents to the island, where many were injured when the surf dashed them against the sharp rocks. A small flotilla of thirty Chinese junks and sampans suddenly appeared and, at the risk of being shot by the Japanese, began hauling the British soldiers aboard; the Chinese boatmen treated the prisoners kindly, giving them clothing and what little food they had; Japanese landing parties soon reclaimed the escapees and took them to Shanghai. Others were taken aboard Japanese vessels and stuffed back into the holds of the ships.

On 5 October all the prisoners who had been recaptured were assembled on the Shanghai docks and a roll call was taken. Of the original 1,816 prisoners aboard the *Lisbon Maru*, only 970 answered the call; 846 had perished, most of them in the hold of the freighter when it sank a day after being torpedoed. It was later learned that six or seven men had managed to escape, aided by the Chinese.*[6]

UP to this point in the war, the American submarine force had not been used anywhere close to its maximum potential; it was more akin to a disorganized bunch of snipers than a potent military force working in concert. A few random submarines had sunk a few random transports and warships, but there had been no truly coordinated effort to mold the ever-growing sub force into an entity to be reckoned with.

The captains and crews of America's submarine force had shown no want of courage in going after their prey despite their almost total lack of confidence in their primary weapon: the torpedoes. If only we had some reliable fish, the captains and crews thought, and a better strategic doctrine that would put our bravery and aggressive spirit to the best use, we could begin to rack up impressive scores.

But when, if ever, would it happen?

The S-boats, armed with the older but more reliable Mark X torpedoes, had acquitted themselves reasonably well, but it was clear that the S-boats were too slow, too clumsy, too unreliable mechanically and electrically, and too old. The new Fleet boats that began to replace the superannuated S-boats were equipped with several technological innovations that would prove to be of inestimable value. One innovation was SJ radar, which allowed a submarine to find and accurately plot surface targets, no matter what the weather or visual conditions. The SJ was also a boon for navigation. Up to this time, the older submarines were equipped

* The British held no grudges against the American submarine, but the responsible Japanese were tried on war-crimes charges after the war. (www.hamstat.demon.co.uk/Hong-Kong/Lisbon_Maru)

only with SD radar, which was nondirectional and useful only for detecting aircraft. Using the new radar equipment in a trial off Formosa in August 1942, *Haddock* (SS-231), piloted by Arthur H. Taylor, sank three (downgraded to two after the war) ships.[7]

The less-than-effective Admiral Robert English, ComSubPac, was also coming under increasing fire, but mostly from subordinates, who carried little weight. As Clay Blair notes, "Bob English had not distinguished himself in command of Submarines Pacific. He failed to organize a hardheaded and persistent strategic war against Japanese shipping in the home islands, allowing his submarines to be shunted to Alaska, Truk, and elsewhere on missions that produced little. He had ignored the Mark XIV torpedo problem, leaving it for Lockwood, a newcomer to the Pacific, to solve. His management of submarines during the Battle of Midway had been less than professional. Few of his skippers respected him. One reason was that English continued to write negative and harsh endorsements for patrols . . . that were aggressive yet unlucky or bedeviled by torpedo failures. The skippers resented being second-guessed by a man who had little understanding of the fleet submarine and who had never been on one in combat."[8]

But English's job was safe for the time being, for a new crisis arose. Another fierce confrontation in the Solomons was shaping up between the American and Japanese navies—a savage confrontation that would be known as the Battle of Cape Esperance.

On the dark night of 11–12 October 1942, in the seas around Guadalcanal's northwest tip, the two sides blindly traded blows, recalling the earlier Battle of Savo Island. In the melee, the Japanese lost a heavy cruiser and a destroyer, and had another cruiser damaged; the United States lost the destroyer *Duncan*, while the light cruiser *Boise* was severely battered.

Also battered was Nimitz's faith in Vice Admiral Ghormley's abilities and aggressiveness; after the battle, he relieved Ghormley as commander of the South Pacific Area and replaced him with fire-breathing William Frederick "Bull" Halsey Jr., a 1904 graduate of, and a former fullback for, the U.S. Naval Academy, whose weather-beaten face was crowned by a thicket of eyebrows shading a glowering stare. His reputation as a hard-driving commander was already legendary; it was his task force that had taken *Hornet* and Jimmy Doolittle's bombers on their mission to hit Tokyo.

Halsey had barely gotten his feet wet in his new post when he was faced with a major test. After failing to defeat the Americans during the Battle of Cape Esperance, Yamamoto had assembled another enormous force he was convinced would win back complete control of the Solomons and oust the Americans once and for all. On 26 October 1942, the task force, built around the aircraft carriers *Junyo, Zuiho, Zuikaku,* and the repaired "wounded bear,"

Admiral William F. ("Bull") Halsey.
(Courtesy National Archives)

Shokaku—all accompanied by five battleships, fourteen cruisers, and forty-four destroyers—plunged like a tsunami into the understrength American fleet around Guadalcanal. This fight would be called the Battle of Santa Cruz Islands—250 miles southeast of San Cristobel—as tough and as bloody a naval battle as has ever been fought.

The clash of warships was enough to unnerve even the steeliest of warriors, but the Americans hung on, took a pounding, and fought back. The emperor's dive-bombers cascaded in waves upon the carriers *Hornet* and *Enterprise*, and the destroyer *Porter* was sunk by a submarine. American planes, rising up from the two carriers and Henderson Field on Guadalcanal, were slapped out of the air like so many flies. Yet enough of the Yank pilots got through that *Shokaku* and *Zuiho* sustained serious damage, as did a cruiser and two destroyers. Still, it was not enough to make up for the fact that *Hornet* had gone to the bottom and *Enterprise* had been badly damaged. However, when the smoke cleared on 27 October and Yamamoto's ships headed back to Truk, the bruised American fleet—and the American flag flying over Henderson Field—were still there. Everyone wondered, though, just how much more they could take.[9]

It was obvious to Halsey that the submarines that were supposed to be blockading Truk simply weren't getting the job done. There were too few of them. It was like Navy fielding only six defensive players against Army when they needed eleven. And they needed to stop playing tag football and start hitting the ball carrier coming through the line. In accordance with his two personal mottoes: "Kill Japs, kill Japs, kill more Japs," and "Hit hard, hit fast, hit often," Halsey practically demanded that Nimitz tell English to clear the substitutes' bench and transfer all the submarines based on the far side of Australia to Brisbane, closer to where they were needed. By November, Halsey had eighteen submarines added to his team and he stationed them around Truk and southward in the Solomons.[10]

Although the number of submarines in the area increased dramatically, the number of sinkings of enemy ships did not. Plenty of convoys were sighted and fired upon, but the torpedoes refused to cooperate. The war patrols seemed more like peacetime training exercises, leaving the skippers hopping mad. Part of the problem was the torpedoes; the other part was the submarine commanders themselves.

At the beginning of the war, many of the submarine skippers were "old-timers"—career naval officers in their mid to late thirties, schooled in the outdated submarine doctrine of the post–World War I era, and lacking in youthful, aggressive spirit. Others were simply out of their element. The case of red-haired Lieutenant Commander Marvin G. "Pinky" Kennedy was typical.

Before being assigned to take command of the *Wahoo* (SS-238) in early 1942, Kennedy had been executive officer on the old monster sub *Argonaut*. Formal, standoffish, and possessing several quirks and senseless rules that inspired one author to describe him as "Queeg-like," due to his resemblance to the martinet protagonist of Herman Wouk's novel *The Caine Mutiny*, Kennedy was not well liked by the other officers and crewmen of the *Wahoo*. More importantly, he was not respected, and his frustrating penchant for avoiding fights with enemy ships became corrosive to the morale aboard *Wahoo*; at least one of the officers was studying the *Navy Regulations* to determine if a "legal mutiny" was possible.

Fortunately, a mutiny was not necessary. In November 1942, after

Kennedy picked a 5,300-ton freighter out of a convoy and sank her but refused to press his luck and go after other nearby targets, two of his boat's officers, Dudley Walker "Mushmouth" Morton, a former stand-out on the Naval Academy football team (class of 1930), and Richard Hetherington O'Kane (class of 1934), conspired to get him "fired" for his lack of aggressiveness; Kennedy was transferred to command the destroyer *Guest*. On New Year's Eve 1942, Morton replaced Kennedy and O'Kane became Mush's exec. Both Morton and O'Kane, not to mention *Wahoo*, would become Navy legends.[11]

LIKE a dog that refused to let go of a favorite bone, Admiral Yamamoto, after the Battle of Santa Cruz Islands, was determined to hang on to Guadalcanal. He would make one last all-out effort to blow the Americans, still entrenched on and around the island, out of the neck of the Solomons bottle—no matter how high the cost.

Because most of his carrier force had been decimated, Yamamoto had to rely on land-based aircraft and his navy's old reliables—the battleships and cruisers, supported by scores of destroyers—as an iron wedge that would finally shove Halsey and his fleet back to Hawaii. Aboard his flagship, the *Yamato* anchored at Truk, Yamamoto directed Vice Admiral Hiroaki Abe, commanding the Raiding Group, to precede the landing of 12,000 soldiers onto the American-held islands with a naval assault of two battleships, *Hiei* and *Kirishima*, a light cruiser, and fourteen destroyers. Abe's group would be followed by the Main Body, led by Vice Admiral Nobutake Kondo. Yamamoto fixed Thursday, 12 November 1942, as the date for the start of what would become

Dudley Walker Morton, commander of *Wahoo*.
(Courtesy Naval Historical Center)

known as the Naval Battle of Guadalcanal—the pivotal fight for control of the South Pacific.

As it happened, Rear Admiral Richmond K. Turner, in command of Task Group 67.1, was on that date in the process of reinforcing and re-supplying the 1st Marine Division on Guadalcanal, which, after more than three months of fighting not only the fanatical Japanese, but also insects, disease, torrential rains, heat, humidity, festering wounds, and malnutrition, was about at the end of its rope.

Turner's transports were finishing the process of dropping off fresh men and supplies at Lunga Point when an aerial armada of Rabaul-based Mitsubishi G4M1 "Betty" bombers and aircraft from the carrier *Hiyo*, somewhere to the northwest, were sighted heading for Guadalcanal. Turner pulled his transports away from the beach, had all the antiair-craft guns manned, and arranged the ships in a defensive formation that would leave them less vulnerable to aerial attack. Enemy planes dropped their bombs and torpedoes, but caused little damage. Marine aircraft from Henderson Field rose up like aerial knights to joust in a deadly tournament in the sky. A disabled Betty chose *San Francisco* on which to make its suicide dive, killing or wounding fifty sailors and causing tremendous damage but failing to knock out the ship.

Later in the day, Turner's transports returned to finish the unload-ing, but few believed the Japanese were gone. Nervous lookouts scanned the sky and the sea, searching for any sign of the enemy's return. Soon Intelligence reported that, indeed, the Japanese were on their way back. Halsey received word—thanks again to the "Magic" code breakers, who acted like spies in the other team's huddle—that Abe's flotilla was steam-ing toward Guadalcanal, and he passed the word to Turner.

Knowing what the enemy is planning on doing and stopping him from doing it are two different things. The forces at Turner's disposal were tired, battered, and held together with bailing wire and spit. Halsey called upon his single operational aircraft carrier—Rear Admiral Thomas C. Kinkaid's patched-up *Enterprise*, undergoing repairs at Nouméa—to head back to Guadalcanal as soon as possible.

For his part, Turner ordered the transports away, to be shepherded to the safety of Espíritu Santo by Rear Admiral Daniel J. Callaghan's Sup-port Group. In Callaghan's command were two heavy cruisers, *Portland*

and the damaged *San Francisco;* three light cruisers, *Atlanta, Juneau,* and *Helena;* and fifteen destroyers. Callaghan then returned and arrayed his ships across a twenty-mile-wide strait between Guadalcanal and Florida Island dubbed "Ironbottom Sound," due to the many warships that had already made it their graveyard, and waited for the enemy.

Unaware that the American ships were setting an ambush, Abe's task force of two battleships, plus a light cruiser and eleven destroyers, came steaming down the Slot past Savo Island at about 0100 hours on 13 November. Forty-five minutes later, although visibility was zero in the dark, radar gave the Americans an idea of the enemy's positions and night was turned into day as the gunners opened fire. Caught by surprise, Japanese vessels switched on their searchlights in an effort to find targets—an act that turned them into targets themselves. For the next half hour, rival munitions ripped back and forth across the strait, the shells holing hulls and bulkheads, crashing into bridges and gun positions, sending men and hot shards of steel flying, and ships to their doom. Few if any naval engagements have ever been so intense or so destructive in such a short period of time and at such short range.

In the opening minutes of the fray, the cruiser *Atlanta,* serving as flagship for Rear Admiral Norman Scott, commander of Task Group 64.2, was struck and physically lifted out of the water by a torpedo fired point-blank from the destroyer *Akatsuki;* the *Akatsuki* was itself sunk when it was smothered by return fire from Callaghan's flagship, *San Francisco.* Then *Atlanta*'s bridge was blown apart by a salvo of eight-inch shells from *San Francisco,* whose gunners were trying to hit an enemy ship on the other side of her; Admiral Scott and his staff were killed, and *Atlanta* was left dead in the water.

The two sides resembled blindfolded boxers standing toe-to-toe and flailing away at each other. *San Francisco* came under a torrent of fire from *Kirishima;* seventy-seven of her crewmen, including Admiral Callaghan, were killed. *Portland* and *Helena* both received extensive damage but kept fighting. The American destroyers took a beating; three were sunk (*Cushing, Monssen, Laffey*) and five damaged, including *Buchanan,* which was mistakenly blasted by friendly ships but remained afloat. The enemy also suffered with the sinking of the battleship *Hiei* and two destroyers as the dark morning continued to be brightened by flashes of scores of guns and the bursts of orange-colored balls from shells that found their marks. Men from both navies were blown into the sea or jumped willingly—heedless of the shark-infested sea—their bodies aflame. The waters of the strait were coated with fuel oil, floating debris, and the mangled, intermingled corpses of Japanese and American sailors.

Evidently losing his nerve in the wild melee, Admiral Abe, at 0200 hours on 13 November, ordered his battleships to break off contact—*Hiei*'s rudder was damaged—and head north while his smaller ships screened the withdrawal. The respite brought no relief for the Americans, who were engaged in dousing fires on over a dozen warships and pulling wounded men from the sea. At dawn, with two admirals dead, Captain Gilbert C. Hoover of *Helena* found himself the highest-ranking officer still alive and took command of what was left of the task force.

As the eastern sky slowly lightened, each man wondered: *If the Japs return, how much more punishment can we take?* They would soon find out.

As Friday the thirteenth wore on, it became obvious that the Japanese were not quite finished with their efforts to retake Guadalcanal. Another Japanese battle group of six cruisers and six destroyers was on its way to bombard Henderson Field while Admiral Raizo Tanaka's eleven transports, bulging with a fresh division of invasion troops, and accompanied by a fearsome armada under Admiral Nobutake Kondo that included the undamaged *Kirishima,* were determined to land at Guadalcanal.

The forces clashed again in midmorning, and at 1100 hours, the enemy sub *I-26* torpedoed the light cruiser *Juneau*, exploding her magazine and taking to the bottom nearly 700 crew members, including the five Sullivan brothers, Albert, Francis, George, Joseph, and Madison.*

American ships and sailors absorbed everything the Japanese could throw at them in an all-day battle but refused to yield; each man knew the importance of denying the strait to the enemy. There was no rest for

---

* Two hundred and forty sailors aboard *Juneau* reportedly survived the sinking, but after twelve days afloat, all but seven had either died of exposure or were eaten by sharks. (Ruhe, 172)

anyone that night as Yamamoto's ships returned after dark on 13–14 November for what they hoped was the final thrust. Japanese cruisers and destroyers closed in and blasted Henderson Field and the American ships, but with the dawn, the Yanks were still fighting back with unbroken resolve, unleashing once more their aircraft to duel with the enemy.

Like the cavalry riding to the rescue in a Hollywood Western, Hoover's hard-pressed ships, and the Marines on Guadalcanal, were about to be saved by Admiral Kinkaid's Task Force 16, headed by his wounded carrier *Enterprise* and two battleships, *Washington* and *South Dakota* (the latter having been damaged during the Battle of Santa Cruz Islands), under the command of Admiral Willis A. Lee Jr., rushing up from the south.

But Kinkaid and Lee would not reach the area before the fourteenth. The only force left to hold off the attackers was the pitifully small PT boat squadron based at Tulagi. Into the night of 13–14 November roared the tiny, plywood boats, ready to do or die trying. Although their torpedoes made no hits, they scared the much larger ships, which had been bombarding Henderson Field, and forced them to turn tail. At the risk of their own safety, the PT boat crews had managed to buy time for the embattled leathernecks.

At dawn on the fourteenth, Marine and Army aircraft from Henderson and Espíritu Santo, as well as from *Enterprise*, filled the sky, determined to pay back the enemy in spades. The planes found the cruisers *Kinugasa* and *Isuzu*, along with several other ships, and gave them a terrific pounding; *Kinugasa* was sunk and the remainder were damaged. Tanaka's troop-filled transports were also strafed and blasted by American fighters, dive-bombers, and B-17s, and seven of them were sunk.

As night fell on the area, however, the battle was still undecided. The Americans had fought back fiercely and had not only given the Japanese as good as they got, but forestalled the amphibious landing on Guadalcanal. There were still two main protagonists who had yet to appear onstage, however: Kondo's Emergency Bombardment Group and Lee's two battleships and four escorting destroyers. They waited in the wings, anxious for their cue.

Up to this point, the twenty-four American submarines that Halsey had specifically gathered and sent to the Guadalcanal area had seen no action. Inexplicably, all but one remained idle and never fired a single torpedo. That one sub was *Trout*, which had earlier saved the Philippines' gold. Now captained by Lieutenant Commander Lawson P. "Red" Ramage, *Trout* single-handedly took on Kondo's group during the afternoon of the fourteenth, firing three torpedoes (none of which hit their targets) and striking fear into the admiral's heart that he was in dangerous waters.

In the darkness of 14–15 November, Kondo had regained his nerve and sent his task force sailing back toward Guadalcanal, where he was on a collision course with Lee's group moving up from the south. They would meet head-on to the south and west of Savo Island shortly before midnight. Radioing other friendly ships in the vicinity with his battle cry and Naval Academy nickname—"This is 'Ching Chong' Lee. Stand aside, I'm coming through"—Lee, aboard *Washington*, plowed into Ironbottom Sound—and into history. In the no-holds-barred contest that followed, both sides blasted torpedoes and broadsides at each other, illuminating the inky blackness with fiery explosions, flares, searchlights, and webs of crisscrossing tracers.

As with the previous two nights' battles, the damage and carnage were stupendous. When the sun came up on 15 November, three American destroyers (*Walke*, *Preston*, and *Benham)* were below the waves and *South Dakota* was badly damaged, but *Washington* had barely been scratched. With Admiral Lee aboard, *Washington* took off after the enemy like a mad terrier, forcing Kondo's group to retire. Thus ended in dramatic fashion Japan's latest (but not final) attempt to drive the U.S. Marines off Guadalcanal and the American Navy from the southeastern Solomons.

Naval historian Samuel Morison writes, "The Battle of Guadalcanal was decisive, not only in the struggle for that island, but in the Pacific War at large." After being informed of the American victory, President Roosevelt correctly declared that the Battle of Guadalcanal meant "that the turning point in this war has at last been reached." Just five days earlier, British forces in North Africa had defeated the Germans at the Battle of El Alamein and Winston Churchill's famous phrase—"This is not the end, or even the beginning of the end. But it is, perhaps, the end of the beginning"—was as applicable to Guadalcanal as to El Alamein.

The victory also marked the point when the American submarine force in the Pacific was about to end its tenure on the substitutes' bench and finally get into the game to prove what it could do.[12]

FROM the middle until the end of November 1942, the Japanese made one last attempt to regain control of the Guadalcanal area. Known variously as the Battle of Tassafaronga, the Battle of Point Cruz, and the Fourth, Fifth, and Sixth Battle of Savo Island, 15–30 November marked a series of confrontations in the air and on land and sea between the forces of the United States and Imperial Japan.

With the chance of reinforcement becoming less likely by the day, the dwindling Japanese army on Guadalcanal faced annihilation; and with their warriors' code forbidding surrender, the Nipponese troops became increasingly more desperate in their efforts to hold off the growing strength of the American forces. Rear Admiral Tanaka's attempts to land additional troops were driven off, but not before his ships inflicted heavy damage on Rear Admiral Carleton H. Wright's Task Force 67.

Naval historian Samuel Eliot Morison writes, "Tassafaronga, last major sea battle in the arena of the Southern Solomons, ended four months of vicious hull-to-hull slugging the like of which neither the Americans nor the Japanese had ever seen. No man who fought in those bloody waters can forget the apprehension, the exultation and the terror he experienced, the hideous forms of death that he witnessed, or the self-sacrificing heroism that gave him a new respect for his fellow seamen. 'Savo,' 'Guadalcanal,' 'Tassafaronga' are no mere battle names to the survivors; they are the flaming banners of deathless deeds."[13]

BY December 1942, the submarines were beginning to hit their marks, despite the malfunctioning torpedoes. On the eighteenth, *Albacore* (SS-218), commanded by Richard C. Lake, sank a freighter and the light cruiser *Tenru*. *Greenling*, after sinking four ships off the coast of China, sank another four on her way to Brisbane. *Triton* sent two ships to the bottom, while *Guardfish* nailed three, and the venerable *Nautilus* sank a freighter, damaged another, and clobbered a tanker.[14]

Gudgeon, now under the command of William Stovall Jr., was assigned to a different, but equally important mission. On the night of 27 December 1942, seven Filipino "mess boys" came aboard while the sub was docked at Fremantle, but they were hardly there to serve the crew. The mess boys were, in reality, disguised Filipino soldiers and intelligence officers, led by U.S. Army Major Jesus Villamor. *Gudgeon*'s top secret mission was to deliver the soldiers, plus several tons of arms, ammunition, communications equipment, and other supplies, to the strategic Philippine islands of Mindanao and Panay, to aid the Philippine guerrilla forces in their resistance against the Japanese occupation. Throughout the course of the war, American submarines regularly slipped into Philippine waters to bring much-needed supplies and manpower.*[15]

ALL this—the nearly one year of pitiless air, land, and seaborne combat, from Pearl Harbor to Tassafaronga—had taken place before Ron Smith, like millions of other young Americans who had joined the service when he did, could get into the war.

Many of them were worried the war would be over before they would have their chance to participate in it. They need not have worried. There was plenty of war left.

Gudgeon, under the command of Robert A. Bonin, would be reported missing near the Marianas Islands on 18 April 1944 while on her twelfth war patrol. (Blair, 567–568; www .history.navy.mil/faqs/faq82-1.htm)

CHAPTER 8

READY FOR WAR

IT was a thing of beauty.

Eighteen-year-old Seaman First Class John Ronald Smith watched with fascination as the ancient artist—he must have been fifty or sixty—intently traced the inked, stenciled outline and converted the drawing into a gorgeous, three-color tattoo. Taking shape was an American eagle, its wings spreading across six inches of Smith's right forearm, its talons clutching a four-inch-high anchor upon which was emblazoned the letters *USN*.

All the booze that Smitty and his pal Bud Shineman had consumed during their night of hell-raising in downtown San Diego helped to dull the killer-bee-attack pain of the four reciprocating needles that jabbed away like a sewing machine in slow motion, riding along the black lines and squirting tiny droplets of color just beneath the skin. Occasionally the artist would wipe off the blood that beaded to the surface from each epidermal perforation.

Shineman, perhaps the more sober of the two, looked on with some trepidation. "Tattoos are against regulations, Smitty," he had earlier warned his friend in an effort to dissuade him from going through with the procedure. "You could get syphilis from it," he added.

Smith scoffed. "It's not against regulations to get a tattoo—only to get syphilis," he replied. Smitty recalled how often he had studied his dad's tattoo, garnered while he was a sailor during World War I, and could hardly wait for the day when he could get his own. For many sailors, getting that first tattoo was as much a rite of passage into manhood

Smitty (left) and his friend Bud Shineman.
(Courtesy Ron Smith)

as that first sea voyage or that first exchange of gunfire with an enemy warship or that first visit to a whorehouse.

When he was done, the artist told Smitty to keep the tattoo well greased with Vaseline until the scabs came off—which would take about three or four weeks. His arm aching as though he had just been wounded by a tiny Japanese machine gun, Smitty smiled bravely, paid the artist three dollars, and walked out with Shineman into the cool San Diego night, hoping that he would soon have the chance to go home on leave and show his dad his proud new work of arm art before his submarine—whichever one he might be assigned to—shoved off into the vast Pacific on missions unknown.

Smitty and Shineman were about to graduate from Submarine School. Once they got their orders, they would head for Mare Island, near San Francisco, and be assigned to boats.

It was 20 December 1942, a little over a year since Pearl Harbor.

Much had happened during that year—both to Smitty and to the rest of the world. The worst was over, but victory remained elusive and could not yet be seen beyond the horizon.

On this night, the city of San Diego, trimmed in wan Christmas lights, hummed with the sounds of dozens of tattoo machines whirring away, accompanied by the sounds of hundreds of drunken sailors vomiting in alleys, or urinating in doorways, or picking fights with Marines or soldiers or civilians, or haggling with thousands of prostitutes. There was a war on, a great and glorious Navy war, and thousands of young soldiers, sailors, Marines, and airmen just like Ron Smith, many of them far from home, were getting drunk, getting tattooed, and getting laid—sowing their wild oats, as the phrase went—for none of them knew when they might go to sea, or if they would ever return.

SUBMARINE School at San Diego was at last concluded, but there were no ceremonies—not even a piece of paper or certificate of graduation. Because they might receive their orders at any time, Smitty and his fellow graduates were confined to the receiving station, killing time, allowed only four-hour liberties in the evenings, from 1800 to 2200 hours. *Cachalot* had cast off from its dock and was headed to New London, Connecticut, where it would again become a floating classroom, and freshly tattooed John Ronald Smith was nursing a sore arm. But he didn't mind; he and the other eight graduates were waiting for their orders.

Finally, on Christmas Eve, the orders came down, and the next day, the nine Submarine School graduates found themselves on a train, heading north to Mare Island, California. After dark, the passengers were required to keep the window shades drawn. "By military order, no lights were allowed to show on the ocean side of the train," Smitty recalled. "There were Japanese submarines operating off the West Coast and the military didn't want them to see the train or anything it might silhouette. All of the Japanese-Americans who lived on the West Coast had been rounded up and put into camps farther inland; there wasn't time to figure out who was a fifth columnist and who was a loyal American."

Smitty felt that the entire West Coast was ripe for invasion. "The civilians didn't know it but everyone in the military realized that the

Japanese could have invaded us anytime they wanted. We had virtually no defense on the West Coast; they prayed that the Japanese wouldn't find out how easy it would be." Of course, by the end of 1942, after suffering one naval defeat after another, and forced onto the defensive far from American shores, the Japanese no longer had the strength to mount a full-scale invasion.[1]

The Japanese, however, did have enough resources to keep nervous West Coast inhabitants on the verge of panic. Shortly after Pearl Harbor, nine Japanese submarines had begun patrolling the U.S. Pacific coastline, seeking targets of opportunity near Los Angeles, San Francisco, Seattle, San Diego, and elsewhere. For the next few months, a number of oil tankers and merchantmen were shot at; some were hit and some Americans lost their lives. On 23 February 1942, the Japanese submarine I-25 had fired thirteen shells at an oil refinery at Goleta, near Santa Barbara, California. On 21 June of that year, I-25, with its 5.5-inch deck gun, shelled both Fort Stevens and Fort Canby, guardians of the mouth of the Columbia River in Oregon and Washington, respectively; no injuries or serious damage were inflicted. The I-25 also carried a tiny seaplane with folding wings in a hangar built onto its deck. On 9 September 1942, the seaplane dropped incendiary bombs on Mount Emily, near Brookings, Oregon, in hopes of starting massive forest fires; the plan failed.

Also during the course of the war, the Japanese launched 9,300 incendiary "fugo" balloons from Japan that were supposed to cause great fires when they drifted across the ocean and crashed to earth in the United States. These hydrogen-filled balloons came down in Washington, Oregon, Idaho, Wyoming, Michigan, Iowa, Nebraska, Kansas, Texas, Alaska, eastern Canada, and even central Mexico. One landed near the facility at Hanford, Washington, that was involved in the top-secret operation to develop an atomic bomb, and caused a brief electrical outage. Of the 300 balloons that eventually reached the U.S. West Coast and Canada, only one caused any casualties*[2]

---

* On 5 May 1945, six people were killed by one of the fugo bombs. The Reverend Archie Mitchell and his wife had taken a church group on a Sunday picnic to Gearhart Mountain, near Bly, Oregon. One of the children found a strange metallic object, and when he

The Los Angeles area was especially worried about an invasion, or at least enemy aerial attacks. The Lockheed aircraft plant in Burbank was considered a prime target, so much so that Warner Bros. studios, whose nearby soundstages looked from the air like a factory, painted a large arrow on the roof of a building and the words LOCKHEED—THAT-A-WAY. (Lockheed reportedly returned the favor by painting an arrow on one of its roofs pointing in the opposite direction with the message: WARNER BROS.—THAT-A-WAY.)

Hollywood historian Harlan Lebo notes, "Most of the large film studios developed ingenious plans to camouflage their operations. Studio painters, construction crews, and nursery departments were prepared to create elaborate artistic schemes that overnight could shroud an entire complex. By combining paint, greenery, and netting, the crews could produce a clever re-creation of the natural landscape, so a studio could 'disappear' from view by air—practically at a moment's notice."[3]

Of course, from his train, Ron Smith was unaware of this. "We traveled first class," he recalled, noting that the train had a luxurious feature: Pullman bunks. During the day the bunks were seats facing each other; at night the porter converted them into bunks, one up and one down. Each bunk had a curtain that could be closed and snapped shut for privacy.

The sailors found their way to the dining car, enjoyed a civilized meal, and then wandered into the club car, which was a rolling bar, to play cards. Smitty noted, "The club car was a great place to pick up women, and Jim Caddes did." The rest of the weary gobs had retired to their Pullman bunks for the night when they were awakened by the sounds of Caddes and the girl climbing into his lower berth. Smitty had just drifted back to sleep when there came a loud thud. He poked his head through the curtains to see Bill Partin lying in the aisle, moaning.

---

disturbed it, it exploded, killing him, four other children aged eleven to thirteen, and the minister's wife, Elsie. (www.members.tripod.com/~earthdude1/fugo)

Smitty jumped down to help his buddy and asked what had happened. "I was hanging out of my berth," Partin told him, "trying to peek down in Caddes's berth to watch him with the broad. His curtains were snapped tight, so I reached down to pull the snap with both hands when I lost my balance and fell."

Everyone in the car, with the exception of Caddes, howled with laughter. "You guys think it's funny. Well, it's *not*. She has her clothes back on and I didn't even *finish*."[4]

The laughter broke out anew.

ABOUT thirty miles northeast of San Francisco, in San Pablo Bay, the Mare Island Naval Shipyard sprawled along a spit of land on the western side of the Napa River, across from the Navy town of Vallejo. It was truly a veritable beehive of wartime activity.

In 1859, Mare Island became the birthplace of the first American warship to be built on the West Coast, the frigate U.S.S. *Saginaw*. Houses, barracks, workshops, docks, ordnance manufacturing and storage facilities, and other buildings soon sprouted in the California sun.

In 1891, after nineteen years of construction, a second dry dock, 508 feet long, was finally completed. It took another eleven years to construct a third dry dock, this one 740 feet long. In 1919, the battleship U.S.S. *California*, which would be badly damaged at Pearl Harbor on 7 December 1941 but refloated and repaired, was built and launched here. During the 1920s, Mare Island Naval Shipyard became one of the Navy's primary facilities for the construction and maintenance of submarines, and the goal was to build one new submarine here each year for ten years.

By the late 1930s, more than $100 million had been invested in the Mare Island Naval Shipyard, the largest single industrial plant west of the Mississippi. Before the outbreak of the Second World War, some 6,000 people were employed on the base in the construction and repair of ships; after Pearl Harbor, there would be 35,000 more.

During World War II, Mare Island was a place of vital importance. By the end of the war, the facility would produce hundreds of vessels, including more than 300 landing craft, thirty-one destroyer escorts, four

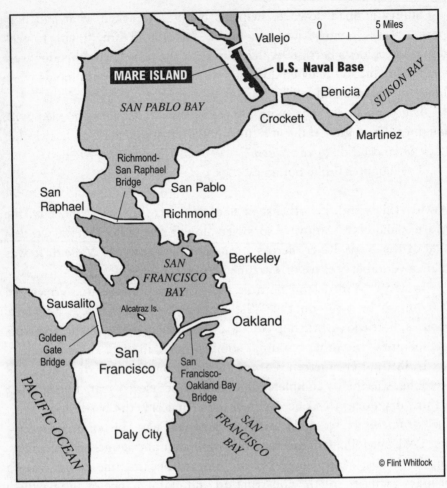

San Francisco area, showing Mare Island Naval Base.

submarine tenders, and seventeen submarines. (As an aside, the shipyard set a record by constructing the destroyer U.S.S. *Ward* [DD-139] in 1918 in just seventeen and a half days.*)

---

* *Ward* became renowned on 7 December 1941 when it fired America's first shots of the Pacific War after sighting and sinking a Japanese midget submarine operating near the mouth of Pearl Harbor a few hours before the surprise assault began. In a strange piece of irony, while supporting the invasion of the Philippines, *Ward* was struck and badly damaged by a suicide pilot on 7 December 1944, exactly three years after Pearl Harbor. After

Aerial view of Mare Island Naval Base, California. The city of Vallejo is at the top of the photo.
(Courtesy Naval Historical Society)

Detraining at Crockett, the nearest depot to Vallejo, Smitty and the other eight sailors, after unsuccessfully trying to buy beer on a Sunday, hopped on a bus that took them to the base. There they were assigned a temporary barracks while they waited for the Navy to assign them to boats. While waiting, they got paid; they had gone without pay for nearly two full paydays and were rewarded with over a hundred dollars each. Wealthier than sheikhs, Smitty and Jim Biggars took the ferry into Vallejo for a little R&R. "It was a busy little town," Smitty recalled, "bustling with Navy yard workers and sailors. You could see the Navy yard across the small bay of water, running full blast with welding flashes spewing everywhere. It sprawled for as far as you could see in either direction."

---

the crew abandoned ship, the destroyer U.S.S. *O'Brien* (DD-725) was called in to sink her. In a further irony, the captain of *O'Brien* was William W. Outerbridge—the same officer who had commanded *Ward* at Pearl Harbor. (members.tripod.com/obrien)

To Smitty, Vallejo, California, seemed to be one giant drinking establishment. On Georgia Street, both sides of the street were solid with beer joints. Not just a *few* bars, but *dozens* of bars, with names like "Porthole" and "Bloody Bucket" and "Crow's Nest," as if having a name with some nautical association was mandatory.

Smitty and Biggars strolled into one of the bars and ordered two beers. "The bartender never even asked to see our IDs. These people were in a different world that had its own set of rules. 'If you're old enough to fight, you're old enough to drink,' seemed to be their attitude, which was okay with me and Jim. It was a real Navy recreation area for submariners. Civilian police were nonexistent; Army MPs always came with a Shore Patrol escort if they were looking for AWOLs or deserters. The Shore Patrol was present in force. Their only weapons were nightsticks, and every sailor knew they were there to protect you."

Smitty glanced around at the few women in the place and thought they looked "well worn." A soused and grizzled motor machinist's mate with silver dolphins on his sleeve came over and bought both of the lads a beer.

"I suppose you two are headed for the pig boats?" he said. Smitty hadn't heard that term for submarines since his dad had told him about the World War I subs being dubbed "pig boats" because of their odoriferous interiors.

"Yep, we just graduated from Sub School," Smitty told him.

"Oh, you guys just in from New London?"

"No, we went to school in San Diego."

The older man chuckled. "Don't try and bullshit a bullshitter. There ain't no Sub School in Dago."

Biggars chimed in. "They just started it. We were in the first graduating class."

The old salt wasn't buying it. "They ain't got no subs in Dago," he insisted. "They're all here, right over there," he said, waving in the general direction of the naval base. "This is the main sub base on the West Coast. Aw, who cares? Hey, barkeep—give these boys a couple more beers." He slapped two quarters on the bar, then went off to make time with one of the "well-worn" female patrons. The two teenagers just looked at each and smiled.[5]

THE new year did not start well for the Silent Service. Although John Pierce's venerable *Argonaut* had found a Japanese convoy bound from Lae to Rabaul on 10 January 1943 and sank one destroyer and damaged two other vessels, the enemy subjected *Argonaut* to a severe depth charging that burst her forward ballast tanks and caused her to pop to the surface. Helpless, *Argonaut* received murderous fire from the destroyers and she sank; Pierce and his crew of 106 were killed. It was another reminder of the dangerous world in which the submariners lived—a world that Ron Smith couldn't wait to experience.[6]

BILL Trimmer, who had survived the attack at Pearl Harbor while serving aboard the battleship *Pennsylvania*, and had also gone through the battles of the Coral Sea, Guadalcanal, and Midway with her, was transferred to submarines. In late 1942, he had been sent to Submarine School at New London, and the gyro and battery schools. In January 1943, he was assigned to the *S-37* in San Diego. "When I first saw her," he said, "I almost died. She was in refit, an old, small submarine commissioned in 1923. Her test depth was only 200 feet. I went below and introduced myself to Gunners Mate First Class Hurt; he was Chief of the Boat."

Trimmer was wishing he had never left the *Pennsylvania*. "There wasn't any shower aboard," he lamented. "Only one small washbasin in the after-battery compartment, which was also the galley and mess hall. There was one small table without seats. We ate anywhere we could find a place to sit down. Most of the time we stood up and ate."

S-37 operated with the Sub School and took students out on training runs. The submarine was then ordered to Dutch Harbor in the Aleutians, but broke down about halfway there, limping back to Hunters Point, a shipyard just outside San Francisco.

Then Trimmer caught a break: appendicitis. "Thank goodness the *S-37* broke down or I would have been at sea when my appendix ruptured." He spent twenty-six days in the base hospital; *S-37* sailed without him. While he recuperated and waited for a new assignment, he became engaged long-distance to Irene Sprinkle, a girl from Orange, Virginia.

It was not until the spring of 1944 that he finally went back out to sea on a newly commissioned Fleet submarine of the *Balao* class, the U. S.S. *Redfish*.[7]

By the end of January 1943, American submarines were racking up impressive scores against enemy shipping. *Nautilus* sank a small freighter north of Bougainville on the ninth and *Guardfish*, under skipper Thomas B. Klakring, sent a patrol boat, destroyer, and cargo ship to the bottom. In the Bismarcks, Hank Bruton's *Greenling* torpedoed an ammunition freighter that went up in spectacular fashion. *Gato* (William G. Myers) holed two cargo ships and *Swordfish* (Albert C. "Acey" Burrows) sank another. *Growler*, from her base in Brisbane, added to the total by downing a 6,000-ton passenger-cargo ship but lost her valiant commander, Howard W. Gilmore, a month later, in dramatic fashion.[8]

On the night of 7 February 1943, while running on the surface to charge *Growler*'s batteries, Gilmore, on the bridge, spotted the *Hayasaki,* a 900-ton armed merchantman, a mile away. Just as Gilmore ordered the sub to dive, *Hayasaki* charged her, blasting away with its deck gun. Shells killed two men on the sub's bridge and wounded three others, including Gilmore. Gilmore, trying to avoid a collision, ordered left full rudder, but it was too late; the two vessels crashed into each other and the collision was so violent that eighteen feet of *Growler*'s bow was bent to port at a ninety-degree angle. After directing the men in the conning tower to carry the other two wounded men below, Gilmore ordered, "Take her down!" The executive officer hesitated for a few seconds; should he save the boat or the captain?

With a heavy heart, he relayed Gilmore's final order, *Growler* dove, and the skipper was washed away to his death. Amazingly, despite the severe damage, *Growler* managed to make it back to Brisbane, where she was repaired by 1 May. For his courage, Gilmore was posthumously

The bent bow of *Growler* after her collision with an armed Japanese freighter, photographed in Brisbane, Australia. *Growler*'s commander, Howard W. Gilmore, lost his life in the incident and earned the Medal of Honor posthumously.
(Courtesy National Archives)

awarded the first Medal of Honor given to a submariner in World War II, and passed into Navy legend.[9]

THE days went by slowly, but still no orders arrived for the nine Sub School graduates at Mare Island. Smitty began to think again about putting in an application for flight training; was he ever going to get into the war? Then somebody found out that there were dollar-an-hour jobs available at the nearby Oakland Ship Yard. If the chief had no details for them after morning muster, the sailors donned dungarees, jumped on a bus, and rode into Oakland.

"They hired anyone for all sorts of menial jobs," Smitty recalled, "like fire watches or sweepers. All you had to do as a fire watch was to stand by a welder with a fire extinguisher and put out any little fires that started." Smitty found out quickly that the main thing you had to do at Oakland was to hide out for eight hours and then collect your money at the end of the day. Occasionally a boss would catch someone goofing off and assign him to some other detail, but for the most part, it was a screw-off deal. The money started piling up fast—forty dollars in just five days. That was almost two-thirds what Smitty and his mates were making every month in the Navy![10]

THE plane, an amphibious Pan Am Clipper on loan to the Navy, took off from the waters of Pearl Harbor and banked to the east, on a heading for San Francisco. It was 20 January 1943. On board was Admiral Robert English, ComSubPac, and three of his most-trusted staff officers: John J. Crane, William G. Myers (former skipper of *Gato*), and John O. R. Coll, along with a handful of other officers and the civilian flight crew. While in San Francisco, English planned to visit the submarine base at Mare Island.

As the Clipper neared the California coast, it was engulfed in a fierce winter storm and the pilot lost his bearings. The radio also failed. When communications were finally reestablished, it was discovered that the plane was 115 miles off course north of San Francisco, struggling through a stiff wind, heavy rain, and a blanketing fog. Contact was again suddenly lost—this time permanently. It was ten days before the charred and mangled wreckage of the plane was discovered in the remote, inaccessible mountains east of Ukiah; Admiral English and the other eighteen persons on board had perished instantly.

The entire Submarine Service reacted to the news as if they had been bludgeoned. While the admiral had his shortcomings and de-

Admiral Robert English, ComSubPac, killed in a plane crash on 20 January 1943.
(Courtesy National Archives)

tractors, no one felt he deserved this ending. Much speculation arose as to who English's successor would be. Chief of Naval Operations Admiral King ended the speculation when he appointed Charles Lockwood to the post of SubComPac; Rear Admiral Ralph Christie replaced Lockwood in Perth-Fremantle.[11]

A new day was about to dawn for the submarine force.

CHAPTER 9

AT HOME IN THE CABOOSE

IN the wake of Admiral English's death, the American submarine force stepped up its efforts to take the war to the enemy. In January 1943, *Wahoo*, with Lieutenant Commander Dudley "Mush" Morton—a man of iron nerve and even stronger determination—set out from Brisbane on her third war patrol to attack the Japanese supply base of Wewak on the northern shore of New Guinea.[1]

Morton was, by all accounts, adored by his men. George Grider, one of the officers on board *Wahoo*, wrote, "Mush . . . was built like a bear, and as playful as a cub . . . The crew loved him." Morton's exec, the aggressive Richard O'Kane, was viewed with some suspicion, as he was even more outspoken than Morton in his hatred of the enemy and his desire to throw caution to the winds in pursuit of them. Of O'Kane, Grider said, "He talked a great deal—reckless, aggressive talk—and it was natural to wonder how much of it was no more than talk."[2]

But the crew must have thought Morton crazed when he penetrated Wewak Harbor—a nest teeming with enemy freighters, destroyers, submarines, and patrol craft. Inciting one of the destroyers into charging *Wahoo*, Morton fired two torpedoes at her, both of which missed or failed to detonate. At the last moment, a third torpedo fired at a range of 800 yards did the trick. The next day Morton came across a convoy of several ships and began picking them off, one by one.

After the attack Grider noted, "We surfaced in a sea of Japanese survivors. They were on every piece of flotsam, every broken stick, in lifeboats, everywhere, and as we cruised among them, they looked at us with expressions beyond description. There were about twenty boats of every type in the water, from large scows to little rowboats. The water was so thick with enemy soldiers that it was literally impossible to cruise through them without pushing them aside like driftwood. These were troops we knew had been bound for New Guinea, to fight and kill our own men, and Mush, whose overwhelming biological hatred of the enemy we were only now beginning to sense, looked about with exultation at the carnage."[3]

What happened next has been a source of controversy ever since Morton submitted his official report. Surfacing, Morton ordered his men to stand by the four-inch deck gun and machine guns and to fire at the lifeboats. If any return fire was received, then *Wahoo*'s gunners were to blast them to eternity; small-arms fire was received from one lifeboat. In his biography of O'Kane, William Tuohy writes, "In reply, *Wahoo*'s machine guns drove most of the Japanese soldiers in life-jackets from the splintering and sinking boats. The 4-inch gun crew demolished the bigger Japanese boats. Some crewmen reported the water was so thick with enemy soldiers that it was impossible to cruise through them without brushing them aside like driftwood. O'Kane knew they were uniformed troops bound for New Guinea to fight and kill Americans, and the officers sensed Mush Morton's overwhelming hatred of the enemy." The firing lasted, by O'Kane's account, no more than fifteen minutes. As far as Morton and O'Kane were concerned, the lifeboats and the men in them were legitimate targets, just as much as enemy soldiers in a convoy of trucks would be to airmen or artillerists.[4]

At last, with the need to resume chasing the escaped ships a priority, Morton ordered cease fire and *Wahoo* steamed away through the bloody water in a plume of diesel exhaust. The number of Japanese troops who died in the water that day is not known.

Late in the day, Morton finally caught up with the two escapees and sank both the tanker and the freighter. Out of torpedoes, *Wahoo* set course for Pearl Harbor, where she, Morton, and the crew were celebrated as heroes after they docked. Lockwood called Morton "The One-Boat Wolf Pack," and awarded him the Navy Cross, while the Army's

Distinguished Service Cross was bestowed upon him by General Douglas MacArthur. Clay Blair notes, "This patrol, one of the most celebrated of the war, gave the whole submarine force a shot in the arm—or kick in the pants." The killing of the enemy troops in the bobbing lifeboats did not trouble anyone; this was war, and the gloves were off.[5]

"REPORT by 0800 1 February 1943 to U.S.S. *Skipjack* (SS-184), Mare Island Navy Yard," is all the typed orders from BuPers—the Navy's Bureau of Personnel in Washington—said on the sheet of paper Smitty held in his trembling hands. At last he was assigned to a submarine!

Smitty checked with his other former classmates. They, too, had received their orders, and each was going to a different boat. Stuffing all their worldly possessions into their seabags—the Navy's version of the duffel bag—the group reported to the submarine base headquarters, where an officer met them and drilled into them for over an hour the need for absolute secrecy about their new assignment. Under no circumstances, he told them, were they to tell anyone—not even their immediate families—what they did or where they were going. "By the time the commander was finished," Smith related, "we knew we were definitely in the 'Silent Service.'"

After reporting to the submarine barracks area and stowing their bags, Smitty shook hands and wished his friends farewell, then went down to the docks to find *Skipjack*. The activity at the docks was organized bedlam. Everywhere darted gray-painted jeeps and trucks and sailors in dungarees, going about their official business. Giant gantry cranes overhead swung to and fro. There was yelling, the banging of rivet guns, the crisp sizzle and pop of welding torches, the tooting of horns. The electric atmosphere was charged with the underlying sense that there was a war on, and that everyone and everything in the area was dedicated to just one thing: victory.

Skipjack was wedged into the docks amid a dozen other subs, each undergoing some stage of maintenance or repair. Smitty stepped over hoses and cables and walked across the small gangway laid from dock to boat, dodging workers coming and going. He followed Navy custom and saluted the stern, even though no American flag was flying that day, then reported to the "doghouse," a small wooden shack temporarily constructed on the sub's deck just forward of the conning tower. The guard, a friendly gunner's mate, directed Smitty to Chief Hickman on the barge tied outboard of the sub. Each boat undergoing overhaul had a barge alongside that acted as temporary living quarters and parts-storage facility; Smitty thought the barge looked like a large garage full of junk and bunks.

Smitty introduced himself to Chief Hickman, who seemed friendly and glad to have him on board. "The chief of the boat," Smith explained, "is the leading enlisted man on a sub and is basically in charge of the crew. He has a lot of power, even more authority in many ways than the junior officers—the ensigns and lieutenants." After learning that Smitty had recently graduated from torpedo school, Hickman invited him to give a future class to the rest of the boat's torpedomen on the latest torpedo technology. The chief then assigned him to the aft torpedo room and introduced him to a sailor named Snavely, who would be Smitty's immediate boss. The two hit it off well. Unlike the cold, unfriendly sailors on *Cachalot*, Smitty felt welcomed by *Skipjack*'s crew.

For the next three weeks that *Skipjack* was undergoing overhaul at Mare Island, Smitty learned every nut, bolt, line, gauge, and hatch of her. He learned that *Skipjack* was the last of the *Salmon*-class boats, and had been built in 1938 at the Electric Boat Company in Groton, Connecticut. Like the other *Salmon*-class boats, *Skipjack* was 308 feet in length; displaced 1,450 tons; could test-dive to 265 feet; had a capacity of 110,000 gallons of diesel fuel; had four torpedo tubes in the bow and four in the stern; and carried a ship's company of eight officers and seventy men. She previously had been part of the Asiatic Fleet based in Manila, but had relocated to Australia when the Philippines fell. Its commander at the outbreak of war, Larry Freeman, was relieved of command after he missed a Japanese carrier, a tanker, and a seaplane tender on two patrols; James Wiggins "Red" Coe, formerly commander of the *S-39*, became the new skipper. Although she was considered obsolescent, *Skipjack*—and Coe—had proven their mettle by sinking three ships off the coast of Indochina in April 1942. Despite his good fortune, Coe felt he could have done even better had the Mark XIV torpedoes functioned properly; it was his report in 1942 that had sparked Admiral Lockwood's torpedo tests.[6]

Not content to do battle over torpedoes alone, Coe also became well known in Navy circles for his wonderfully humorous 11 June 1942 letter to the Mare Island supply officer regarding the cancellation of an order for toilet paper. The matter was this: on 30 July 1941, the previous captain, Freeman, had submitted a requisition for the bathroom necessity through channels, but for unknown reasons, the Mare Island supply officer on 26 November 1941 stamped the requisition "Canceled—Cannot Identify" and sent it back to *Skipjack*. When Coe assumed command of the sub, he was determined to get to the bottom of the problem. Wryly parodying military bureaucrat-ese, he included a small swatch of toilet paper with his letter to the base supply officer:

> During the 11-3/4 months elapsed from the time of ordering the toilet paper and the present date, USS SKIPJACK personnel, despite their best efforts to await delivery of the subject material, have been unable to wait on numerous occasions, and the situation is now quite acute, particularly during depth-charge attacks . . .
>
> Enclosure 2 is a sample of the desired materials provided for the information of the Supply Officer, Navy Yard, Mare Island. The Commanding Officer, USS SKIPJACK, cannot help but wonder what is being used at Mare Island in place of this unidentifiable material, once well known to this command.
>
> SKIPJACK personnel during this period have become accustomed to the use of "crests," i.e., the vast amount of incoming non-essential paper work, and in so doing feel that the wish of the Bureau of Ships for reduction of paper work is being complied with, thus killing two birds with one stone.
>
> It is believed by this command that the stamped notation "Cannot Identify" was possible error, and that this is simply a case of shortage of strategic war material, the SKIPJACK probably being low on the priority list.
>
> In order to cooperate in the war effort at a small local sacrifice, the SKIPJACK desires no further action be taken until the end of the cur-

rent war, which has created a situation aptly described as "War is hell."[7]

—J. W. Coe*

While *Skipjack* had its engines worked on and received a new conning tower and deck guns, the rest of the crew practiced their drinking during their off-duty hours. And formidable drinkers they were. The youthful Smitty was awed by their worldliness, their raunchy language, their ability to hold their liquor. A hundred years earlier, Smitty thought, these foul-speaking, hard-drinking submariners would have been right at home on a full-masted man-of-war in the king's navy. Or on a pirate ship, with a parrot on each shoulder. One night in San Francisco, one of *Skipjack*'s crewmen decided to make a man out of Smitty and taught him how to down several glasses of bourbon; all he did was end up making a very sick sailor out of the teenager, who had to be helped back to the base, drunk as a skunk.

A few days later, a yeoman approached Smitty with the news that a set of new orders awaited him back at the barracks. "You're being transferred to *Seal*," the yeoman said.

Smitty was dumbfounded; he hadn't even gone to sea with *Skipjack*. "Some guy on *Seal* got sick," the yeoman said, "so there was an opening. They're a sister boat to us, like *Salmon*. They're going to be ready to go before we are. Division picked you because you were handy and already knew a lot about *Skipjack*."

It was true. Smitty knew and liked *Skipjack*. "I was just beginning to make friends on her. Besides, what kind of name is that for a submarine—*Seal*. A seal isn't even a fish. Shit." But orders were orders, and he was just a minor cog in the giant Navy wheel; he did what he was told and reported to *Seal*.

---

* This incident was written into the 1959 Cary Grant film, *Operation Petticoat*. Unfortunately, Red Coe did not live to see the movie; he and all hands were lost when his new boat, the submarine U.S.S. *Cisco,* was sunk on 28 September 1943 in the Sulu Sea. (www .csp.navy.mil/ww2boats/cisco)

Like *Skipjack*, *Seal* was awash in both civilian and Navy personnel almost frantically getting her ready for sea. Equipment was being moved in through hatches, welders were sending sparks flying, and electrical cables as thick as a man's arm snaked from shore to sub and disappeared into the interior. Once aboard, Smitty was introduced to Chief Weist, a friendly man of medium height and build, with a round face, round nose, and red cheeks; he reminded Smitty a little of the Santa Claus–like Chief Evans at torpedo school. Weist had the rolling gait common to men who spent a lot of time at sea.

Weist took Smitty on a brief tour of the boat, ending up in his new home—the after torpedo room, also known as the "caboose." The cramped space was crammed with an array of shiny steel and polished brass hardware that sparkled dazzlingly under the harsh glare of the bare bulbs. Smitty was handed over to a five-foot five-inch torpedoman named John Adam Kaczmerowski—"Big Ski" for short—his immediate supervisor, and another torpedoman, Dillingham, nicknamed "Seagull." Big Ski looked like a lumberjack—no, make that a short, squat, thickly muscled oak tree, while Seagull was thin, almost willowy. There was another veteran in the after torpedo room, Maylon Pembroke "Woody" Woodard. Smitty worried that he would be treated like the outsider in this tightly knit group, which had made five war patrols since 7 December 1941, but his new mates welcomed him with open arms.

Someone showed Smitty *Seal*'s battle flag with its cartoon depiction of a pugnacious seal, boxing gloves on its flippers and sitting on a torpedo. Smitty hoped it accurately captured the fighting spirit of the crew.

While at Mare Island, *Seal* had received new periscopes and periscope shears, the previous ones having been nearly torn off during a collision with an enemy ship. The cigarette deck aft of the conning tower, where sailors could smoke while surfaced, also had been enlarged at Mare Island and a new deck added forward of the conning tower. Both decks had been outfitted with twenty-millimeter Orlikan machine guns, and ammunition lockers were built into the conning tower. It was obvious that *Seal* was expecting more surface action.[8]

Smitty's new mates regaled him with stories about *Seal*'s history and wartime adventures. The sub's keel, Smitty learned, had been laid on 25 March 1936 in Groton, and she was launched on 25 August 1937. *Seal*

Woody Woodard, a *Seal* crewman.
(Courtesy Ron Smith)

was not an S-boat; she was one of the early Fleet boats of the *Salmon-Sargo* class that formed a link between the S-boats and the later *Gato-Balao* class boats. Her first skipper had been Lieutenant Commander Karl G. Hensel; in the spring of 1940, Lieutenant Commander Kenneth C. Hurd replaced Hensel. Her first war patrol began on 14 December 1941; she left Manila and, north of Lingayen Gulf, sank the 850-ton freighter *Hayataka Maru*—the last Japanese ship sunk in 1941.[9]

The fifty-three-day patrol ended at Surabaya, Java. *Seal* then went to Tjilatjap (pronounced "chill-a-chap") for refit. While *Seal* was in the latter port, the Japanese launched a series of aerial assaults. *Seal* escaped being hit but some of the natives weren't so lucky; *Seal*'s crewmen told Smitty of watching the slaughter of innocent villagers during the raids. "They said the island natives crawled on top of their thatched huts built on poles about eight feet off the ground," Smith recounted. "It was their natural behavior when confronted with danger, which normally consisted of animal predators or floodwaters. Our guys said the natives looked like sitting ducks on top of their huts. The Japanese pilots had a field day, strafing and killing natives by the hundreds."

Big Ski and Woody told Smitty of the heroism of Eugene "Jeep" Peña, who had cradled a fifty-caliber machine gun in his arms and downed a Zero. Peña still bore scars on his forearm where the hot barrel of the gun had seared his skin.

After surviving four days of air raids at Tjilatjap, *Seal*'s refit was completed, and on 19 February 1942, *Seal* began her second hunting expedition—in the Java Sea, Flores Sea, Makassar Straits, and off the south coast of Timor. On 20 February, *Seal* came upon a convoy of four freighters escorted by three destroyers. Submerged, *Seal*'s crew launched four torpedoes at the biggest target and heard two explosions, but when they surfaced, the ships were gone and the crew could find no evidence that anything had been sunk or damaged.

Near the end of her forty-nine-day patrol, *Seal*, along with *Seawolf* and *Sailfish*, was ordered to disrupt the Japanese amphibious assault landings at Bali; shortly thereafter, during the Battle of the Java Sea, *Seal* reported having damaged a light cruiser. *Seal* then retired to Fremantle for replenishment of her stores—and to await her next assignment.

On 12 May 1942, *Seal* left Fremantle to search for targets off the coast of Indochina. While en route to the patrol area, Hurd sighted and hit a cargo ship, the *Tatsufuku Maru*; the nearby *Swordfish** finished off the crippled freighter, and both subs shared credit for the sinking.

Seal's fourth patrol, which began on 10 August 1942 from Albany, West Australia, was jinxed from the beginning. Although she damaged one cargoman and sighted numerous other vessels, torpedo problems prevented her from adding any more enemy ships to her battle flag. Out of fuel, food, and ammunition, she returned to Fremantle for refitting.

The fifth war patrol began on 24 October and took *Seal* to the Palau Islands; by the middle of November she was wading in a rich hunting ground ripe with potential trophies. Sighting two destroyers escorting nine freighters, *Seal* blasted away with her tubes. The rest of the convoy scattered like a covey of frightened quail, but the 5,477-ton *Boston Maru* charged in *Seal*'s direction and a crash dive was all that saved the sub from destruction. There was a terrible noise as the cargo ship's hull scraped the descending sub's conning tower, bent both periscopes, damaged the shears, and sent the submarine into a fifty-degree list. But the collision ripped open the freighter's hull like a tin can, making *Seal* the only submarine to be credited with sinking an enemy vessel with her periscope shears.

For several hours, the blind and wounded submarine was subjected

---

* *Swordfish* would be reported missing south of Kyushu, Japan, on 12 January 1945. (Blair, 782)

to a horrendous depth charging but managed to survive in 250 feet of water. Once the enemy had gone, *Seal* limped home to Pearl Harbor for emergency repairs. But the damage was too great for Pearl's facilities, so she was ordered to Mare Island for more extensive work. It was then that Commander Harry Benjamin Dodge, Naval Academy class of 1930, replaced Hurd, who had distinguished himself while in command of *Seal*.[10]

Chief Weist took Smitty to meet *Seal*'s new skipper, whom he described as being "an aloof man, quiet, but with an easy smile. Medium build with blue eyes, a ruddy complexion, and a nose as pointed as a bird's beak. Born of a well-to-do family, he had the demeanor of an aristocrat. He was always in control of his emotions, and although not the most aggressive submarine skipper, he was by no means lacking in courage and, as I heard and would later discover for myself, conducted himself well in battle. A true leader."

There was no question in Smitty's mind that he was joining a battle-hardened boat and crew. Now, at the end of March 1943, *Seal*, with new torpedoman Ron Smith aboard, was almost ready to again take to the

Seal Commander Harry B. Dodge makes friends with a gooney bird.
(Courtesy Ron Smith)

seas and do battle with the enemy. All *Seal* needed was to pass the dive test—which would prove to be easier said than done.[11]

AFTER undergoing major repairs, submarines needed to be tested before they left on patrol to make certain that the work was completed satisfactorily; the middle of the Pacific is not the place to find out that a new seal or gasket or hatch was improperly installed.

Thus, on a cold, dark March morning, *Seal* prepared for her test dive in the chilly, choppy waters of San Francisco Bay. Commander Dodge guided the sub from her berth at Mare Island to a place between Alcatraz Island and Goat Island that was deep enough for a stationary test dive to check for leaks and make sure that all systems were working properly.

Smitty was handed a set of large headphones and a throat mike and told to stand near the torpedo tubes to relay orders and information between the officers and tubes aft, as his station was called.

Dodge took up his station inside the conning tower. As *Seal* reached the location for the test, Control announced over the battle circuit, "Stand by to dive." Smitty repeated the command so that the skipper would know that the order had been correctly received; misunderstandings could be fatal.

In the center of the boat, in the control room, all eyes were on the "Christmas tree" and its red and green indicator lights. As hatches were closed, the indicator lights went from red to green. Only one light stayed red—the engine exhaust indicator light.

"Dive, dive," said Lieutenant Jack Frost, the diving and engineering officer, and the awful, nerve-jangling *aaaaooogaa!* claxon shrieked throughout the boat. The roaring diesels abruptly went silent as the electric motors took over the job of propulsion; the engine exhaust indicator light went green as the vent closed.

Frost ordered that high-pressure air be drawn into the boat. Eardrums popped and the barometer showed that *Seal*'s seal was holding. Frost reported to the skipper in the conning tower, "Green board, pressure in the boat."

"Very well," replied Dodge. "Take her to sixty-five feet."

"Sixty-five feet, aye." That was *Seal*'s periscope depth.

"Flood negative," said Dodge.

"Flood negative, aye."

The ports on the ballast tanks were opened to release the air, and tons of seawater filled the tanks, angling the boat sharply downward.

"Flood bow buoyancy."

"Flood bow buoyancy, aye."

The two sailors on the bow and stern planes, studying the bubble indicators and large depth gauges in front of them, turned the big chrome-steel wheels that controlled the angle of the dive.

"Small leak in pump room," someone suddenly reported over the circuit.

"Very well, pump room," answered Frost calmly.

Someone in the forward torpedo room called, "We got a little water coming in around number two soundhead but we're tightening the packing. Ain't no problem."

"Very well, tubes forward."

After a few minutes at sixty-five feet, Dodge ordered the boat down to one hundred feet.

Seal had just reached that depth when something went seriously wrong. Water began gushing from the crew's lavatory at the forward bulkhead of the after torpedo room as though a fire hydrant had just split open; Woody and Big Ski took off running for the head. "Surface! Surface!" yelled Ski, and Smitty repeated the words to Control. Instantly the claxon sounded three times and Control began blowing the water out of the ballast tanks to gain positive buoyancy and return the boat to the surface.

Lieutenant Frost asked Smitty, "Tubes aft, what's your condition?"

"Don't know, Control. We're getting a lot of water coming in from the washroom overhead."

"Okay, tubes aft. Is the bulkhead door closed?"

"Tubes aft, aye." Before the dive began, all hatches and doors had been sealed tightly shut; if the after torpedo room flooded, the caboose would become a tomb for Smitty and his mates. It was just one of those hazards everyone on board came to accept; you died so your buddies—and the boat—would live.

Meanwhile, Big Ski, Woody, and a civilian from the Navy Yard, along for the test, were soaked to the skin as they tried to find a wooden plug of the approximate right size and wedge it into the hole through which was pouring ice-cold seawater. A few swings of a mallet and the gusher was reduced to a trickle.

Once *Seal* had surfaced, Lieutenant Frost came back to the caboose to inspect the situation. Woody spoke up. "Looks like someone put a bad patch on that three-inch hole that was left when we removed the escape buoy mechanism." Frost agreed, and Dodge set *Seal* on a course to return to Mare Island.

After *Seal* had docked, inspectors went over every inch of her and came up with another chilling finding: someone had deliberately punched or drilled holes in the trim line, a large pipe that extended the entire length of the sub. Had the trim line failed, the sub could have experienced a loss of control during the dive and everyone on board would have perished.

There was only one explanation: sabotage.

The crew members themselves removed the damaged trim line and installed a new one. They suddenly didn't trust the Navy Yard workers.

A second test dive a few days later showed no problems, and a week of drills brought the crew up to fighting trim; *Seal* was nearly ready to head out to sea for her sixth war patrol.

Smitty was filled with a quiet, nervous excitement. It was April 1943—nearly a year and a half since the United States had entered the war, and ten months since he had enlisted in the Navy. At last he was going off to combat, and it thrilled him. Yet there was a subcurrent of anxiety, of fear. He had never been subjected to a depth charging before; would he crack under the strain? He had heard enough war stories from the older sailors to know it was going to be tough, demanding, and very risky. A submarine, once at sea, has few friends. It was like an infantry platoon crossing alone into enemy territory on a suicide mission. Your own forces could attack you as quickly as the other side, because all submarines look alike, and you can't come up and wave an American flag. In addition, if you don't get depth-charged or bombed or strafed, the sub could get stuck on an underwater reef, or somebody could always forget and leave a hatch open during a crash dive, or screw up during a critical operation, and the whole boat, crew and all, would be lost.

* * *

ON 13 April 1943, Commander Dodge gave all but a skeleton crew a final liberty before shoving off the next day. Smitty, alone with his thoughts, went into San Francisco. His status as a virgin still bothered him and he hoped to find a young woman who would alter the situation before he sailed into battle. He hit a few bars, downing a few shots of liquid courage before being directed to a brothel above one of the saloons. After a desultory few minutes with a kindly and attractive "older" woman, he got dressed and headed back to Mare Island, still lost in his imaginings of the war that lurked beyond the horizon.

Comforted by the booze and the departure of his virginity, Smitty had slept like a baby, but now he was up before dawn with the rest of the crew, making ready for the voyage. "Set the sea detail," came the order from the bridge over the bullhorn. Men who had been on deck climbed down into the sub and dogged the hatches shut behind them, in order, from fore to aft, like a well-rehearsed team.

WITH the morning sun just beginning to peek over the California hills to the east, *Seal*, on the surface, slipped beneath the orange-hued Golden Gate Bridge. It was Wednesday, 14 April 1943, and *Seal* was heading west, first to Hawaii and then to wherever the secret orders locked into *Seal*'s safe directed.

The crew began the sea detail watches—four hours on, eight hours off, twenty-four hours a day, seven days a week. Whenever the sub was surfaced, men were stationed on the bridge and equipped with high-powered binoculars with which they constantly scanned the sky and the horizon for signs of aircraft and other ships. Some crewmen wore special polarized sunglasses that enabled them to stare directly at the sun without fear of damage to their retinas as they searched for Japanese aircraft who loved to attack from out of the solar ball. Standing watch was intensely boring and uncomfortable duty—four hours without a break—but it was also necessary duty, for no one knew when or from what quarter the enemy might appear.

During the voyage, Commander Dodge constantly put the crew through drills and practices—Battle Stations Submerged and Battle Stations Surface—to keep their combat reflexes sharp. Occasionally the claxon would unexpectedly jolt everyone's nerves, followed by the command "Dive, dive!" as the skipper, stopwatch in hand, worked on cutting the time it took to submerge. If an enemy plane suddenly swooped down upon them, *Seal* would need to be underwater in less than fifty seconds; anyone still on deck, including the skipper himself, risked being left behind to die.[12]

As *Seal* was steaming steadily toward Hawaii, on 18 April 1943, a significant event took place far to the southwest. Navy code breakers had learned that Admiral Yamamoto would be making an inspection tour of Rabaul and Bougainville. Perhaps, thought the planners on Nimitz's staff, there might be an opportunity to ambush the admiral and shoot him down. The nearest American air base to Rabaul and Bougainville

Submariners on watch.
(Courtesy National Archives)

was Henderson Field, Guadalcanal, some 400 miles away. It was too far for single-engine fighters, but the twin-boom P-38 "Lightning," if fitted with larger fuel tanks, could make it there and back.

The 339th Fighter Squadron, under Major John W. Mitchell, was alerted, and mechanics worked late into the night of 17 April to modify the fuel tanks and give the P-38s the range they needed. After studying the translation of the admiral's detailed itinerary, Mitchell decided to take eighteen planes and intercept Yamamoto on his approach to Kahili aerodrome on Bougainville. At 0933 hours, Mitchell spotted two Naka-jima G4M2 "Betty" bombers, accompanied by six Zeros; Mitchell did not know which bomber carried the admiral, so both became targets and the P-38s banked into the attack. At approximately the same moment, the Zeros' pilots saw the Americans and turned to drive them off; the two Bettys headed for the deck with P-38s hot on their tails. Lieutenant Rex T. Barber pounced on one of the bombers and sent it flaming into the jungle; Barber then went after the other Betty, sending it crashing into the ocean. As it turned out, Yamamoto was aboard the first plane shot down; he died immediately from rounds from Barker's machine guns.*[13]

In retrospect, the death of Isoroku Yamamoto probably had little effect on Japan's prosecution of the war for, by April 1943, Dai Nippon's strength had been eclipsed by the rising military and industrial power of the United States. As a moral victory for the Americans, however, it was a tremendous moment, for the architect of the Pearl Harbor raid was now dead.

IN order to save fuel, *Seal* was running on the surface with only two of her 1,600-horsepower engines operating. Had she been going wide open—flank speed—with all four engines running, she could make a maximum speed of twenty-one and a half knots, but with two engines she could still cruise at a respectable fifteen knots. *Seal* guzzled fuel oil, getting an average of 12.9 miles per gallon. The boat followed a zigzag

---

* Naval historian Samuel Morison gives credit for one of the downings to Captain Thomas G. Lanphier. (Morison, *Breaking the Bismarcks Barrier,* Vol. VI, 128)

course that further slowed her but, it was hoped, made her less of an easy target for any nearby Japanese submarines.

Most of the men lost track of the days. Smitty recalled, "Inside the boat you couldn't tell if it was day or night anyhow, unless the diesels were running. Then it was probably night and you were surfaced to charge the batteries while it was dark."

Seal's first stop was Hawaii. It took her five days to get there, and Smitty was seasick for the entire cruise, fighting with other seasick sailors for use of the single toilet in the aft of the sub. So wretchedly ill was he, Smith said, "Death would have been a pleasant relief."

His buddy Woody warned him, "Two things you never do in this man's Navy: you don't puke in the bilges and you don't piss in the bilges." The bilge was the space beneath the torpedo tubes into which any water on the deck drained. Smitty tried to obey this commandment, but it wasn't easy, especially with eighty men on board, half of whom needed to use the head at one time or another.

A few hours east of Oahu, a Navy destroyer rendezvoused with *Seal* to escort her into Pearl Harbor. An order came over the internal communications system: "Line handlers topside. Secure from sea detail."

Along with the rest of the aft-torpedo-room crew, Smitty climbed out the hatch and stood in the bright sunlight on the fantail, lines in hand, ready to help with the mooring. He couldn't help noticing that, off their port side, a few remains of the U.S. Pacific Fleet still lay. Many of the torn ships—*California*, *Nevada*, and *Maryland*—had already been salvaged, repaired, and were back in the war, but *Arizona*, the hardest hit of the battlewagons, sat with her main deck and guns below the waterline, her superstructure tilted at an odd angle, her gray paint scorched black. Behind *Arizona*, wrecked planes at the Ford Island Air Station were piled in a heap, like so many broken toys. It seemed that everywhere in the harbor, workers by the hundreds were cutting, drilling, welding, and still attempting to salvage the remains of the decimated fleet. Out of sight of *Seal* was Smitty's father's old ship, *Utah*, now lying on her side and growing a patina of rust.

"The base at Pearl Harbor was still a mess," Smith recalled. "The superstructures of sunken ships sticking up out of the water were grotesque reminders of what had happened here—and why I had joined the Navy."

Seal headed toward the submarine docks on the eastern shore of the harbor—past the Ten-Ten Dock, 1,010 feet long—with Lieutenant Commander Frank Greenup, the exec and most experienced submarine officer on board, in charge of the docking. He deftly guided *Seal* through the maze of small boats going every which way and toward her berth. Greenup, on the bridge, couldn't resist showing off a little for the crew and the small knot of officers and sailors waiting on the dock. It is not easy to bring a 1,500-ton submarine, as long as a football field and with a draft of eighteen feet, into a dock, even if the waters are calm, with no tides or currents, but Greenup evidently was skilled at his craft.

"Steady on the helm," Greenup called down to the helmsman below, who then relayed the order to the men on the maneuvering board in the control room. Greenup then barked, "Left twenty degrees rudder, port stop."

"Left twenty degrees rudder, port stop, aye," said the helmsman. It took a couple of seconds but the boat reacted accordingly.

As the bow swung around, just before it lined up with the dock, Greenup ordered, "Helm amidships, all ahead one-third."

"Helm amidships, all ahead one-third, aye." *Seal* seemed to respond by itself to the verbal command, almost as though the boat were a well-trained, living creature.

"All stop," directed Greenup, and *Seal* drifted straight for the dock, and for a moment, less trusting observers feared that the boat would ram the dock. But then Greenup commanded, "All back full," and the diesels roared to life as the props, spinning in reverse, bit into the water, sending the boat sliding perfectly sideways, barely kissing the dock, in a beautiful demonstration of how to parallel-park a submarine.

"Smart-ass," Big Ski muttered to Smitty and the other crewmen on the fantail. "One of these days he's going to miss and we'll end up in the middle of ComSubPac," jerking his thumb in the direction of the palm-surrounded building that housed the offices of Admiral Lockwood, commander of Submarines Pacific, and his staff.

"All stop," Greenup commanded, and the engines shut down. "Throw over the bowline," he said, and the men at the bow tossed the monkey fist, or "heavy," a five-pound lead weight attached to twenty-one thread—about the thickness of a clothesline—to men on the dock waiting to catch it. The twenty-one thread was secured to a three-inch manila hemp mooring line, and this in turn was wrapped around a large steel cleat bolted to the dock. The same procedure was repeated for the stern line. The line stretched and screeched as *Seal*'s stern was slowly pulled toward the dock and secured.

For the purpose of going ashore for liberty, the officers and men of *Seal* were divided into two groups. Luckily for Smitty, he was in the first group. Before anyone could go ashore, however, they must first shower, shave, wash a week's worth of crud off their bodies, and look presentable. A large, freshwater hose was brought aboard and the crew lined up outside the showers for a personal scrub-down. The crew's tailor-made white uniforms had been mashed into wrinkled messes in the tiny lockers, so Smitty and his mates brought them ashore to be pressed at a laundry on their way into Honolulu, and then bought several more sets of whites at a nearby tailor shop.

The gobs trooped over to King Street, downed a few drinks, flirted with the prostitutes, then headed back to the boat; their liberty was up at 1800 hours, when curfew went into effect. Their short shore leave was less exuberant and carefree than it might otherwise have been; after they tied up, scuttlebutt* on the dock had it that three Brisbane-based submarines, *Amberjack*, *Triton*, and *Grampus*, had all been lost.

The rumors turned out to be accurate. *Amberjack*, under Lieutenant Commander John Bole; *Grampus*, captained by John Craig; and *Triton*, under George K. Mackenzie Jr., had started out on patrols from Brisbane back in February and none had returned or been heard from. (It has since been learned that *Amberjack* was sunk by the Japanese torpedo boat *Hiyodori* on 16 February off Rabaul; *Grampus* was likely sunk by destroyers off New Georgia in the Solomons on 5 March; *Triton* went down forever on 15 March north of the Admiralty Islands. At the time, however, no one knew exactly how, where, or when the submarines and their total of 217 officers and men met their fates.)

---

* Navy jargon for drinking fountain; i.e., a place to pick up the latest gossip.

In addition, *Gato,* skippered by Robert J. Foley, had been seriously damaged during an engagement with an enemy destroyer in February and barely made it to a friendly port. Salvos of depth charges had rocked her, sending *Gato* plunging a harrowing 380 feet before leveling off and eventually resurfacing. Although her propulsion system was damaged and barely operable, she somehow managed to crawl back to Brisbane.[14] As he listened to these stories, Smitty's worry meter went up an extra notch.

Seal wasn't in Pearl Harbor only for crew liberty and to stock up on food and fuel. Serious training was also on the schedule. For three days the submarine operated alongside a destroyer in Hawaiian waters. Besides giving *Seal* protection from "friendlies" who might have otherwise mistaken her for the enemy, the destroyer also got in some good practice time, pretending to attack *Seal* while *Seal*, in turn, pretended to attack the destroyer. The deck gunners also got a chance to see what their twenty-millimeter guns could do against a towed target. And to give new men like Smitty an idea what a real depth charge sounded like, one day the destroyer dropped one of the devices—dubbed "shit cans" and "ash cans"—at a considerable distance from *Seal*. The shock wave reverberated throughout the sub, ringing her like a bell. Smitty, who nearly hit the overhead at the blast, wondered what a depth charge would sound and feel like if it were dropped right next to *Seal*.

It wasn't long before *Seal,* sporting a new camouflage paint job of blue and gray splotches, was ready for her sixth war patrol. A ton of food in crates had been hauled aboard and stowed wherever the boxes would fit. Fuel tanks were topped off, ammo lockers were full, and sixteen torpedoes—eight fore and eight aft—were tucked into their berths. The men shaved and took the last showers they would have for weeks.

And in spite of his trepidations, Smitty was ready to see firsthand what war was like.

AT the end of April 1943, *Seal* cleared Pearl Harbor with a destroyer escorting her for the first hour at sea, heading due north. Then she was all alone in the wide, trackless ocean.

Seal's crew had been practicing trimming seconds off the time it took the boat to dive, and when Commander Dodge reached the designated area where they would submerge, the crew managed the dive—from surface running with the diesels to ninety feet below the surface on batteries—in just forty-five seconds.

Not even the captain, until he opened his secret orders locked inside the sub's safe, knew where the boat was to go or what he was supposed to do when he got there. As soon as he had a look at the orders, Dodge announced over the intercom what everyone wanted to know—*Seal* was going first to Midway and then back to Palau, scene of her fifth patrol— a distance of over 5,000 miles—where the Japanese had a major naval base and a stout defense against submarines.

It took three days for *Seal* to reach Midway; the base didn't look much better than it had immediately after the Japanese had finished pounding it the previous June. But, although little effort had been made to freshen the cosmetics, the base was operational—a vital installation supporting the American effort to retake the Pacific. Airplane hangars, maintenance sheds, barracks, and offices had been patched up, but many still bore the scars of battle. Some roofs were still missing, having been blown away by Japanese bombs, and there were very few windows that still had glass in them. But the Stars and Stripes still fluttered from the flagpole in the hot breeze in front of headquarters. It was a sight that heartened everyone.[15]

Admiral Lockwood noted that a great deal of work had already been expended into making Midway a first-class submarine base, but that a great deal more needed to be done. He planned for the submarine base to eventually be able to refit three or four submarines simultaneously. He also noted that recreational facilities on the island were substandard, but that improvements were under way.[16]

Smitty and a sailor named Weekly, in charge of the forward torpedo room, took a launch to the torpedo shop on Sand Island, one of two islands that made up Midway; the other was Eastern Island, where the airstrip was. The lagoon between them was ringed by coral reefs with only one safe opening, making it a perfect natural harbor and one of the prime submarine bases in the Central Pacific.

Sand Island was just a few hundred feet long, with one unpaved road going up the middle and a few palm trees, scrub plants, and a little sand grass. They trudged past the former Pan American Airways Hotel, where passengers of the amphibious Pan Am Clippers in prewar days spent the night before continuing on their journey either to or from the Orient.

The island was home to thousands of birds, some strange and exotic, others just strange. One, a beautiful snow-white bird with a crimson plume sticking out in back, caught Smitty's eye. There were others, too—green or blue or brown. Midway's most famous avian inhabitant, however, was the clumsy "gooney" bird, which, in actuality, was the Laysan albatross—a magnificent bird with trifold wings and a wingspan of over ten feet. Waddling erratically along the ground when young, the albatross inspired some long-forgotten visitor to tag it with the "gooney" label, but in flight they were graceful.

Weekly and Smitty entered the torpedo shop through a large bomb hole in one of the walls that served as a doorway and asked a sailor for some gaskets for the torpedoes' high-pressure air-filler valve. You would have thought they had asked for a cold beer and some beautiful women. "What the fuck," growled the less-than-helpful swabbie, "you think we grow parts here?"

Realizing he wasn't going to get his gaskets, Weekly simply said, "Thanks, anyway," and left. Wondering why his older pal—Weekly was twenty-two—didn't get angry, Smitty was told that the guys on Midway had been there for over a year. "Most of 'em haven't seen a woman in all that time," said Weekly. "This is gonna be a long war, so don't pay any attention to them bastards. Before you judge, consider the source."

Smitty nodded, realizing it was good advice.

THE next morning, Dodge assembled all his officers and men on the deck of *Seal* aft of the conning tower. "Men, I'll make this brief," he began. "I must tell you before we leave Midway that if you are taken prisoner, you understand all you're required to tell the enemy is your name and serial number. If you still have dog tags, get rid of them. If you are captured, you will probably be sent to work in the salt mines in Japan." The men nodded grimly; broadcasts from Japan by Tokyo Rose had already warned them of that possibility.

"You're all volunteers," Dodge went on, "so if any of you want to change your mind, you still can." No one moved, but some wondered about the new ensign, Franz, who had come down with an attack of appendicitis and would be staying behind.[17]

Everyone knew that once a submarine began a war patrol, there would be scant opportunity for someone stricken with appendicitis or an impacted wisdom tooth or a broken leg to receive proper medical attention. Submarines did not carry doctors; the only medical personnel was one pharmacist's mate per boat, who could dispense aspirin or patch a minor cut but was unprepared with either education or equipment to handle anything more serious.

The exception to that rule was what happened aboard *Seadragon*, the "red submarine," on 11 September 1942. Submerged in 120 feet of water off the coast of Indochina in the South China Sea and hundreds of miles from friendly territory, *Seadragon* became home to one of the most amazing stories to come out of the Submarine Service in World War II. Seaman Darrel Dean Rector was in agony from an infected appendix. Twenty-two-year-old Pharmacist's Mate Wheeler Bryson "Johnny" Lipes of Virginia was not a doctor, but he and the sub's skipper, Pete Ferrall, knew that unless an emergency appendectomy was performed, Rector would die.

Turning the ward room into an operating suite, Lipes and two officer assistants—one of them, surprisingly enough, Harry B. Dodge, the future commander of *Seal*—sterilized their improvised instruments with boiling water and donned "operating gown" pajamas sterilized by soaking them in "torpedo juice," the alcohol usually reserved for fueling *Seadragon*'s tin fish. With no proper surgical instruments on board, Lipes bent spoons to serve as retractors to hold open the incision and abdominal muscles. Lipes placed Rector on one of the dining tables and went to work. Dodge dripped ether onto a gauze pad on a tea strainer that acted as an anesthesia mask over Rector's nose and mouth. One of the sailors guided Lipes by reading the procedures from a medical textbook.

Lipes made his incision using only the blade of a scalpel—he lacked the full instrument—and discovered the gangrenous appendix was five inches long and adhering in three places to the lining of the intestine. If the appendix broke, it would pour pus into the abdomen and likely kill

Darrel Dean Rector.
(Courtesy Ron Smith)

the patient. For two and a half hours, Lipes worked slowly and gently to cut the appendix free from surrounding tissue and remove it.[18]

Remarkably, everything went smoothly, and Rector was back at his duty station within two weeks.* Two other similar incidents on other submarines became part of the lore of the Silent Service.[19]

As far as Ron Smith was concerned, Midway Island was the "worst place on earth to pull a liberty, let alone an R&R. The topography is simple: SAND, nothing but SAND, along with a few scraggly trees and palms. Midway first became important to man as the halfway point for the first airline service across the Pacific Ocean. The Pan Am 'China Clippers'—the famous 'flying boats'—had to stop at Midway to refuel and give the passengers a rest. The airline built a hotel for the passengers and appropriately named

---

* Both the *Chicago Daily News* and *Life* magazine carried articles about the operation, and Lipes earned considerable praise in some quarters for his improvised techniques. He also received criticism from Navy physicians angered by his actions, although he had obeyed his captain's orders to perform the surgery. Even the U.S. Surgeon General was outraged by what Lipes had done, and subsequently set protocols for appendectomies aboard submarines. In a much-belated recognition, Lipes, who remained in the Navy and rose to the rank of lieutenant commander, received the Navy Commendation Medal in February 2005. He died on 17 April 2005 at age eighty-four from pancreatic cancer and was buried in Arlington National Cemetery. (*Denver Post*, 4/20/05)

The operation was incorporated into another Hollywood submarine drama, 1943's *Destination Tokyo*, also starring Cary Grant.

Sadly, the patient Rector would die in 1944 when his submarine, *Tang*, was sunk by its own malfunctioning torpedo. (*Washington Post*, 4/19/05)

it the Pan Am Hotel. We renamed it the Gooney Bird Hotel. This was the rest spot for submarine crews between war patrols."

After the periodic excitement of a month or two at sea, and getting occasionally bombed and depth-charged, the primitive but peaceful accommodations at Midway were a welcome relief. But, for young men seeking some "action," Midway was also boring in the extreme. "No woman had set foot on this godforsaken place since the last civilian plane left in 1941," Smitty related, "so sex was not a viable option. All that was left was gambling and drinking warm beer."

Smitty noted that the Pan Am/Gooney Bird Hotel "was a V-shaped building with a fairly large entry or lobby area, with officers on one side of the hotel and us ne'er-do-wells on the other." During the war, it was the "Las Vegas of the Pacific." Green-felt-covered tables for craps, poker, and roulette filled the lobby. Gambling went on twenty-four hours a day, seven days a week. It was not unusual for pots to get as large as three thousand bucks—no small thing since the average player made less than a hundred dollars per month. "As usual," Smitty related, "the Navy displayed its normal duplicity. They allowed the gambling, but you could only buy one fifty-dollar money order to send home. Usually, the heavy winners would trust their 'poke' to a buddy who was going back to the States, as he was supposed to then send it to the winner's family. What do you think the odds of *that* happening were?"

Everyone was paid in cash—and each man received a beer ration: one twenty-four-bottle case of beer per week. "The brand was some shit called 'Green River,'" Smitty said. "The label said it was made in California. Now, everybody knows them California prune-pickers can't make real beer, but we drank it, anyway." There were no coolers or ice, so the sailors parked their cases of beer in the water beneath the stern planes of *Seal* to cool it off. With the waters at more than eighty degrees, it didn't help much.

"The powers that be wouldn't allow any 'girlie' pics in the place, not even *Esquire*," moaned Smitty. "There were several thousand Marines guarding the place and they had been there for so long that they were half crazy—what we called 'rock happy.' Masturbation was a favorite pastime for the jarheads."

There were frequent attempts by rock-happy sailors and Marines to build makeshift rafts that, they hoped, would enable them to desert and get back to the States. Most of their rafts were made of scraps of wood, empty milk cartons, anything that would float. "It was rumored that a lot of guys drowned trying to get off that hellhole," Smitty said.

The beaches, though, were beautiful—white sand and clear blue water, a living embodiment of a South Seas island tourist brochure. "You could see a hundred feet or more down into the water, it was that clear," said Smitty. "These beaches were covered with *millions* of 'cat's-eyes.' They were formed in clams the way pearls are formed in oysters. They looked just like an eyeball, with a colored center and a white outside, rounded on the front and flat on the back. They came in a multitude of colors and sizes, from less than a quarter inch to as big as two inches. When we weren't gambling or getting drunk on the shitty California beer, we tried to find pairs of matching 'cat's-eyes.' Some guys found some really neat matches."

The Japanese, on occasion, reminded the sailors and Marines that there was still a war going on. "They kept sending planes over to 'stir the shit,'" Smitty recalled. "One night Ted Sharp, one of our gunner's mates, and I were guzzling down our tepid beer when the air-raid sirens went off. First thing the Navy did when an air raid occurred was to shut off every light on the islands. Great—you couldn't see a thing. Ted and I went running down this dirt road (they were *all* dirt roads) looking for an air-raid shelter we had seen. These 'air-raid shelters' were just holes dug in the sand, covered with some wood and more sand piled on top. We were running and sucking on one bottle and carrying another under our arms. We must have run for an hour, stopping every now and then to swig some more beer. The antiaircraft guns were blasting away and every once in a while a bomb would explode. Finally, we were so exhausted we just said, 'To hell with it,' and sat down on a sand pile to watch the show. Things finally settled down. We finished our beer and fell asleep on the sand pile. When we woke up the next morning, we discovered that we had been sleeping on *top* of an air-raid shelter. Such is life."

Smitty recalled that the most fun and excitement he had during the entire two weeks at Midway was a baseball game between the crews of *Seal* and *Snook* (SS-279). "Everybody got all beered up and the game ended in a free-for-all between the two crews. There were just a few knots on the head and bloody lips until someone from *Snook* pulled out his deck knife—we all carried them—an eight-inch blade in a leather sheath on your belt. This guy stuck his knife through the foot of one of our torpedomen. That ended the game."*

Fortunately, before anyone else could get hurt or lose any more money at the gaming tables, on 14 April 1943, *Seal*, full of food, fuel, and beer-bloated sailors, headed back out to sea for her sixth war patrol.[20]

Worried about the growing shortage of Mark XIV torpedoes, submarine commanders had been warned by ComSubPac to go easy on the expenditures of tin fish. Admiral Lockwood noted that the available stocks of the unreliable Mark XIV torpedoes were so low that he ordered the next three boats leaving on patrol to eschew torpedoes for mines. All were hoping that supplies of the wakeless Mark XVII electric torpedo would soon reach Lockwood's command, but were dismayed to learn that the Mark XVII was considered low priority by BuOrd. This additional problem had Lockwood steamed.[21]

Seawolf, which left Midway for the same area ten days before *Seal* sailed, had, according to scuttlebutt, registered six kills in just two days.†

Seal's voyage from Midway to her combat station was long, uncomfortable, and uneventful in the extreme. Smitty stood more than his fair share of watches—manning the radar scope inside the stifling submarine or spending many days under the broiling sun scanning the vast sea and sky for any signs of ships or aircraft, friendly or hostile, until his eyeballs felt scorched.

On occasion Smitty also wore the sonarman's earphones and was fascinated by the myriad and varied sounds of the teeming undersea parade of aquatic life picked up by the sensitive microphones of *Seal*'s

---

* *Snook* would be reported missing near Okinawa in April 1945, possibly the result of an encounter with an enemy submarine. (Blair, 809; www.history.navy.mil/faqs/faq82-1)

† This time, scuttlebutt was wrong. *Seawolf*'s report for her eighth war patrol indicates that, with Royce L. Gross in command, she sank three ships worth 13,100 tons; postwar corrections reduced those numbers to two ships and 5,300 tons. She was lost with all hands on 3 October 1944 after being sunk in error by the American destroyer U.S.S. *Rowell* off Morotai. (Blair, 712; www.fleetsubmarine.com/ss-197; www.history.navy.mil/faqs/faq82-1)

sonar heads. He soon learned to tell the difference between the whistling and chattering of schools of porpoise and the strange screeching of whales. A school of fish could sound like a flock of birds. From unknown fish or mammals came burping sounds, belching sounds, and even sounds that were indistinguishable from flatulence and gave Smitty a chuckle. Some of the most awesome sounds were the deep, disconcerting rumbles of an underwater earthquake caused by the earth's tectonic plates rubbing together, or the roaring eruption of a volcano thousands of feet below the surface. The world beneath the sea, Smitty came to appreciate, was friendly and frightening, both at the same time.

A sonarman needed a sharp, discriminating set of ears in order to separate the odd natural sounds from what he was primarily interested in hearing—the faint *shoosh, shoosh, shoosh* made by the propellers of a ship. "Lumpy" Lehman, *Seal*'s regular sonar operator, had such a set of ears. He could detect the faint shooshing of screws from as far away as twenty miles and tell the officers how many ships there were, what types of ship were in the convoy, how fast the ships were going, and even in what direction they were heading. Some wags aboard *Seal* swore Lumpy could even tell what the registration numbers of the ships were.

At night, when *Seal* was running on the surface to recharge her batteries, and with hatches open to suck fresh air into the sub's interior, she left a brilliant phosphorescent trail in the dark water, as though she trailed in her wake millions of tiny Christmas lights. One night, while Smitty was standing watch on the bridge, Lieutenant John Hanes, the gunnery officer, explained that the glow came from a chemical in the algae. Smitty privately worried that an enemy plane could easily spot them just by tracking the wake, as if someone had painted a sign on the ocean: U.S.S. SEAL—THAT-A-WAY.[22]

CHAPTER 10

ABORTIVE ATTACK

IT took eight days for *Seal* to reach her assigned station in the Philippine Sea. Once there, Lieutenant Duryea, the communications officer, decoded a radio message from ComSubPac back at Pearl Harbor, directing *Seal* to raid enemy installations on the island of Anguar on 29 April. A tiny speck of an island at the southern tip of the reef that encircles most of the Palau Archipelago, and looking like the dot on an exclamation point, Anguar was important to Japan because of its deposits of phosphate, used for the manufacture of ammunition and explosives. Scuttlebutt had it that every boat on station had orders to hit some Japanese base, from the Aleutians to near Australia, on that date.

Dodge pointed *Seal*'s nose south toward Palau and Anguar. Smitty was excited and a little nervous, too, at the prospect of his first combat.

Within a few days *Seal* stealthily approached Anguar and stood partially submerged a few miles offshore to make observations. The first pale fingers of dawn were streaking over the horizon as *Seal* lay off the barren, coral-studded coast at periscope depth, with Skipper Dodge and the other officers studying the western shore of the island. Just north of the island's only sizable town, Saipan,* stood a phosphate plant.

---

* Not to be confused with the island of Saipan in the Marianas, north of Guam. The designation of "Saipan" or "Saipan Town" for the settlement on Anguar Island was a World War II–era term, and appears on World War II–period military maps. Except for elderly survivors of the Pacific War, however, present-day Palauans are generally not familiar with it. (Ballendorf correspondence with authors)

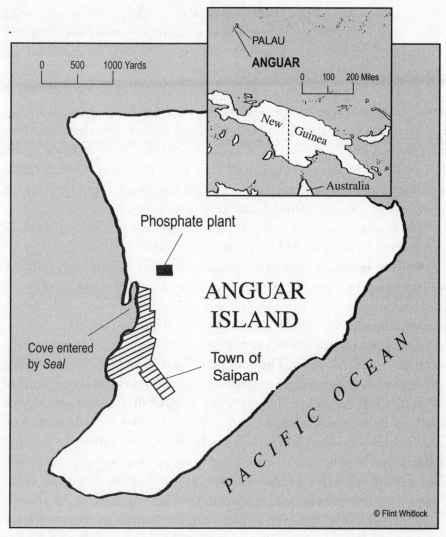

Location of Anguar Island, scene of aborted raid by *Seal*, 29 April 1943.

In a small cove about a hundred yards from the plant was a dock where a single freighter of about 5,000 tons could be seen being loaded with phosphate.

The cove was not very large and was formed by a small tonsil of land dangling down from the north, with the phosphate plant on a slight rise above the northeast corner of the cove. Two Japanese patrol boats could be seen crisscrossing the mouth of the cove. The deck-gun crews, one of which Smitty was a member, were told to memorize every building and land feature, for the attack would come at night and the crews would need to pick out targets in the dark.

"Here's our plan," explained Lieutenant Hanes like a football coach to the gun crews gathered in the mess hall. "We want to hit them fast and get the hell out. We'll move submerged close to the shore south of the town exactly at sunset. We'll surface and you men then come up on deck and get the guns ready. For Christ's sake, keep it as quiet as possible. Then we'll put all four engines on line and make a speed run to the north end of the bay, hitting the targets as we go by."

The men grinned and nodded; they thought the hit-and-get-the-hell-out-of-there attack sounded like a very good plan.

At 1800 hours, the gun crews assembled in the control room. Smitty was a little jittery about his first engagement but tried not to show it. He very much wanted to prove himself to his crewmates and hoped his youthful courage would not wilt in the heat of battle.

As the sun dipped below the horizon, *Seal* nosed her way toward the southern tip of the island. The command "Battle Stations Surface" rang throughout the boat and the submarine tilted upward. Someone climbed the ladder and opened the hatch; water dripped in. Commander Dodge was the first man out, with the gun crews scrambling to their battle stations right behind him; Smitty was on the aft twenty-millimeter. He and the men on the other guns were going through their well-practiced routine, getting ready for battle. Adrenaline was flowing like beer as the guns were primed and aimed at their darkened targets along the shore.

"All ahead full!" directed Dodge, and the four diesel engines roared to life, propelling the big boat forward with a lurch as it began its run parallel to the shore. Everyone knew they had only one chance to get it right.

Just seconds before the order came to commence firing, Lieutenant Hanes began screaming "Secure all guns! Clear the bridge!"

Smitty was unsure why the attack was being aborted, but began stuffing the unused ammunition back into its watertight locker.

"What the hell's wrong?" somebody shouted.

Seal crewmen engage in a gunnery drill with the five-inch deck gun as Ron Smith (circled) observes.
(Courtesy Ron Smith)

"Look—there," shouted another sailor, pointing to the port side. The two patrol boats the crew had spotted on their earlier reconnaissance were steaming directly toward them, their searchlights flicking across the water, on a *Seal* hunt.

"Down ladder!" the men above yelled before sliding down the ladder like firemen coming down a fire pole, their hands and feet on the outside of the vertical struts, with Lieutenant Hanes the last man down. "Secure the hatch," he directed one of the enlisted men as his feet hit the deck. The dive alarm sounded.

"What about the skipper?" someone asked.

"He's staying topside," Hanes replied, then turned and called to the diving officer in the control room: "Flood down. Just leave the bridge out of the water. Captain's staying topside to steer us out of the cove. Take her down to sixty-five feet."

Everyone looked at everyone else. They couldn't believe that their skipper was putting himself in harm's way in order to save the boat and the crew. Thoughts of Howard Gilmore's final and fatal act of courage on *Growler* flooded into their heads.

Lady Luck was riding with Dodge. By slow and careful maneuvering he managed to prevent the patrol boats from spotting the sub as he guided *Seal* into open water. When they were clear, the sub surfaced and Dodge went below while the regular lookouts assumed their stations topside. Everyone could breathe easily again.[1]

WHILE *Seal* was on her patrol to Anguar, Admiral Lockwood was in Washington dueling with the top brass over the torpedo issue. In a meeting with Captain Merrill Comstock, the Submarine Material and Operations Officer on Admiral King's staff, the conversation grew heated when the subject of the malfunctioning fish came up. Lockwood fired a broadside, demanding that if the Bureau of Ordnance could not provide his boats with a reliable torpedo, he wanted the Bureau of Ships to design a "boat hook" that they could use to rip the hull plates off of enemy ships. Comstock was not amused by Lockwood's sarcasm.[2]

FOR the next few days, *Seal* swam back and forth across her patrol area, seeing nothing. Then, at 0700 hours on 4 May, as part of the crew was eating breakfast, the alarm was sounded: "Battle Stations Submerged!" A convoy had been spotted on the far horizon. The motormen shut down the diesels, the electricians in the maneuvering room switched to batteries, and the sub glided silently beneath the surface.

All routine activity aboard *Seal* ceased as every man hustled to his battle station. In the aft torpedo room, the reloaders quickly removed the bunks and stowed them in the aft engine room. Horizontal I-beams were then swung into place across the room, front and rear, to support the four extra torpedoes stored in the room in the event reloading was necessary. Smitty took up his battle station—seated between the aft tubes, eyes focused on the TDC—the torpedo data computer transmitter—mounted on the rear bulkhead, with headphones on his ears, a microphone pressed against his throat.

While the sub continued on its way to the intercept point, Smitty glanced around at his fellow sailors in the tight space—a scruffy, unmilitary-looking lot. All wore ragged, cut-off dungaree shorts; sandals, no socks; an assortment of dirty skivvy shirts with the sleeves cut off or brightly colored Hawaiian shirts. Everyone was dripping with sweat. A few covered their stringy, unwashed hair with dark blue Navy baseball caps. Those old enough to shave had full beards; a few young guys, like Smitty, sported the first scraggly suggestions of facial hair. Yet each man was a pro, an expert at his deadly craft. There was Big Ski, looking confident, like a quarterback in a close game. Behind him, acting as backup, was Woody Woodard, a reliable man in a sub–ship duel. There was skinny Dillingham, nicknamed "Seagull," a torpedoman without peer. Two other sailors, one named Brown and the other nicknamed Dead Eye, stood by, ready to lend a hand and their considerable muscle with the reloading. Each man had an insouciant, almost cocky look to him, as if to say, "No big deal; we've done this a hundred times before," masking any tension they might have felt and helping calm Smitty's tightening stomach.

Control had already begun the plot as *Seal* moved to intercept the convoy. The TDC was being fed the distance, angle, and speed of the target, information that was entered into the torpedoes' primitive "brains." It was Smitty's job to line up the marks on the dial of the TDC transmitter to the one going into the fish; he would push the big brass firing lever only if, after receiving the command to fire, the marks, or "bugs," were perfectly aligned. An accurate plot would make the pickles more likely to hit their targets, but no one could be certain, even if the bugs were right on, that the torpedoes would actually detonate.

Over the headset, Control alerted the boat to stand by for action, and Smitty passed this news along to those around him. While the forward torpedo room was put on alert, the aft torpedo room was told to stand easy.

Once the range and distance to the target—a fat oiler with the distinctly un-Japanese name of *San Clemente Maru*—had been entered into the TDC, the order to "Fire one" was given to the forward torpedo room and the boat suddenly lurched as though it had collided with a brick wall.

"Fire two. Fire three." Two more lurches as 2,000 pounds of compressed air pressure from the "impulse bottle" violently kicked the tin fish out of their tubular homes.*

Lumpy Lehman, the sonar man, reported over the circuit, "All fish running hot, straight, and normal." Now they all waited; would the torpedoes strike home, or would there be nothing but silence? Some men crossed their fingers or fingered the crucifixes that hung from their necks or played with some other sort of talisman thought to bring them luck.

A few of *Seal*'s crew may have given a moment's thought to the enemy sailors at whom the torpedoes were being directed, oblivious to the fact that their world was about to be shattered, that their lives were about to come to a sudden and violent end. Like the Americans, these sailors had girlfriends, wives, mothers, fathers, and children back home. Like the Americans, most of these sailors were just doing a job that someone in higher authority had decreed they must do. Like the Americans, most of these sailors would have preferred spending their youth in other, more peaceful pursuits. But the Americans felt it was not healthy to dwell on such thoughts, to think of the enemy in human terms.

No, the business of war demanded that they think of the enemy as exactly that—the *enemy*—and attempt to kill as many of them as possible. After all, it was the *Japanese* who had bombed Pearl Harbor without warning; the *Japanese* who had invaded Korea and China and Malay and the Philippines; the *Japanese* who had raped and tortured and murdered hundreds of thousands of civilians in Shanghai, Nanking, and elsewhere; the *Japanese* who had turned thousands of Korean girls and young women into their sex slaves; the *Japanese* who had beheaded captured Australian and British and American soldiers and airmen; the *Japanese* who had slaughtered their American and Filipino POWs along the march from Bataan; the *Japanese* who had committed atrocities every bit as horrible as those being perpetrated by the Nazis on the other side of the world. Thinking of the enemy as "human" was simply an unprofitable exercise. And so the men inside the *Seal* pushed such

---

* In the forward torpedo room, tubes one, two, and three were made ready for firing; tube four was almost always held back and used only in an emergency. In the after torpedo room, tubes five, six, and seven were employed, while number eight was normally held back.

thoughts—if they had them—out of their minds and waited with eager anticipation to hear the explosions that would signal that the despised Japanese enemy sailors—the "dirty Japs"—were plunging in agony to their deaths.

The men in the aft torpedo room focused on the second hand sweeping around the shiny bulkhead chronometer.

"First one missed," Woody muttered as the time for the intercept came and went. The second and third torpedoes also passed into the silence of failure.

Commander Dodge swung the sub around so the aft torpedoes could be fired while the forward torpedo room reloaded, and Smitty heard Lieutenant Hanes's voice in his headphones say, "Tubes aft, stand by."

"Tubes aft standing by," Smitty replied, making his posture just a little more erect, a little more military. "Stand by," Smitty repeated for the benefit of his crewmates. Here he was, the newest and youngest member of the crew, issuing orders to these "old salts." He was at last being given a chance to show what he could do. He hoped he would not fail this, his first big test. The crewmen moved quickly to their firing stations. They had no idea what their target was—a carrier, battleship, cruiser, destroyer, oiler, tanker, freighter, or transport—nor did it particularly matter.

"Tubes aft, stand by five, six, and seven," said Hanes.

"Tubes aft, standing by five, six, and seven," repeated Smitty.

Hanes directed, "Tubes aft, open outer doors on five, six, and seven."

"Tubes aft, aye," said Smitty, and repeated the command for Big Ski and Seagull. They opened the valves from the "water round torpedo"—a tank located just below the torpedo tubes—and flooded the three firing chambers with seawater to equalize pressure to the sea.

"Control, outer doors on five, six, and seven open," Smitty reported.

"Tubes aft, switch on firing circuits on five, six, and seven," said Hanes, and Smitty repeated the directive.

Seagull threw the switches that armed the torpedoes, then gave Smitty the "okay" sign. "Firing circuits on for five, six, and seven," Smitty told Hanes.

"Very well, tubes aft. Set depth twelve feet."

"Set depth twelve feet, tubes aft, aye," Smitty said as the dials on the tubes were set to the depth ordered.

"Stand by five."

"Stand by five, tubes aft, aye." Smitty watched the dials and waited for the marks on the TDC to line up.

"Fire five."

As the bugs came into alignment, Smitty mashed the tube firing button at the same instant that Hanes pushed the firing button for number five, making sure that the torpedo fired even if the electric circuit failed.

There was a loud *whoosh* of compressed air, a deep-throated boom, and a spray of water that spurted in from around the tube's gasket as the torpedo was launched. The same procedure was followed for tubes six and seven, although Smitty was angry at himself for launching number six just as the TDC marks went out of alignment by two degrees; he knew that torpedo number six would miss its target.

Big Ski was having trouble with the number seven tube right after the fish was fired and was cursing a blue streak. An eight-inch stream of water was pouring in and sloshing down into the bilges. Not a critical problem yet, but one that couldn't be ignored.

"Hit the emergency valve," Woody yelled over the noise of the rushing water. "Shut 'er down!"

Big Ski moved over to tube seven and with great effort turned the manual control wheel. The stream of water was gradually pinched off, but not before Ski was a soaking, dripping mess.

"Tubes aft, close outer doors," Hanes commanded.

"Tubes aft, close outer doors, aye," Smitty relayed, and Big Ski and Seagull cranked the outer doors closed.

"All fish running hot, straight, and normal," reported Lumpy Lehman on sonar.

Then someone who was clocking the first torpedo announced that it had missed. The crew in the aft torpedo room slumped. *Damn these defective fish*, they collectively thought.

A few seconds later there came a thumping roar followed by a jolt that felt as if the sub had been struck with a giant sledgehammer.

"We hit the son of a bitch!" shouted Big Ski. It was number six, the one Smitty knew for sure was going to miss.

The crew members began whooping and hollering and jumping up and down and slapping one another on the back, just as if their team had

A submarine skipper uses the periscope to target an enemy vessel while the Executive Officer (foreground) uses the manual "Is-Was" computer.
(Courtesy National Archives)

scored the winning touchdown. *How lucky can you get?* Smitty wondered to himself.

"Tubes aft," said Hanes, "start your reload. And good shot, Smitty."

"Tubes aft start reload, aye," said Smitty. "And thanks, Hanes."

The periscope was raised, then lowered. Greenup, the executive officer, came over the intercom. "We just sank a large transport freighter," he announced. "Looks like a lot of men in the water." Cheers erupted again in the aft torpedo room and more celebratory dances were conducted. The crew gave Smitty a new nickname: Warshot.

Infantrymen can tell if their bullets are hitting their target just by looking; artillerists, too, can watch the results of their salvos. Airmen on bombers can scan the landscape below and note their bombs striking home, and gunners on surface ships can observe the havoc their shells cause. But submariners, with the exception of the officer manning the periscope, are denied visual confirmation of their marksmanship and must rely on aural evidence alone. Even without sonar headphones, the men in the submarine could hear the 7,354-ton *San Clemente Maru* breaking up as it sank. Then the boilers exploded—*Ka-THWOOMP! Ka-THWOOMP!* The shock waves hit the *Seal,* shaking her and rattling the chinaware in her galley. Then they heard cracking and popping noises as the freighter's bulkheads caved in while the ship sank deeper into the ocean. *So that's what a dying ship sounds like,* Smitty said to himself with morbid fascination.

Greenup again: "There are two escorts up there looking for us now. Rig for depth charge. Rig for silent running. Close all watertight doors."

Without the waste of a second, *Seal*'s crewmen did what they had

practiced a thousand times. The watertight doors between compartments were swung shut on their heavy hinges and dogged down. The
bulkhead flappers that passed air between compartments were closed.
Big Ski climbed up into the escape hatch to make sure it would not spring
open from the shock of the depth charges and flood the interior. The air-
conditioning was shut off.

Seal plunged to 200 feet, where the oceanic pressure on the hull was
ninety pounds to the square inch, and the electric motors were silenced
so that not even the slow turning of the propeller screws would give their
position away. Talking, walking around, dropping a tool, doing anything that might make the slightest noise was strictly verboten. This was
the moment that every submariner feared and dreaded. The worm had
turned; the hunter had become the hunted.

While they sweated it out down below, the crew knew that the enemy's destroyers were crisscrossing above them, doing their best to locate
them. Sonar operators on the destroyers, using submarine-locating equipment, were "pinging"—sending electronic signals into the deep water and
listening for the telltale echo that would tell them that a large metallic
object was down there. Once that echo was heard, depth charges would
begin to cascade down on the immobile prey. Sometimes there would be
only a handful of charges; at other times the depth charging would go on
for hours. No one could be certain when—or how—it would end.

Japanese depth charges were generally regarded as less powerful
than the American variety—containing 242 pounds of explosive and
detonating at a relatively shallow depth—about 150 feet at the maximum. By diving to 200 feet or more, the submarines were generally safe,
but not always. The "shit cans" could still be plenty lethal; no one knew
how many submarines did not return because a lucky shot had split the
pressure hull or damaged the propulsion or steering mechanism or
wrecked a valve on a ballast tank, making it impossible for a sub to gain
positive buoyancy and return to the surface.

Smitty and his mates in the aft torpedo room suddenly discovered they
had a problem—a big one. When the order to rig for depth charges came,
torpedoes had already been loaded into tubes five and seven, but the torpedo for tube six was only halfway in. As *Seal* dove to 200 feet, the outer
pressure compressed the steel hull just enough to make it a tight fit for the

torpedoes; consequently the torpedo in number six tube was stuck. Everyone knew that a depth charge going off near the stern might jar open the outer door to tube six and cause a sudden inrush of seawater. If the blast were severe enough, it might even rip the outer door off its hinges, blow the torpedo back into the compartment, and cause the aft torpedo room to flood, killing everyone in the sealed-off compartment and making it hard, if not impossible, for the sub to surface. The crewmen manhandled the fish, trying to shove it home, but it wouldn't budge.

Somebody had once told Smitty that he would hear a click just before the depth charge detonated; it was the trigger mechanism and would give those in the boat only a fraction of a second to grab something, grit their teeth, and hang on. Then it happened.

Click . . . KaBLOOM! As feared, a depth charge went off close to the stern, and water immediately began pouring into the compartment from around the protruding torpedo. *Click . . . KaBLOOM!* Another one, then another. The lights flickered off and on, and the whole sub lurched and rocked as though some giant sea creature were pummeling the *Seal* with its monstrous fists.

Click . . . KaBLOOM! With each explosion, the glass faces of gauges throughout the sub shattered; lightbulbs popped, sizzled, then went out. Cork insulation and chips of paint flew. Cockroaches scurried for safety. The boat's welded seams seemed ready to split apart, and water continued to gush in from around the half-inserted torpedo.

"Get that goddamned thing in there before the whole fucking ocean pours in!" yelled Woody. Brown and Dead Eye did their best with the block and tackle but the fish wouldn't move. Big Ski went to lend a hand, grabbing the line in front of Dead Eye, but Dead Eye called him a dumb Polack and shoved him out of the way. Big Ski slipped on the wet deck and came up with a tube-door crank in his hand, ready to split Dead Eye's skull. Dead Eye grabbed a mallet, and for a minute it looked as if the two Americans had declared war on each other.

Click . . . KaBLOOM! Click . . . KaBLOOM!

Two more charges went off nearby, shaking the *Seal* violently and bringing the two combatants back to their senses. More water gushed in; the outer door could blow at any moment.

Big Ski dropped the crank handle, shoved past Dead Eye and the others, and yanked the chock and block and tackle from the rear of the torpedo. He then pulled a wiping rag from his back pocket, placed it against the rear of the fish, and, grunting and straining with almost superhuman effort, shoved the torpedo into the tube all by himself. Everyone watched with stunned disbelief. It was a miracle; no one, especially not someone five-feet-five, could do that alone.

Click . . . KaBLOOM!

Coming out of his momentary stupor, Seagull slammed shut the inner door to tube six as Smitty cranked it around into the dogs and locked it closed. Exhausted, Big Ski dropped to the deck, sitting with his head between his knees, sweating hard, his breath coming in clumps, the veins in his forearms and neck bulging like snakes. Everyone moved around him cautiously and quietly, not daring to say a word.

Click . . . KaBLOOM! Click . . . KaBLOOM!

The depth charges continued to rain thick and fast, and Smitty prayed that they would soon cease. After another ten or fifteen explosions, the hammering stopped. The entire battle had lasted about four hours, but to Smitty it seemed like several eternities.

Finally, Smitty spoke quietly into the throat mike: "Control, tubes aft. All tubes reloaded."

"Very well, tubes aft. Stand easy."

The sub hunters had gone and *Seal* swam silently out of the area, propelled at a slow but steady three knots. Eventually the order came to secure from depth charge and silent running. The boat surfaced, fresh air poured in, and the bunks were returned to their places in the torpedo rooms. Exhausted men fell into them.

Smitty took stock of himself. It had been his first combat, and he was surprised to find that he had been excited but not terribly frightened—he had been too busy to be really scared. He also noticed that he was more exhausted than he ever remembered being. As soon as a bunk came available, he slid onto it, just a stiff mattress covered with green plastic, his nose only three inches from the oil pan under the thirty-horsepower electric motor that powered the stern planes. Heedless of the motor's noise, he fell asleep in seconds.

Moments later he felt someone tapping his bunk. "Time to take the watch, Smitty." It was Big Ski.

"I just got into bed," Smitty groaned.

"Been two hours," Ski said. "Your turn."

As soon as Smitty climbed out of the rack, Big Ski slid in—"hot bunking" at its finest—and was immediately in dreamland.

Smitty's two-hour watch went by uneventfully—just a black, endless sea and a black, endless sky speckled with the brightest stars he had ever seen. He looked up and wondered if there was a God somewhere out there who was watching over him and his mates. He returned to the torpedo room to sack out again, this time for six hours.

Upon awaking, with his stomach growling, he headed to the mess hall. There he joined Rick "Big Wop" Bonino from the forward torpedo room and an electrician from the maneuvering room called "Hopalong" Cassedy, whose brother Hiram was commander of *Searaven* (SS-196). After eating his fill, Smitty lit a cigarette, leaned back with a self-satisfied look on his face, and declared to his two tablemates, "You know, I didn't think that was so bad." He could hardly wait to write and tell his dad and Shirley about it.

Bonino grinned. "Shit, Smitty, that was nothing. We lucked out all the way."

"Yeah," added Cassedy. "You ain't seen nothin' yet. Just wait'll we get one of those Jap skippers who knows what he's doin'. He'll put those shit cans right down our hatch."

Smitty gulped and a small tingle of fear scampered through him. He didn't know if the guys were just giving him the business to see if he'd sweat or if they meant it.

"Funny how you always get scared after it's over," Smitty said, "you know, like when you almost have a car wreck? You keep control while it's happening, but when it's over, you shake like a dog shitting razor blades. You know what I mean, Wop?"

"Sure, but like Hopalong says, you ain't seen nothing yet."

SEAL patrolled back and forth across her station for several more days, but the pickings were slim. The few contacts they made turned out to be not worth wasting a torpedo on. The war got boring again.[3]

ADMIRAL Lockwood was still scratching his head over the torpedo problem. He conceded that the Bureau of Ordnance was pulling out all the stops to solve the magnetic-exploder problem and noted that on 10 May an expert from the Alexandria torpedo factory came to Pearl with modifications to the Mark XIVs that BuOrd felt would solve its many problems. Lockwood resolved to test the modifications, but if the problems persisted, he would request permission from CinCPac to inactivate the magnetic exploders.[4]

AFTER forty days at sea, with food and fuel running low, Dodge turned *Seal* back to the barn at Midway. The crew had started out eating fresh fruit and steaks, but now they were down to the nonperishables—powdered eggs and canned potatoes.

As soon as they reached the middle of nowhere, "nowhere" being anyplace in the Pacific that had no ship traffic or was out of sight of land, *Seal* ran on the surface twenty-four hours a day.

During the quiet periods, when he wasn't on watch or performing maintenance down below or drilling with the aft gun crew, Smitty studied hard for his submarine qualification test. Each man had six months in which to qualify; if he failed, he would be booted from the submarine service.

It was easy to qualify; all you had to do was go through the boat with a qualifying officer and be able to identify every gauge and valve, tell where every hatch led to, describe whether there was water, fuel, or air in every line and pipe, and be able to explain in full detail the job of every other man on the boat, including the officers. Simple.

"Think you're ready?" asked Lieutenant Hanes after Smitty had told him he was prepared to take the test.

"I'm as ready as I'll ever be, Hanes."

Hanes walked Smitty through the sub, from bow to stern, pointing at nearly every valve, gauge, dial, indicator, switch, lever, wheel, electric line, hydraulic line, high-pressure air line, low-pressure air line, and water line, and asked Smitty to identify it and explain what purpose it served.

"How'd I do, Hanes?" Smitty asked, when the walk-through was complete.

Hanes was noncommittal. "I'll let you know," was all he said.

Two days later Smitty was told to report to the ward room and see

Lieutenant Commander Frank Greenup, the executive officer. More than a little nervous, Smitty, accompanied by Hanes, squeezed into the small room the officers used for eating, meetings, and playing cards and cribbage. Greenup was seated at one of the tables, his face giving nothing away. Smitty hoped there would be good news.

"Smith," Greenup said, pausing dramatically for effect, "Mr. Hanes passed you for qualification. I'll order it put into your record." Smitty and Hanes exchanged smiles. "One other thing. Mr. Hanes also recommended you for torpedoman third class. I concurred and Captain Dodge has approved it. Congratulations, Smith."

Greenup extended his hand and Smitty shook it. "Thank you, sir," he said, visibly puffed with pride.

"Don't thank *me*, Smitty. You earned it."

Smitty was feeling great, on top of the world. As he went back to the caboose, he just had to tell everyone he saw that he had qualified and been promoted. The congratulations were sincere. For the most part, he was liked by his fellow crew members. A little cocky sometimes, they said, but a good man in a fight.

SEAL was within two days of ending her sixth war patrol, and Smitty was about to end his first. It felt good to be part of the *Seal* team. It was a little like being on the Hammond High football squad, but the stakes were bigger, much bigger. There was no trophy or league championship to play for, and no scoreboard clock to tell them how much time was left in the game. There wasn't even a scoreboard to let them know if they were ahead or behind. And if you lost, you weren't dejected, depressed, or downhearted. You were *dead*.

Instead of a trophy, the future of his country—the future of the whole world—was on the line. If everyone on board *Seal* did his job, they just might make it home alive and start to build a better world, a world where people could get along, where one country wasn't always trying to take over some other country and start a fight that would eventually force the United States to get involved, like his big brother, Bob, used to protect Smitty from bullies. That would be some swell world, Smitty thought. Maybe, just maybe, it might happen if you got enough really good people to sit around a big table and discuss the problems and work things out. War was exciting, no doubt about it, but it was stupid, too, and a lot of good people were getting killed. Eighteen-year-old John Ronald Smith tried to make sense of it all—the whole idea of geopolitics and hegemony and national identity and the subjugation of the weak by the strong—but it was too big a concept, too complex for his young brain to totally grasp.

More sailors filed into the small ward room, filling it with cigarette smoke and their body odor, the level of which was approaching that of a decomposing whale. The tension that had been palpable throughout the boat during the depth charging a few days earlier had been replaced by an air of convivial jollity and comradely horseplay, each man bragging about how he had personally been responsible for the death of the transport and the hated enemy on board her. Jokes were swapped and men tried pulling one another's legs.

Big Ski was a great joke teller. "Hey, I just got a report," he declared to the assembled smelly crew.

"What report?" a man named Dolly asked.

"It seems the Japs have this big meat locker on one of these islands."

"What *kind* of meat locker, Ski?" said Dolly, going along with the story.

"Well, it's for these cannibals. Y'know, they still got 'em out here. Anyhow, the cannibal chief goes into the meat locker and asks the Jap clerk, 'How much for that strong young Marine hangin' there?' The clerk, he says, 'Marines are five dollars a pound.' The old chief says, 'Too much,' then sees this pilot from an aircraft carrier hangin' there and asks how much. The clerk says 'Four bucks a pound.' The old chief says, 'Too much. You got anything cheaper?' The clerk points to a sailor. The chief asks, 'How much?' The clerk says, 'For you, fifty cents a pound.' 'How come so cheap?' the chief wants to know. "'Cuz he's a submariner. You ever try to clean one of them sons a bitches?'" The room broke up laughing.

When the bull session finally ended, Smitty drifted up to the forward torpedo room for a brief visit with Big Wop, then was heading back to the stern when he passed through the control room. The sailor manning the radarscope suddenly yelled out, "Radar contact! Dive, dive!" as he stomped on the alarm button at his foot.

Aaaaooogaa! blared the alarm throughout the sub, sending men scrambling to their battle stations. Lieutenant Frost, the diving officer, flooded negative tank with eight tons of seawater and the screws bit into the ocean, sending *Seal* on a steep downward descent. It was organized chaos in the narrow passageways as men bumped into one another, dashing in both directions. Smitty found himself running uphill toward the stern on a thirty-degree slope. An officer's voice came over the intercom: "Rig for depth charge! Rig for depth charge!" Smitty squeezed through the watertight door openings of each compartment just seconds before they were slammed shut and dogged down.

He had just entered the caboose when a tremendous blast threw him like a rag doll across the room, smashing his legs against one of the heavy steel I-beams that crossed the room about a foot above the deck. Big Ski, already in the compartment, grabbed onto a bunk frame while Woody was knocked flat on his skinny ass. Men who had been asleep in the bunks were wide-eyed and wide-awake, fear and confusion written on their faces. Smitty, prone on the deck and in intense pain, looked down; blood was streaming from his shins and he thought he could see white bone.

"Shit," exclaimed Big Ski, looking at the depth gauge. "That was too close. We just made ninety feet when that bastard hit us."

The "bastard" turned out to be a Japanese aircraft that had come roaring down on them from out of the sun. If the radar operator hadn't picked him up when he did, *Seal* and everyone on her might have been dead.

After the attack, Smitty hobbled off to see the pharmacist's mate, who clucked his tongue and shook his head at the sight of the gashes. "I don't know how it kept from breaking your legs," the corpsman said, " 'cause these cuts are deep, all the way to the bone." The PM put some antiseptic on the cuts that burned like hell, then bandaged them. Smitty limped back to his duty station, grateful that his injury wasn't more severe.

Seal remained submerged all day, poking her nose up only after sunset to recharge her batteries. The following day, 3 June 1943, *Seal* put into Midway for refitting, with *Searaven* right behind her. Commander Dodge and *Searaven*'s Hiram Cassedy—Hopalong's brother—had a happy college reunion in the bow of the launch that took the officers and men to shore. Smitty, his legs still aching, stood in the rear of the launch, and watched the two officers, clad in tailored and starched khakis, exchanging laughs and grins. Dodge had graduated from Annapolis in 1930, Cassedy a year later. *Searaven* had just completed her seventh war patrol, and Smitty thought the two skippers were probably comparing scores.

Although he had been in the Navy for less than a year, Smitty was beginning to feel the enlisted man's usual jealousy and resentment toward officers in general. All of the American submarine commanders were white, Anglo-Saxon, mostly Protestant, and graduates of the Naval Academy—the military's version of "Ivy League." Many—perhaps most—Annapolis graduates came from well-off families who lived near the ocean and had had plenty of time (and money) to go sailing or yachting while growing up. Smitty resented the special privileges that the officers received—the better pay, the better uniforms, the better accommodations, the better off-duty facilities. Had there been women on Midway, Smitty knew that the officers would have had their pick of them. He shook his head at the unfairness of it all. If he had been selected to go to aviation school and become a pilot, he would have been an officer and one of the privileged few. *Luck of the draw,* he grumbled to himself.

The launch docked alongside a submarine that was tied to the submarine tender *Bushnell,* which itself was secured to the dock. *Seal*'s complement of men walked the short distance to the Gooney Bird Hotel and were assigned rooms. Smitty shared the spartan room with three of his mates. The shower felt good.

Their bodies at last clean, *Seal*'s crewmen were paid two months' wages in scrip, issued a chit for a case of warm Green River Beer, trooped off to the laundry to get their uniforms cleaned, got their hair cut and beards trimmed (Smitty still didn't have much facial hair but got himself a nice Mohawk haircut), and went to the Base Exchange to buy the brightest, loudest Hawaiian swim trunks they could find. Smitty also saw a doctor for his leg wounds, then limped down to the beach, chased some aggressive gooney birds out of the shade of a war-scarred palm tree, and stretched out on the white sand. He gave some thought to writing some letters home; his dad, his grandmother, and Shirley had all written to him and asked why he hadn't replied. *What do I say?* he thought. *If I say I haven't written because I've been on patrol for two months, the censor will cut that out. If I say I haven't had time, they'll think it's an excuse. Damned if I do, damned if I don't. What would I say, anyway? Even if I could tell them what I'm doing, they wouldn't understand.*[5]

Lying there, gazing up at the gently waving fronds and the blue sky and puffy white clouds beyond, he thought about the war; scuttlebutt had it that both *Pickerel* and *Grenadier* were overdue. Scuttlebutt, as usual, turned out to be accurate. *Grenadier* had gone down fighting on 21 April off Penang on the west coast of Malaya. A Japanese plane had spotted *Grenadier*, which had been chasing a couple of ships, and dropped a bomb that wrecked her stern, bent the propeller shafts, and ignited an electrical fire. The next morning, with *Grenadier* dead in the water and no hope of rescue, the skipper, John Fitzgerald, ordered the crew to scuttle *Grenadier*, abandon ship, and swim to shore. As this was taking place, another enemy plane swooped in for the kill. Blazing away from the bridge at the attacking plane with a Browning Automatic Rifle, Fitzgerald chased off the pilot. He and his men were then captured, tortured, and sent to spend the duration of the war in the notorious Ofuna POW camp in Japan. For his steadfastness in the face of the enemy, Fitzgerald would later be awarded the Navy Cross.[6]

One of those taken prisoner was Robert York, a chief petty officer aboard *Grenadier*. He recalled, "We all survived but were taken prisoner. We were taken to Penang and the Light Street Convent, where we were held incommunicado for about three or so months while the Japs interrogated us."[7]

While everyone soon learned what had happened to *Grenadier*, the fate of *Pickerel* and skipper Augustus H. Alston's crew remains unknown to this day. She left Midway on 22 March to hunt off Honshu and was not heard from again.[8]

Beneath his palm tree Smitty also pondered *Seal*'s three narrow

escapes on his first patrol—slipping undetected out of the harbor at Anguar; the fearsome depth charging they had received after the sinking of
the *San Clemente Maru*; and the close call when the Japanese aircraft
nearly bombed them into oblivion—and wondered if his luck—and
Seal's—would continue.[9]

He wouldn't have long to wait to find out.

CHAPTER 11

JUST STAY LOOSE

It was June 1943, and the tide of war around the world was gradually shifting in favor of the Allies.

The Germans and their Fascist partners, the Italians, had been soundly defeated in North Africa; the survivors fled to Sicily, off the northeast coast of Tunisia, and were bracing for an invasion by the Americans and British. Hundreds of tons of bombs were devastating German cities and industrial facilities as American and British bombers flew missions day and night through the flak-studded skies over the Third Reich.

On the Russian front, the Germans were still recovering from the crushing loss in January of their Sixth Army at Stalingrad. Slowly but surely, foot by foot, town by town, the Soviet troops were beginning to reclaim their country from the invaders.

In the Pacific, the Australians steadfastly continued to beat back attempts by the Japanese to take Port Moresby, while American forces had finally wiped out enemy resistance on Guadalcanal and wrested control of the Solomons from the Japanese. U.S. Marines began their relentless reconquest of the Pacific, landing on Woodlark and Kiriwina Islands in the Trobriand group, as well as Rendova Island.[1]

The enemy, however, was handed a victory by an unthinking congressman, Andrew Jackson May, a member of the House Military Affairs Committee. After returning from a fact-finding junket to the Pacific in June 1943, the sixty-eight-year-old Kentuckian told reporters that the

Japanese did not know how deep American submarines could go and that, consequently, the enemy fused their depth charges to go off at too shallow a depth. Naturally, Japanese agents in the United States picked up the story and relayed it back to Japan, where the Imperial Navy ordered that depth charges be set to explode deeper. When Admiral Lockwood learned of May's indiscretion, he was understandably livid. After the war, he would declare that by giving away secret information, the congressman had probably cost America ten submarines and the lives of 800 sailors.[2] The Japanese, thanks to this leak of secret information, upped the amount of explosive in their depth charges from 242 to 357 pounds and modified them so they could be detonated as deep as 500 feet.[3]

By the middle of 1943, the entire United States was on a total war footing. Virtually all of the nation's disparate elements could be seen marching shoulder to shoulder toward victory. At a time when the very survival of the United States hung in the balance, the American people came together as never before—and never since—to recognize the danger and face the common enemy. No sacrifice seemed too profound to make, no personal inconvenience too trivial to set aside, no hardship too extreme to endure for the good of the country.

By the spring of 1943, the American Army had grown from a paltry force of fewer than 500,000 men before the war to 4.3 million battle-ready soldiers; that figure would nearly double by the end of the year.

There was no shirking, either. Recruiting centers were swamped with young men wanting to join the service and "do their part." Being rejected by a branch of service because of a physical or psychological impairment was as devastating to many would-be warriors as being rejected by a lover. Being "in uniform" was the patriotic thing to do, and many young men of draft age who *weren't* in uniform saw themselves as pariahs within American society, even though they may have tried their best to enlist or were exempt from the military because they were physically unfit or were employed in an "essential" war industry.

Scores of professional sports figures and Hollywood movie stars and directors voluntarily gave up their high salaries and cushy jobs to join the military. So many baseball stars—Ted Williams, Bob Feller, Joe DiMaggio, Ralph Kiner, Eddie Yost, Yogi Berra, Hank Greenberg, Warren Spahn, Stan Musial, and hundreds more—had traded their flannel for khaki that an all-women's league was formed to fill the shortage. Even the heavyweight champion of the world, Joe Louis, enlisted in the Army. Popular musicians and bandleaders such as Glenn Miller switched from entertaining the teens to entertaining the troops, many of whom *were* teens.

Established box-office notables such as Eddie Albert, Douglas Fairbanks Jr., Glenn Ford, Clark Gable, Robert Montgomery, Paul Muni, Ronald Reagan, Mickey Rooney, and Jimmy Stewart (as well as men who, like Tony Curtis, Jack Lemmon, Lee Marvin, Walter Matthau, Cameron Mitchell, Hugh O'Brian, Jack Palance, Aldo Ray, Jason Robards Jr., Robert Ryan, and Telly Savalas would become stars after the war) eschewed their safe, glamorous lives to take part in the war. Famous directors, screenwriters and producers—Frank Capra, John Ford, John Huston, Budd Schulberg, George Stevens, and Darryl F. Zanuck among them—lent their talents to the making of training films, documentaries, and war propaganda movies necessary for the maintenance of home-front morale.

From the long soup-kitchen lines peopled with discouraged workers at the depths of the Great Depression just a decade earlier, the United States, thanks almost entirely to the war, had rebounded by 1943 into an unprecedented period of prosperity and full employment. Factories that had been closed for years suddenly sprang to life to fill orders for war goods. Cotton and wool mills worked around the clock making khaki, olive-drab, and Navy blue uniforms. Miners in the coal, iron, oil, and related industries were digging and drilling as never before. Carpenters, electricians, and plumbers who previously had been able to find only odd jobs and part-time work suddenly found their skills in high demand as military bases and other temporary government facilities sprouted up across the country.

Nineteen forty-three was also a year of unprecedented social change. As millions of men enlisted or were drafted into the armed forces, millions of women took their places in the work environment. Economically disadvantaged African-Americans from the South migrated northward to cities such as Chicago, Detroit, and Newark in response to the need for both skilled and unskilled laborers.

But not all the news was good. Racial tensions in big cities flared, and strikes and riots often broke out when blacks were hired or promoted over whites. Racism and segregation, even in the military, was rampant.

By 1943, civilian goods had practically disappeared, except on the black market. New tires were impossible to get. Gasoline and oil were also severely rationed in order that America's highly mechanized military would be assured of having enough fuel and petroleum products to power and lubricate their vast array of vehicles, ships, and aircraft.

Through ads and posters asking "Is this trip necessary?" the government admonished civilians not to use mass transportation frivolously in order to free up the buses, planes, and trains for the movement of soldiers and sailors and airmen across the country. Farmers who had survived the dust-bowl days could not grow fast enough all of the food needed to feed the troops and keep the homeland cupboards stocked; the inevitable shortages of meat, sugar, coffee, and other items left grocery-store shelves half empty.

But Americans did what they could to avoid having their attention deflected from the ultimate national goal: victory. Housewives saved cooking fat and turned it in at collection centers so that it could be converted into the chemicals needed to produce explosives. Secretaries were told to squeeze a few more copies out of each sheet of carbon paper. With shoe leather rationed, civilians stuffed paper inside their shoes to plug holes in the soles. Women went without nylons and silk stockings—material needed for parachutes—and instead painted their legs with "leg makeup." Boy Scouts scoured neighborhoods, searching vacant lots and knocking on doors collecting scrap aluminum, steel, and cast iron that could be converted into the matériel of war. Men, women, and children bought "Victory Bonds" and "Victory Stamps" to help finance the war. Community blood drives brought in millions of gallons of blood and plasma for America's wounded fighting men.

It was virtually impossible to pick up a magazine without seeing scores of advertisements from companies apologizing for their inability to supply consumer goods but, at the same time, praising themselves for their contribution to the war effort.

Ford, General Motors, Hudson, Studebaker, Willys, and all the other automobile makers, along with thousands of small, anonymous companies, had ended the production of civilian goods in early 1942 and converted their plants exclusively to the output of war equipment: tanks, jeeps, cargo trucks, command cars, weasels, half-tracks, howitzers, trailers, engines, generators, and airplanes—bombers, fighters, patrol craft, flight trainers, and the parts to keep them running.

Under prodding by the War Production Board, formerly fierce competitors worked together for the good of the nation. Willys had designed the jeep, but Willys and Ford shared the contract to build the versatile vehicle. Farm-implement companies such as International Harvester assembled M-1 rifles and torpedoes. The Baldwin Locomotive Works built tanks; Cadillac developed engines to go into those tanks. Western Electric and Motorola churned out thousands of military radios and telephones. Wooden-propeller manufacturers, their industry having dried up as a result of aviation's progression to metal props, made hickory skis for the nation's only mountain division.[4]

AMERICA'S shipyards, working twenty-four hours a day, seven days a week, continued to turn out ships of all descriptions: carriers, battleships, cruisers, destroyers, destroyer escorts, oilers, transports, tankers, corvettes, gunboats, frigates, Liberty ships, PT boats, minelayers, minesweepers, store ships, hospital ships, ammunition ships, repair ships, yard craft, landing craft, amphibious craft, repair and salvage ships, net tenders, seaplane tenders, submarine tenders, submarine chasers, and, of course, submarines.

In the summer of 1943, with the boatbuilding facilities at Portsmouth, Groton, Manitowoc, Mare Island, and Philadelphia all operating at full capacity, dozens of new submarines were launched. But it was still torpedoes—and submarine sailors—that were in short supply, for the losses among the Silent Service continued to mount.

BESIDES relaxing on the beach, chasing birds, gambling away their hard-earned money at Midway's Gooney Bird Hotel and Casino, and getting soused on the lousy beer, Smitty and the crew of *Seal* spent time on the water in training, sharpening their combat skills and getting ready to return to the war. There were also a few new replacements to train, men who had come in to relieve sailors who had been transferred to other boats, or gone back to new construction, or who had failed to earn their dolphins.

On 24 June 1943, *Seal* backed away from the sub tender *Bushnell* at Midway to begin her seventh war patrol. According to the secret orders in the sub's safe, *Seal* was to patrol in Japanese home waters off Honshu, some 3,000 miles from Midway—a very dangerous place.

After five days at sea, zigzagging to present less of a target to any enemy subs that might be lurking along the route, *Seal* ran into a typhoon—the Orient's version of a hurricane. Plunging into waves as tall as houses convinced the crew that this was no ordinary storm. The boat was rolling thirty degrees from side to side and everything loose within the sub had to be lashed down or securely stowed. Sleeping men even had to be tied to their bunks to keep from being dumped onto the deck. Everyone except the saltiest of old salts got violently seasick. At the height of the storm, Smitty volunteered for a watch as starboard lookout topside. "I couldn't sleep and I couldn't eat," he said. "Might as well do something useful."

The storm was the most powerful, violent thing Ron Smith had ever experienced. The wind was blasting the rocking sub at speeds up to a hundred miles an hour, and the rain, instead of coming from just one direction, seemed to be coming from *all* directions at once. *Seal* was batted from one monstrous wave to another like a shuttlecock. Smitty fastened a lifeline around his waist, secured it to the railing, and held on. The binoculars were useless.

"A swell would form like a hole in the ocean fifty to seventy feet deep," Smitty said, "with a black wall on the other side just as high. *Seal* would fall into the hole like an airplane in a free-fall dive, then slam into the wall of water on the opposite side, shuddering as she wallowed back up and over it."

Most of the wave washed over the boat and Smitty shut his eyes and held his breath, hanging on with all his might when he saw it starting to crest over him. Then down the black wave would crash, smashing into him like a giant wet fist, trying to rip him from the safety of the boat and throw him into the sea. It reminded him of one of the rides at Chicago's Riverview Amusement Park. But this ride was anything but amusing.

There was one redeeming feature to the storm: if any enemy ships were out there in the roiling sea, the Japanese sailors would be in the same stew—fighting Mother Nature instead of the Americans.

After enduring several hours of being banged around in the storm and soaked to the skin, he was at last relieved and struggled to get below, where it was dry. Smitty retreated to the mess hall that was pitching back and forth and grabbed a mug of hot coffee that kept sloshing all over him. He then dripped his way to the control room. "Why're we riding this out on the surface, Chief?" he asked Red Servnac, an old salt and veteran submariner. "Why don't we just submerge and get out of this shit?"

"Didn't know it was gonna be this bad," Servnac answered. "It'd be hard to dive in this now. We'd prob'ly take as much air into the tanks as water. Not sure we *could* dive."

Lieutenant Jack Frost, the engineering and diving officer, leaning against the gyrocompass table to keep his balance, joined the conversation. "It's better we ride it out on the surface, Smith," he said. "*Seal* can take it. She's a tough girl."

Still skeptical, Smitty headed back to the caboose, stripped off his sopping clothes, wrung them out, and put them back on before sliding into a bunk and strapping himself in. *At least my clothes got washed,* he thought, sighing with resignation about the situation.

After three days, the storm moved on and *Seal* once again swam in calm seas.

AAAAOOOGAA! Aaaaooogaa! went the diving alarm for the umpteenth time. "Dive, dive," said Control. Dodge was really putting the crew through their paces with one drill after another until even the old salts began to complain. It had been going on for five days now—diving and surfacing, and Battle Stations Submerged and Battle Stations Surfaced.

"That must be ten times today," Big Ski bitched to Smitty as he moved instinctively to once more push up the big lever that engaged the Waterbury speed gear to the stern planes. The gear was supposed to engage automatically by electric solenoid, but it hadn't worked for so long that it had become second nature for the torpedoman on watch to push the handle until the gears caught. *Seal* tilted down at a steep angle.

"Just stay loose," Smitty recalled Seagull once advising him. He tried to stay loose, but it was getting hard.

AFTER a week, half of which had been spent struggling against the storm, *Seal* finally arrived on station—off the northeast coast of the main Japanese island of Honshu, the enemy's front yard. With daylight lasting twenty hours a day at this latitude, Dodge kept *Seal* submerged most of the time, coming up for only about four hours in the darkness to charge the batteries. It was a risky thing to do, for if she were spotted by the enemy, *Seal* would have to dive and get out of there fast—and who knew what might happen if the batteries didn't get a full charge?

Being this close to Japan, the ship traffic looked to Smitty like the Chicago Loop at rush hour. Ships went left and ships went right, but Dodge bided his time, staying low, refusing to shoot. Everybody wanted to know what the hell they were waiting for.

One day the dim thumping of depth charges detonating a long way off reverberated throughout *Seal*, but no one knew why. "Ask Control what's going on," one of the torpedomen directed Smitty, who was on the headphones.

"Control, tubes aft. We're hearing explosions back here. What's going on?" Smitty asked.

"Tubes aft, Control," said Cowboy Hendrix, a sailor manning the phones in the control room. "We hear it, too. Don't know what it is, but it's definitely not for us. Too far away."

"Ask him if anyone else is close," Big Ski told Smitty.

Cowboy reported that Mr. Greenup thought *Runner* was nearby, to the south of *Seal*.

The tempo of the explosions picked up, like the final minute of a Fourth of July fireworks show, but still at quite a distance.

"Sounds like they're working someone over pretty good," said a sailor named Abelardo Lago. Men just stared at the bulkheads or the deck and listened.

At about 2100 hours, the thumping stopped and the crew in *Seal* relaxed a little. Then, about forty-five minutes later, Lumpy Lehman came on over the circuit; he had picked up an emergency signal. "Sounds like the *Runner*. Weak signal, hard to read. Sounds like they are saying they're stuck in the mud or something. Can't make it out."

Lieutenant Hanes's voice came on. "Sound, Control. Maybe they've run aground. Keep listening."

"Sound, aye," said Lehman.

The men of the *Seal* were silent. The signs were clear—*Runner* had probably gone down.* A sister submarine was dying. Or dead. *Seal* was filled with a sobering silence. They knew that it could be *their* fate, too.

AT 2200 hours on 7 July 1943, *Seal* surfaced again in darkness to recharge her batteries. All four diesels ran at full power to squeeze as much juice back into the lead-acid cells as possible during the short time available.

At 0340 hours the next morning, radar picked up the blips of a large convoy steaming north at twelve knots: three big transports, five or six smaller ships, and perhaps a few escorts. The convoy was hugging the coastline, exposing only the starboard side and giving *Seal* little maneuvering room. Dodge thought it was risky but worth a shot; he put *Seal* on a northerly course at flank speed on the surface in order to intercept the convoy. Throughout the boat, men practiced their procedures of preparing to engage. When *Seal* got to the ambush point, she went to battle stations submerged and dove to periscope depth. Target range, speed, and distance was fed into the TDC. Everything was ready for the attack.

Lumpy Lehman suddenly reported, "Small fast screws closing from port side." It was a Japanese sub homing in for the kill.

"Drop her to one-fifty feet," Dodge commanded. Lieutenant Frost ordered all ballast-tank vents opened, sending *Seal* on a steep plunge.

---

* A postwar search of Japanese naval records did not confirm a depth-charge attack on an American submarine during this period; speculation at the time was that *Runner* may have been sunk by floating mines known to have been sown in thick profusion off northeast Honshu. The true identity of the sub being depth-charged may never be known. (www.csp.navy.mil/ww2boats/runner)

202 THE DEPTHS OF COURAGE

The command had not come a moment too soon, as all hands on board heard the distinctive, high-pitched *screeeeeooooom* sound of a torpedo ripping through the water just above them. Smitty nearly jumped out of his skin at the noise.

"Periscope depth," ordered Dodge, and *Seal* rose at his command. They were still going to attack the convoy!

"Stand by, tubes forward," said Hanes.

"Tubes forward standing by, aye," said Big Wop with a hint of glee in his voice.

Smitty listened intently on his headphones as Dodge maneuvered *Seal* into position for a shot from the bow tubes. In his mind's eye he could see his counterparts in the forward torpedo room doing everything needed to prepare for the attack.

"Fire one," said Dodge, and *Seal* lurched under the kick of compressed air. Two more torpedoes left the sub in quick succession. "All ahead full," directed Dodge. "Tubes forward, start your reload. Take her down to a hundred feet."

"Tubes aft, stand by," said Hanes. "Open doors five, six, and seven."

"We're going *under* the son of a bitch!" exclaimed Big Ski.

"If those first three fish hit him, he'll come down right on top of us!" yelled Lago.

"Knock that shit off, Lago," shouted Woody. "The Old Man knows what he's doing." The torpedomen began cranking open the outer tube doors.

It was now clear to everyone. Shoot from the bow tubes, go under the target, and then hit him again from the other side with the stern tubes. It was a brilliant maneuver, one that, as far as Smitty knew, no one had ever tried before. But weren't they too close to the shore? Wouldn't *Seal* run aground once she got on the other side of the target ship?

There was no time to worry as Hanes's voice crackled in Smitty's headphones. "Tube aft, Control. Stand by to fire five."

"Tubes aft standing by to fire five, aye," said Smitty as he intently studied the TDC box, waiting for the bugs to come into line.

Suddenly *Click . . . KaBLOOM! Click . . . KaBLOOM! Click . . . KaBLOOM!*

Three shock waves smashed into and through *Seal*. The caboose was plunged into total darkness as the lightbulbs blew out. It quickly became very cold and very wet as water began spraying from pipes burst by the force of the torque that had twisted the ship. Men were yelling, swearing, giving commands, shouting warnings.

Instinctively Smitty reached out and grabbed anything he could find in order to steady himself and keep from being tossed around the blackened room with all its hard, protruding surfaces. He felt the boat tilt upward at a sickening angle. At that moment the emergency lighting came on.

"Holy Mother of God," gasped Big Ski as he stared at the depth gauge. "Three hundred sixty-five feet!" The old hull groaned under the weight of 200 pounds of pressure per square inch. Everyone knew *Seal's* maximum test depth was ninety feet shallower; she had never been this deep before.

Click . . . KaBLOOM!

"Rig for depth charge! Rig for silent running!" came the order from Control. Smitty, scared out of his wits, repeated it.

"A little late for that," somebody cracked as the aft torpedo crew dogged down the watertight door, closed the bulkhead flappers, and secured the outer tube doors.

Click . . . KaBLOOM!

"What the hell happened?" somebody demanded to know.

"The sons of bitches caught us with our pants down," Woody replied.

Click . . . KaBLOOM!

Seal shuddered as though being beaten with a baseball bat the size of a smokestack.

"We're getting gangbanged," shouted Dead Eye as he hung on to a loading rack.

Water continued to spray into the compartment from ruptured lines. With the upward slant of the deck, the icy water was knee-deep down near Smitty's station and getting deeper.

Click . . . KaBLOOM! Click . . . KaBLOOM! Click . . . KaBLOOM!

Although the men of the *Seal* didn't yet know it, seven Japanese destroyers had positioned themselves between the convoy and the coast, invisible to *Seal*'s periscope and radar. At the first salvo of torpedoes, the enemy tin cans had swung through the convoy, pinged *Seal*, and started dropping their deadly munitions. As Big Ski and Hopalong had predicted, they had run into a captain—or seven of them—who could drop depth charges "down the hatch."

Click . . . KaBLOOM! Click . . . KaBLOOM! Click . . . KaBLOOM!

Sound and pressure waves reverberated through the hull, and Smitty was amazed that he could actually *see* the steel bend and move with each shock as though the sub were made of aluminum foil. The men in the caboose tried to climb higher, away from the rising water, but the deck, slick with an oily film, prevented traction. The water, only a couple of degrees above freezing, chilled the air and the men could see their breath clouds.

Click . . . KaBLOOM! Click . . . KaBLOOM! Click . . . KaBLOOM!

Damage reports from the different sections of the boat were coming in thick and fast over Smitty's headphones. He relayed the depressing information to his mates: "Forward torpedo room flooding; a gasket on the sound head is leaking bad. Forward battery room is okay. Conning tower has a few minor leaks. Control room is dry but the pump room is flooded almost to the control-room hatch. After battery room has some water, still about eight inches from the batteries."

This last bit of news was especially ominous, for if the water reached the batteries, it would combine with the acid to create chlorine gas and kill everyone on board.

"Forward engine room reports minor leaks, not much water in bilges," Smitty continued repeating. "After engine room flooded to the decks; the donkey engine* is almost underwater."

It was Smitty's turn to report. "Control, tubes aft. Outer doors closed, water about halfway up the deck, stern depth gauges reading three hundred sixty-five feet."

"Very well, tubes aft," came the calm response from Control. Smitty wondered how Hanes could be so unflappable at a time like this, but the

---

* The donkey engine was a 500-horsepower auxiliary engine located belowdecks used to provide emergency power.

officer's calmness helped to settle Smitty's nerves. Maybe things aren't as bad as they seem, he said to himself.

"What time is it?" Hopalong asked Smitty, who moved so he could see the chronometer.

"Zero seven-twenty," Smitty replied. It was 9 July 1943. He wondered if he would live to see 10 July.

"It's been less than an hour since the attack started," Woody said quietly in disbelief. It seemed as if they had been under fire for hours. Somebody mentioned that the depth charging had ended about a half hour earlier. They were starting to breathe easier, but were still worried about water reaching the batteries.

"All compartments, we're going to try to correct our trim," Control said, but no sooner were the valves noisily opened than another rain of depth charges cascaded down.

Click . . . KaBLOOM! Click . . . KaBLOOM! Click . . . KaBLOOM!

"The sound of a depth charge cannot be described," Smitty later said. "There is no other sound like it. Worse than the loudest thunder, ten times louder than a large bomb, a sound so powerful that it goes through the spectrum of physical sound that the ear can hear and turns into a pressure wave."

Click . . . KaBLOOM! Click . . . KaBLOOM! Click . . . KaBLOOM!

"It don't get no closer than that," Brown growled as his knuckles turned white from holding on to an I-beam.

The charges kept coming in a seemingly endless deluge. *Click . . . KaBLOOM! Click . . . KaBLOOM! Click . . . KaBLOOM!* There were so many depth charges, the men began to think that the enemy destroyers were returning to port, reloading, and coming back to drop more. Maybe all the depth charges in Japan were being used to sink *Seal.* Smitty started to grow really scared. His fellow crew members were the best in the business, but they had no way to fight back, no shield to deflect the blasts, no magic wand to make the enemy disappear and the bombing stop.

Click . . . KaBLOOM! Click . . . KaBLOOM! Click . . . KaBLOOM! When, dear Lord, will it end? ran through each man's mind. How much more of this shit do You expect us to take?

The diving officer was unable to change *Seal*'s awkward angle by correcting her trim. Each time they tried pumping water from the tanks, the Japanese sonar men would hear the noise and more depth charges would come fluttering down. The enemy definitely had *Seal* pinned to the mat and were not about to let her up.

Three more hours passed, but there was no cessation in the assault on nerves and eardrums.

"Sound, can you tell us anything?" Control asked Lumpy Lehman at one point.

"Control, I make seven destroyers and some smaller craft nearby, probably destroyer escorts." This was the first anyone had heard about the number of hunters who were up there. No wonder the cannonade never seemed to cease.

"Very well, Sound," Control acknowledged, again without emotion, almost as if he had just been given a weather report for fair skies and calm seas.

It was getting colder by the minute in the aft torpedo room. *Is this my tomb? Is this where I'm going to die?* Smitty thought. He wondered how his dad would take the news. And Shirley. *They won't even have a body to bury.*

Lumpy Lehman gave his assessment of the situation. "Sounds like they're circling us and takin' turns runnin' across the circle and droppin' a load on us."

Smitty repeated what he heard and Brown tried to lighten the tension: "Sounds like the Indians got our wagon train circled." The men in the caboose laughed a little harder than they might ordinarily have done. Then the room grew quiet again. Each man in the group would close his eyes and lower his head every once in a while. The others knew he was praying, as they all were.

Smitty issued his own silent prayer. *Please, dear God, please help me, please help us. I don't mind dying if it will help get this war over, but I don't think it will. Please give me the strength to do whatever I have to do.*

Lago tried to relieve the tense atmosphere with a dirty joke, but it fell flat.

Click . . . KaBLOOM! Click . . . KaBLOOM! Click . . . KaBLOOM!
Woody also made a contribution, but before he could get to the

punch line, he was interrupted by *Click . . . KaBLOOM! Click . . . KaBLOOM! Click . . . KaBLOOM!* Everyone went temporarily deaf.

Suddenly a new sound—a sharp, loud *POING!*—rang through the hull as though the *Seal* had been turned into a large gong.

"Sonar," said Dead Eye. "He's pinging on us."

"That son of a bitch really has us now," offered Big Ski, standing up and facing the bulkhead. It was the first time Smitty had seen Big Ski scared. The destroyers had zeroed in on *Seal* with their active sonar and were echo-ranging, bouncing the signal off the massive steel hull of the helpless sub and calculating her position. It was the only sound that submariners dreaded more than the sound of depth charges. It meant the destroyers knew exactly where *Seal* was, as though she had a giant flashing neon target painted on her side.

A new sound greeted the submariners' vibrating ears: *Pop-pop-pop-pop-pop-pop-pop-pop-pop-pop.* It sounded like a string of large, underwater firecrackers.

"Shit. Depth bombs," Woody said.

Eight more depth charges went off, and a lot more bombs.

"They probably got an airfield near here," said Hopalong.

"Yeah, and a goddamn bomb factory, too," said Big Ski, "and we're right at the end of the assembly line."

Big Wop Bonino, in the forward torpedo room, was keeping score of the number of charges dropped and would periodically report his count quietly over the circuit. "Two hundred and twelve," came the latest total.

Somehow, incredibly, they were all still alive. Since their demise no longer seemed imminent, thoughts of living took over, especially thoughts of food.

"I'm starved," said one.

"Me, too," said another.

Suddenly the men started pulling cans of food out from secret storage places, such as from behind the spare torpedoes, and pooled their wares. There were several cans of Dole pineapple, some sardines, and a tin of soda crackers. The sailors broke out their knives and cut open the cans. "It would have made a nice picnic except for the freezing cold and the continuing explosions of the depth charges," Smitty later said.

Click . . . KaBLOOM! Click . . . KaBLOOM! Click . . . KaBLOOM!

"Boy, those bastards just ain't givin' up," Big Ski said, his mouth stuffed with crackers.

The hours dragged by, but the Japanese destroyers refused to slacken their efforts to kill the picnickers. Strangely, it was becoming as routine as being bombed and depth-charged could become. And, surprisingly, despite *Seal*'s odd upward angle, Dodge was managing to keep the submarine moving at reduced power, hoping to slip away from the ever-alert enemy destroyers.

Damage reports came in from various parts of the sub. The pump room was flooded and out of commission, some vents were damaged, and engine mufflers had been blown away. Worse, the fuel tanks had been punctured and *Seal* was leaking diesel fuel; the oil would form a shiny rainbow ribbon on the ocean's surface, making it very easy for enemy destroyers to track her movements.

At 1430 hours, Smitty decided to make a foray to other parts of the boat to check on conditions. After handing the headphones to Ski, he opened the watertight door and slipped out. Because of the boat's steep upward tilt, it took several men in the caboose to shut the door behind him.

Smitty climbed uphill through the maneuvering room, chatted briefly with the men there, then commiserated with Ginny Ginero, dejected over the fact that his donkey engine had drowned.

Next Smitty banged on the door to the forward engine room and its keeper, a sailor named Phillips, opened it. The room looked okay. "How's it going in here?" Smitty asked.

"You don't want to know," Phillips replied. "The water is getting closer to the battery hatch." Not good news.

Smitty hurried on, next reaching the crew's mess, where a dozen or more men had gathered to smoke and talk quietly. Smitty gave them the news from the aft torpedo room, then made himself a ham sandwich. Everyone was in relatively good spirits, but beneath the forced cheerful banter they all knew the situation they were in.

"Thank God the Japs don't have hedgehogs," said a sailor. Everyone nodded. American destroyers in the Atlantic were armed with an underwater munition known as a hedgehog that fired two dozen rockets in a pattern, each with an armor-piercing head three inches in diameter. They were blowing nasty holes in the hulls of Nazi submarines.

Control ordered everyone to open five-gallon cans of a white powder and spread it around. It was carbon dioxide absorbent that would help preserve the sub's gradually depleting supply of oxygen. Cigarette breaks were cut down to five minutes every hour. When the "smoking lamp" was lit, Smitty tried lighting a cigarette but found that the lack of oxygen made the burning of tobacco nearly impossible.

Smitty said his farewells to the men in the mess hall and, to the accompanying drumroll of more depth charges, headed downhill and back to the caboose. He retrieved the headphones from Ski and continued monitoring the situation throughout the boat. He learned that conditions in the forward torpedo room were deteriorating; water was continuing to pour in from around the damaged sound head gasket and gradually filling up the room. If anyone opened the hatch, the water would pour out into the forward battery compartment and cause a disaster.

Click . . . KaBLOOM! Click . . . KaBLOOM! Click . . . KaBLOOM!
Would it never cease?

Smitty slowly began to realize that their chances of making it out alive were diminishing by the minute. Not only was the oxygen running out and the water getting closer to the batteries, but the Japanese could continue to bomb and depth-charge them from now until the end of time. After all, they were sitting just off the coast of Japan. When a destroyer ran low on depth charges, it could just pull into the nearest port and reload. How stupid was Dodge for attempting this stunt? How stupid was the Navy for sending them practically into the emperor's bathtub?

Smitty was sitting on the inclined deck, his bare knees drawn up and his arms wrapped around them, his teeth chattering from the cold. How stupid was *he* for not bringing any warm clothes on this patrol?

Bitter thoughts ran through his head. *Why did we have to get involved in this war, anyway? The Japs attacked us because we tried to keep them from getting the oil and rubber and steel they wanted. What business was that of ours? If they had done the same to us, wouldn't we have attacked them first?*

Smitty thought, *Why should I have to die for something I didn't start? After all, it doesn't make any difference what kind of government*

U.S.S. *Seal*, photographed March 1943.
(Courtesy Naval Historical Center)

you have as long as you have enough food, have a wife and kids, and are left alone. I bet the poor, dumb bastards in Japan and Germany feel the same way. I don't mind dying if it would make a difference, but it won't. Why are we humans so stupid? We're all going to die and it won't make a damn bit of difference in this war. Hell, we didn't even sink the target!

Smitty's mind wandered on, trying to make some sense of the situation. *I'm only eighteen and I haven't even had a chance to live. I'd like to get married and have kids. I haven't even really been with a woman.*

And just think of all the money this war is costing. Just this submarine cost millions of dollars. What a waste. Shit, one torpedo costs more than fifteen new cars. I could buy fifteen new Pontiacs and have money left over.

As if he could read Smitty's mind, Big Ski broke into his thinking. "Smitty, you're a fool. You should be going to your senior prom about now instead of being out here on this stinking boat."

Smitty looked at him with pleading eyes. "Ski, are we gonna make it out of here?"

"Sure, kid. You'll live to be fifty-five and bounce your grandkids on your knee. Keep the faith. Remember what Seagull says: 'Stay loose. Just stay loose.'"

Smitty wished it were that simple. *I'm glad I didn't have to fight the Germans. At least they're Christians. These heathen Japs, what the hell are they? They think their emperor is God. They should all be killed, these dumb shits who think they'll go to heaven if they die for their em-peror. I wish I had that son of a bitch Hirohito here right now. I'd show them he was human.*

Click . . . KaBLOOM! Click . . . KaBLOOM! Click . . . KaBLOOM!

The seven sub hunters hung around all day, taking turns gleefully bombarding *Seal*, like bullies beating a puppy. The air in *Seal* was getting really foul, with oxygen levels dropping and carbon dioxide levels rising. Nobody tried to smoke; cigarettes wouldn't stay lit, anyway. The batteries, too, were running out. Might not even last two more hours. Smitty didn't know if there was even enough high-pressure air left to blow the ballast tanks and bring her to the surface. They were, Smitty knew, as good as dead. The destroyers just had to stay up there a few more hours and it would be all over. Maybe he should just close his eyes and give up.

Click . . . KaBLOOM! Click . . . KaBLOOM! Click . . . KaBLOOM![5]

CHAPTER 12

FEATHER MERCHANT THIRD CLASS

THE sun, when it was rising, was a symbol of Japanese supremacy in the Far East. It was now setting behind the Kitakami Mountains that rose above the coastline of northeast Honshu. Perhaps this was also a symbol, or at least an omen.

The hours, punctuated by depth charges that punched and jarred the sub like a massive boxing glove, passed slowly within *Seal*, still trapped below the sea. It was 9 July 1943. The chronometer read 2300 hours; *Seal* had been submerged for eighteen hours, and many of the men wondered if this would be the day of their death.

Lieutenant Commander Harry Benjamin Dodge had other ideas. To him, it was time to bring *Seal* to the surface, despite the presence of the enemy's destroyers, and try to make a run for it. If he didn't, he and his crew would certainly all have their names carved into a memorial slab somewhere. The chances of being able to outrun the enemy ships were slim to none, but they were better than lying 365 feet beneath the surface and waiting for the inevitability of asphyxiation.

Suddenly the order "Battle-surface crew, report to the control room" came over the headphones. Startled, Smitty repeated the command and stood up.

"What the hell is this?" grumbled one of the other sailors in the caboose, but he also stood up because he, too, was on the battle-surface crew. In fact, everyone in the aft torpedo room except Big Ski had some function on the battle-surface detail, and they all filed out. Smitty was the last to leave the compartment, and as he did, he turned to Big Ski, who was holding the watertight door open for him. Their eyes met. For a moment Smitty thought he might never see Ski again, at least in this life.

"You gonna be okay?" Smitty asked. He hated leaving his friend alone.

"It's okay, Smitty," Ski said, holding out his hand and shaking the youngster's, almost as though he knew what Smitty was thinking. "Give 'em hell, kid."

When Smitty reached the control room, lit only by dim red bulbs to preserve night vision, it was already packed with the others on the gun crews. He looked around at the disheveled bunch. In place of regulation uniforms they had on an assortment of Hawaiian-print swim trunks, cut-off shorts, sandals, sheathed deck knives, and submarine jackets. They wore beards, Mohawks, and colored rags tied around their heads, arms, legs, and necks. They looked more like Barbary Coast pirates than a group of elite U.S. Navy submariners.

Commander Dodge climbed a couple of rungs up the conning tower ladder so he could see and be seen by his sailors. "Men," he began earnestly. "I'm proud of all of you. We're not going to stay down here and die like rats. We're going to wage this battle on the surface, and if we die, we die fighting, like Americans. Bring her up, Lieutenant Frost."

"Aye, aye, sir," said the diving officer, and ordered the ballast tanks to be blown. There was the sound of air trying to push tons of seawater out of the tanks to give the boat positive buoyancy, but the sound was fainter than anyone remembered hearing it. Would the old girl be able to make it? Everyone's eyes focused on the depth meter, using all their combined willpower to force her to the surface. The electric motors, nearly completely drained of their energy, strained weakly to push *Seal* upward. At a depth of a hundred feet, *Seal* seemed to hang, unable to make the last few fathoms to the life-giving air above, ready to slip back down in a death dive. Then, without warning, she gave one last lunge, and the periscope broke through the waves, followed by the bridge and the conning tower.

"Open the main induction!" commanded Dodge. There was the re-assuring metallic *clank* of the main air-induction valve slamming open, drawing oxygen into the diesel engines. "The huge engines pulled a vac-uum in the boat that felt like it would suck your guts out through your nose," Smitty said.

"Start number one," Greenup called out, and the diesels cranked and turned over with their familiar roar, followed by a forward lurching mo-tion.

Dodge scrambled up the ladder, cracked open the hatch, and a blast of cool, fresh air, along with a small torrent of cold seawater, rushed into the superheated interior, instantly turning the atmosphere inside the con-trol room into a fog so thick that it was impossible to see. But no one needed to see, for every man was sprinting up the ladder behind his com-mander, spilling out onto the deck, running for their guns, eager to hurt the enemy before they died.

Smitty slipped and slid across the wet deck as he dashed for his twenty-millimeter aft of the conning tower. He opened the ammo locker and began retrieving shells as fast as he could, feeding them to the gun-ner. Any second now Japanese shells would rake *Seal*, for the destroyers had been there all day, licking their collective chops, just waiting for *Seal* to surface.

The three-inch gun swung on its mount, the gunners looking for targets. The same for the twenties. Fingers tensed around triggers. It was now or never.

There was only one problem.

The seven Japanese destroyers were gone.

The men scanned this way and that, straining to force their eyes to find targets in the dark. But there was nothing, no one, not a sign of any-thing. The sea around them was black, vacant, empty.

The crew was happily perplexed. Perhaps the enemy had run out of depth charges and depth bombs. Perhaps they had concluded that *Seal* was lying dead on the bottom of the ocean. Or perhaps they had just gotten bored and gone home. For whatever reasons, the Japanese had vanished, leaving *Seal* totally and miraculously alone beneath the stars.

Everyone was silent as they secured from battle stations, cleared the decks, and returned to the sub's interior. They felt they had just experienced something that was beyond words, beyond comprehension.

SEAL, battered, bruised, and dented, limped back to Midway. Seal's radioman received messages from ComSubPac, inquiring as to her condition, but could not send an acknowledgment; in the wake of silence ComSubPac assumed that Seal was lost, and when she appeared as if by magic at Midway on 20 July 1943, there was great joy and relief.

A team of experts went over the sub from stem to stern, compared notes, and shook their heads; the damage was more extensive than their limited facilities could handle. Seal would need to go back to Pearl for further evaluation; if Pearl couldn't handle it, then a trip to Mare Island would be in order. No one on Seal was terribly upset about having to take some time off from the war; there actually had been some grumblings about a mutiny if Seal had been ordered to return to sea again without a break.

The trip back to Pearl was a rough one. Something was seriously wrong with Seal; when underwater, she swam erratically, listing heavily to port and then to starboard and back to port again. She would unexpectedly plunge like a whale and then broach like a runaway porpoise, requiring all the strength of the bow and stern planesmen to restrain her. She definitely could not return to combat until her condition was corrected.

A band was on the dock playing patriotic marches as Seal limped into her berth at Pearl on 24 July. As with every returning sub, there was an official greeting, then the men showered; slipped into their white uniforms that they had kept pressed beneath the springs and plastic-covered mattresses of the bunks; were subjected to a cursory physical; were given their fill of fresh fruit; received their pay—their regular pay plus 50 percent submarine pay and an additional 10 percent overseas pay—and were told that they had rooms waiting for them at the Royal Hawaiian Hotel, a plush hostelry on Waikiki Beach leased from the Matson Company by the Navy for the war's duration. There was enough space at the hotel to accommodate 150 officers and a thousand enlisted men at a time.[1]

Once they received their passes, Smitty and Big Wop Bonino piled into a taxi parked outside the gates of the base, just past Hickam Field, and told the driver to take them into Honolulu.

Smitty and Bonino could hardly believe it—the taxi ride into town seemed like a dream. Here they were, actually in Hawaii—not on another endless patrol on an endless sea inside a stifling, stuffy, stench-filled submarine. Flower-and-pineapple-scented air flowed in through the taxi's open windows. Outside, lines of palm trees in neat rows rushed past. They saw no bombed-out buildings like the ones on Midway. No one was trying to kill them. Everything was neat, clean, civilized. Free of the constant tension and worry, they could finally relax, kick back, have a beer or twelve (not that Green River crap), watch the sun set, and live the good life for a week or two, maybe more, depending on how long the repairs took. Smitty looked at Bonino and they both grinned as if they were sharing the same thoughts, the same wonderful vision.

Passing a uniform store, the pair told the driver to stop and drop them off. They went in and bought several sets of whites; after all, they couldn't very well be seen in Honolulu in their uniforms that looked and smelled like moldy dishrags. Smitty had the tailor sew on his third-class rate with the dolphins on the lower right sleeve. They waited an hour for the uniforms to be tailored to their slim builds, had the new duds pressed and wrapped in brown paper, then grabbed another taxi to the hotel.

The elegance of the Royal Hawaiian took Smitty's breath away as he and Bonino stepped out of the cab. There it was, the famous "Pink Palace of the Pacific" in all her outlandish coral-pink-stucco glory. Smitty thought only Chicago's Edgewater Beach Hotel approached the grandness of the Royal Hawaiian. Built in the Moorish style and ringed by tall, stately coconut palms, Oahu's 500-room beachfront edifice had been a favorite of millionaires and movie stars ever since it opened in 1927. And now it was the rest and recuperation center for the exclusive use of weary U.S. Navy submariners. Only the sandbagged foxholes and armed guards and barbed wire along the beach in front gave any hint that there was a war on.

Then they saw it.

There, walking across the street from the hotel, the sailors caught sight of something they hadn't seen for months. In fact, it was something that they had almost totally forgotten existed.

It was . . . a *woman*!

Smitty and Big Wop were frozen in their tracks, staring in disbelief at this curvaceous creature in lipstick and high heels. They could almost smell her perfumed hair from where they stood. "And she wasn't even pretty," Smitty admitted. All of a sudden the primordial male sexual urge, suppressed for so long, came rushing at them like an enemy destroyer.

But first, before they could get that urge satisfied, they had to clean up their act. The Shore Patrol didn't take kindly to sailors in rumpled clothing looking as if they had just fallen off the boat. Checking into the hotel, the pair rushed up to their room, showered, shaved, and donned the best-looking of their new uniforms. Then it was off to the notorious Hotel Street red-light district. But the lines of horny sailors outside each establishment were long, and so Bonino guided his younger companion to a more discreet house he had frequented on earlier visits to Honolulu. There Smitty's horns were expertly removed by a small Portuguese woman.

Navy nurses pose with surfboard on Waikiki Beach in front of the Royal Hawaiian Hotel.
(Courtesy National Archives)

THE Navy-Yard engineer just clucked and shook his head. He had never seen anything quite like it. Several of the two-inch-thick brass vents on the tops of the saddle tanks had hairline cracks nearly invisible to the naked eye. Each vent had two hydraulic arms that opened and closed them, and the cracks had been just enough to cause the vent doors to bind because of the unequal pressure on the hinge pins. That was the reason why *Seal* had behaved so erratically when she dove during the trip back to Pearl. "Must have taken one hell of a force to crack that brass," the engineer said to Lieutenant Jack Frost. "Probably take two weeks to replace 'em. And fix all the other stuff that's broken." Frost told him to get busy; *Seal* needed to get back out to sea as soon as possible.

While the repair team went to work, *Seal*'s sailors continued to relax. Interspersed with drinking and whoring and just lying on Waikiki Beach to darken their pale skins, the sailors drank, whored, and lay around on Waikiki Beach.

One day, while downing another cold beer and soaking up the rays, Smitty said to Big Wop and Big Ski stretched out beside him, "This is the life. Big Wop, I could get used to this."

"Well, don't get *too* used to it, Smitty," Bonino said. "I have a hunch we're going to be back at sea very soon. And, Smitty, would you do me a favor?"

"Sure, Wop, anything."

"How about not calling me 'Big Wop' anymore? My name's Rick."

Smitty was taken aback. He hadn't realized that he had been insulting Bonino all these many months. "Sure, sure. I'm sorry. I didn't mean to offend you. It's just that . . ."

"It's okay. Forget it."

"Sure, Wo . . . I mean, Rick." Smitty felt terrible.

THE repair work was finished quickly and Dodge was ready to put *Seal* through her paces. Seven or eight new men reported for duty to replace the seven or eight veterans who had been transferred to other boats or sent stateside to become instructors at the submarine schools.

Many combat veterans have talked about the fact that, at some point, they have heard a small voice in their heads telling them that their "number is up," that the next bullet, bomb, or shell "has their name on it," that they are not going to survive the war. Smitty recalled something similar—a fatalistic sense that he would not live to see the peace. He said, "The general feeling was that the war was probably going to last another five years or so. In 1943, we were losing one submarine out of three. It didn't take a rocket scientist to do the math—in less than five years, you're probably going to die. So we in the Submarine Service just sort of accepted our fate. It wasn't a death wish at all; we just accepted the fact that we probably were not going to live through this thing—and we didn't give a shit. Maybe it was kind of a callous attitude, but so what? You couldn't do anything about it, anyway."

ONCE the sea trials were complete and *Seal* was certified fit enough to return to battle, Smitty was told to report to the skipper in the ward room. Lieutenant Hanes and Lieutenant Commander Greenup were also there. It looked like a "captain's mast"—akin to a court-martial. Smitty wondered what he had done wrong.

"At ease, Smith," Dodge said. "Lieutenant Hanes said that you might be interested in attending the Naval Academy."

"Yes, sir," said Smitty, breathing a sign of relief. On the return trip from the last patrol, he and Hanes *had* discussed the possibility. The nerve-racking patrols had started to get to him, and he was hoping to find some way to get off *Seal* without being branded a coward. Because of Smitty's high boot-camp test scores, Hanes thought he might make an ideal Academy candidate.

"Much as I hate to lose you," Dodge continued, "in talking with Greenup and Hanes, we all agree that you have the makings of an officer. So we're transferring you to the relief crew here at Pearl so you can enroll in the prep school and try for the Academy."

Smitty was dumbfounded. Sure, he had talked with Hanes, and Hanes had promised to pull some strings, but he never really believed that the lieutenant would actually follow through. For the first time Smitty felt that the officers knew who he was, that he wasn't just some anonymous face in the crowd of sailors on board *Seal*.

Still stunned, Smitty shook hands with the three officers and wandered back to his locker in a sort of happy daze, already picturing himself as one of *them*. He began removing his belongings from the tiny locker and stuffing them into his bag. Big Ski and Woody came by and stopped.

"What the hell you doin'?" asked Ski.

"I'm leaving. Getting off. Transferred." Smitty sensed that the other two already knew, for they just grinned. Leaving *Seal* was hard. He had learned to like most of the men. A few of them were as close to him as his brother Bob. He would have died for them. But leaving *Seal* meant that he would live. He felt a pang of guilt and shook hands with his two mates and wondered if they would make it through the war. He wondered if he would ever see them again.

Struggling with a surge of mixed feelings, he slung his bag over his shoulder, climbed the ladder to the conning-tower hatch, saluted the colors at the stern, and walked briskly across the gangway that connected *Seal* with Hawaii. He tried not to look back, for he wasn't sure that he could keep his emotions in check.

The next day, however, he returned to watch *Seal*, full of his friends, pull away from the dock and head for the open sea. It was 15 August 1943 and *Seal* was off on her eighth war patrol. A large lump filled Smitty's throat and he could feel moisture building up in his eyes.

"Godspeed," he whispered to *Seal* as she hove out of sight.

A sailor without a ship, Smitty was temporarily assigned to the base torpedo shop, under a man named Deason, an old Chief Torpedoman who was in charge of all torpedo maintenance, overhaul, storage, and loading for the base. Deason assigned him to the main engine shop, where he worked with a number of other sailors for several days until a lieutenant came looking for him.

"Smith, John R.?" the lieutenant called out.

Smitty raised a grease-covered hand, put down his tools, and walked over to the officer.

"Yes, sir?"

"Smith, I've got some good news and some bad news for you," the lieutenant said.

"Sir?"

"Standing orders from ComSubPac. The bad news is a qualified submariner like you can't stay in the relief crew. The good news is that Captain Blair, the division commander, has picked you to work for him. I'm on his staff and he sent me down to find you."

"What are my duties, sir?"

"You're going to be his personal driver, aide, 'gofer,' bodyguard, whatever."

"What about the prep school for Annapolis, sir?"

"Don't worry—Captain Blair will take care of that."[2]

THE problems with the Mark XIV's magnetic exploder would not go away; Admiral Lockwood had had enough. Late in 1943, he ordered the exploders deactivated—an order that angered "Mr. Torpedo," Admiral Christie. As submariner Robert Beynon writes, "The underlying problem of the controversy was that Admiral Christie had been the principal architect of the Mark VI exploder. He believed so strongly in its efficiency and reliability that the complaining submarine captain was 'put to blame.' Any skipper who was too adamant in his criticism was put ashore, soundly admonished and relieved of command . . .

"Admiral Christie was a strong-willed individual who believed in his torpedo. In fact, his position was so immovable that Admiral Lockwood, Christie's superior, had to step in and order the magnetic exploder deactivated. This order enraged Christie to the point of not obeying Lockwood's directive. The dispute continued with boats under Christie's command using the activated exploder and boats operating out of Pearl Harbor using deactivated exploders. The issue was finally settled by Admiral [Thomas C.] Kinkaid [head of the Seventh Fleet]. The exploder was 'deep-sixed,' not to be used."[3]

Lockwood noted that the Mark XIV steam torpedo's upgrade, the Mark XVIII electric, was also problem plagued and was giving his men fits. He called the Mark XVIII "a man-killer at sea," but refused to become downhearted. Believing that, with time, his men could overcome the problems, he temporarily suspended issuing electric torpedoes to submarines heading out on patrol while his experts looked into fixing the fish. He and his men badly wanted the electric torpedo because it left no telltale wake and made it virtually impossible for the targets to know from which direction the torpedo had come.[4]

THE torpedo controversy no longer concerned Smitty, who was out of submarines and leading a soft new life, free from danger. As the captain's chauffeur, he had a great deal of freedom and a life of relative luxury. He slept in an airy barracks with soft, fragrant tropical breezes wafting through the open windows. He wore a clean uniform every day and could shower as many times as he wanted. He read the daily newspaper and listened to the radio. He ate well in the mess hall and drank to excess at the beer hall.

His duties consisted of driving Captain Blair from his spacious home in Aiea to his headquarters at the Pearl Harbor base administration building and back again. Most of Smitty's day was spent waiting to take Blair to wherever he wanted to go. For a half hour or so he would stand in the shade of a palm tree and wipe the dust off the captain's car, a Chevrolet station wagon painted an un-Navy shade of maroon. When that difficult job was done, he would smoke and chat with the other enlisted men who were also detailed as drivers for other senior officers.

If Blair didn't need him for a few hours, Smitty would spend a warm, sun-soaked afternoon at the beach or at the beer garden on the submarine base, getting soused. "The beer was good, cold, and cheap," he recalled, "only ten cents for a quart bottle." It was a pleasant way to pass the day.

At other times, Smitty would drive back to Blair's quarters, where he and Aguan, the Guamanian mess boy who had once served as a mess boy aboard the *Seal*, would hang out, gorging themselves on food from the captain's plentiful pantry and guzzling the captain's private stock of hard liquor.

Smitty, on occasion, found himself the object of affection of young female officers—Navy nurses—who might have had a little too much to drink at parties at the captain's home and who made passes at the handsome sailor when he drove them back to their quarters. Realizing that fraternizing with female officers could get him tossed into the brig, Smitty wisely steered clear of them. To take care of his sexual needs, he would on occasion drive into Honolulu during the day, spend an hour or two romancing the painted ladies, then head back to the headquarters in time to pick up the captain and take him home. "It was a tough life, but somebody had to do it," Smitty said, laughing. Smitty had become a "feather merchant"—the Navy's derisive term for anyone who pulled noncombat duty in the safety of a rear area.[5]

Although Smitty was no longer an active participant in it, the war continued on its inexorable path. Glum news floated around the beer garden—both *Cisco* and *Pompano* were declared lost and were stricken from the rolls of active Navy vessels.* The submarine sailors at the beer garden raised their glasses solemnly and toasted the memory of those who had gone down with their boats, wondering if and when *their* turn would come.

---

* *Cisco* was last heard from in mid-September 1943, having apparently gone down in the Sulu Sea; *Pompano* was reported lost on 3 September after patrolling near Honshu. It is assumed that she fell victim to mines in the area. (Blair, 433, 474; www.history.navy.mil/faqs/faq82-1)

CHAPTER 13

THE ROAD TO TOKYO

In late November 1943, the scuttlebutt at the beer garden hit Smitty like a depth charge: *Sculpin* had been sunk.* His friend Bill Partin, whose wedding he had attended in San Diego, was a crewman aboard *Sculpin*. Smitty also heard that a number of men supposedly had survived and had been picked up by the Japanese; he waited anxiously to hear if Bill was among them.

The good times he had spent with Bill at San Diego came back to him. Smitty recalled the night when Partin had fallen out of the upper berth of the train from Dago to Mare while trying to get a peek at Caddes having sex with that girl he had picked up in the bar car.

Smitty remembered all the goofy, practical jokes Bill had played on him and the others, his quick wit, and his seriousness when he buckled down to study. He pictured Bill sitting across from him at the Pearl beer hall just a few weeks earlier, a thick, black beard covering his young face, showing Smitty a photo of his newborn son, all the while laughing and joking and acting like the war was a big lark, just before *Sculpin* sailed for the last time.

He couldn't get the two images out of his head: that of Bill and Mary on the evening of their wedding in the Destroyer Base chapel, and how happy each of them looked that night, and the other image—the photo

---

* It was later reported that the Japanese destroyer *Yamagumo* sank *Sculpin* off Truk on 19 November 1944. (www.history.navy.mil/faqs/faq82-1)

of the baby who would grow up never knowing his father. And now Bill was missing at sea. Smitty wondered how Mary got the news, and how she was taking it. He thought maybe he should write to her, but he didn't have her address. And he didn't know what he would say, what he *could* say, that would make the pain any less. *It must be awfully hard on everyone who finds out that something has happened to their son or husband,* he thought. *If you get killed, then you don't have any more worries. But it's your survivors who suffer.*[1]

THE loss of *Sculpin* was one of the most dramatic chapters of the war in the Pacific, and any account of heroism among submariners would be incomplete without recounting the death of that boat, half her crew, and the self-sacrifice of Captain John Philip Cromwell, commander of a Submarine Coordinated Attack Group, who went down with the *Sculpin* during Operation Galvanic, the invasion of Tarawa and Makin Islands in the Gilberts.

Cromwell, born in 1901, graduated from the U.S. Naval Academy in 1924 and served on the battleship U.S.S. *Maryland* before serving in several submarines between the world wars. At the beginning of the war, he was on the staff of ComSubPac, where he was in charge of Submarine Divisions 44 and 203. He was later assigned the additional command of Submarine Division 43.

In November 1943, after its successful conclusion of the Solomons campaign, the United States prepared to invade Bougainville, Tarawa, and the Makin Islands. A group of submarines* took up station in the Marshalls and Gilberts to counter any Japanese moves to interfere with the operations. Cromwell was a part of the Tarawa operation and he made the *Sculpin*—on its ninth patrol and commanded by Fred Connaway on his first—his flagship.

Historian Edward C. Whitman notes, "Captain Cromwell possessed secret intelligence information of our submarine strategy and tactics,

---

* These were the U.S.S. *Apogon* (SS-308), *Blackfish* (SS-221), *Corvina* (SS-226), *Drum*, *Nautilus*, *Paddle* (SS-263), *Plunger*, *Sculpin*, *Seal*, *Searaven*, *Skate* (SS-305), *Spearfish*, and *Thresher*. The *Corvina*, captained by Roderick Rooney, was lost during this operation, sunk off Truk by the Japanese sub *I-176*. (Blair, 490–497)

scheduled Fleet movements, and specific attack plans . . . As a senior officer, Cromwell was completely familiar with the plans for Operation Galvanic and knew a lot more about Ultra*—and its source—than anyone else on *Sculpin*."[2]

Sculpin arrived on station east of Truk on 16 November. Two nights later *Sculpin*'s radar picked up a large Japanese convoy steaming at high speed towfard Truk. Connaway submerged for a dawn attack, but his periscope was spotted by the enemy, who drove the *Sculpin* deep; by the time the sub resurfaced, the convoy was gone. An enemy destroyer, the *Yamagumo*, lagging behind, pounced on *Sculpin,* forcing Connaway to again dive and remain below for several hours. During the fearsome depth-charge attack, the sub's depth gauge was broken; when she attempted to come to periscope depth, the diving officer, mistakenly thinking she was still 125 feet below the surface, brought her completely up, where she became a target for the lurking destroyer. More depth charges followed, which distorted the hull, sprang a number of severe leaks, and badly damaged *Sculpin*'s steering and diving-plane gear.

Unable to control the boat below the waves, Connaway decided that his only hope was to surface and shoot it out with the *Yamagumo*. It was a brave but foolhardy decision, for the submarine's puny deck gun proved to be no match for the enemy's heavier and more abundant armament. The destroyer's first salvo blew apart the *Sculpin*'s bridge and conning tower, killing Connaway, his executive and gunnery officers, and the watch team; the deck-gun crew was also wiped out in the exchange of fire. With *Sculpin* in imminent danger of sinking, Lieutenant G. E. Brown, a reserve lieutenant and now the officer in charge of the boat, ordered her to be scuttled and abandoned.

Whitman notes, "This action left Captain Cromwell facing a fateful choice. With his personal knowledge of both Ultra and Galvanic, he realized immediately that to abandon ship and become a prisoner of the

---

* *Ultra* was the general term used to describe the intelligence derived from the interception and decoding of Japanese and German messages.

Captain John P. Cromwell chose to die aboard *Sculpin* rather than risk capture.
(Courtesy Naval Historical Center)

Japanese would create a serious danger of compromising these vital secrets . . . under the influence of drugs or torture. For this reason, he refused to leave the stricken submarine." His last words to Lieutenant Brown were "I can't go with you; I know too much."

Whitman said, "Cromwell and eleven others [including Bill Partin] rode *Sculpin* on her final plunge to the bottom, where her secrets would be safe forever." Ensign W. M. Fielder, the diving officer whose actions had led to the *Sculpin*'s erroneous surfacing, was one of those who chose death over capture.[3]

Lieutenant Brown, two other officers, and thirty-nine enlisted men were picked up by the Japanese; one badly wounded crewman was thrown overboard by his rescuers and drowned. To heap even more tragedy upon the situation, the aircraft carrier *Chuyo,* transporting half of the *Sculpin* survivors, was torpedoed and sunk by the submarine *Sailfish* on 4 December 1943; only one American from this group was rescued.* In all, twenty-one survivors from *Sculpin* finally made it to a prison camp, where they remained for the rest of the war.

When Admiral Lockwood learned after the war from *Sculpin*'s survivors about Cromwell's selfless action, he recommended the captain for the Medal of Honor, the nation's highest military award for valor. Congress concurred and Cromwell's widow was presented with the medal after the war.[4]

---

* In probably the Pacific Theater's ultimate irony, in 1939 it was *Sculpin* that had assisted in the raising of the sunk *Squalus*—which was renamed *Sailfish.*

* * *

IT took a few weeks before the list of prisoners who survived *Sculpin*'s sinking was received and promulgated at Pearl. Bill Partin's name was not on the list.

The not-unexpected news hit Smitty with unexpected force—almost as much as the death of his mother. At least with his mother, her long illness had braced him and the rest of the family for the inevitability of her passing; and while submariners knew that they could die at any moment while at sea, the reality of Bill's death—the *finality* of it—struck home with a staggering blow. *He's so young,* Smitty thought, *maybe only a year older than me. How could this have happened?* Smitty found a private place and shed a tear for his lost friend—and for everyone who had thus far made the ultimate sacrifice.

Once he had pulled himself together, Smitty went to Captain Blair and confided to him about the loss of *Sculpin* and Bill's death. Blair seemed callous and unconcerned. "War is hell, son," is all the senior officer said, then went back to reading a report. At that moment Smitty had to restrain himself from leaping over the captain's desk and attacking him. "Don't you give a shit?" Smitty wanted to scream. "Don't you care that people like Bill Partin are dying in this goddamn war while your fat ass is nice and safe here in your goddamn leather-covered chair?"

While he was attempting to rein in his emotions, it suddenly became obvious to Smitty that he could no longer continue living the soft, safe life at Pearl while his friends were putting their lives on the line every minute of every day. *What makes me think I'm so special that I get to sit out the war like Blair in beautiful Hawaii?* he asked himself. *I joined the Navy so I could fight the Japs, so what the hell am I doing here,* not *fighting the Japs?*

A great surge of anger was welling up in him—an anger at Blair's uncaring response, an anger at himself for taking the easy way out, and an even more white-hot anger at the Japanese who had caused the war and caused Bill's death. "You can't do that to my buddy," a voice in his throbbing head wanted to yell out loud enough that it would be heard across the ocean, all the way to Tokyo. "It has nothing to do with patriotism or flag-waving or being a loyal American or wanting to win a medal. It has to do with loyalty to my buddy. Well, listen up, Tojo. I'm coming back and I'm going to kill every last one of you sons of bitches, even if I have to die in the process!"

Stiffening to attention, Smitty said to the unconcerned captain, "Sir, I request that my pending appointment to the Naval Academy Prep School be withdrawn. I'd like to go back to submarines."

Blair didn't even look up. "Request granted," he said, almost as though he had been expecting this for a long time. Then he verbally slapped Smitty with the remark, "I'm not sure you're officer material, anyhow, Smith."

Smitty saluted briskly, performed a perfect about-face, and marched out of the office. He was certain that, had the captain looked up, he could have seen smoke coming out his ears.[5]

OPERATION Galvanic—the invasion of Tarawa Atoll, consisting of thirty-eight small islands, principally Betio and Makin—began the day after *Sculpin*'s sinking—20 November 1943. Because of his superb performance during the fight for Midway a year and a half earlier, Nimitz installed Rear Admiral Raymond A. Spruance to command Galvanic.

Tarawa was another of the many Pacific land battles that brought new meaning to the word *savagery*. Ever since the fall of Guadalcanal, Imperial Japanese Marines and Korean slave laborers under the island's principal commander, Rear Admiral Keiji Shibasaki, had been engaged in building an airfield on Betio and fortifying the atolls in anticipation of an American attack. And now that time had come. Emplacing four of the heavy coastal artillery pieces captured from the British at Singapore, Shibasaki planned to blow any invasion fleet out of the water, boasting that "a million men could not take Tarawa in a hundred years."

The actual landings on Makin Island were relatively easy. Six thousand Marines came ashore, opposed by 300 Japanese troops and 500 Korean workers who had been forced at gunpoint to fight. During the brief engagement, all of Makin's defending soldiers were wiped out, plus half of the Koreans; the rest surrendered. Sixty-four Americans died.[6]

But Betio proved to be a tougher nut to crack. Following a three-hour saturation bombardment by three battleships, five cruisers, and

Marines battle for Tarawa.
(Courtesy National Archives)

nine destroyers in the early morning hours of 20 November, the 2nd Marine Division was ready to come ashore on Betio's lagoon side. A greeting party of some 4,800 battle-hardened Imperial Japanese Navy Marines, augmented by 2,300 armed Korean and Japanese laborers, was lying in wait for them. The laborers had done a masterful job of turning Betio into a deadly fortress made of reinforced concrete pillboxes covered with coconut logs, from which the defenders could pour an intense concentration of artillery, mortar, and machine-gun fire at the invaders.

Compounding the difficulties was the fact that someone on the American side had screwed up royally and gotten the tides wrong. The six transports, crammed to the gunwales with Marines, were sitting ducks for the Japanese shore batteries. As if that weren't enough, the naval bombardment ended early and the carrier pilots were late. "The thirty-minute airstrike," Manchester says, "lasted seven." When at last the Marines climbed down into the Higgins boats—plywood landing craft whose flat steel bows could be dropped to let the troops out into shallow water—they got hung up on the coral reef at low tide, forcing the troops to wade in for over a mile, where they were raked by enfilading fire.

With nowhere to take cover, the wading Marines, trudging toward shore as if in the slow motion of a bad dream, were easy targets for the Japanese gunners. Although the first wave of Americans was nearly totally destroyed, more Marines came on, delivered into the killing zone by Higgins boats and "amphtracs"—armored amphibious vehicles that held twenty men. Somehow, they got to the beach.

William Manchester observes, "The Marine dead became part of the terrain; they altered tactics; they provided defilade, and when they had died on barbed-wire obstacles, live men could avoid the wire by crawling over them. Even so, the living were always in some Jap's sights . . . As the day wore on, the water offshore was a grotesque mass of severed heads, limbs, and torsos."

Men were paralyzed by the sight of so much death and destruction, and by the wholesale slaughter of their officers and noncoms. Movement forward seemed as impossible as leaping up and touching the moon. Somehow, someway, though, small bunches of frightened men summoned up courage they did not know they possessed, said "Let's go" to their equally frightened buddies lying next to them, and crawled across the blood-soaked sand to engage the entrenched enemy with rifles, pistols, grenades, flamethrowers, bayonets, knives, bare hands.

The enemy fought with unbelievable tenacity, a characteristic that prompted Manchester to write, "At the time it was impolitic to pay the slightest tribute to the enemy, and Nip determination, their refusal to say die, was commonly attributed to 'fanaticism.' In retrospect it is indistinguishable from heroism. To call it anything less cheapens the victory, for American valor was necessary to defeat it."[7]

The battle offshore was equally savage. The carrier *Liscome Bay* was torpedoed by a Japanese submarine and 644 sailors died.[8]

It didn't take a million men a hundred years to overcome the nightmare of Tarawa. It did, however, take 35,000 American fighting men three days to utterly wipe out the defenders; only seventeen Japanese or

Koreans were taken prisoner. Shibasaki and his staff committed suicide. Fifteen hundred Americans died during the battle. It was a terrible toll compressed into just seventy-two hours. But America was another island group closer to Japan—and victory.[9]

LOCKWOOD's submarines had done a creditable job during November. Although the bugs in the Mark XVIII electric torpedoes had yet to be worked out, the crews were doing yeoman's service with the revamped Mark XIVs. During the month, three enemy warships and forty-eight merchant vessels—displacing a total of 232,333 tons—went to the bottom, sent there by American subs.[10]

SEAL's ninth war patrol turned out to be an easy reconnaissance mission to the Marshall Islands in preparation for the upcoming Operation Flintlock—the offensive against the Marshalls and Truk Island. Between 17 November and 15 December, Seal scouted the proposed invasion beaches and photographed through her periscope the visible Japanese defenses on fifty-six of the ninety-six islands that make up the chain. After refit at Midway, Seal proceeded to Pearl for dry-docking to replace a malfunctioning screw.

Smitty went down to the Ten-Ten Dock a week before Christmas 1943 to greet his shipmates as Seal returned from her patrol with no new additions to her battle flag. Approaching Chief Weist as he was coming off the boat, Smitty said, "How'd it go, Chief?"

"Don't ask, Smitty," Weist said. "A big fat zero. We made one torpedo attack but didn't hit anything. And later, when we made a routine dive, some asshole left the conning-tower hatch open. Nobody checked the Christmas tree, otherwise they'da seen the red light. Water poured in and shorted out most of the electrical equipment, including the air compressors, the air-conditioning motors, the gyrocompass, the pumps, the blowers, you name it. We had to repair the compressors at sea using a jury-rigged system just so's we could operate the boat and fire the torpedoes."

"Chief, I want back on Seal," Smitty blurted out.

Weist gave him a wry smile. "What's the matter—shore duty too rough for you?"

"Yeah, sitting on my ass all day, getting drunk and getting laid, has worn me out."

"Well, I think maybe I can get you back on *Seal*. Your replacement turned out to be a screwup, anyway. I'll talk to the old man and see what I can do."

"Thanks, Chief."

Weist was as good as his word. Following her refit, *Seal* was ready once more for combat and, with Smitty back on board in the aft torpedo room, sailed on her tenth war patrol on 17 January 1944. Her mission this time was twofold: to gather information about conditions in the Ponape Island area of the Marianas, near Guam, Wake, Saipan, and Tinian, or about 1,000 miles south of Japan, and to act as a lifeguard and pick up any aircrew members who might be shot down during Operation Flintlock.[11]

As 1943 came to a close, American air forces began making concerted attacks on the enemy's strongly defended air and naval bases at Rabaul. Although the Japanese were prepared to make another fight to the death, the Americans decided merely to isolate Rabaul and let it "wither on the vine." In December, too, American Army and Marine units launched the invasion of Cape Gloucester, New Britain, with the purpose of taking airfields away from the enemy; so difficult was the terrain, climate, and enemy resistance, though, the job would not be finished until April.

Nineteen forty-four in the Pacific began much like 1943 had ended—with steady American gains in territory paid for by steadily rising American losses in men and matériel.

Sixteen American submarines had been lost during 1943—up from just a half dozen the previous year—but Lockwood's force had reported sinking 422 enemy vessels during that twelve-month period.*

The United States was gearing up to push deeper into Japanese-held territory. On New Year's Day 1944, aircraft from Rear Admiral Frederick C. "Ted" Sherman's carrier task group bombed a Japanese convoy escorted by cruisers and destroyers off Kavieng, New Ireland; the next

---

* Downgraded to 336.5 ships after a postwar check of Japanese records.

day U.S. Army troops landed at Saidor, New Guinea. On 8 January, Task Force 38, under Rear Admiral Walden L. "Pug" Ainsworth, bombarded Japanese shore installations on Faisi, Poporand, and the Shortland Islands in the Solomons. Three days later, Navy aircraft based in the Gilbert and Ellice Islands bombed Japanese shipping and installations at Kwajalein in the Marshalls in preparation for invasion.[12] On 14 January, the Japanese destroyer *Sazanami* was sunk by the submarine U.S.S. *Albacore* in the Central Pacific. The new year was off to a good start for the Americans.[13]

HALF a world away, important developments were also taking place in the moribund Italian campaign. In mid-January, the Allies launched the first of the four attacks it would take to dislodge the Germans from atop Monte Cassino. On the twenty-second, in an attempt to break the stalemate, a combined U.S.-British amphibious force landed at the Anzio-Nettuno coast of Italy in Operation Shingle. It would soon get bogged down and Rome would not be taken for more than four months. Five days after Shingle began, the 880-day German siege of Leningrad was finally broken.[14]

Back in the Pacific, the American submarine force continued to make important contributions to victory. *Tinosa* landed personnel and supplies in northeast Borneo while *Bowfin* laid mines off the southeastern Borneo coast; Smitty's previous boat, *Skipjack,* sank the Japanese destroyer *Suzukaze* in the Carolines.[15]

Following the capture of Makin and Tarawa in the Gilberts, the Americans aimed for the Marshall Islands, 700 miles to the northwest of the Gilberts. Prior to the First World War, the Marshalls had belonged to the Germans; after Germany was stripped of her Pacific colonies following the war, Japan was given the mandate by the treaty makers at Versailles to rule them—hence their other name: the "Eastern Mandates." Now the Americans—Rear Admiral Richmond K. Turner's 5th Amphibious Force and Major General Holland M. "Howlin' Mad" Smith's V Amphibious Corps—under the overall command of Vice Admiral Raymond Spruance, were set to revoke the mandate.

The Japanese had greatly reinforced the Marshalls to make any at-

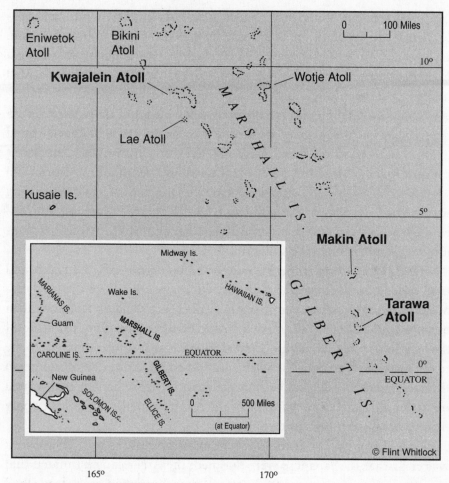

Marshall and Gilbert Islands.

tempt at retaking them expensive for the United States; it would prove to be a waste of effort on the part of the Japanese. Although Admiral Masashi Kobayashi, the regional commander, had 28,000 troops to defend the Marshalls, he had only 110 aircraft there—a shortage that would cost him dearly. On 29 January, American carrier planes attacked the enemy airfield on Roi-Namur, destroying ninety-two enemy aircraft in the opening moves of Operation Flintlock.

Expecting the Americans to attack the outermost islands first, Kobayashi had entrenched most of his defenders on Wotje, Mille, Maloelap, and Jaluit Atolls. The Americans learned of this deployment through Ultra decryptions of Japanese communications, and thus Nimitz decided to bypass these outposts and strike directly at Kwajalein.

Kwajalein Island is less than three miles long and only about half a mile wide. For such a small space it was to be the scene of concentrated death. Learning from their many mistakes at Tarawa, the Americans pulled off the Kwajalein operation with almost textbook precision. On 31 January 1944, with complete mastery of the air and sea, the landing units—the U.S. Army's 7th Infantry Division and the Marines' 4th Marine Division—stormed ashore on Kwajalein and Majro Atolls, swamping the 5,000 enemy troops dug in there.

The landings were superbly supported by carrier-based aircraft and land-based aircraft from the Gilberts. On the north side of the atoll, the Marines captured a number of small islets. The airfield on Roi was taken quickly, and Namur was overwhelmed the next day. Only fifty-one of the original 3,500 Japanese defenders of Roi-Namur survived to be taken prisoner. The worst setback came when a Marine demolition team threw a high-explosive satchel charge into a Japanese bunker that turned out to be full of torpedo warheads. The resulting explosion killed twenty Marines and wounded dozens more.

By 1 February 1944, the second day of operations on Kwajalein, it was clear that the Japanese were doomed; the Americans estimated that almost all of the original 5,000 defenders on Kwajalein were dead. By 3 February, only a handful were left, and it was all over except for the burying of the bloated dead.[16]

MEANWHILE, *Seal's* problematic H.O.R. engines were nearly worn out, and it was time to replace them with new Fairbanks-Morse diesels—an overhaul that would require a trip back to Mare Island.

Although the majority of the crew was excited about a return to the States, Smitty was not. "There really wasn't anything waiting for me back there. Shirley had written to tell me that she was engaged to a sailor, so I had no 'love interest' back home to worry about. Besides, I still hadn't avenged the death of Bill Partin. We hadn't sunk any Jap ships on *Seal*'s last three patrols. I began to think about transferring to some other boat."

One day while downing a cold one at the Pearl Harbor beer garden, Smitty ran into an old buddy, Eugene "Jeep" Peña, the sailor who still bore burn marks on his forearm from the time he had fired a machine gun at the Japanese planes at Tjilatjap before Smitty joined *Seal*'s crew. Peña now wore the insignia of a chief petty officer.

"Hey, Jeep, what're you doing here?" Smitty asked, surprised.

"Just came in with the *Robalo*." Peña then gave Smitty a brief rundown on *Robalo* (SS-273). She was a *Gato*-class boat built at Manitowoc, Wisconsin, and had been floated down the Mississippi to the Gulf of Mexico, then through the Panama Canal and over to Pearl Harbor, where she was put into commission.

"No shit? That's great! And I see you're chief of the boat, too?"

"Yep. I got transferred off *Seal* to join *Robalo*. Hey, what the hell are you doing these days?"

Smitty gave Peña an abbreviated version of his life. The chief then said, "Smitty, I got a real problem. Less than a third of the crew is qualified. I gotta find me some guys who know their shit. Guys like you."

"Yeah? Sounds interesting."

"Our boat has all the latest gadgets," Peña offered. "We got power-operated doors on the tubes now. Even the air-conditioning works! Besides, you'll really like our skipper. He's Admiral Kimmel's son."

"No shit?" Smitty was intrigued. In the official congressional inquiry that followed the Pearl Harbor debacle, Admiral Husband E. Kimmel was blamed for letting the Navy's guard down and allowing the Japanese to raid Pearl Harbor. Surely the bad luck that dogged the admiral wouldn't follow his son.

"Listen, I'll get you torpedoman first class and put you in charge of the after torpedo room. What do you say?"

"Well—okay. You talked me into it."

"C'mon, let's go down to the dock and look her over."

The two submariners finished their beers and strolled over to where *Robalo* was tied up. She looked fresh and new, not war weary like *Seal*. A big "273" was welded onto her conning tower.

The two men crossed the gangway, saluted the colors, and requested permission to come aboard. As he slipped down through the hatch, Smitty's eyes grew big. Brightly polished brass and chrome gleamed everywhere, like burnished gold and silver in a sultan's treasure room. The bulkheads were wood-grained, giving *Robalo* an almost yachtlike appearance. She even smelled new; her decks and bulkheads were not yet permeated with the stench of sailor sweat.

Smitty was amazed that the new generation of *Gato*-class submarines had outclassed the old boats to such a degree. Then Jeep took him to meet the skipper, Lieutenant Commander Manning M. Kimmel, class of 1935.[17]

Although only thirty years of age, Manning Marius Kimmel was already an old salt in submarines. From 1935 to 1938, he had served aboard the battleship *Mississippi,* then attended Submarine School at Groton. His first submarine assignment was aboard the ancient *S-38* before he transferred and helped put *Drum* into commission in early 1942; he served on *Drum* during her first three war patrols. He became part of the precommissioning crew of *Raton* (SS-270) and was her executive officer after her commissioning in July 1943. After two war patrols with *Raton,* Kimmel was given command of *Robalo,* still undergoing construction at the Manitowoc shipyard.[18]

Smitty was impressed with Kimmel and the feeling was apparently mutual; the officer invited Smitty to transfer off *Seal* and join his crew. All that was needed was the approval of the officer for whom Smitty had been the chauffeur.

But, the next day, Blair turned down Kimmel's request, saying that *Seal* had the right of first refusal for Smith's services. If they did not want him back, then Kimmel could

Manning Marius Kimmel, skipper of *Robalo.*
(Courtesy National Archives)

A large crowd watches U.S.S. *Robalo* being launched at the Manitowoc
Shipyard in Manitowoc, Wisconsin, 9 May 1943.
(Courtesy National Archives)

have him. Smitty glared at the captain. "If looks were punishable," he
said, "I would have gotten ten years."

"Sorry, Smith," said Kimmel after they had left Blair's office. "I
would have liked for you to have been part of our crew. Maybe someday."

"Yes, sir. Maybe someday." Smitty saluted and the two men parted.[19]
Neither one could know that, on 26 July 1944, *Robalo,* Manning Kimmel, and fifty-five others on board would die when the boat struck a
mine off Palawan, west of the Philippines. For some unknown but fortunate reason, Jeep Peña would be transferred off *Robalo* before the
sinking. Four men would manage to escape the stricken boat, swim to
shore, and be taken captive by the Japanese. Their fate remains unknown to this day.[20]

* * *

WHILE waiting for *Seal* to leave Pearl for California, Smitty was rousted out of his bunk in the relief-crew barracks by Deason, the chief torpedo-man of the submarine base. The chief said he had a big problem—one of *Salmon*'s torpedoes had been accidentally fired while the boat was moored and the fish was jammed partway out of the tube. Smitty got dressed hurriedly and grabbed his swim trunks.

As they rushed to the dock, Deason went into detail: One of the tor-pedomen had gone into the caboose to show some new men how to fire a torpedo. For some reason the interlocks that keep the torpedo from fir-ing when the outer door is closed were unlocked. "We're not sure how it happened," Deason said, "but the damn thing fired—rammed the tor-pedo right through the outer door and wedged itself between the outer door and the superstructure door. It's a real mess. Fortunately the fish didn't arm itself."

"That's a relief."

"We're moving a barge into place for you so you can work on her."

"Why me?"

" 'Cause you're qualified on *Seal*. She's a sister ship to *Salmon,* same identical boat, same class."

Smitty couldn't disagree with Deason's logic. "Okay, but I'll need some help."

"You name it."

"How about Ferry and Lewis? They're on the relief crew, too, and they're qualified torpedomen."

"I'll get them right now," Deason said, peeling off and heading back to the barracks while Smitty continued on to *Salmon*. She was down a little at the stern, and a raftlike barge with floodlights was lashed to her. A number of sailors were milling around the scene.

Smitty surveyed the situation, then slid down the hull to the raft. Slipping a waterproof flashlight into his belt, he removed his shirt and shoes and dove into the water, swimming up into the space between the hull and the plates that made up the outer superstructure. Holding his breath, he clicked on his light and ducked beneath the water. What he saw didn't look good. The big warhead was protruding halfway out of the heavy brass, partially opened torpedo tube door and wedged up against the door built into the superstructure; the warhead had a couple of good-size dents in it. The exploder mechanism looked okay, but Smitty couldn't tell if there was any additional damage to the warhead.

Smitty surfaced and pulled himself up onto the small barge. Warren Lewis and Jack Ferry were there by then. He told them what he had seen and got everyone's opinion as to how best to solve the problem. Working in a very tight space, they would first have to turn the torpedo enough to be able to get at the exploder and remove it. Assuming they could do that, they next had to remove all the bolts to detach the 600-pound warhead from the air flask. Finally, the warhead would have to be lifted out with a crane.

"Okay, let's get to work," Smitty said, and his two helpers jumped into the water to begin the process. Somehow, the three of them managed to turn the 3,000-pound torpedo enough to give them access to the exploder. Deason had chased all nonessential personnel from the area—not because there was any danger of the warhead detonating, but the air flask, with its charge of high-pressure air at 2,000 pounds per square inch, certainly could. It took all night with the men working with the care of brain surgeons to remove the exploder.

The next day the trio took off the bent hinges and bolts from the outer door and removed it; the hinge pin alone weighed nearly 150 pounds. Always there was the danger of one of the heavy parts slipping and crushing somebody's arm or leg, so the men worked with extreme caution, not rushing any aspect of the operation.

After working for seventy-five hours straight, breaking only for sandwiches, Smitty, Ferry, and Lewis finally removed the superstructure door. Attaching it to the big hook dangling by a steel cable from the crane, Smitty gave the signal to haul away, but the 800-pound door lurched outward and then back, straight for him. Only his quick reflexes kept him from being squashed; the door banged against the pressure hull, leaving a deep gouge in the steel.

Finally, the three sailors pushed the half-protruding torpedo back into its tube and their job was done; the rest would have to be repaired in dry dock.

Treating themselves afterward to a few drinks at the beer garden, Smitty, Ferry, and Lewis heard that three submarines—*Wahoo*, *S-44*, and *Dorado*—were overdue.* "Gentlemen, we are certainly in a hazardous business," Smitty said as he lifted his glass in salute to the 212 missing men.

Word was passed that the hospital ship U.S.S. *Mercy* would be arriving at Pearl Harbor that evening loaded with hundreds of Marines wounded in the savage fighting for Tarawa. Smitty went down to the dock where *Mercy* was moored and was struck by the enormity of the casualties—an unending procession of stretchers being carried down the gangways. "The gray Navy Packard ambulances were lined up as far as you could see," Smitty said. "As soon as one was loaded, it took off for the hospital and another one moved up."

At around midnight, a black Packard limousine drove onto the dock next to the hospital ship and out stepped a slim, somber-faced, white-haired officer, Admiral Chester Nimitz, Commander in Chief, Pacific. Smitty recalled, "He went back and forth to each gangway, talking to the wounded men on the stretchers as they were brought down. At one point the admiral was just a few feet in front of me and I could see the moisture in his eyes. I could also feel the respect and admiration the wounded men had for *him*. He was a real human being."

The next day a troopship full of Marines from Kwajalein entered Pearl Harbor and the word was the Marines were willing to trade war souvenirs for cigarettes. Smitty and his friend Lewis bought armloads of cartons, went down to the dock, and began tossing them up to the Marines on the ship. Smitty didn't want any souvenirs; he was just glad to be a "good Samaritan" and provide free smokes. But a grateful Marine threw down what looked like a dirty and stained rolled-up Japanese flag that landed with a thump at Smitty's feet.

---

* *Wahoo* was lost on 11 October 1943 in Soya Strait, Japan; *S-44* was sunk by an escort ship off Paramushiro, Kurile Islands; the Atlantic-based *Dorado* was probably sunk accidentally by U.S. aircraft in the Caribbean Sea. (www.history.navy.mil/faqs/faq82-1)

Smitty unrolled it and out fell a soggy mass of hair and blood. The stench was overwhelming; Smitty kicked the gruesome bundle into the harbor, not wanting to know if it was a pair of bloody Japanese ears, a scalp, or part of a head.

What in God's name are we coming to? he wondered as he walked away in disgust.[21]

DESPITE the improvements in the new submarines, life for men in the Silent Service had not grown easier or less dangerous, and courageous captains and crews were still needed to man the boats. In late June, early July 1944, immediately after the Battle of the Philippine Sea, Admiral Lockwood had formed four multiple-boat "wolfpacks" and sent them into the Luzon Strait, which was teeming with targets. One of the packs, consisting of three submarines—Slade Cutter's *Seahorse* (SS-304), Anton R. Gallaher's *Bang* (SS-385) and the repaired *Growler*,* under

Slade Cutter, skipper of *Seahorse*, and recipient of four Navy Crosses.
(Courtesy National Archives)

Thomas B. Oakley Jr.—enjoyed especially fine hunting. The trio reported a total of six ships sunk and several more damaged; the other three wolfpacks also scored well, sinking twelve ships during the same period.[22]

Midshipman Slade Deville Cutter had won the bitterest rivalry in college sports when his field goal defeated Army, 3–0, in the 1934 Army-Navy game. Once war broke out, Cutter—described by Lockwood as his "pride and joy"—went on to even bigger victories. In command of *Seahorse*, Cutter had already been awarded three Navy

---

* *Growler* would be lost on 8 November 1944 as a result of enemy action in the South China Sea. (www.history.navy.mil/faqs/faq82-1)

Crosses "for extraordinary heroism."

Now, in July 1944, after penetrating heavy and unusually alert
escort screens in enemy-controlled
waters near the Philippines, Cutter
launched a series of torpedo attacks
and sank six enemy ships totaling
37,000 tons, while damaging an
additional ship of 4,000 tons.
Avoiding the enemy's best effort to
depth-charge him into oblivion,
Cutter brought *Seahorse* safely
back to port. For this courageous
patrol, he received his fourth Navy
Cross.

July 1944 was shaping up to be
an excellent month for American

Lawson P. "Red" Ramage (photo taken
in 1967), skipper of *Parche* and
recipient of the Medal of Honor.
(Courtesy Naval Historical Center)

submariners. On the eighteenth, *Guardfish* surfaced inside an immense
convoy in the Luzon Strait—the largest convoy that skipper Norvell G.
"Bub" Ward had ever seen. He radioed Dave Whelchel's *Steelhead* (SS-
280) and Red Ramage in *Parche* (SS-384) and invited them to come over
and share in sinking the flotilla. On 30 July, dodging Japanese planes,
Steelhead and *Parche* moved in for the kill. *Steelhead* fired her ready
tubes then withdrew to reload while *Parche* took up the attack under
cover of darkness.

As Clay Blair describes it, "The next forty-eight minutes were
among the wildest of the submarine war. Ramage cleared the bridge of
all personnel except himself and steamed right into the convoy on the
surface, maneuvering among the ships and firing nineteen torpedoes.
Japanese ships fired back with deck guns and tried to ram. With con-
summate seamanship and coolness under fire, Ramage dodged and
twisted, returning torpedo fire for gun fire . . . The attack mounted on
the convoy by Red Ramage was the talk of the submarine force. In
terms of close-in, furious torpedo shooting, there had never been anything like it."

Whelchel, his tubes now reloaded, came charging back into the fray until enemy fire got too hot and both subs were forced to submerge and withdraw.

For his bold actions during that encounter, redheaded "Red" Ramage earned the Submarine Force's third Medal of Honor.[23]

CHAPTER 14

THE FINEST SUBMARINE COMMANDER

THROUGHOUT 1942, in the landlocked state of Colorado, a twenty-two-year-old married college student by the name of Clayton O. Decker— "Deck" to his friends—had been undergoing a personal crisis. For weeks he had agonized over the biggest decision of his life: Should he drop out of school to join the service and leave his wife, Lucille, and their two-year-old son, Harry, behind? On one hand he knew that he was safe—at least for now—from the long arm of the draft board; the military was calling up only younger, single men. On the other hand, his conscience told him not to be a shirker when his country was in danger and at war.

All during the school year, he had gazed distractedly at his textbooks while trying to study at the Agricultural College of Colorado in Fort Collins, but couldn't concentrate. So many of his friends had already been drafted or had enlisted. What was he doing here in this "ivory tower" campus setting, far from the shells and bullets and falling bombs? Why wasn't he on the front lines with his buddies? Why wasn't he doing something to keep his wife and son and homeland safe? The issue was burning through him like a welder's torch.

At last, after pacing all night, he made up his mind. "I decided to join the Navy," he declared. "I was told that the Navy had the best chow of any of the services, and you took your bed along with you." And, because submariners got extra pay, Deck volunteered for submarines. Lucille would just have to understand.

She didn't, of course. His place was with her and Harry; if he eventually got drafted, well, fine. You couldn't do anything about that. But there was no point in rushing off to a war and perhaps getting himself killed. Then where would she be? The $10,000 government insurance policy would only go so far—maybe a year, or a few months longer. She would be a widow and little Harry would grow up without a father. Was that somehow worth the show of manly bravado that joining the service represented?

They had argued about it, but Clay Decker's mind was made up. In December 1942, he went down to the local recruiting office, signed the papers, passed the physical, and after a tearful farewell with Lucille and baby Harry at the train station, was on his way to boot camp.

Like Ron Smith and every other Navy recruit, Deck found boot camp a living hell, but he endured it, and when he graduated and was assigned to torpedo school at Norfolk, Virginia, he was pleased. Then it was off to three months of submarine training in New London, Connecticut. He knew he would have no problems, like so many others did, with claustrophobia; he was used to dark, confined spaces. After all, he had worked the past couple of summers digging coal in a mine near his hometown of Paonia, Colorado.

Upon graduation from Submarine School the following September, Deck received his orders: he was assigned to new construction, the U.S.S. *Tang* (SS-306), which had just been launched at Mare Island.

Once he arrived in California, Decker found an apartment for Lucille and Harry; his wife and son would share the apartment with the wife and son of another *Tang* crewman, George Zofcin.

"California was sort of a second home to me," Decker said. "My parents had moved to the Menlo Park–Redwood City area when I was seven and I went to grades one through eight, and my first year of high school, there."

With his family's housing arrangements worked out, he then reported to the submarine docks at Mare Island, found *Tang*'s berth, and looked her over. From the pointy bow to the rounded stern, *Tang*, named for a tropical fish, gleamed in all her gray-painted loveliness.[1]

Sailors have always had a special love for their first ship, and Clay

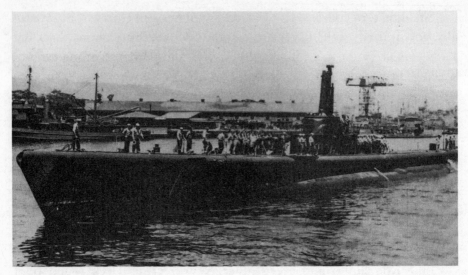

U.S.S. *Tang* pictured at Mare Island.
(Courtesy National Archives)

Decker was no different. Although she looked identical to every other *Balao*-class submarine, except for the "306" in large block numerals welded to her conning tower, to Decker *Tang* was a thing of beauty. She was 312 feet long, had a beam of twenty-eight feet, a surfaced keel depth of sixteen feet, displaced more than 1,500 tons, and carried twenty-four torpedoes. Even better, as one of the new, thick-hulled *Balao*-class of Fleet submarines, *Tang* could dive to an unheard-of test depth of 438 feet—safely below the range of any known Japanese depth charge.[2]

Decker walked up to *Tang*'s berthing space at Mare Island, showed his orders to the armed guard at the dock, crossed the narrow metal walkway, smartly saluted the America flag fluttering from her stern, then saluted the bridge.

"Torpedoman Clayton Decker reporting for duty," he announced to the guard on board, and again showed his papers.

The guard directed Decker to report to Bill Ballinger, the chief of the boat. Ballinger, formerly of *Tunny*, also gave him a hearty welcome.

Very shortly, *Tang* would begin her shakedown cruise to make certain she was seaworthy, and Clay Decker would be a part of that shakedown crew. "Whenever you put a boat or ship in commission," he said, "you're declared a 'plank owner.' I was on the commissioning crew, so I owned a 'plank' on *Tang*."

Decker was escorted around the boat by Ballinger and introduced to the skeleton crew (the rest of the crew would come aboard after the boat passed her shakedown; no use risking the lives of a full crew if something went tragically wrong during the final test) and made a cursory inspection of his new home. As the two men walked from one end of the submarine to the other, Deck was impressed by the newness of every gauge and switch, the smell of fresh paint and diesel oil, and the friendliness of the crew. Once his initial tour was complete, Deck was taken to meet the skipper.[3]

Lieutenant Commander Richard Hetherington O'Kane was a short, handsome, energetic officer who had already compiled a fine service

Clay Decker, photographed in Hawaii, 1943.
(Courtesy Clay Decker)

record. Born on 2 February 1911, in Dover, New Hampshire, not far from the Portsmouth Navy Yard, O'Kane, the son of a professor at the University of New Hampshire, developed a great love of the sea. As a boy and young man, he spent his summers sailing all manner of craft in the waters near his home and dreaming of a career in the Navy. In 1930, his dreams began to come true when he received an appointment to the United States Naval Academy. Graduating four years later, O'Kane was immediately assigned to sea duty, and spent his first four years in the Navy as a lieutenant (junior grade) aboard the *Northampton*-class heavy cruiser *Chester* (launched in 1929) and later the old destroyer *Pruitt*, built in 1920.

O'Kane became interested in

submarines and in 1938 attended Submarine School at New London. Upon graduation, he was assigned to *Argonaut* and then, as a lieutenant, with war having broken out, became part of the precommissioning crew of the new *Wahoo* in May 1942, in which he served as her executive officer under Pinky Kennedy, and against whom he nearly mutinied. When Mush Morton relieved Kennedy, O'Kane blossomed into the aggressive, hell-bent-for-leather officer that would later make him a legend in the Submarine Service.

Tang was commissioned on 15 October 1943 and sailed for her test dive/shakedown cruise off San Diego. The tale is told that O'Kane, after taking *Tang* down to 450 feet, where the pressure blew out a few lines and hoses, ordered her to surface, plugged the holes with potatoes, and immediately submerged again—this time to 525 feet—just to see what her high-tensile steel hull could take. As one might expect, a few more problems developed. These were quickly repaired and the next day *Tang* dove again, this time even deeper.[4]

"I thought the skipper was going to put her through the ocean floor," recalled Decker of this dive.[5] O'Kane sent *Tang* to 600 feet—and beyond. No one really knew exactly how deep she went, because a peg on the depth gauge kept the needle from moving past 600 feet. The new sub wheezed and groaned but she stayed intact, and many of the crew began to wonder if they were being led by a suicidal maniac.[6]

Clay Decker had no such doubts. He said, "Dick O'Kane was without a doubt the finest submarine commander in the entire Navy—an absolutely first-class officer." Nothing boosts morale more than a commander praising a subordinate, and Deck was proud of the times when O'Kane went on a white-glove inspection of his area. "There never was a time when he wouldn't say to me, 'Good job, Decker; you're doing a fine job.'"[7]

Dick O'Kane also became a man on a mission. Three months after he left Mush Morton and *Wahoo* to command *Tang*, *Wahoo* was lost. It happened at some point after *Wahoo* had made her final kill in the Sea of Japan on 9 October 1943; Morton and his crew were never heard from again. In *Submarine!*, the author and ex–Navy commander Edward L. Beach wrote *Wahoo*'s eulogy: "Like so many of our lost submarines, she simply disappeared into the limbo of lost ships, sealing her mystery with her forever. This has always been a comforting thought, for it is a sailor's death, and an honorable grave. I like to think of *Wahoo* carrying the fight to the enemy, as she always did, gloriously, successfully, and furiously, up to the last catastrophic instant when, by some mischance, and in some manner unknown to living man, the world came to an end for her."[8]

If Dick O'Kane smoldered with a hatred of the Japanese *before* the loss of his friend and mentor Mush Morton, he was positively incendiary now. He made it his personal crusade to wipe as many of them and their ships as possible off the face of the earth. To accomplish this goal, he would have to take *Tang* and her crew deep into harm's way and fight with a fury seldom seen in the Silent Service, or any other service.[9] If there had been a way to cram more than twenty-four torpedoes into *Tang*, O'Kane surely would have done it, for he despised the fact that, on each patrol, he could get no more than twenty-four shots at the enemy before having to return to base to reload.

O'Kane was a man with a total disdain for danger, and he expected the same from his officers and men. For his executive officer and navigator, O'Kane picked Murray B. Frazee Jr.—five years his junior and unquestionably a ferocious tiger. Frazee had already made seven patrols aboard *Grayback* and had gained a reputation as a tough, aggressive officer. The other officers were the usual assortment of old salts and enthusiastic young bucks ready to make their mark on the war, including engineering and diving officer Lieutenant William Walsh; Lieutenant Frank Springer, in charge of torpedo fire control; Lieutenant Bruce "Scotty" Anderson, responsible for deck and auxiliary maintenance; Ensign Henry "Hank" Flanagan, a former enlisted man who had risen through the ranks, a veteran of seven patrols on other boats, and now in charge of *Tang*'s torpedoes; and pink-cheeked Ensign Fred M. "Mel" Enos Jr., eager for his first duty in subs.[10]

Just as an orchestra conductor stamps his own personality on his musicians, and a football coach does the same on his players, the officers and men of every ship and submarine quickly adopt the personality traits of their commander—or they don't last long. And so it was on

Tang; soon each of the eighty-six other officers and men on board became an amalgamation of themselves and Dick O'Kane.

Determined to turn *Tang* into the highest-scoring submarine in the U.S. Navy, O'Kane trained his crew incessantly, day and night. There was endless drilling in Battle Stations Surface and Battle Stations Submerged, in trying to clip seconds off the time it took to clear the bridge and submerge. "We got to the point," Decker said, "where we could do it all blindfolded, if need be."[11]

ONCE *Tang* was squared away, declared seaworthy, filled with food, fuel, torpedoes, and stalwart sailors, she departed Mare Island for Pearl Harbor on New Year's Day 1944, arriving in Hawaii a week later.

Normally a newly arrived sub took at least three weeks of additional training at Pearl to be deemed ready-for-sea, but O'Kane was itching to get back into combat. *Tang* passed her operational tests and was ready to sail in a record-setting eight days. On 21 January, she headed for enemy-held Wake Island, 600 miles west of Hawaii. There she was assigned to "lifeguard duty"—standing ready to pick up any downed aircrew members during strikes against Japanese installations. Such a prosaic assignment rubbed O'Kane the wrong way; he would have preferred to be putting a few tin fish into enemy ships, but orders were orders.

For nine long and boring days and nights, *Tang* stood off Wake, reconning the coastline and waiting to rescue any downed fliers; none were downed. Finally, *Tang* was released and permitted to go hunting; off she went to cover a 5,000-square-mile area north of Truk. Once she arrived and looked around, the ocean seemed devoid of any enemy traffic. *Tang* stayed on the surface, the sonar operators' sharp ears searching for the faintest sounds of propellers, her lookouts with their eyes pressed against binoculars, scanning the unbroken horizon for any telltale sign of black smoke coming from coal-burning engines; there was none.

For ten days the fruitless search went on, then fifteen, then twenty. At last *Tang*'s luck changed. Intercepting a coded radio message from Pearl to *Skate* (SS-305) and *Sunfish* (SS-281) informing them that a convoy would be leaving from Gray Feather Bank the next morning, 17 February, O'Kane decided to try poaching; he put the spurs to *Tang* in order to beat the other subs and arrive in the just right spot for an ambush. At 0230 hours *Tang* was spotted on the surface by a destroyer but dove to 500 feet—well below the temperature gradient layer that submariners counted on to deflect enemy sonar—and swam at full speed underwater to slip inside the convoy's protective destroyer screen.

Fifteen hundred yards dead ahead of him, O'Kane discovered the 6,874-ton cargo ship *Gyoten Maru*, rising like a ghostly apparition, and launched four torpedoes at it; three detonated and the cargoman sank like a concrete block. It is likely that one of the tin fish also hit an oiler, the 5,184-ton *Kuniei Maru*, for the Imperial Japanese Navy reported that that ship was lost at the same location on the same day. The escorts dashed around in a fury, pinging madly, trying to locate the intruder, but *Tang* quietly slipped away from the hostile reception.

The next day O'Kane was ordered to head for Saipan and take up station with four other subs; again wanting to beat the others to the prey, *Tang* took off for the area at eighteen knots.

Arriving first and immediately spotting a five-ship convoy, the skipper decided to make a night surface attack; four torpedoes blasted the 3,581-ton auxiliary *Fukuyama Maru* out of the water. Not content to leave with the job partially finished, O'Kane had the forward tubes reloaded and went after the 6,777-ton *Yamashimo Maru*, raising her from the sea, as he put it in his report, "as you would flip a spoon on end, then plunged by the stern, engulfed in a mass of flames."

Because of leaks caused when the *Yamashimo Maru* exploded, *Tang* went deep—below 600 feet—to escape the ensuing depth charges, and almost didn't rise again. Serious flooding in the forward torpedo room was experienced, but after fourteen hours of careful maneuvering and overworking the bilge pumps, *Tang* finally surfaced in an empty sea. Divers repaired the outer gasket of the door to torpedo tube five and soon everything was again shipshape.

On the night of the twenty-fourth, *Tang* caught up with another convoy, and O'Kane put three fish into the 2,424-ton *Echizen Maru* before scampering off. The following morning, after tracking a small freighter and its escort all night long, a very weary captain and crew finally sent the 1,790-ton *Choko Maru* to the bottom.

Instead of heading for home as some cautious submarine commanders on their first patrol might have done, O'Kane, with a few torpedoes

A dramatic view taken from the bridge as a submarine closes in on a burning
Japanese cargo ship.
(Courtesy National Archives)

still on board, resumed the hunt. Near Pagan Island in the Marianas, he
expended *Tang*'s remaining fish at another convoy but hit nothing. Out
of ammo and content with five (or possibly six) kills to her credit, *Tang*
set course for Midway.[12]

Clay Decker was unhappy—not with the results of his first patrol
but with Bill "Boats" Leibold, *Tang*'s boatswain's mate. "Boats was in
charge of all the 'right-arm ratings,'" Deck said, "and my rating of torpedoman was a 'right-arm rating.' For some reason he and I didn't hit it
off at the beginning. He really cracked the whip and went by the
book—I thought the guy was related to Hitler! Anyway, after our first
patrol, he busted me down to seaman first class and sent me to the
'black gang' to work the throttles in the engine room. Later on, we got
to be good buddies, but there was a time when I couldn't stand his
guts."[13]

Tang pulled into Midway on 3 March 1944 for refitting. The crew
was not given a full liberty, for O'Kane wanted the sub serviced in a

hurry so they could get back to the war. He did take the time, however, to have a strictly nonregulation "crow's nest" installed atop the periscope shears so that a lookout could be stationed up there and have a commanding view of the surrounding sea with the specific purpose of spotting enemy submarines.

On the eleventh, *Tang*'s refit was finished and O'Kane took her out for some training runs to shape up new personnel who had just come aboard. On 15 March, *Tang* departed Midway, with O'Kane eager to add a few more "meatballs" to her battle pennant. He needn't have hurried; for the next forty-eight days, *Tang* wandered the Pacific without seeing anything worth shooting at. "We began to think that maybe Japan had dropped out of the war," said Decker.[14]

Japan most assuredly had *not* dropped out of the war, but her power was waning as America's was increasing exponentially. America's Pacific strategy of "island hopping" was bringing Yanks ever closer to Japan, although the term *island hopping* suggests a lighthearted frivolousness that was far from reality. Reclaiming islands from the Japanese was a dirty, deadly business, and a very costly "butcher's bill" had to be paid for each one.

Perhaps nothing symbolized the decline of Japan's once-dominant position as "ruler of the Pacific" as much as the attack by John Scott's *Tunny* on the giant 65,00-ton (nearly 73,000 tons fully loaded) battleship *Musashi*. On 29 March 1944, *Musashi* was at sea near Palau when a torpedo from *Tunny* struck the giant ship just below the port-side anchor. The flooded compartment was quickly sealed off and counterflooding measures were taken to prevent listing; the mighty *Musashi* crawled back to Kure for repairs without further incident.[15]

MEANWHILE, Ron Smith was sailing back to California in *Seal*, which had an appointment to get new engines and a complete overhaul at Mare Island. Sailing beneath the Golden Gate Bridge was a heartwarming experience, and every man who wasn't needed below was on the sub's deck, waving up at the pretty girls far above them who were waving down on them. Tears coursed down bearded cheeks.

As *Seal* entered San Francisco Bay, Smitty reflected on the time he had spent away from home. There had been times when he thought he would never make it back alive, and there was still no guarantee that he would return from future patrols.

Once *Seal* tied up at Mare Island on 3 April 1944, and the announcement was made that all those who did not have duty could go ashore, Smitty said, "The exodus of bodies leaving *Seal* reminded me of rats running from a sinking ship." No barracks for him; he checked into the Casa de Vallejo, the best hotel in town, and enjoyed a hot, hourlong shower. He then got dressed in his best uniform and took the elevator down to the lobby, where the bar was located. That evening he picked up a girl at the bar and they did what horny sailors and lonely married women did during wartime. The romance lasted one night.

A few days later, Easter Sunday 1944, Smitty met another young lady, this one a dark-haired lass named Marilynn, who was leaving a church service with a girlfriend. After some initial hesitation on her part ("Nice girls don't talk to sailors—besides, I'm engaged to one," she told him), she and Smitty struck up a conversation. He talked her into lunch. He found out that she worked as a file clerk at the base administration building and lived at home in Vallejo with her parents. He was struck by her young, fresh beauty and could not stop looking at her. He felt like a grubby little street urchin who had just found a brand-new shiny penny.

They began dating, and against his better judgment, he fell crazily in love with her. He kicked himself for doing it, but he couldn't help himself. She apparently felt the same, for she had broken her engagement to the other sailor without even knowing what Smitty's plans for the two of them were. To him, things like marriage and kids—a normal life—were not

Smitty and Marilynn, 1943.
(Courtesy Ron Smith)

possible. At least not now, with him in the Navy and a war on. He loved her but didn't know what the future held. He was never going to make it through this war and it wasn't fair to leave a woman widowed, as Bill Partin had done. But he couldn't stop seeing her.

Meanwhile, Marilynn was having trouble at home. Nothing serious; just the kind of stresses and strains that sometimes develop between a mother and a headstrong, teenage daughter. One night Marilynn told Smitty that she wanted to leave home and move in with her aunt Mary in the southern Colorado city of Pueblo. The news hit Smitty hard. If she left, he might never see her again. But he played it cool, even offering to put in for a thirty-day leave so he could visit his dad in Hammond and escort her on the train to Pueblo. To his surprise, she agreed to his plan.

On the cross-country train ride, they made love for the first time—and then second and third and . . . He felt she wanted him to propose but he just couldn't make himself commit. *It wouldn't be fair to her if anything happens to me,* he kept thinking, reflecting on Mary Partin, a widow at twenty, with a fatherless son.[16]

APRIL 1944. The time to liberate the Philippines had come, and the first step was to dislodge the enemy from the Marianas. To this end, General MacArthur's soldiers were poised to invade Hollandia on the north central coast of New Guinea, supported by Admiral Marc Mitscher's Fast Carrier Task Force 58, under Admiral Spruance's Fifth Fleet. Task Force 58 consisted of five large aircraft carriers of the *Essex* class, plus the two remaining prewar carriers—*Enterprise* and *Saratoga*—along with eight light fleet carriers of the *Independence* class. These, plus a full armada of supporting ships, prompted naval historian Samuel E. Morison to write, "The age of steam has afforded no marine spectacle comparable to a meeting of Fast Carrier Forces Pacific Fleet. Now that the seaman's eye has become accustomed to the great flat-tops, and has learned what they can do to win command of the sea, they have become as beautiful to him as to his bell-bottomed forebears. They and the new battleships with their graceful sheer and boiling wake evoked poetic similes."[17]

Six submarines—*Tang, Archerfish, Bashaw, Blackfish, Tullibee,* and

Tunny—were on station to play a small but significant role in the operation: keeping vessels containing enemy reinforcements out of the area and picking up any carrier-based fliers who might be forced to splash down. It was this latter role for which *Tang* would become renowned.[18]

THE train pulled into Pueblo, but Marilynn had second thoughts about moving in with her aunt. Instead, she and Smitty got on the next train to Chicago and from there took the South Shore Railroad down to Hammond. As they climbed out of the taxi hand in hand and looked at his home on Jackson Street, the feelings swelling inside Smitty threatened to overwhelm him. This was the house where he was born and the house where his mother had died just six years earlier—a lifetime ago. This was the place he had left to go off to war, a place he feared he would never see again. Here he was, back where it all began, holding hands with a beautiful girl who wanted to be his wife.

Little Rex banged through the screen door and flew down the steps, yelling "It's Ronnie! It's Ronnie! He's home! He's home!"

THE leave seemed as much too short as too long. There were interminable, uncomfortable moments with his stepmother, Dorothy, whom his father had married a couple of years before Smitty had joined the Navy and whom he felt he still didn't know. There were his dad's and Dorothy's two daughters, five-year-old Judy and the baby, Carol, who seemed like tiny strangers.

Smitty's old school chums, too, seemed oddly disconnected with his life. Most of the girls who had been his friends in high school were either married or off to college. Most of his male friends were in the service; those who were still around were 4-F—unfit for military service—and wore a stigma that said they somehow weren't good enough to be in uniform. A few asked him what it was like to serve on a submarine and go into battle, but Smitty declined to elaborate; they wouldn't understand.

Even his aunts and uncles and cousins were out of touch with what was going on in the Pacific, and complained mostly about how scarce things like meat and butter and shoe leather and tires and gasoline were now, because of the severe wartime rationing. Smitty felt a little guilty that he and the Navy never seemed to lack for anything, and he realized it was because of all the sacrifices on the home front.

About half the houses on Jackson Street had small red-bordered pennants with blue stars hanging in the front windows, indicating that a family member was in the service. A couple of pennants had gold stars, which indicated that that family member had died while serving his country, and Smitty said a silent prayer for them.

Ernie laid down the law, telling his son that there would be no "hanky-panky" in a house with three young children; Marilynn slept in Judy's room and Smitty stayed in his old room in the basement next to the fire-breathing coal furnace. Their lovemaking was confined to the backseat of Ernie's 1938 Pontiac.

After they had been in Hammond for a couple of weeks, Marilynn gave Smitty some bad news—she had missed her period and thought she was pregnant. Great, simply great, thought Smitty. "I guess we'd better get married, then," he said to her, knowing that's what nice boys did in 1944 when they got nice girls "in trouble."

"Yes, I guess so," she responded happily.[19]

On 27 April 44, *Tang* was afloat east of Truk when a flight of American B-24 "Liberator" bombers flew overhead and released their eggs on Japanese positions. The jungle went up in flames and smoke and mushrooms of flying dirt. For three days the aerial pounding continued; on 30 April, some enemy gunners got lucky and shot down a bomber. *Tang*'s crew plucked three grateful men from the water, handed out some booze and blankets to warm them, and found space for them belowdecks.

With the coming of night, more wet airmen were picked up. Another distress call was received but *Tang*, taking fire from shore and on the alert for a prowling enemy sub, was unable to locate the life raft. The following day, *Tang* continued her role as lifeguard, rescuing several other raft-bound groups. None of this was done without risk to herself and her crew, but O'Kane and every sailor on board performed their tasks with heroic aplomb. One pilot, weak and dehydrated, was spotted on the coral of the atoll's shore; O'Kane scraped *Tang*'s hull to practically crawl up on shore to rescue the flier—despite the danger of being hit by enemy fire from nearby bunkers. Nine more aviators were extracted from a crippled Kingfisher aircraft. Another raft was spotted in the dark by night-fighter aircraft and the men brought on board.

With *Tang* crammed to the overhead with twenty-two welcome-but-uninvited guests, Clay Decker recalled that the sub's already tight living quarters got even tighter. "We had a crew of eighty-seven and now we suddenly had twenty-two more. Talk about hot-bunking! But we fed them and treated them well, just as they would have done for us had the situation been reversed. Admiral Halsey wanted all those fliers back in service as fast as he could get them."[20] *Tang* stayed on patrol for several more days before heading back to Pearl; she sank no ships.[21]

Tang reached Hawaii on 15 May 1944 with her boatload of aviators; by now the sailors and the fliers were fast friends. Admirals Nimitz and Lockwood and other notables were at the dock to greet *Tang* and its human cargo with much fanfare.

Normally, at least one enemy ship had to be sunk while on a war patrol in order for a submariner to receive a star to his combat pin. Even though *Tang* had not sunk a ship, Admiral Lockwood bent the regs to ensure that every crewman was awarded a star for the second patrol. They also received something else. Clay Decker said, "Later, Halsey gave every man of the *Tang* crew the Navy Air Medal. You can imagine what kind of comments and funny looks I get at a submariners' convention when I'm wearing my Air Medal!"[22]

ON the same day that *Tang* arrived back at Pearl Harbor with her cargo of aviators, another submarine, U.S.S. *Tullibee* (SS-284) was reported overdue and presumably lost. One survivor, Gunner's Mate C. W. Kuykendall, after the war told the chilling tale of *Tullibee*'s demise—a tale that was eerily similar to what would happen to *Tang*.

Back on 5 March 1944, Commander Charles F. Brindupke had guided *Tullibee* out of Pearl to begin her fourth war patrol, stopping at Midway to top off her fuel tanks. Her destination was the sea north of Palau, where she was to remain in support of a carrier strike in the area. Kuykendall said that the boat arrived on station on 25 March and the next night, during a rain squall, made radar contact with a seven-ship Japanese convoy. Closing in on the convoy, Brindupke selected a large

Richard O'Kane is surrounded by twenty-two airmen rescued by *Tang* crew members.
(Courtesy National Archives)

transport as his first target but held his fire until he could get a good visual fix on it.

Tullibee's presence, meanwhile, was noticed by the escorts who went on the attack, dropping depth charges. Undeterred, *Tullibee* stayed in the area, finally launching two fish at the transport. The first torpedo evidently struck the transport and sank it, while the second, behaving erratically, swung around in a circle and hit the submarine. Kuykendall, who had been on the bridge as a lookout, was blown into the water—the boat's only survivor. He was picked up by a Japanese vessel and beaten when he refused to divulge anything more than his name, rating, and service number. Taken to Ofuna Naval Interrogation Camp near Yokohama, Japan, he remained there until 30 September. He was then sent to work for the duration of the war as a slave laborer in the copper mines of Ashio.[23]

ALTHOUGH Clay Decker's rating when he came aboard *Tang* was torpedoman third class, it was later changed to motor machinist's mate when Executive Officer Frazee discovered, as crewmen cross-trained in other specialties, that Deck had a talent as a bow planesman and rescued him from the Black Gang.

Decker recalled, "Murray Frazee selected me to be the permanent bow planesman whenever we were submerged. He said he selected me because I had a 'knack for catching the bubble.' That's a glass tube with a bubble in it that showed whether we were level or not, kind of like a carpenter's level. I sat in the control room on a bench with the big wheel in front of me that looked like a huge steering wheel. When we started to dive, my job was to rig the bow planes—they look like big elephant ears that stick out from the side of the hull. They act the same way a fish's fins or an airplane's elevators work—they make the sub either dive or surface." Against his back was the ladder leading to the conning tower.[24]

Clay Decker didn't know it, but being wedged into that tight space would soon save his life.

ON 20 May 1944, a beautiful spring day in the Calumet region, as northwest Indiana is known, Smitty and Marilynn said their vows in front of a small group on the front lawn of the Hyde Park Methodist Church. (It turned out that Marilynn was not pregnant—at least not yet.) After a short honeymoon trip to central Illinois to visit some of Smitty's aunts and uncles, the newlyweds prepared to return to Hammond and then back to California, but not before an uncle who owned a used-car business gave them a 1940 red Chevrolet convertible as a wedding present. Another uncle, who was on the ration board in Hammond, gave them a stack of gas coupons "under-the-table" to help fuel their return to the West Coast.

On the trip back to California, Smitty and Marilynn stopped in Salida, Colorado—her hometown; during Smitty's leave, her mother, stepfather, and two brothers had moved back there from Vallejo. After a few days with them it was time to get back on the road.

Once again at Mare Island at the beginning of June, Smitty and his bride found an apartment. Smitty reported in at the submarine base and checked on *Seal*'s overhaul. The sub sat on huge wooden blocks in a dry dock large enough for a cruiser, looking like a small toy boat in a large, empty bathtub. A narrow catwalk connected her deck with the wall of the dry dock. Smitty noticed a few changes in *Seal*. The twenty-millimeter gun on the forward cigarette deck was still there, but the three-inch gun on the aft deck had been replaced by two five-inch guns—one forward and one aft of the conning tower—and the twenty-millimeter gun on the after cigarette deck had been replaced by a forty-millimeter gun. *She's beginning to look more like a small, sleek destroyer than a submarine*, thought Smitty, surveying all the new armament, and wondering if the admirals were planning to use the submarines in more surface battles.

He went down inside her and looked approvingly at the four Fairbanks-Morse diesels that were being installed. They were things of beauty—all closed in with head covers over the valve lifters—and no copper and steel lines running like spaghetti all over the place, as on the old H.O.R.s Smitty was used to seeing. He had to step over tools and engine parts and manuals and stay out of the way of the dozen workers and mechanics and engineers who were still putting the engine room back together, but he marveled at *Seal*'s transformation. She was going to be one tough submarine. *This is for you, Bill,* he vowed silently to his dead friend. *Now we're really going to get those sons of bitches.*

Chief Weist appeared through a bulkhead hatch. "Hey, Smitty! I heard you was back! Scuttlebutt has it you got hitched."

"That's right, Chief," he said, holding up his left hand so the chief could see the gold wedding band.

"Well, congratulations!"

"Thanks. Say, *Seal*'s looking pretty good."

"Yep, she is. We're scheduled to get back in the war in July. And we're getting a new skipper. Name's Turner, John Turner. Dodge is going to new construction—a boat called *Brill*."

"Wow, no shit? Lots of changes. Say, Chief, what do you need me to do?"

"Get into some dungarees and help the boys scraping her hull."

By tradition, all hands except officers went over the side hanging from bos'un's chairs to scrape old paint and waterproofing from the hull. That was one of the worst, if not *the* worst job when a sub was in dry dock. "Aww, Chief, do I have to?"

"Smitty, I don't have time to argue. You've been goofing off on your honeymoon for a month, so it's time you got back to work. Plus, working out in that healthful California sunshine will get rid of your sickly bedroom pallor." Weist smiled a knowing grin.

Smitty grumbled but changed into old dungarees, for the job was guaranteed to get him sweaty and filthy. It was hot, dirty work dangling forty feet above the concrete floor of the dry dock, scraping the black, tar-like goop from the sides and bottom of the sub. After three days everyone realized *Seal* was a lot bigger on the outside than she seemed from the inside.

Smitty and the other torpedomen soon escaped most of the scraping on the pretext that they had to "sight the tubes"—a simple but necessary procedure to ensure that the periscope crosshairs were aligned dead center with each tube. The torpedo-room crews dragged out the procedure as long as possible so they wouldn't have to go back to scraping.[25]

IN late May 1944, another submarine was about to leave her port in Fremantle and sail into history. U.S.S. *Harder* (SS-257), named for a species of South Atlantic mullet and under the command of Sam Dealey, had built a reputation of being an aggressive, fighting sub. If ever a Navy skipper was beloved by his men, it was Sam Dealey, born in Texas in 1906, and a 1930 graduate of Annapolis. It is said that if the devil had ships in hell, and Dealey decided to attack them, his men would have followed unquestioningly.

Mike Geletka, a Clevelander and an engineer aboard *Harder*, was one of Dealey's many fans. "I thought Captain Dealey was a fantastic officer, a prince. He came from a nice, well-to-do family. We respected him and we all thought the world of him. He'd go through the boat and talk to you; he knew every man on the boat by name. He would always take the time to show us on the chart table where the boat was, and tell us what our orders were and what we were going to do. After an engagement he would always explain the attacks and tell us what we did.

"He was sharp and he had a good set of officers—Lieutenant Mauer, Lieutenant Frank Lynch, Samuel Logan. They were well trained, well, the whole crew was. He trained the hell out of us. We had no problems; never had any trouble. And it paid off. The officers got along well with the crew. In fact, every time we came in from a run, we'd hang out with each other for a couple of days and we'd go wild. After our first three runs we pulled into Pearl Harbor. Stayed at the 'Pink Lady'—the Royal Hawaiian. We'd get together for a day or two, playing baseball and all that. After our second patrol, we had a big ball game—beer, steaks, everything. Afterward, none of us felt no pain."

Geletka recalled that the "old man" was his size—about five-foot-seven, 155 pounds. "The old man was an ex-fighter—a pug—from the Academy. Bantamweight, or something like that. One day while we were on R and R at the Royal Hawaiian, he grabbed me and said, 'C'mon, Geletka, let's put the gloves on.'

Sam Dealey, skipper of *Harder,* and recipient of the Medal of Honor, posthumously.
(Courtesy Naval Historical Center)

"I looked at him and said, 'Captain, I'm a lover, not a fighter. And I know you're a fighter.' But he talked me into it. So I said, 'If you stick me, Captain, pull your punches.' So we put the gloves on and we start sparring around, and the next thing I know, he hit me square in the face— he didn't pull the punch. He hit me and I flew about six feet and fell on my butt. I wiped my nose and there was a little blood, and I said, 'Goddamn you, Captain, you hit me too hard! I said to pull your punches!' He helps me up and I take off the gloves and throw them at him. I'm bitching like hell and cussing at him, and when I went by him, I kicked him in the shins.

"The next morning we're still at the hotel and I go down for breakfast and the yeoman says to me, 'The old man wants to see you.' So I went in there and he apologized, and I said, 'Captain, forget about it. I don't remember a damn thing.' I didn't find out until years later that he had broken my nose."[26]

Sam Dealey didn't pull his punches on board *Harder*, either, and wasn't afraid of going after the enemy's destroyers, even though the submarines generally avoided them. Bob Beynon writes, "The pride of the Japanese navy was her heralded destroyers. Early in the war, the American submarine deemed this type of war vessel as the most dangerous of the enemy's armament. The value of the destroyer as a war target was not considered very high. Its value to the Japanese was as a deterrent to the attacking submarine. It carried extremely high firepower and was used to fend off the submarines from destroying the cargo-carrying freighters and the ever-precious oil and gasoline tankers."[27]

Author Edward L. Beach also notes: "The destroyer or escort vessel is the bane of the sub's existence, for it is commonly considered too small to shoot successfully and too dangerous to fool around with. Besides, sinking a destroyer was not ordinarily so damaging to the enemy's cause as sinking a tanker, for example . . . Ordinarily, you avoid tangling with one."[28]

But, like a man who gets satisfaction out of wrestling alligators, Sam Dealey welcomed the challenge. Knowing that the Japanese were critically short of destroyers, and the ones they did have were operated to exhaustion in order to protect the precious cargomen, transports, and fuel ships plying the sea-lanes, Dealey deliberately decided to target the tin cans.

On 26 May 1944, *Harder* departed Fremantle on her fifth war patrol, sailing for the Celebes Sea and Tawi-Tawi, the southernmost island province of the Philippines, close to Borneo, where a large enemy convoy was reported to be assembling for an attack against the Americans' Saipan invasion force. *Harder*'s role was simply to be that of observer, but things turned out quite differently.

Moving *Harder* close to the enemy's Fleet Operating Base at Tawi-Tawi in the Sulu Archipelago, Dealey hoped to draw the destroyers into a fight. Mike Geletka recalled, "We were sent out there just to observe, and when the Jap fleet started moving, we were to break radio silence."[29]

IT was 4 June 1944. Half a world away, as the submariners would soon learn, Rome was the first of the Axis capitals to fall to the advancing Allies. Two days later the Americans, British, and Canadians stormed the beaches of Normandy, launching an invasion that would not stop until it reached the heart of Germany eleven months later.

On that day, 6 June 1944, the radio in the Smith's apartment in Vallejo announced the historic news: "Allied ground forces, supported by strong Allied naval and air forces, landed this morning on the northern coast of France."[30]

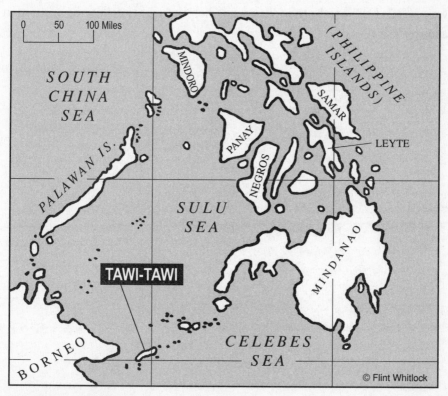

Location of Tawi-Tawi.

It was "D-Day"—the beginning of the end for the Nazis in Europe. Smitty hustled down to *Seal*, which had finished her makeover and was ready for sea trials. *Who knows? With this news the Japanese might be ready to give up,* Smitty thought.[31]

TANG on 6 June was moored at her berth in Pearl Harbor, taking on torpedoes and supplies, and preparing for her third patrol. Clay Decker recalled that *Tang*'s crew celebrated D-Day in a happy but subdued fashion. "The invasion made it seem that the war in Europe might be over any day now, but we wondered what effect, if any, it would have on the Japanese. Would they give up, or would they just fight harder?"[32]

Dick O'Kane also mused briefly about the Normandy landings. He would later write, "I had anticipated that the Allies' return to the Continent would be a moment of great elation, but like others, found that I could not cheer and pray at the same time. If Godspeeds can carry halfway around the earth, then *Tang* was helping eighty fellow fighting men ashore."[33]

CHAPTER 15

THE FATE OF THE EMPIRE

DURING a night chase of a convoy on 6 June 1944, Sam Dealey in *Harder* noticed a destroyer in an attacking mood coming fast astern. Submerging to periscope depth and making a hard turn to port, Dealey waited until the onrushing tin can was perpendicular to his stern tubes, fired, and blasted the target—the *Minazuki*—into the hereafter. Dealey then resumed chasing the convoy but was soon spotted by another destroyer. Unlike his predecessor, the captain of this destroyer was on the alert and zigzagging to avoid the fate of his comrade. The range and direction kept fluctuating, making drawing a bead on the destroyer difficult.

Dealey at last gave the command to fire and a barrage of fish flew out to greet the tin can. The enemy skipper saw the wakes of the torpedoes spearing toward him and took evasive action while simultaneously trying to locate *Harder*'s position in order to drop his ash cans on her. *Click . . . KaBLOOM!* went the first depth charge as *Harder* dove, followed by *Click . . . KaBLOOM! Click . . . KaBLOOM! Click . . . KaBLOOM! Harder* and her crew were rattled but unhurt.

But something went wrong. The stern planesman, new at his job, made a drastic mistake. He turned his big wheel the wrong way, sending *Harder* plunging downward in a steep dive. The diving officer shoved the panicked planesman out of the way and pulled with all his might on the wheel, but it is not easy to stop the death dive of a 1,500-ton submarine in an environment where the downward pressure increases with every foot. The depth gauge fell to 200 feet, 250, 300, and still she was on the decline. The boat's hull groaned loudly and threatened to burst.

Dealey shouted over the intercom, "All hands to the aft—on the double!" hoping that the shift of internal weight might help curtail the plunge. Immediately the boat was filled with sailors running to the stern; those in the control room remained at their duty stations. Somehow the maneuver worked; *Harder*'s dive began to slow, then she leveled off. Dealey glanced at the depth gauge: 400 feet.

Then the boat tilted upward and the forty men who had run to the stern to counter the dive realized the tilt was too extreme and began filtering back to the center of the boat to balance her. Tense moments passed before *Harder*, like a runaway sea horse, could be brought back under control.

The destroyer above had not gone away. The ship's pinging revealed the fact that the sub was coming back up and the enemy's depth charges were ready and waiting. As *Harder* neared the surface, the depth charges began to fall again with a steady hammering. Miraculously Dealey and *Harder* managed to avoid the explosions and slip away.

The next day, while resting from their close call, the crew of *Harder* was once more called to battle stations; another destroyer was spotted rushing toward her periscope and closing at a fast rate of speed. Sonar then picked up a second tin can, also coming at the gallop, from a different heading. Dealey decided to take care of the first one—the *Hayanami*—now only 700 yards off the bow. Two torpedoes were launched in a risky "down the throat" shot, and Dealey ordered a hard turn to starboard just as the fish struck home, obliterating the target; it sank almost instantly.[1]

Harry "Bud" Dunn from Baltimore was a very young torpedoman aboard *Harder*; he had joined the Navy when he was sixteen by falsifying someone else's birth certificate. He described this patrol as being "very exciting."

"This one torpedo was a down-the-throat shot," Dunn said, "that caused the destroyer's magazine to blow up, and it came down on top of us." He watched in amazement as the explosion jolted *Harder* and caused the heavy deck plates in the forward torpedo room to jump. "They didn't go back down in place, of course—they were all askew. There wasn't that much room between the tubes but I was all black-and-blue on my shoulders where I bounced off them.

"One man I'll never forget; he was a gunner's mate third class. He got hit a glancing blow by a chain block coming out of the overhead and needed more than twenty stitches in his head. I believe that Commander Sullivan was the exec; the gunner's mate asked him if he thought he would get the Purple Heart for his wound. The exec said, 'I don't know, son. The way that citation reads, I believe that the wound has to come from direct action of the enemy.' And the gunner's mate says, 'Well, who the hell do you think was up there?' "[2]

Harder now homed in on the other sub hunter. The angle was not good, and through the periscope Dealey could see the Japanese crewmen on the stern, preparing to launch their depth charges. Dealey took *Harder* down again just as the ash cans began splashing the waves above her. *Click . . . KaBLOOM! Click . . . KaBLOOM! Click . . . KaBLOOM!* The thundering symphony went on for four hours as Dealey attempted every maneuver he could think of to cease being the pursued and turn again into the pursuer.

At last shaking the enemy, *Harder* swam out of the area, surfaced, and came startlingly close to not one but *six* enemy destroyers headed straight for her! Although his instinctive reaction was to go on the offense and attack the enemy ships, discretion became the better part of valor; Dealey pulled the plug, submerged, and *Harder* escaped.

Harder was then ordered by ComSubPac to head for northeast Borneo and pick up six Australian coast watchers who were in danger of being captured by the Japanese. Throughout the war, coast watchers performed heroic duty in spotting the movements of enemy ships and convoys and reporting their sightings back to the Allies. Second only to the *Magic* code breakers, the coast watchers were the Allies' most valuable intelligence source—a source that the Americans, British, and Australians couldn't afford to lose.[3]

With the coast watchers safely on board, Dealey continued his hunt of the enemy's destroyers and, on 9 June, sent the tin can *Tanikaze* to the bottom; the following day *Harder* hit and wounded another. The pickings then became slim and *Harder* was ordered to sail to Darwin, on Australia's north coast, instead of to her base at Fremantle.

"Why we were ordered to Darwin, we didn't know," said Mike Geletka. "But we soon found out. As we came close to Darwin, one of the quartermasters was looking out through the periscope and yelled, 'Jesus Christ, there's somebody up there with a lot of gold braid. I think that's Admiral Christie!' So the admiral came on board—he wanted to go on patrol with us so he could get a combat pin."

The admiral soon became known as "Pain-in-the-Ass Christie." Geletka said, "We were sent in between Borneo and New Guinea to sink a ship carrying nickel. We would run a sweep—every fifteen minutes they'd run the scope up, take a look around, and then bring it back down. We found the ship, but from what I understand, we were too far away. The admiral was a pain in the butt. He was up in the conning tower, where they didn't want him to be. On one of the sweeps, the O.D. saw a beautiful sailing ship up there, a full-masted schooner or something. The admiral wanted the old man to battle-surface and fire at it, but the old man said no—we're in too close to shore, so we're not going to battle-surface.

"The admiral wanted a gun battle—he wanted to get that submarine combat pin. He and the old man were having a discussion, but then it got a little hot. The old man was pissed. He said, 'Admiral, I want to see you in my stateroom.' They came back a little later, but we didn't battle-surface, and all of us said, 'Whew.'"

Harder sailed on the surface into enemy waters, where she was spotted by a Japanese aircraft. The diving alarm sounded and the men topside began scrambling for the ladder. Unbeknownst to anyone, Christie had been on the cigarette deck having a smoke. As the first man down the ladder from the conning tower into the control room, the admiral was coming down slowly, one rung at a time. Geletka said, "The men above on the bridge were dropping down on him and nearly killed the poor bastard."[4]

Bud Dunn was one of those who landed atop the admiral. "When I dropped through the hatch I was right on the admiral's shoulders. He said, 'I don't blame you, son—I wouldn't want to be left up there, either.' "[5]

Captain Dealey came running into the control room and helped the admiral to his feet. Geletka reported that Dealey said to the junior officer of the deck, " 'Did you know the admiral was up there?' and the junior O.D. said, 'No, Captain.' The captain told him point-blank, 'Admiral Christie, when you go up on my bridge, I don't care who you are, you get permission from my O.D., because he's got the responsibility of every man on that bridge. He's got to count heads.' Well, the admiral never went up again."[6]

The crew topside had not come down a second too soon, for a storm of depth charges began falling as *Harder* went deep. For what seemed like forever, explosions rocked the sub, popping lightbulbs, shattering gauge faces, snapping lines, and turning everyone into nervous wrecks. The battering finally ceased and *Harder* once more escaped, continuing on her mission.

Two days later, in a smooth sea devoid of enemy ships, *Harder* was suddenly jumped by another Japanese plane. Only a quick dive prevented the aircraft's bombs from reaching her. That night, still itching for a fight, Sam Dealey returned to Tawi-Tawi. A convoy soon appeared, and as Dealey looked through the periscope at what appeared to be a huge warship, the ship was suddenly engulfed in smoke and flames; some other nearby submarine had struck it! Dealey suddenly spotted a destroyer heading at full speed in his direction and took steady aim at the tin can's bow as the range grew shorter.

Harder was like a car parked on a railroad track, its occupants watching with morbid fascination as the train gets ever closer. The soundman detected another destroyer rushing to the scene, but Dealey was intent on dealing with his first target. The command to fire was given as Destroyer Number One closed within 1,500 yards. A second fish was launched, then a third for good measure. At the last second Dealey gave the order to dive.

A minute after the first torpedo was launched, a tremendous shock wave rocked *Harder* as the tin can disintegrated above her. The second destroyer arrived on the scene and began bubbling the ocean

with depth charges. Two more enemy ships showed up, along with a
depth-bomb-dropping aircraft. For two hours the unrelenting pummeling went on, and the men below held on to anything they could in
order to maintain their balance and their sanity.[7]

Click . . . KaBLOOM! Click . . . KaBLOOM! Click . . . KaBLOOM!
They lost count of the explosions around them. The battering went on for
hours, with each explosion yelling out, *DOOM! DOOM! DOOM!*
DOOM! DOOM!

Mike Geletka recalled the tension belowdecks during that depth
charging. "Two of our boys were in a corner. One of the boys was a
Catholic; he had a rosary, and he was praying on it. I think I was praying with him. There was another boy next to him; I don't know if he
was Protestant or Jewish, but he looked over at the Catholic boy and
asked him what he was doing and the Catholic boy started explaining
all about the rosary, and the other boy said, 'Never mind that bullshit;
just give me the other half!' I think all three of us were praying on the
same rosary. It must have worked, 'cuz I'm still here."[8]

At last, after sunset, the brave, battered *Harder* came up for air. The
enemy was gone, however, having retreated back to the safety of his anchorage at Tawi-Tawi.

Once *Harder* returned to Australia, the crew was feted with a wel-
coming ceremony that had been arranged for the submarine that had
sunk five enemy destroyers on one patrol—one of the most remarkable
feats of marksmanship in the history of the American submarine force.
Modestly, Dealey gave credit to the boatbuilders in his patrol report:
"It is amazing that the ship could have gone through such a terrific
pounding and jolting around with such minor damage. Our fervent
thanks go out to the Electric Boat Company for building such a fine
ship."

For the fifth patrol, Dealey received the Medal of Honor, every man
in the crew was decorated appropriately with the Navy Cross, and even
General MacArthur bestowed the Army's Distinguished Service Cross
on the sub's commander.[9]

Geletka said, "MacArthur also gave Admiral Christie a Silver Star
for that patrol—for sitting on his ass and doing nothing. The crew didn't
like that, you know. I didn't find out he got a Silver Star for making the

trip with us until years later. He claimed he was assistant O.D. on that run, which was baloney."[10]

EACH sea trial uncovered new and different problems that delayed *Seal*'s return to combat. Finally she was tightened up and declared seaworthy. Lieutenant Commander John H. Turner, Naval Academy class of 1936, introduced himself to the crew as Dodge's replacement. Smitty found him to be sharp and competent, but he, like all submariners, would reserve judgment until they could observe their new skipper under fire.

Food, fuel, ammunition, torpedoes, toilet paper, and other necessities were brought aboard *Seal*. The only thing left to do before shoving off was to have every officer and enlisted man undergo a thorough physical examination.

"I'M afraid I have some bad news for you, Smith," the physician said to Smitty at the base hospital.

"Sir?" A slight wave of unease lapped at Smitty's stomach.

"You seem to be running a low-grade fever. The tests have been inconclusive, so we need to keep you here for a few days, run a few more tests, and find out what's causing it."

"But, sir, my boat leaves tomorrow."

"Well, it can't be helped. Can't have you out in the middle of the ocean and develop more serious problems, now can we?"

"No, sir, I suppose not, but—" Smitty wanted to explain to the doctor why he needed to go back out on patrol, why he needed to kill more Japanese and avenge Bill Partin's death, but the words wouldn't come.

"Smith, some sailors would give their eyeteeth to get out of combat duty."

Smitty couldn't reply, just nodded his head yes. He walked down to *Seal*'s dock in a daze. It was 8 August 1944—departure day. The final crate of fresh fruit was being brought aboard and the whole boat seemed to be swarming with last-minute activity. Smitty found the chief and gave him the news.

"That's a damn shame," said Weist, patting Smitty on the shoulder. "We'll have to grab some torpedoman off the relief crew. We'll miss you, Smitty, but get well fast and we'll see you on the next patrol."

"Right, Chief. Right."

Smitty left *Seal* and all his friends that day, looking back with an odd mixture of joy and regret.

"OH, honey, that's wonderful!" Marilynn said when he broke the news to her that evening, and she began to sob. He knew why she was crying—at least for the next month or two, her chances of becoming a widow had just dropped to zero.

He held her in his arms and let her cry.[11]

ON the afternoon of 8 June 1944, with no sign that the Japanese were about to give up, *Tang* departed Pearl and, along with Eli T. Reich's *Sealion II* (SS-315) on her first patrol, set a course for Midway Island. There the two subs would pick up a third partner, Don Weiss's *Tinosa* (SS-283), and then head out as a wolfpack to the rich hunting grounds of the East China Sea—the area east of China, south of Korea, and southwest of Japan.

It was an area that American submarines had not patrolled for half a year, and was the site of the loss in late February or early March 1944 of Max Schmidt's *Scorpion* (SS-278); someone would pay dearly for *Scorpion*'s demise.*

On 13 June, as the three subs were making their way to their assigned station, Operation Forager, the American invasion of Saipan—a preliminary bout to what would become the larger Battle of the Philippine Sea—began.

It is recorded that the Battle of the Philippine Sea of June 1944 was the last great carrier battle of World War II. Admiral Marc Mitscher's Fast Carrier Task Force 58, with 896 aircraft distributed across the car-

---

* *Scorpion*, a *Gato*-class sub with sixty officers and men aboard, vanished during her fourth war patrol in the East China Sea–Yellow Sea area, presumably after striking a mine. On her first three patrols, *Scorpion* was credited with sinking ten ships for a total of 24,100 tons, and damaging two others. Ironically, in 1968, a nuclear-powered sub also bearing the name *Scorpion* (SSN-589) was lost in 10,000 feet of water 400 miles southwest of the Azores Islands. Ninety-nine sailors died in that tragedy. (www.txoilgas.com; www.lostsubs.com/SSN-589)

riers divided into four task groups, opened the battle and gained air superiority over the enemy at Saipan and Tinian. American battleships also closed in on the islands and saturated the Japanese defenses with their big guns. This was followed on the fifteenth by an assault force of 71,000 Americans who came ashore at Saipan.

In an attempt to sweep them off the island and cripple the supporting American fleet, Japan sent a large armada, including eight carriers and the two biggest battleships in the world—the *Yamato* and *Musashi*—steaming toward Saipan. To Vice Admiral Jisaburo Ozawa's assembled fleet, the Japanese warlords radioed the following message: "The fate of the empire rests on this one battle. Every man is expected to do his utmost."

American submarines kept watch on the enemy's movements and kept Admiral Raymond Spruance, head of the Fifth Fleet, informed. When it became obvious that the Japanese were heading for Saipan, Spruance reorganized his force and created a flotilla of seven battleships, four heavy cruisers, and thirteen destroyers whose primary duty was to keep Ozawa's fleet away from the American flattops. In turn, the carriers' planes provided the air cover for the battleships.

On 15 June 1944, the patched-up "wounded bear"—the huge carrier *Shokaku*—left its base at Lingga Roads near Singapore and sailed with the Mobile Fleet to take part in the counterattack against the Allied offensive in the Marianas, a clash that would be known as the Battle of the Philippine Sea.

On 18 June, the submarine *Cavalla* (SS-240), on her first war patrol, found the enemy fleet 780 miles west of Saipan and roaring eastward. *Cavalla*'s skipper, Herman J. Kossler, notified Fifth Fleet headquarters of the impending attack and moved into position to disrupt the enemy's movement. At 1123 hours the next day, *Cavalla* fired three torpedoes into *Shokaku*, and at 1510 hours, her magazines blew up and the big carrier went under along with 1,272 of her men; four Japanese cruisers rescued *Shokaku*'s captain and 570 men. It was one of the great American submarine victories of the war.[12]

On that same day, James W. Blanchard's *Albacore*,* on station with

---

* In December 1944, *Albacore*, with Hugh R. Rimmer then at the helm, would be re-

Cavalla, Bang, Finback, Stingray, and *Pipefish* to the west of Saipan, put
another carrier out of action when she seriously damaged the 29,300-ton
carrier *Taiho.*[13]

The Battle of the Philippine Sea quickly evolved into what was
dubbed "The Great Marianas Turkey Shoot," because the now-
obsolescent Zero aircraft, and the inexperienced Japanese carrier pilots
who had been rushed through training following the twin debacles of
Coral Sea and Midway, were no match for the superb Americans and
their Grumman F6F Hellcat fighters. In the first attempt to strike,
forty-two of sixty-nine Japanese planes were sent spiraling into the sea.
The second strike fared no better; of the 128 planes that left their carriers, only thirty made it back. Another attack resulted in the loss of
sixty-eight out of eighty-seven enemy planes. In all, out of 373 planes,
only 130 returned, as compared to twenty-nine American planes lost.
Neither of the monster Japanese battleships played a major role in the
fighting.[14]

It was an overwhelming victory for the United States and a terrible,
crushing defeat for Japan. If "the fate of the empire" depended on that
one battle, then the empire was doomed. The next great sea clash—the
Battle of Leyte Gulf, in October—would seal that fate.

As one island fortress after another fell to the Americans, the Japanese
convoys became more concentrated. Gone were the days when the Imperial Japanese Navy was master of the Pacific, going here and there with
impunity in such numbers and along such diverse paths that the American boats were hard-pressed to locate them. Now the enemy's space was
compressed, his routes known, and American submariners had their
choice of targets.

As the Battle of the Philippine Sea was ending, a hot message from
ComSubPac notified *Tang, Tinosa,* and *Sealion II* that a damaged enemy
battleship would soon be plowing through the area on its way to a repair

---

ported overdue and presumed lost, probably the result of hitting a mine in Japanese home
waters. (www.csp.navy.mil/ww2boats/albacore)

facility at either Kobe or Sasebo. *Tang* took up station near the Koshiki Islands, just south of Nagasaki, at nearly midnight on 24 June to lie in wait for the injured dreadnought. Shortly thereafter, *Tang*'s radar scope sparkled with a large number of bright green blips—indicating a sizable Japanese convoy—and the dive alarm sent everyone scrambling for his battle station. Despite the lateness of the hour and the darkness of the night, O'Kane and his lookouts on the bridge could tell that the convoy was immense: twelve escorts surrounding several large ships—perhaps battleships or heavy cruisers.

O'Kane tried an audacious move—slipping half submerged between the escorts and the escorted. Could he possibly get a shot or two at one of the big boys before his presence was noted and the destroyers went nuts?

Viewed close up, the big targets were not cruisers or battleships but more likely large tankers or freighters. "Both appeared heavily laden," O'Kane noted, "and were most probably diesel-driven, as there was nary a wisp of smoke."

"Make tubes ready for firing," the skipper commanded, and the crew obeyed. O'Kane made some slight adjustments in *Tang*'s attitude, then gave the order to fire. He launched three fish at the leading ship, then, while the torpedoes were on their way, realigned *Tang* for a shot at the second target. Another spread of three fish was fired. Coolly, O'Kane kept the boat on the surface to watch the torpedoes—and to gauge the enemy's reaction. "Evasion would have to wait on the hits and some minutes into the counterattack. In the inevitable confusion, we would find a route out of the area," he said confidently.

Someone with a stopwatch in the conning tower counted down the seconds until the first torpedo was due to strike home: "Torpedo run one minute forty-eight seconds. One minute . . . Thirty seconds."

Then, right on schedule—*KaBLAMMMM!*

O'Kane described the spectacular result: "A whack, a flash, and a tremendous rumble came from the freighter's stern. Then from amidships, and her whole side seemed ripped out. The countdown was resumed only to be smothered in two more explosions. The second ship's stern was a mass of flames, and her superstructure aft crumbled with the second hit. More tremendous explosions and accompanying flashes followed, not timed as our torpedoes, and within minutes escorts were racing through the holocaust, dropping depth charges singly and in patterns. *Tang* was racing, too, for the nearest deep water."

Like a little boy who has just batted a baseball through the neighborhood grouch's window, O'Kane got out of the area as fast as his electric motors would take him. Once safely beyond the reach of angry destroyers, O'Kane sent a message to *Sealion II* and *Tinosa*, telling them what *Tang* had done. Taking credit for two ships, O'Kane didn't know until after the war that a couple of his fish had missed their primary targets and sunk two additional ships beyond them! He never did find the wounded battleship that had sent *Tang* into the area to begin with.[15]

"We were feeling really good about that third patrol," Clay Decker said, "especially since we hadn't sunk any ships during our second patrol. We didn't realize it, of course, but that third patrol was just getting started."[16]

The day after the two sinkings, *Tang* sighted and tracked an unescorted freighter near the island of Bono Misaki, off Kyushu. Closing in for the kill, O'Kane fired two fish, but they both porpoised toward the target, giving the merchantman's captain the chance to see and avoid them; the fish missed and *Tang* swam out of the area.

The next day *Tang, Tinosa,* and *Sealion II* received another alert from ComSubPac, directing the boats to begin hunting along an enemy shipping route off the coast of China. O'Kane picked a spot he thought might be productive and waited. Soon a 5,464-ton armed freighter of the *Tazan Maru* class lumbered into periscope view, aligned itself in *Tang*'s sights, and after a short chase (and some too-deep torpedo misses that O'Kane thought must have "scared the barnacles growing along her keel"), took a torpedo amidships that broke her back. O'Kane had a warrior's admiration for the enemy's courage: "Her gun crew had guts, for from her canting bow came a half dozen well-aimed rounds. How they pointed and trained their gun on that tilting platform will long remain a wonder, and their dedication in keeping up the fire until they went under would be a matter of pride to any nation." *Tang* probed the wreckage field but could find no survivors.

The next day, 1 July, brought more success to *Tang*. Two columns of black smoke were spotted on the horizon and *Tang* slid beneath the surface, heading toward the smoke being made by *Taiun Maru II*, a 270-foot-long armed freighter, and *Takatori Maru*, a 357-foot-long cargoman. Remarkably, no destroyers protected them. *Tang* fired a spread of torpedoes at both ships, and the stern of the smaller freighter shot into the air, accompanied by a great belch of flame, sailors, and debris. Internal detonations—probably a cargo of munitions destined for Japanese infantry on some island—finished the demolition job. Two minutes and twenty seconds after the severed stern disappeared beneath the waves, the upturned bow followed suit.

The *Takatori Maru,* seeing what had happened to its companion, took off with *Tang* in hot pursuit. Staying beyond the range of the enemy's deck guns for several hours, O'Kane tracked the freighter the way an Indian might track a deer. The sun set, the *Tang* rose, and the freighter's last moments as a seagoing vessel were at hand. Two torpedoes bolted from their homes in *Tang*'s bow and struck the enemy ship, setting off secondary explosions that sent it plunging. Still, *Tang*'s remarkable third patrol was not over.

After a couple of days of trolling for targets in the empty Yellow Sea, and watching the same Hollywood Westerns over and over in the wardroom, *Tang* rendezvoused with *Sealion II* to exchange movies and news. Skipper Eli Reich reported that his *Sealion II* had just sunk her first victim on the way to the rendezvous, and that he was now on his way to patrol around Shanghai.

Following *Sealion II*'s departure, *Tang* sailed to Korea, where the crew would get the chance to celebrate the Fourth of July in typical American fashion, complete with fireworks. At dawn, a large ship hove into view. "I liked a part of what I saw," said O'Kane, "the massive bow, broad superstructure and bridge, the great, heavy masts. Perhaps we had forgotten what a big ship looked like, but everything suggested an auxiliary warship. It would take a broader angle, uncovering more details, before we could further identify her." A quick study of ONU-14, the

Warship Recognition Manual, brought a difference of opinion as to what their target might be. Some of the officers said it was the *Kurosio Maru*, but O'Kane wasn't so sure; he thought it might be a conversion to a seaplane tender or perhaps an aircraft transport.

The window of opportunity for an attack was quickly closing; *Tang*'s batteries had only about an hour of juice left in them and the water was shallow—about four fathoms under the keel, or about twenty-four feet—and getting shallower. If the ship was armed—and almost every Japanese merchantman was—*Tang* might have difficulty escaping unscathed.

But O'Kane was nothing if not brave. Nosing in for a closer look, he decided to go after the freighter, no matter what its name was or what it carried. Shortly before 0600 hours, at a range of 2,500 yards, the torpedoes were launched and piloted themselves at forty-six knots beneath the dark waters.

"Hot, straight, and normal," sang out the soundman, alleviating the worry that the fish might be swallowed by mud in the shallows.

Now it was a waiting game. Everyone watched the steady circular run of the second hand skating across the boat's chronometers, wondering when—or if—they would hear the submariners' favorite tune: the sound of an enemy ship in its death throes.

KaWHAM! O'Kane looked through the periscope at the destruction he had wrought: "Only the bow, stern, and masts were sticking out of the water," he said of the fatally stricken ship. "We surfaced, surrounded by thirty-four fishermen, understandably awestricken. They were quick to recover, for in some sampans men were shaking their fists at us while from others came the overhead clasped hands of a boxer's salute. We assumed that they were Japanese and Korean, respectively." A few survivors of the sinking were already crawling into lifeboats. The ship *Tang* had just downed was the 6,886-ton transport *Asukazan Maru*, but the day was just beginning. *Tang* departed and headed farther up the peninsula, where Korea meets Manchuria, to see how many more victims she could claim.[17]

"What a way to celebrate the Fourth," said Clay Decker.[18]

After charging *Tang*'s batteries on the surface for a few hours,

O'Kane came across a freighter steaming south, slipping through a narrow passage between some small islands and the Korean coast. The cargoman was fortunate; O'Kane judged the fit to be too tight and broke off the pursuit.

Another ship was not so lucky. With the sun setting behind Manchuria, lookouts on *Tang*'s bridge spotted the smoke of another transport coming from the west. O'Kane steered a course to intercept the new target, grateful that deeper water was now below his keel. Four torpedoes remained; O'Kane hoped to expend not more than two against this ship. The batteries were another consideration, for they were not yet fully charged. That couldn't be helped, and O'Kane ordered *Tang* to submerge. Like a well-trained circus animal, she complied without hesitation.

The range to the target closed to 7,500 yards—a little over four miles. As the ship zigged and presented her flank to *Tang*, the identification party leafed quickly through the silhouette book but could find no match. It would be learned later that the ship was the 7,500-ton *Yamaoka Maru*, laden with 7,000 tons of iron ore and heading from Tientsin to Kobe.

The range was now down to 3,000 yards, then 2,400. The *maru* zigged again, giving *Tang* a nice wide target. The first torpedo was launched, its run only thirty seconds.

"Shaking explosions rocked us," said O'Kane, "but the great tripod masts were tilting toward each other; the enemy ship's back was broken. Jones took a look and a second later said, 'She's gone, Christ, all of her!' The twisting, grinding, breaking-up noises came over Sound and through the hull in increasing intensity. It was a frightening, sobering noise and should serve to keep any lookout on his toes for weeks to come."

Surfacing and snooping in the floating debris, *Tang* found one frightened but unhurt survivor—a very young sailor—and hauled him aboard. The crew dubbed their prisoner "Firecracker," in honor of the Independence Day holiday.

Tang was now down to two torpedoes. Lesser skippers might have thanked their lucky stars, turned around, and headed for home, preferring to keep their remaining fish for defensive purposes only, but not O'Kane. He was going to stay on the hunt as long as he had a single arrow left in his quiver.

Moving north along Korea's west coast to a rocky jut of land called Choppeki Point, *Tang* found some deep water and staked out a claim. She did not have to tread water for long; at around 2200 hours a blip presented itself on the radar screen. It was a ship moving away from Choppeki Point and heading west, probably a freighter or transport on its way to China. O'Kane wanted *Tang* to be ahead of the target, so he put her on a course that would allow her to outflank the ship and be in position before dawn. That would mean several hours of running at full speed on the surface. Fortunately, there were no antisubmarine forces in the area.

At last O'Kane reached the ambush site, submerged, and waited for the transport, identified as the 4,000-ton *Dori Maru*, to come into range. The last two fish were launched, struck home, and blew out the freighter's side. Within minutes the enemy ship had vanished. There were no survivors. Out of torpedoes, and with destroyers steaming over to see what had happened, *Tang* headed for Midway, some 2,500 miles to the east. Except for outrunning a gantlet of small patrol craft, the return trip was uneventful.

The prisoner, Firecracker, whose real name was Mishuitunni Ka, became a fixture in the sub and was soon conversing via smiles and hand gestures with the rest of the crew, who took him under their wing. The cook went out of his way to boil Ka's rice to his liking; O'Kane restrained himself from reminding the cook that Ka was a prisoner, not a cruise-ship guest. Ka was brought in handcuffs to the wardroom, where he watched the nightly Western movies along with the Americans, and O'Kane remarked that Ka "had become more of a crew's mascot than a prisoner of war." Once *Tang* reached Midway, however, Firecracker was blindfolded, shackled, and taken away by four big Marines. The skipper said that many of the sailors were heartbroken to see him carried off in irons, and "looked like boys who had just lost a pet."[19]

Most of the crew were given liberty and headed off to do whatever young men could do on an island completely devoid of women: they got drunk and gambled away their pay in the lobby of the Gooney Bird Hotel.

ONCE ashore, O'Kane received the congratulations of the island's senior officers, who marveled at *Tang*'s score of eight (later increased to ten) kills on one patrol. Up to that point, only Mush Morton's ill-fated *Wahoo* had sunk eight ships on one patrol. Dick O'Kane was well on his way to avenging the death of his friend, but his mission was not yet over.

While at Midway for rest, recuperation, and refitting, O'Kane said farewell to those moving on to other assignments and conducted the usual training program for new hands coming aboard. There were test dives to trim the time it took to submerge; mock attacks against American warships; and depth-charge indoctrination using an American destroyer dropping ash cans at a safe distance to familiarize the novices on board with what such an attack sounded and felt like. O'Kane also spent considerable time allowing some of his junior officers turns at the helm, for he knew the day was likely coming when they would be transferred from *Tang* to command boats of their own.[20]

Tang's crew also caught up on the war news while at Midway. They learned that, on 20 July 1944, some of Hitler's own staff officers had tried to kill him with a bomb in his forward headquarters at Rastenburg, East Prussia. Although the Führer survived the blast, the action signaled that even his own officers had grown disillusioned with his leadership and were willing to risk their lives to eliminate him in hopes of reaching a negotiated settlement and ending the war.[21]

There was more good news. On 21 July 1944, American soldiers and Marines had landed on the island of Guam, some 1,300 miles east of the Philippines, and overcome stiff resistance by the entrenched enemy. Guam, at the southern end of the Marianas chain, had been captured on 10 December 1941 by the Japanese, who had turned it into one of their most strategic air and naval bases. Few islanders had been treated with more brutality than the Guamanians, and they were especially happy to welcome the Americans to their home. As the historian Martin Gilbert notes, "In the Japanese conquest of [Guam] in December 1941, only a single Japanese soldier had lost his life; now, in a twenty-day battle, 18,500 Japanese defenders were killed, at the cost of 2,124 American lives."[22]

Next to fall was the island of Tinian, which was needed as a base of operations for B-29 "Superfortress" bombers; American Marines took Tinian away from 6,000 of the enemy. It was a grim and grisly business, with napalm—a jellied gasoline that could be dropped in bombs or shot through the air with handheld flamethrowers or specially equipped tanks—being used for the first time in the Pacific Theater; the stench of burning flesh pervaded the soft South Seas air on Tinian.*

Rather than burden their families with the disgrace of being captured, Japanese soldiers blew themselves up with grenades or threw themselves from Tinian's high, rugged cliffs onto the rocks below.[†23]

Inexorably, the once seemingly invincible Japanese Empire was slowly being crushed to death. Reduced now to defending the Home Islands, Formosa, and the Philippines—plus a few outposts such as the Palaus, Okinawa, and Iwo Jima—Japan's military forces were defending a shrinking perimeter. On one hand, this was a boon for the Americans, for it meant they could concentrate their forces and firepower over a smaller area. On the other hand, such a shrinkage brought about a major problem, for it meant the Japanese would fight even more tenaciously as the American enemy closed in on their homeland.

What wasn't then generally known, however, was the fact that Emperor Hirohito had lost faith in General Tojo's ability to conduct the war. Disgraced, Hideki Tojo offered his resignation on 9 July 1944, but it was not until the eighteenth that it was accepted and he was relieved of his many titles and duties—that of prime minister; minister for war, armaments, education; and chief of the Imperial Japanese Army general staff. He was replaced in the latter role by General Yoshijiro Umezu. On the nineteenth, the entire government of Japan resigned, and Emperor

---

* Napalm was developed by a team of chemists at Harvard University in 1942–1943, and was formulated for use in bombs and flamethrowers. The chemicals convert gasoline into a sticky syrup that burns slowly but at a high temperature. (www.napalm.net)

† Some Japanese soldiers disappeared into Tinian's steamy jungles in an effort to avoid being taken prisoner. The last soldier did not emerge until 1960. (Crowl, 437)

Hirohito directed General Kuniaka Koiso to form a new government. The war, however, would go on.[24]

ON 30 July 1944, several of the officers and men of *Tang* received medals and commendations from higher headquarters; O'Kane received the Legion of Merit for the rescue of aviators at Truk and a third Silver Star for his earlier service aboard *Wahoo*.

The following afternoon, gassed up and loaded with food and tin fish, *Tang* cast off her lines and motored out to sea for her fourth patrol, this one to the Japanese Home Islands off the coast of Honshu. O'Kane was handed a personal note from Admiral Lockwood before this fourth patrol. It read:

> Dear Dick,
>
> I want to tell you why I am sending you and your *Tang* right back to the Empire, with hardly a breather. We have had two poor, and now a dry, patrol in these areas, the boats reporting a dearth of shipping.
>
> Intelligence reports indicate that the merchant traffic must be there, and I am certain that *Tang* can rediscover it.
>
> Sincerely, and Godspeed,
>
> C. A. Lockwood

O'Kane was pleased at the trust that ComSubPac had placed in him and his crew to get the job done: "We knew that this note was a compliment to our ship, and offered a challenge to each of us," he wrote.

As *Tang* cruised toward Japan and, according to O'Kane, "continued to enjoy yachting weather, with flying fish skimming away from her bow," the crew's thoughts turned to the upcoming mission. Would fortune continue to smile on them, or did disaster lurk beyond the horizon?[25]

CHAPTER 16

THE DEATH OF INNOCENTS

IN spite of heavy casualties suffered by all branches of service and in all theaters, the war in August 1944 was progressing well for the Allies. The combined American–British–Canadian–Polish–Free French force that had landed in the French province of Normandy in June had finally broken out from the beachhead in an operation dubbed "Cobra" and was pushing south; it would soon turn eastward and Paris would be liberated before the month was out. On the fifteenth, the American Seventh Army would land on the French Riviera in Operation Dragoon and begin its long march northward toward Alsace-Lorraine and the fortified border with Germany. German units occupying Hitler's onetime Axis partner Italy were being slowly squeezed into the mountains north of Rome.[1]

In the Pacific, the Americans were also drawing ever closer to Japan. Carl Vozniak, the electrician's mate first class from Philadelphia aboard *Finback*, recalled that on 1 September 1944, his submarine was on lifeguard duty about seven or eight miles off Iwo Jima. He was frustrated: "Because I was the main power electrician, I was always belowdecks and had never had a chance to see the war. I wanted to see at least a little of it, so one day I had my buddy stand by for me on the maneuvering board and I went up to be a lookout. I saw our planes coming over the island and they let their bombs go. There had been a bunch of houses and buildings with towers on the island, and in two minutes they were gone. That was the first time I ever saw the war. I got to see fifteen minutes of it."

Suddenly *Finback* got word that an American pilot from the carrier *Franklin* had ditched in the sea about a mile from the shore of Iwo Jima. "When we were on lifeguard duty," Vozniak said, "we would put a big American flag on our deck so our planes wouldn't attack us. We started to go pick that pilot up—we're running on the surface now—and we got so close to Iwo that the Japs started shelling us like crazy. They had our range but they didn't have our speed. We went in submerged, spotted the pilot, and he spotted us. He's in a rubber raft, and he wraps a line around our periscope, plus his arms, but he slipped off three times. We had to swing out and come up again. We finally got him out about seven miles from shore and surfaced to bring him aboard. Now there's a pilot who was thankful."[2]

The next day, 2 September, four American Grumman TBF "Avengers" of Squadron VF-51 lifted off the deck of the converted aircraft carrier *San Jacinto*, 1,200 miles northeast of Palau. Their mission was to strike the major Japanese communications installation on the island of Chichi Jima, one of the Bonin Islands, 400 miles south of Tokyo and 150 miles north of Iwo Jima. One of the Avenger pilots was a twenty-year-old lieutenant (j.g.) named George Herbert Walker Bush, flying his fifty-eighth mission.

Nat Adams, a Navy Grumman F6F "Hellcat" pilot from the *San Jacinto*, assigned to protect the Avengers, recalled seeing Bush's plane get hit by a burst of antiaircraft fire just before he could release his four 500-pound bombs. Adams said, "He continued his 200-mile-an-hour dive on the target and released his volley of explosives. I could see his engine flame and then spread to the fuel tanks housed in the wings. As he leveled off and cleared the target area, I followed him from above. His plane continued to spew black smoke. It was apparent that the shrapnel had punctured a fuel line. 'Get out,' I thought, 'before you blow up.'"

Lieutenant Bush ordered his two crew members, Lieutenant (j.g.) William "Ted" White and Radioman Second Class John Delaney, to bail out of the flaming Avenger, which they did; neither survived the fall, however. Then it was Bush's turn. Pushing back the canopy, he struggled to keep the stricken plane level long enough step out onto the wing.

Adams said, "I expected to see the plane explode before George could get out, but he was able to make it to the wing at the last moment. It appeared to me that he pulled his rip cord too soon. He, with his partially opened chute, clipped the leading edge of the plane's tail. I found out later that the blow cut a gash over his eye . . . Because of the damage to the parachute, Bush floated unduly fast away from the stricken plane and to the sea, a couple thousand feet below. Just before he hit the water, the Avenger, now at some distance, exploded in a ball of fire."

Bush managed to inflate his Mae West life jacket and a small yellow life raft that had served as his seat cushion. With blood streaming from his wound, he crawled into the raft. But his problems were not yet over; the wind and currents were pushing him directly toward the shore of enemy-held Chichi Jima and a small flotilla of Japanese boats were heading out to capture him. But Adams and the other Hellcat pilots swooped down with machine guns blazing and drove them off.

It was a close call for the future commander in chief; the Japanese on Chichi Jima were especially ruthless, and there were several reported instances of captured American fliers on the island being beheaded.[3]

Just then *Finback*, which had just arrived from Iwo Jima, surfaced near Bush's raft and the injured pilot paddled over to it. There he was brought aboard, had his wound treated, and was given dry clothes, a bunk, and a hot meal. Of course, no one at that time knew the young pilot would one day become the forty-first president of the United States.

"He was just another snot-nosed kid like me," recalled Carl Vozniak. "He was eighteen when he went into service and was the

Lieutenant (j.g.) George H. W. Bush.
(Courtesy Naval Historical Center)

youngest pilot in the history of the United States Navy. We picked up a total of five airmen around Chichi Jima—three officers and two enlisted men; but he was the first pilot we rescued on that patrol. We had to hot-bunk with them; the boat's officers traded bunks with the pilots. The *Finback* picked up a prisoner of war, too. All of them finished the patrol on board with us."[4]

For two months, Bush stayed aboard *Finback* as she continued on her tenth war patrol and he got to experience submarine life from the inside. *Finback* even sank two ships—the 536-ton Japanese army cargo ship *Hassho Maru* and the 866-ton merchantman *Hakuun Maru 2*.[5] *Finback* was also depth-charged during her patrol, an unnerving experience that Bush later said was "far scarier than an airplane bombing run. At least in the plane you controlled your destiny to some extent, but there, under the water, all you could do was hope like hell that an enemy wouldn't put an explosive on top of you!"[6]

The pilots were eventually brought to Midway at the end of *Finback*'s patrol and flown back to Pearl Harbor for rest and recuperation.[7]

FOR three months that spanned the summer of 1944, the hospital at Mare Island ran nearly every test on Smitty known to medical science, including a spinal tap, but could find nothing physically wrong. Daily Smitty was poked, prodded, and examined inside and out by a team of specialists. They even got inside his head. "Ever have dreams or nightmares?" asked one of them in the psych ward one day.

"Yes, sir. I keep seeing this buddy of mine, name's Bill. Bill Partin. He went down with the *Sculpin*. He was married and had a kid. Sometimes I wake up in the middle of the night in a sweat after dreaming about him, only it's *me* going down in the *Sculpin*, not him."

The doctors huddled. This piece of information seemed to hold the key. A day or two later, the head of psychiatry met with Smitty. "Smith, we think we know what the problem is. We think it's 'battle fatigue.' In the First World War they called it 'shell shock.' "

Smitty took offense. "You think I'm *yellow*? You think I'm *nuts*?"

"Calm down, Smith. No, nothing like that. A lot of very brave men, when they're subjected to the stresses and strains of combat over a long period of time, sometimes have trouble dealing with it mentally. It doesn't mean you're a coward or crazy. It just means the emotional strain is beginning to manifest itself physically. We see a lot of those cases here."

"So how do I get over it, doc? Take some pills? Get a shot?"

"It's not that simple, Smith. There is no known remedy. You may experience symptoms—nightmares, night sweats, nervousness, that low-grade fever—for a short period of time, or for the rest of your life. There's no way of knowing. The most important thing we can do for you now is to take you off sea duty."

Smitty felt like he had just been kicked off the football team—and kicked in the gut. No more sea duty? How could he pay the Japs back for Bill Partin? How could he face his buddies? Would people laugh and point at him and call him a chicken? His face reddened. "Doc, please—just give me a chance."

"Sorry, Smith. You could endanger yourself and your shipmates if we allowed you to go back out to sea."

Smitty thought about it for a moment. "So what does this mean—you're discharging me from the Navy?" The thought of going back to Hammond and hanging out with the other 4-Fs was chilling.

"No, not at all. You'll be reassigned to shore duty. You might want to work as a mechanic here at Mare Island, or have some sort of office job, maybe even become an instructor."

"Instructor? Like where?"

"You name it. I'm sure we can get you transferred to a school wherever there's an opening."

"How about Great Lakes? It's near my hometown of Hammond, Indiana."

"Well, we can probably arrange for that. Give us a little time to work on it. Report to Personnel in about a week."

Smitty took a taxi back to his and Marilynn's apartment in Vallejo, thinking over the whole improbable situation. An instructor. Great Lakes. Yeah, that would be all right. If he couldn't personally kill Japs, at least he could teach *others* how to kill them.

He checked with the personnel office the following week and his orders to become a torpedo instructor at Great Lakes Naval Training Center were there waiting for him.[8]

* * *

AFTER repairs and refitting, Sam Dealey's *Harder* left Fremantle on 5 August 1944. Along with John C. Broach's *Hake* and Chester W. Nimitz Jr.'s *Haddo*, she was to patrol as part of a wolfpack in the South China Sea, east of Luzon. There the three boats would join up with Brooks J. Harral's *Ray* (SS-271) and Enrique D. Haskins's *Guitarro* (SS-363).[9]

Because of a rare excess of engineers on *Harder* for that particular patrol, Mike Geletka was ordered to stay behind with the relief crew in Australia; although he was disappointed at being excluded from the patrol, it turned out to be an order that saved his life.[10]

On the afternoon of 20 August, *Ray*, patrolling in the South China Sea, tracked a large convoy into Paluan Bay, on the northwestern coast of Mindoro. Dealey and Harral held a megaphone conversation from their respective bridges just outside the bay; Dealey's plan was for a concentrated wolfpack attack on the convoy at dawn. *Harder* came alongside *Haddo* at 0130 hours on 21 August and Dealey told the younger Nimitz that at least sixteen enemy ships were holed up in the bay. When the convoy made its exit at dawn (as convoys normally did), *Ray* and *Guitarro* were to approach from the northwest, *Haddo* from the west, and *Harder* from the southwest.

The attacks went off perfectly. Four enemy ships, totaling 22,000 tons, were sunk; it is believed that *Harder* sank one of them. The following day, *Haddo* and *Harder* conducted a combined attack on three vessels off Bataan, sinking all three. *Harder* sank two frigates, the *Matsuwa* and *Hiburi*, about fifty miles southwest of Manila.

On the morning of 23 August, *Haddo* spotted a tanker escorted by a destroyer, and blew the bow off the destroyer in a down-the-throat shot, leaving the tin can flaming and dead in the water. *Haddo* fired her last torpedo in this attack, and in response to urgent calls for assistance, *Hake* and *Harder* rendezvoused with her. Out of ammo, *Haddo* received Dealey's permission to leave the wolfpack and head south to Australia. Dealey and Broach finished off the damaged destroyer and then departed for their next objective.

At 0453 hours the next morning, *Hake* dove not far from Caiman Point, near the west coast of Luzon, with *Harder* in sight 4,500 yards south of her. Broach heard echo ranging to the south and soon sighted two ships: a three-stack light cruiser and a destroyer that, on further inspection, were identified as a three-stack destroyer and a minesweeper of less than 1,000 tons. *Hake* broke off the attack and headed north when the destroyer zigged away and entered Dasol Bay; the minesweeper stayed outside.

At 0647 hours, *Harder*'s periscope was seen cutting a wake at about 600 to 700 yards ahead of *Hake*. *Hake*'s soundman also picked up faint screws on the bearing, so Broach turned toward the south. At this point the minesweeper gave three strong pings, whereupon *Hake* saw her 2,000 yards away, apparently maneuvering toward the two submarines. Broach went deep. The enemy kept pinging, but seemed to have the two subs pinpointed. At 0728, *Hake* heard and felt a salvo of fifteen depth charges, none of them close. By 0955, all was quiet.

Harder never was heard from again. Japanese records revealed that an antisubmarine attack with fifteen depth charges was made by the Siamese destroyer *Pra Ruang* on the same day at *Harder*'s last-reported location. The enemy's records said, "Much oil, wood chips, and cork floated in the neighborhood." Presumably *Harder* perished in this attack.

Harder, Sam Dealey, and his seventy-eight-man crew—brave men all—had fought their final battle.[11]

It is a tragic fact that innocents are often killed or maimed in war. Some are civilians who happen to be in the wrong place at the wrong time: under a stick of bombs, or a salvo of shells, or in the middle of a cross fire. Others are wounded troops whose hospital is accidentally or purposely targeted by the enemy.

Just as tragic is the unintentional loss of life among men who have been taken prisoner and are *hors de combat*. It is estimated that of the 50,000 Allied prisoners of war the Japanese transferred by ship from one POW camp to another, nearly 11,000 died when their unmarked transports were unknowingly sunk by American submarines.

Robert Barr Smith writes, "These vessels were called 'hell ships,' and with good reason. POWs and slave laborers were crammed into stinking

Officers and crew of the gallant, ill-fated U.S.S. *Harder*.
(Courtesy Mike Geletka)

holds, filthy with coal dust, congealed sugar syrup and horse manure left over from previous voyages. Without water, or nearly so, sick, abused and neglected, they baked in unimaginable heat inside their steel prisons."[12]

The Japanese, whether by accident or design, refused to visually mark any of these "hell ships" from the outside, as required by the Geneva Convention. American and British submariners, therefore, had no way of knowing that prisoners of war were the human cargo inside many of the ships they sank. Consequently, thousands of Allied troops died by "friendly fire."

September 1944 was an especially tragic month for POWs. On the twelfth, Eli Reich's *Sealion II* spotted the transport *Rokyo Maru* (also spelled *Raykuyo Maru*) near Hainan Island and attacked—completely unaware that 1,159 Australian prisoners, weak from years of working as slave laborers on a jungle railway, were in its hold. Three torpedoes were fired; two struck home, shaking the ship and triggering a panic. The POWs tried to climb out of the hold and make for the lifeboats and rafts, but the Japanese crew beat them back with sticks, clubs, and rifle butts.

The Diggers, as Australian soldiers are known, refused to be held down. They overcame their guards and jumped overboard, clinging to bits of flotsam and overturned lifeboats. Several attempted to row to Australia, over 200 miles away. Before they could make it, though, a group of Japanese ships arrived and hauled the survivors aboard. The POWs were eventually reincarcerated in the Karasaki prison camp.

On that same day of 12 September, and in the same waters, some 400 Allied POWs perished when *Pampanito* unknowingly torpedoed the prisoner-laden *Kachidoki Maru*. Once the commanders of *Pampanito* and *Sealion II* discovered what they had done, they reversed course and rescued ninety-two Australian and sixty British prisoners from the sea, bringing back not only the prisoners but also the first information about Japanese atrocities committed during the building of the Burma–Thailand Railway—the infamous "bridge over the River Kwai."[13]

Six days later, another "hell ship" met its doom. The *Junyo Maru,* an old, British-built cargoman, was filled with some 2,300 POWs—Americans, Dutch, British, Australians, Indonesians, along with some 4,200 Javanese slave laborers—bound for Padang, on the west coast of Sumatra.

Robert Barr Smith writes that on board *Junyo Maru*, "There was not enough water, and there were no latrine facilities, save for a few boxes suspended outboard on the upper deck. Some prisoners were too weak even to reach these primitive privies, and human excrement accumulated in the holds and dripped down from the hatch covers. Some prisoners remained on the upper deck, exposed to wind and chilly rain at night and brutal tropical sun throughout the day; the rest baked in the iron ovens below. Men sat on cargo derricks and on the hatch covers, from which every other plank had been removed to admit a vestige of air. Before the ship ever sailed, the stench of human bodies and human waste was overpowering. Many prisoners suffered from malaria or

British and Australian prisoners of war are rescued at sea by
Sealion II on 15 September 1944. The POWs had been aboard
Japanese transports en route from Singapore to Japan when
their "hell ships" were sunk by *Sealion II*, *Growler*, and *Pampanito*.
(Courtesy Naval Historical Center)

dysentery or both. Some died; others went mad. The sick and the weak
sank further toward death."[14]

The British submarine *Trade Wind* spotted the transport and moved
in for the kill. In the attack, some 1,500 Western and Indonesian POWs
lost their lives while about 4,000 of the Javanese died. The remaining
survivors were picked up by Japanese vessels and eventually were put to
work on the Sumatran railroad; very few would live to see the end of the
war.

On 21 September, the Japanese freighter *Hofuku Maru* was sunk by
U.S. Navy aircraft north of Subic Bay, Philippines; 1,287 British and
Dutch POWs went down with her. Sixty-three men survived, but not for
long. They were transferred to *Oryoku Maru*, which would also be sunk
off Bataan by American aircraft in December; 1,340 of the over 1,600
men on board the *Oryoku Maru* would survive, only to die when their
next ship, *Enoura Maru*, was sunk by planes. Two more "hell ships,"

known as *PS-3* and *PS-4*, were sunk by Allied forces, the first bombed in Manila Bay, the second torpedoed between Hong Kong and Formosa; some 2,700 prisoners died.

The tragic experiences of the men aboard the transport *Shinyo Maru* were also well documented. On 7 September 1944, the American submarine *Paddle* (SS-263), under Byron H. Nowell, spotted a Japanese convoy heading from Davao to the waters north of Sindangan Point, Mindanao. Picking out a transport from among the multiple targets, Nowell attacked. No one in the submarine could have guessed that 750 American POWs were in *Shinyo Maru*, which was sunk by torpedoes.

Harry Alvey, a torpedoman on *Paddle,* said, "After we sank that prisoner-of-war ship and our skipper found out about it, he kind of went to pieces mentally, and Captain [Joseph P.] Fitz-Patrick took over. We just thought it was a freighter; the Japanese didn't put any signs on them. Like they say, 'War is hell,' so what're you going to do?"

Onnie Clem of Texas, a Marine Corps sergeant who had been captured on Bataan in early 1942, was among the 750 men in the hold of the *Shinyo Maru*, which had been at sea for nineteen days. He described his harrowing ordeal: "Late one afternoon . . . the Japanese pulled the hatch covers off and dropped hand grenades down in there and then turned machine guns down in the hold. Well, just about the time they started that, there was this explosion. A torpedo had hit the ship. Personally, the only thing that I remember was that I saw a flash, and everything turned an orangish-colored red. No feeling, no nothing. Everything just turned a solid color. I don't know if the grenades went off first or the torpedo, because it all meshed together . . . The next thing I knew, I was kind of flying, just twisting and turning, and there were clouds of smoke all around me. I couldn't see anything but these billowy forms, like pillows. I thought I was dead.

"Then I opened my eyes, and reality came back. I was underwater in the hold of this ship, and these pillows were the bodies of other guys in there. Some of them were dead; some of them were trying to get out. The ship was filling up with water, and I thought it had already sunk. I thought I was trapped down in it, and I thought I was going to die. So

I figured the quickest way to get it over with was to go ahead and drown myself. So I opened my mouth and thought I'd drink some water.

"I found that my head was above water, and I was just gulping air. I looked up, and I could see light coming through this open hatch. Then I thought, 'Well, I can get out of here.' In the meantime, all this water was rushing up toward this hatch, and the ship was filling up and sinking. I had actually been forced into a corner and was away from the hatch . . . It was everybody for themselves—survival of the fittest. Everybody was clawing at each other trying to get to the hatch. You'd pull one person out of the way to get a little closer to the hatch. I finally reached the hatch, and two other guys and I pulled ourselves out at the same time.

"Up on the bridge there was a machine gun spraying the hatch. A burst of machine-gun fire caught all three of us and knocked us back down in the hold. We'd all been hit. I got plowed in the skull. Another bullet chipped out my chin. Nevertheless, I was able to work myself back up on deck, and I was eyeing that bridge when I came out that time. The gun was still there, but the gunner was laying out on deck. Somebody had apparently got up there and killed him. At this time I found out that we were out in the ocean about two or three miles from shore. All I had on was a loincloth."

Besides being weak and wounded, Clem was desperately thirsty. "I figured I was in pretty bad shape, but I still wanted to get to shore and get something to drink." He dived over the side. When he surfaced, he saw that the sinking ship had been part of a convoy. "The other ships had put out lifeboats to pick up Japanese, but they were shooting all the Americans. They were shooting them, or some of the officers were taking swipes at their heads with sabers. There were Japs all around me."

Clem also discovered that he was deaf; both his eardrums had been punctured by the concussion of the exploding torpedo. He tried swimming toward a distant speck of land. "We swam and we swam, and my right arm just finally got to where I couldn't swim, I couldn't move it, couldn't pull it over my head. It was completely paralyzed, useless. I found out later that while I had been swimming I'd been shot twice—once in the arm and once in the shoulder."

Clem and two other survivors somehow managed to make it to the beach. The trio crawled into some foliage that rimmed the beach and were later spotted by a friendly Filipino. "He had on a pair of cut-off dungarees, and he took them off and gave them to me, and then he climbed up this coconut tree and got a bunch of coconuts and cut them down for us. We walked about a mile inland and came upon this hut with several Filipinos standing around. They gave us some water—I never could get enough water—and then they took us to a village probably five or six miles away. Then they started to bring other Americans into this village. There were 750 of us on that ship, and only eighty-three of us got ashore."

The survivors were taken to a camp deep in the jungle, where they came under to protection of a guerrilla group commanded by an American colonel named McGee. There a medic removed the bullets from Clem's arm, but declined to take the one out of his back, thinking it too close to the spine. The guerrilla camp had radio contact with Australia and informed the authorities there of the survivors.

"They promised us that the next time they brought in supplies by submarine they would take out the wounded," Clem said. After the ex-POWs had been with the guerrillas about a month they were escorted down to the beach. On 29 October, Filipinos in dugout canoes took all but one of the *Shinyo Maru*'s survivors out to Jack Titus's submarine *Narwhal*; that one man, Joseph P. Coe, Jr., elected to stay behind and become a radio operator on Mindanao for another guerrilla group, this one commanded by Brigadier General Wendall Fertig.[15]

Cletus Overton, another of the survivors, recalled the *Narwhal* rescue: "That moonlit evening about nine P.M., the submarine suddenly surfaced some distance from shore. Excitedly, I watched as two crewmembers came ashore in a rubberized rowboat. As the boat slid upon the sandy beach, one of the two stepped out and asked how many were in the group. Colonel McGee told him. The crewmen flashed a light signal to the submarine. There was an immediate signal back to the crewman who turned and said, 'We will take every damn one of you!' The other crewman . . . jammed in the sand a staff holding the American flag! It must have been a new flag. It seemed as if it were illuminated in the soft breeze and moonlight. The American flag, the symbol of freedom and liberty! What a glorious sight! Each of us, by the grace of God, had finally beaten the Japs in our struggles against their tyrannical brutality.

"We were carried by native rowboats and loaded into the submarine, filling every available space. Five days later, we arrived at a military base in New Guinea. There we were issued shoes, clothes and toilet kits. I'll never forget that good, hot, soapy bath, shave, and haircut. We were fed sumptuously and slept on good, clean beds. The next day, we were moved by torpedo boats to an airbase on another island. We were then flown to Brisbane, Australia, and placed in the 42nd General Hospital." The survivors were sent by ship back to San Francisco, and then taken by train to Washington, D.C., for interrogation by Navy intelligence specialists.

"We who went to Washington," said Overton, "were questioned in minute detail about the treatment received from the Japs and the conditions under which we had lived, as prisoners of war—particularly the many atrocities they had committed against us. After four or five days in Washington, we were given a ninety-day furlough home."[16]

Although a few hundred Allied POWs survived the sinking of their "hell ships," many thousands more did not, making their deaths one of the war's sad and tragic episodes.

CHAPTER 17

RETURN TO THE PHILIPPINES

By the autumn of 1944, Japan's earlier conquests were little more than distant memories as the Americans marched across the wide blue ocean to rip islands and atolls out of the enemy's grasp. General MacArthur had promised to return to the Philippines and now he was about to fulfill that promise.

In preparation for the invasion and liberation of the Philippines, MacArthur's forces hit the island of Morotai, northwest of New Guinea, on 14 September 1944, while Marc Mitscher's Task Force 58 joined up with Admiral Halsey's Third Fleet and Task Force 38 to create a massive striking force against the Japanese in the Palaus, specifically the islands of Anguar and Peleliu in the Palau group.

The Peleliu operation has been criticized as being unnecessary—and unnecessarily wasteful of American lives, for it turned out to be the worst bloodbath of any American amphibious assault landing during the whole of the war. During the eleven-day struggle, 9,171 men of the 1st, 5th, and 7th Marine Divisions were killed; 13,600 Japanese also died. Strategists have argued that Peleliu could simply have been bypassed, leaving the garrison there to wither on the vine.[1]

While American forces mopped up enemy resistance on the islands, and Roosevelt and Churchill met in Hyde Park, New York, to discuss the progress of the supersecret atomic bomb program—code-named "Manhattan Project"—MacArthur's men and Halsey's ships were gathering to

U.S. Marines search for cover during the assault on Peleliu.
(Courtesy National Archives)

assault Leyte from the sea. To accomplish this, the United States would first need to gain control of the seas around the Philippine Islands—a massive operation called King Two that would evolve into the Battle of Leyte Gulf.[2]

On 20 October, 100,000 American infantrymen came ashore at two separate points near Tacloban on the eastern shore of Leyte. The Battle of Leyte Gulf, fought from 23 to 26 October 1944, was actually four separate engagements—the Battle of the Sibuyan Sea; the Battle of Surigao Strait; the Battle of Samar; and the Battle of Cape Engaño—in four separate locations, making it the largest sea battle of all time.

In a desperate move to counter the Americans, Japan threw the bulk of her ships into a last-gasp, do-or-die effort. Enacting a complicated plan known as SHO-1, the Japanese hoped to lure the American carriers away from Leyte and then wipe out the unprotected troops—the 7th, 24th, 77th, and 96th Infantry Divisions, plus the 1st Cavalry Division—on the beaches. The bait would be Vice Admiral Jisaburo Ozawa's Northern Force with its six carriers.

Once Halsey's ships gave chase, as it was hoped they would, Vice Admiral Takeo Kurita's Center Force—with the world's two largest battleships, the *Yamato* and *Musashi*—would plow through the San Bernardino Strait and strike the American landing force. This attack would be reinforced by the cruisers and destroyers of two additional task forces led by Vice Admirals Kiyohide Shima and Shoji Nishimura. "The plan risked almost the entire remaining strength of the Japanese Navy," writes author John Wukovits. "Should it fail, little would remain to halt the growing American naval power."[3]

Preliminary American air strikes on Japan's fighter and bomber bases in the Philippines and on Formosa had essentially crippled Dai Nippon's ability to protect her flotillas from the air; three days of raids by U.S. aircraft destroyed 500 Japanese planes and forty warships while the Americans lost eighty-nine planes in the process.[4] Ozawa's six aircraft carriers could not make up the difference, for they were sacrificial lambs that held a paltry total of only 116 planes.

Despite this handicap, and the devastation of their land-based air fleet—the equivalent of going into the boxing ring with one hand tied behind one's back—the Japanese launched SHO-1 on 18 October. Kurita's armada left Lingga Roads and steamed northward for the Philippines via the Palawan Passage.

Two days later, as American troops hit the beaches on eastern Leyte, Ozawa's decoy carrier force left Kure in the Home Island of Honshu and headed south toward Leyte. On 22 October—the same day MacArthur waded ashore for the benefit of photographers—Nishimura's force departed Singapore to become the fourth claw in the attack.

Meanwhile, two American submarines that had been on station west of the Philippines for several weeks—David H. McClintock's *Darter* (SS-227) and Bladen D. Clagett's *Dace* (SS-247)—were low on food and fuel, and were preparing to return to their base in Australia. Unaware of the Japanese approach toward the Philippines, Raphael C.

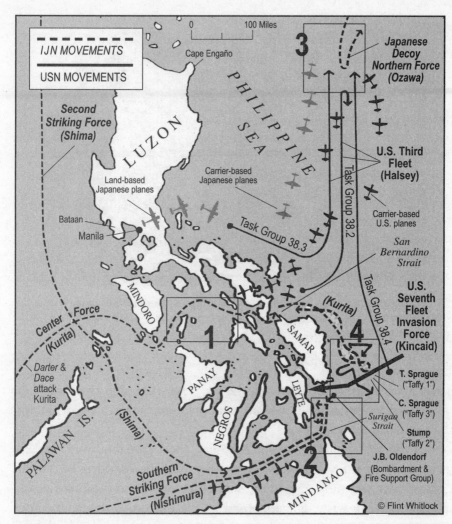

The four major engagements of the Battle of Leyte Gulf, 24–25 October 1944:
1. Battle of Sibuyan Sea
2. Battle of Surigao Strait
3. Battle off Cape Engaño
4. Battle off Samar

(Based on a map in Reports of General MacArthur, *Center of Military History, Pub. 13-3, 1994 reprint, Vol. 1, Plate 60)*

Fulfilling his promise to return to the Phillipines, General Douglas
MacArthur wades ashore with aides at Lingyan Gulf, 22 October 1944.
(Courtesy National Archives)

Benitez, an officer aboard *Dace*, said, "Our thoughts were more on
[Australia], on fresh food, mail from home, and the two weeks of shore
leave than on the war."

Shortly after midnight on 23 October, their thoughts were suddenly
thrust back to the war when lookouts spotted the outriders of Kurita's
Center Force steaming toward the southern entrance to the Palawan Passage. Disregarding the dangers posed by the numerous shoals and coral
reefs, *Dace* and *Darter*, along with Franklin G. Hess's nearby *Angler* (SS-
240), Haskins's *Guitarro*, and Wreford "Moon" Chapple's *Bream* (SS-
243), went hunting for Kurita's ships. The sub commanders were in for a
pleasant surprise. Instead of surrounding his convoy with the typical
screen of prickly destroyers, Kurita was plunging ahead with his cruisers
in the lead.

At 0324 hours, *Bream* fired six torpedoes toward the cruiser *Aoba*,
hitting it twice and causing extensive damage. *Dace* and *Darter*, near the
northern end of the Palawan Passage, spotted Kurita's onrushing main

body and set up an ambush. The two subs did some impressive damage, sinking the heavy cruisers *Maya* and Admiral Kurita's flagship *Atago*, and inflicting serious harm on the cruiser *Takao*.

Claggett, viewing the action through *Dace*'s periscope, exclaimed, "It looks like the Fourth of July out there! One is burning. The Japs are milling and firing all over the place. What a show! What a show!"

To say that the loss of *Atago* and the 360 men aboard it created confusion within the task force's ranks would be a major understatement; Kurita had to jump overboard to save his own life and was picked up by the destroyer *Kishinami*. During his absence, Rear Admiral Matome Ugaki on *Yamato* assumed temporary command. The all-out Japanese effort to forestall America's return to the Philippines had gotten off to a disastrous start.

Shortly after midnight the following morning, while in pursuit of the wounded *Takao* retreating to Brunei, *Darter* ran aground on a coral reef on Bombay Shoal and could not get off; *Dace* came to the rescue and brought her crew aboard.

But the beached *Darter* could not just be left there for the Japanese to scavenge and use as they saw fit; the decision was made to scuttle her. Codebooks and other classified material were burned, communications gear was smashed, and armaments were disabled prior to the boat being rigged with explosives to render her useless.[5]

Crewman Jim Clepper was setting the demolition charges throughout *Darter* to prevent the Japanese from getting anything from her. He had started at the aft torpedo room and was working his way forward, placing demolition blocks at all the strategic places. As he entered the galley, Clepper saw a strange sight. The cook was urinating on several pans of freshly baked bread. When Clepper asked what the cook was doing, the cook responded, "Ain't no fuckin' Jap gonna eat any of *my* fresh baked bread!"[6]

Shortly thereafter, Darter's crew was taken into *Dace*, and the explosive charges were detonated but failed to go off properly. *Dace* tried to help by firing her remaining torpedoes at *Darter*, but they hit the reef and exploded; *Dace*'s deck gun also did little damage. The nearby submarine *Rock* (SS-274) swam over and lent a hand, but her torpedoes, too, struck the coral before they could damage *Darter*.*[7]

Darter was not the only submarine to be lost on 24 October. *Shark II* (SS-314), commanded by Edward N. Blakely, went down in hostile waters near Hong Kong that same day, with eighty-seven men on board.

TWENTY-FOUR October 1944 also marked the opening of the main phase of the Battle of Leyte Gulf when aircraft from the Third Fleet's carriers spotted the remainder of Kurita's still-powerful Center Force, slowed but not stopped by the submarine attack, steaming into the Sibuyan Sea. Before the Americans could launch their strike, however, Rear Admiral Ted Sherman's Carrier Task Group 38.3, on station east of Luzon, came under assault by land-based aircraft and was soon fighting for its life. Attacking in waves of fifty to sixty aircraft, the Japanese airmen braved the sheets of antiaircraft fire and pounded Sherman's ships unmercifully.

The Battle of Leyte Gulf heated up to the boiling point. The leviathan battleship *Musashi*, with the damage inflicted during its encounter with the *Tunny* on 29 March at last repaired, came roaring into Leyte Gulf, hungry for battle, only to be swarmed upon by hundreds of American planes, like a wildebeest being stung to death by wasps. Nineteen aerial torpedoes and seventeen bombs crashed into *Musashi*'s decks, its two-foot-thick armored hull, superstructure, 18.1-inch gun turrets, and antiaircraft gun tubs, blowing its bridge apart and starting raging fires that consumed its fuel and exploded the magazines. At 1915 hours, four hours after the first hit, *Musashi* keeled over and sank, taking with it 1,376 sailors; another 1,023 survived.[8]

The death of *Musashi* did not signal the end of the Battle of Leyte Gulf, but it must have struck fear and despair into the hearts of the Japanese sailors who watched the giant ship being pummeled even as they battled to save their own skins.[9]

---

* On 31 October, *Nautilus* was called upon to help destroy the beached sub; fifty-five shots from her six-inch deck gun finally did the trick. *Darter*'s captain and entire crew were kept together and assigned to the U.S.S. *Menhaden* (SS-377), which was then still under construction. (www.subnet.com/fleet/ss227)

American sailors aboard the light carrier *Princeton* were also battling to save *their* skins. A Yokosuka D4Y "Judy" dive-bomber singled out *Princeton* during the melee and dropped a 550-pound bomb on her. The bomb tore through the wooden flight deck, severed the main gasoline line used for fueling aircraft, pierced an auxiliary drop tank under the wing of a torpedo plane, then exploded in the crew's galley on the second deck. Within seconds, *Princeton* became a floating inferno.

While simultaneously trying to keep enemy aircraft at bay, several other ships, including the cruiser *Birmingham,* took turns pulling alongside *Princeton* in an effort to douse her fires. But the heat and flames were too intense, and their efforts were for naught. Suddenly, more than four hours after the Judy's bomb struck, 200 feet of *Princeton*'s stern and flight deck were blown off by a huge explosion; the *Birmingham,* lying hull to hull with *Princeton,* also went up in a massive, wrenching burst. Neither ship sank, but casualties were enormous. The carrier lost 347 men killed, 552 wounded, and four missing; the cruiser had 230 dead, 408 wounded, and four missing. One of *Birmingham*'s crewman, Harry Popham, had his leg blown off, and as he lay wounded, all he could see was "a deck strewn with body parts and flowing with rivers of blood."[10]

Meanwhile, Bull Halsey, befitting his nickname, was charging off toward the red cape—Ozawa's decoy carriers—just as the Japanese had hoped he would, sending his three available carrier groups, including all six of his battleships, north in pursuit of the enemy flattops. This act was in contravention to an earlier Nimitz directive ordering him to remain at Leyte to protect Vice Admiral Thomas Kinkaid's Seventh Fleet. Halsey's impulsiveness was nearly a fatal error, for it weakened and left exposed the Seventh Fleet, which stood off the beaches in support of the amphibious operation. Kinkaid apparently had no idea that Halsey's Third Fleet had departed, nor that a large enemy force was bearing down on him in a pincer movement through both the San Bernardino and Surigao Straits. Nimitz, too, was unaware what Halsey was doing and sent a message: "Where repeat where is Task Force 34? The world wonders."[11]

With TF 34 gone hunting, Kinkaid had only a relatively weak force of small carriers left at his disposal, but he did have a fleet of destroyers and forty-five PT boats in the Surigao Strait armed with torpedoes and the ability to sound the alarm in case of enemy incursion.

On the night of 24–25 October, Surigao Strait was suddenly thick with warcraft, for the next armada to arrive was Shima's Second Striking Force and Nishimura's Southern Force, which both ran headlong into Kinkaid's unexpected screen of destroyers. As with Kurita's ships, however, the Southern Force brusquely plowed through the impudent tin cans and roared ahead, closing in on the unprotected Seventh Fleet.[12]

The Southern Force came on; Admiral Jesse B. Oldendorf's Bombardment and Fire Support Group was ready and waiting. As Gerald Astor describes it, "Searchlights, star-shell bursts, muzzle flashes, red, white, and green tracers, and fiery, deafening detonations splintered the night. The duel, which began shortly before dawn on 25 October, lasted two hours. It ended with the Southern Force shattered and in retreat. The Japanese, lacking a coordinated attack by the Center Force, withdrew, minus two battleships and two destroyers sunk and with major damage to other vessels. The Americans chased the fleeing flotilla and blasted several more ships, notably the cruiser *Mogami*."[13]

Kurita's Center Force also entered the San Bernardino Strait on the night of 24–25 October before running into the picket line of PT boats. Boiling the water with wakes of explosive fish, the little plywood combatants gave it their all but to no avail; only one torpedo of the dozens launched struck home. The attack barely slowed the enemy flotilla, which brushed the small boats aside and raked them with both large- and small-caliber fire.

A task unit known as "Taffy 3," built around the small escort carriers *Saint Lô* and *Gambier Bay*, and commanded by Clifton Sprague, was now the last line of defense, and was directly in the path of the Central Force as it charged through San Bernardino Strait. Shortly after sunrise on 25 October, Kurita's fleet of twenty battleships, cruisers, and destroyers—including the *Yamato*, *Kongo*, *Nagato*, and *Haruna*—came charging through the mist and fog off Samar Island, bound for Leyte Gulf.

The ships of Taffy 3 swung into action and the escort carriers launched their aircraft, as did those of nearby Felix Stump's Taffy 2, and Thomas Sprague's Taffy 1 farther to the south. The airmen performed yeoman service, bombing, torpedoing, and strafing the Japanese fleet until their munitions were exhausted. Despite the pilots' best efforts to protect the carriers, however, *Gambier Bay* was hit, set afire, and was listing badly. Doomed, she would need to be abandoned. Fortunately, the majority of her 800-man crew was rescued.[14]

The escort carrier *Saint Lô* was not as lucky. A Japanese suicide pilot crashed his aircraft through her flight deck, igniting the fuel tanks, detonating the bombs below, killing 114 of the 860-man crew, and sinking the flattop.[15]

But the Japanese Center Force could not withstand the punishment and turned tail, escaping back through San Bernardino Strait. *Kongo* was especially hard hit but stayed afloat.

Admiral Clifton Sprague said, "At 0925 my mind was occupied with dodging torpedoes when, near the bridge, I heard one of the signalmen yell, 'They're getting away!' I could hardly believe my eyes, but it looked as if the whole Japanese fleet was indeed retiring. However, it took a whole series of reports from circling planes to convince me. And still I could not get the fact to soak into my battle-numbed brain. At best, I had expected to be swimming by this time."[16]

Although it ended as an American victory, the Battle of Leyte Gulf saw the first large-scale employment of a new and deadly tactic. The Japanese, growing increasingly desperate, had trained a corps of young men willing to sacrifice themselves while inflicting heavy casualties on their enemies—a tactic that would be copied five decades later in the Middle East. Scores of suicide pilots, known as *kamikaze*, or "divine wind" (a reference to a typhoon that miraculously saved Japan from an invading Mongol fleet in AD 1281), were shot down and sent plunging into the sea without accomplishing their deadly missions.

But many other kamikaze found their marks—carriers, battleships, cruisers, destroyers, oilers, auxiliaries—wreaking havoc and visiting death upon those aboard ships. By the time the war ended, the kamikaze would claim 400 American ships and 9,724 American sailors, at a cost of 5,000 men of their own. William Manchester notes, "Anyone who saw a bluejacket who had been burned by them, writhing in agony under his bandages, never again slandered the sailors who stayed on ships while the infantrymen hit the beach."[17]

FARTHER north, the fourth and final episode of the Battle of Leyte Gulf was reaching its thunderous climax; Halsey's Third Fleet caught the enemy's decoy carriers east of Cape Engaño and sank all six.

The Battle of Leyte Gulf was over. It was another stunning, hard-won victory for the United States and another devastating defeat for Japan. Because of the sacrifice of the Navy, the American soldiers who were landed on Leyte were able to begin their campaign to reclaim the islands and liberate the long-suffering Filipinos.[18]

The Submarine Force had also played a prominent role. One hundred

Kamikaze attack.
(Courtesy National Archives)

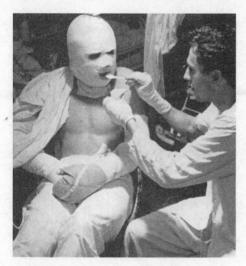

A badly burned sailor, swathed in pressure bandages, is fed by a medical orderly.
(Courtesy National Archives)

and thirteen submarine war patrols were conducted during the months of September and October, which resulted in the reported sinking of 205 ships—205 ships that could not be used to deliver troops and supplies to enemy strongholds. And by sinking Admiral Kurita's flagship, they had served notice of the brutal beating that would await the Japanese at Leyte Gulf.[19]

The invasion of the Philippines had opened the door for the invasion of Japan, a door the Japanese could no longer bar.

RON Smith missed the Battle of Leyte Gulf, for in October 1944 he was living in Kenosha, Wisconsin, and teaching aspiring torpedomen all about the latest torpedoes at the Great Lakes Fleet Torpedo School.

In September 1944, he and pregnant Marilynn had moved from Vallejo to Kenosha, just north of the Illinois state line, and he commuted to work by car pool every day. "I had a lot of trouble with the regimentation while there," he admitted. "I guess that happens to a lot of guys when they go from a combat assignment, where you have a lot of freedom, to a more structured setting in which you're always supposed to be at a certain place at a certain time, and salute the officers and call them 'sir.' You just get immersed in a whole lot of chickenshit rules and regulations on a base. Because of my 'limited duty' status, there wasn't much they could do with me."

The Smiths were in Kenosha for a couple of months when Marilynn moved to Salida, Colorado, to stay with her mother and stepfather and have the baby, which was the common practice at that time.

Smitty and Marilynn ran into some unexpected financial complications. "In addition to her allotment, I had been sending her extra money," he said. "When I went down there for a visit in March of '45, I found she had spent it all feeding her family—her mother and two brothers. Her stepfather had disappeared and left the family destitute. What else could I do?"

It wasn't the only problem they would have, however.[20]

CHAPTER 18

DISASTER AT SEA

DURING the Battle of Leyte Gulf, Dick O'Kane's *Tang* was on station some 600 miles north of Leyte. It was *Tang*'s fifth war patrol, this one in the Formosa Strait, between the island of Formosa (today known as Taiwan) and Foo Chow, China. No one could know that it would also be her *last* patrol.

"We used to hate to patrol there because it was so shallow," Clay Decker said. "There are a couple of places where it is shallower than 200 feet. We weren't that fearful of a depth charge going off above us or to the side of us, but if it went off *below* us, it would blow the water out of our ballast tanks. If that happened, it would give us positive buoyancy and we'd pop to the surface like a cork. We'd be sitting ducks for whoever was up there gunning for us."[1]

Tang had been on station in the Formosa Strait for about a week and a half. At 0200 hours on Tuesday, 25 October 1944, while running on the surface to recharge her batteries, the blips on *Tang*'s radar screen blossomed into a huge convoy of thirty-five ships approaching through the strait. The radar operator could hardly believe his eyes and called the exec Frazee over to double-check that his vision was accurate.

O'Kane was awakened and informed of the sighting. Excited, he threw a bathrobe over his shorts and headed for the control room to confirm the contact for himself. It was true. The blips on the radar screen looked like a large covey of bright green quail taking flight.[2]

Aaaaooogaa! Aaaaooogaa! Everyone was sent rushing to his battle station as O'Kane dived and set the sub on a course to intercept the convoy. Decker recalled, "Our troops had landed on Leyte and we assumed that this convoy was heading there to resupply and reinforce the enemy. Skipper ordered flank speed, and we took off to make an end run and get in front of the convoy."

As *Tang* reached the interception point and submerged to wait for the targets to come into range, O'Kane noticed that the convoy was coming on in single file without the usual zigzagging. "It was just like a shooting gallery for us," said Decker, who was manning the bow planes and could hear and see all the activity in the control room.

O'Kane kept his eye glued to the periscope. As the sky gradually lightened, he saw the ships moving quickly, black smoke billowing from their stacks. It was an embarrassment of riches—there were so many targets it was difficult to decide which to shoot at first.

Decker recalled, "There was one troop transport among all those thirty-five ships. There were also a goodly number of destroyers, and destroyer escorts, which we didn't like, because those were the guys with the depth charges." But everyone was excited at the prospect of another engagement. *Tang* had already sunk eighteen ships on her first four patrols; how many more could be added to that score this morning?[3]

As the first big target came within range and centered itself in the periscope, O'Kane went through the familiar litany of submarine commander in action. The command "bearing—mark" was Frazee's cue to check the azimuth reading on a brass ring that circled the base of the periscope. Frazee called out the bearing: "Zero one zero."

Next O'Kane requested the range; the radar operator sang out the yardage from the sub to the target: "One thousand yards and closing."

"Open outer doors," directed the skipper and the order was conveyed to the forward torpedo room, which immediately complied. A couple more range and bearing checks took place before O'Kane shouted, "Fire one!"

The first fish was launched. Seconds went by, then a heavy *thump*. The enemy ship went up in a giant chrysanthemum of flame and smoke, sending debris and sailors flying into the predawn sky. The destroyers, the watchdogs of the convoy, immediately went on the prowl, rushing madly about, eager to sink their blunt, 242-pound teeth into their unseen adversary.

"Fire two! Fire three! Fire four!" O'Kane commanded without removing his eye from the periscope's rubber eyepiece. With each command *Tang* lurched. Soon the shock of torpedoes leaving the sub became indistinguishable from the shock waves of exploding torpedoes detonating against Japanese hulls and the shock waves of bursting boilers inside those hulls.[4]

Clay Decker, being buffeted at his battle station, could only imagine what the scene on top was like—crumpled ships on fire slipping beneath the waves, men jumping overboard to escape the flames and detonations, oil burning on the water, sheer panic, death and destruction being heaped upon the hated enemy. The mood inside *Tang* was one of grim celebration. *Tang* was paying back the Japanese for Pearl Harbor, Cavite, Bataan, and a hundred other places.

The destroyers dashed about in great confusion, unable to locate *Tang* as one ship after another exploded in a display of submarine marksmanship seldom, if ever, equaled. The thirteenth ship sunk by *Tang* was the lone transport, which Decker said O'Kane estimated as holding at least 5,000 troops.

Decker said, "When the fire-control party looked at a silhouette in the book of all the enemy's ships, they could determine the type of ship and how much water it drew. If we'd have hit a target at, say, water level, all we'd have done is blow a hole in it. They have watertight compartments and they'd seal off that compartment and stay afloat. But if you hit him just above the keel, you'd break his back and sink him. So they set the depth they wanted into the memory of the torpedo, somewhere from a foot to two feet above the keel.

"We had hit the transport in the stern with our twenty-second torpedo and stopped its propulsion, but didn't sink it," Decker continued. "With two torpedoes left, numbers twenty-three and twenty-four, both in the forward tubes, we approached that crippled transport. I'm sitting at the bow-plane wheel just below the hatch that goes up to the conning tower;

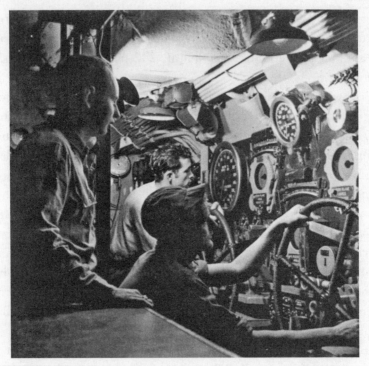

Two planesmen operate the wheels that control the angle of
ascent and descent under the watchful eye of the diving officer.
(Courtesy National Archives)

there's a fire-control party up there and the skipper is now up there, too,
on the bridge, giving all the orders. I can hear everything that's going on
over the intercom; it was like listening to a football game on the radio."

Usually, Decker said, they would fire their torpedoes at a range of a
thousand to fifteen hundred yards. "Well, this time we went in on that
target at a range of 700 yards. Skipper gave the command 'All stop.'
Normally we would have one or two knots on the screws, but now we
were all stopped. The reason for him doing this was, *Tang* was like a big-
game rifle and he's got two shells left and there's a big bull elk out there.
The transport is sitting dead in the water, and the skipper didn't want to
miss. So we aimed the boat at the transport and fired those last two torpedoes. Number twenty-three went out straight and hot and hit the target amidships."[5]

For insurance, the twenty-fourth and last torpedo was fired. Torpe-doman Third Class Pete Narowanski, in the forward torpedo room, re-membered that he had just pressed the firing plunger and called out, "Hot dog! Course zero nine zero—head her for the Golden Gate!"[6]

But something went terribly wrong. Instead of running below the surface straight for the target, number twenty-four began broaching as it ran, then circled to its left.

Seeing the torpedo coming back toward *Tang*, O'Kane, on the bridge, yelled an order for "all ahead emergency" and a "right full rudder" in a desperate bid to get *Tang* out of the way of her own errant missile.

The command came too late to get *Tang* moving again. Roaring in at forty-six knots, the out-of-control fish struck the submarine's port side just ahead of the after torpedo room. The blast from the 500-pound warhead was terrific and immediately flooded the three aft compart-ments, together with number six and seven ballast tanks.

O'Kane found himself blown off the bridge and into the water along with the two other lookouts, the soundman Floyd Caverly and Boat-swain's Mate First Class Bill Leibold.[7]

Jesse DaSilva, a motor machinist's mate second class in *Tang*'s after engine room, had left his station a few minutes before the blast to get a cup of coffee in the crew's mess. "I never really liked coffee," said DaSilva, "but that's one coffee break I'm glad I took." He had been standing between the after battery and the mess when the wayward torpedo struck. He recalled, "Two other men were with me. One had headphones and was keeping us posted." Suddenly, after the last tor-pedo was fired, there came the order, "All Ahead Emergency! Right full rudder!"

DaSilva said, "The torpedo hit between the after torpedo room and the maneuvering room. I clutched a ladder to keep from being pitched off my feet. Someone dogged down the water-tight door between the after and forward engine rooms. The *Tang* was settling quickly by the stern and water was pouring in from the open doorway that connected the crew's mess with the control room. I thought to myself, 'Let's get this door shut!' Two or three of us seized the door and, with a great effort, shoved it closed, cutting off the flow of water."[8]

The explosion was the most jolting, violent thing Clay Decker had ever experienced. It threw men across the control room, sending them smashing into gauges, switches, tables—breaking bones, splitting skulls, and knocking out teeth. Somehow he avoided being tossed about like a kitten in a cement mixer.

"The lads who were standing in the compartment where I was sitting were thrown across the compartment against the bulkhead," he said. "It was terrible. The explosion knocked out all the lighting, and we immediately began sinking by the stern. The hatch above me was open and water was gushing in. Those lads in the conning tower fell into the control room, a drop of eight or ten feet. I heard them falling and hitting the steel deck."

Like every qualified submariner, Decker knew exactly where the emergency lighting switch was, felt his way to the switch, and flipped it on. The sight appalled him. "At the bottom of the ladder, we had one man with a broken back, one with a broken neck, two with broken arms, and another with a broken leg. They were just lying there in a heap, moaning and bleeding."

"The last man who came down the hatch from the conning tower had a broken arm," Decker said, "but with his good arm he grabbed the rope lanyard that was attached to the hatch. A piece of wood was tied onto the end of the lanyard. You'd grab that piece of wood and pull down to close the hatch, which is spring-loaded. Well, he's coming down and the water is pouring in and he pulls on the lanyard and lets go. But the wooden end flips up and gets caught in the rubber gasket around the hatch opening. He got the hatch closed but not sealed, so we still had a stream of water pouring in on all the casualties piled up around the bottom of the ladder."

He said, "Below the deck of the control room there are the bilges, storage lockers, arms lockers, a couple of air compressors, and some huge air tanks, so we knew it would take a while before the water would reach the deck. But we're sitting at a forty-five-degree angle. We knew that the bow was sticking out of the water because we could hear the waves slapping against the hull and we're rocking back and forth. It wouldn't be long before the Japs started shooting at it. We also knew that we had to have the *Tang* level so that the men could go up to the forward torpedo room where the escape chamber was."

Getting *Tang* level was another story. The chief of the boat, Bill Ballinger, had been hurt during the explosion. Decker said, "He had been standing watch by the 'Christmas tree' and was thrown when the torpedo hit us. He was lying in the corner, bleeding from the forehead, so I went over to help him. He had a big gash but he was conscious. He said, 'Deck, we aren't going to be able to get forward unless we get her level.' That was all the order I needed."

To lower the bow and make the boat level, Decker knew he had to flood the forward ballast tanks. "All the hydraulic controls could also be operated manually. The manual lever to open the valves on the forward ballast tanks was located directly above the chart desk in the control room. But it took a lot of force to move that lever, so I crawled up on the desk that was now at an angle, pulled the pin, and threw my legs around that lever. It swung down. The valves opened and the *Tang* just leveled out and sat on the bottom."[9]

Pete Sutherland, historian of the *Pampanito*, shows the emergency lever of the type that Clay Decker used to level the *Tang*.
(Whitlock photo)

Unknown to Decker at that time was the fact that Skipper O'Kane, Caverly, and Leibold had been blown off the bridge; Engineer Officer Lieutenant Larry Savadkin had been in the enclosed conning tower operating the torpedo data computer. When *Tang* went down, Savadkin found an air bubble at the top of conning tower. It was only about thirty or thirty-five feet from the hatch to the surface, so Savadkin decided to make a swim for it. Knowing how to turn his pants into a life preserver, he removed them, knotted the legs, blew up the pants with his breath, and sealed the top with his belt. He then took a deep breath, opened the hatch, and made it to the surface, where he joined O'Kane and the two other survivors.[10]

Dazed and distraught, the quartet managed to stay afloat while enemy destroyers stampeded about, firing their deck guns and dropping depth charges. O'Kane recalled the moment when he saw his boat go under: "*Tang*'s bow hung at a sharp angle above the surface, moving about in the current as does a buoy in a seaway. She appeared to be struggling like a great wounded animal, a leviathan, as indeed she was. I found myself orally cheering encouragement and striking out impulsively to reach her. Swimming against the current was painfully slow and interrupted momentarily by a depth-charging patrol. Now close ahead, *Tang*'s bow suddenly plunged on down to Davy Jones's locker, and the lonely seas seemed to share in my total grief . . . My heart went out to those below and to the young men topside who must now face the sea," wrote O'Kane in his memoir.[11]

Before long O'Kane and the others were picked up by the Japanese, who were eager to exact revenge against the submariners who had just sunk thirteen of their ships.

MEANWHILE, down inside the crippled sub, Decker and Ballinger began assembling the "walking wounded" and herding them toward the bow. "Everyone aft of the control room was apparently dead," Decker assumed.

On their way through the passageway, the two men came across Ensign Mel Enos in the skipper's stateroom, trying to set the codebooks on fire in a wastebasket. Decker grabbed the codebooks from the officer's hands. "I said, 'Mr. Enos, you can't do that! We need every bit of air we've got! We can't have a fire going! Besides, the batteries are right below us—you can't have any sort of spark near them!' "

"But we have to destroy the codebooks," Enos replied.

"Stuff 'em in the batteries," the injured Ballinger offered. Popping the hatch in the deck, Decker crawled down into the battery room, removed the top to one of the huge batteries, and dropped the codebooks into the sulfuric acid, then scrambled out and closed the hatch.

The forward torpedo room was crowded with survivors, some bleeding, some burned, some nursing internal injuries. Clay Decker determined to look and act bravely in order to instill some calmness in the others, as well as in himself.

Submarine sailor aboard *Narwhal* demonstrating an early
model of the Momsen Lung. Photo taken July 1930.
(Courtesy Naval Historical Center)

He was gratified to see that, while the fear in the tight compartment
was palpable, there was no panic among his shipmates. Each submariner
is a volunteer, and each knows the hazards of his chosen branch of service. Two officers—Mel Enos and Hank Flanagan—were in charge. The
depth meter said they were at 180 feet. Men began pulling brand-new
'Momsen Lungs' out of storage lockers and removing them from their
cellophane bags.

"The Momsen Lung," Deck explained, "was invented by a Navy
officer, 'Swede' Momsen, before the war. It was designed to help crewmen escape from sunken subs. We had over a hundred of them on
board."

"The Momsen Lung* was an ingenious device," Decker said. "It was a black rubber bladder that strapped to your chest, and it had a hose that went up to a mouthpiece that you put in your mouth. There was a nose clip to keep you from breathing in water through your nose. The bladder had a little valve on it, like a bicycle tire, and you charged the bladder with oxygen before you used it. There was also a canister of soda lime in the lung, and the carbon dioxide you exhaled would go through the soda lime, which absorbed the free carbon and created free oxygen. It also had a little flat rubber piece on it, a relief valve, right below the mouthpiece that would let air out but wouldn't let water in. Once you got to the surface, you would close the relief valve and use the lung like a 'Mae West' life preserver."

George Zofcin, whose wife and child were living with Decker's wife and son back in San Francisco, helped Deck put on his Momsen Lung; Deck returned the favor.[12]

Jesse DaSilva recalled, "The Japanese came over us and continued to drop depth charges for some time. There were now about twenty of us in the mess room and crew's quarters. We knew that we couldn't stay here because of chlorine gas. We knew, too, that our one chance of escape was in reaching the forward torpedo room. But we had to pass through the control room to get there. This meant opening the control room door and, for all we knew, it might be flooded. Yet, we had to risk it.

"Someone cracked the door—water gushed in and rose around our legs, then gradually subsided. We discovered that the control room was only partially flooded. One by one, we moved up forward, knee deep in water. We filed into the control room and destroyed all the secret devices. I noticed at this time the depth gauge was at 180 feet. I thought to myself that there was still a chance [to get out] if we could reach the es-

---

* Charles "Swede" Momsen, of Danish-German heritage, was born in New York in 1896 and graduated from the Naval Academy in 1919. A submariner, he began experimenting with underwater breathing devices that could help men trapped below the surface in relatively shallow water to survive. In 1939, he was in charge of the rescue attempt to free thirty-three sailors inside the sunken *Squalus*. The depth of 243 feet was too great for use of the Momsen Lung, but the McCann Rescue Chamber, which Momsen had also helped to develop, was successfully used instead. (www.onr.navy.mil/blowballast/momsen)

cape hatch located in the forward torpedo room. We passed through the officers' quarters and into the torpedo room.

DaSilva noted that there were already twenty-some men in the in the forward torpedo compartment. "With our arrival, we brought the number to forty-five. There were some injured men, and the air was foul and breathing was difficult. Everyone was given a Momsen Lung. There had already been several attempted escapes and now they were going to make another."[13]

Clay Decker said, "With the number of guys we had in the forward torpedo room, we figured we had only about four or five hours of air left. We had to do something within that period of time or we'd all die."

Those sailors who were unhurt or only slightly injured set about making their wounded shipmates as comfortable as possible. The hanging bunks in the forward torpedo room were put back into place and the most seriously injured sailors were gently laid in them. A pharmacist's mate bandaged those with lacerations and splinted those with broken bones. Those with broken necks were immobilized as much as possible with bolsters improvised from blankets and pillows.

"There was no use in any of them even trying to escape," Decker said of the seriously injured. "There was no way any of them could have made it. It's tough enough if you're *not* injured."

Decker remembered that *Tang* had "a couple of loudmouths, a couple of know-it-alls. This one loudmouth and a chief torpedoman had crawled up into the escape chamber before the rest of us could get organized. They didn't have a Momsen Lung, or a Mae West on. They just flooded the escape chamber, opened the hatch, and went out on their own. We never saw them again. Lieutenant Flanagan took charge after that. He said, 'We go in groups of four.' "

Ballinger called out, "I'm going in the first group. Who wants to go with me?" Clay Decker's hand shot up, and he turned to George Zofcin. "C'mon, George, let's go with Bill."

But Zofcin held back. "I can't go, Deck," he said.

"For Christ's sake, George, why not?"

"I have a confession to make—I can't swim."

It was true. Decker suddenly recalled the times when they had lounged on Waikiki Beach; George never went into the water. Now, with the situation in *Tang* growing more desperate by the minute, Decker tried a couple more seconds of persuasion, but Zofcin just crawled onto a bunk, as though he were waiting to die.

"Let's go, Deck," Ballinger said, grabbing him by the arm.

Decker gave George one last glance before climbing up the ladder and into the dimly lit, phone-booth-size escape chamber, along with two other men, newcomers to *Tang*. It was the last time he would ever see George Zofcin.

Inside the escape chamber were three main gauges. "One's the fathometer that shows how deep you are," explained Decker. "One's a gauge that shows the air pressure inside the chamber and the third shows you what the external pres-

Pete Sutherland looks up the ladder that leads to the escape hatch in the after torpedo room of *Pampanito*.
(Whitlock photo)

sure is out at sea. What we had to do was close the bottom hatch that leads into the torpedo room, then let in seawater up to our chins. Then we opened another valve to let the air pressure build up and create an air pocket that exceeds the sea pressure by five pounds. That way, the hatch that opens to the sea will open as easily as opening a door in a room. Otherwise, you'd never be able to open it.

"Once the hatch is open, you let out a wooden buoy about the size of a soccer ball that has a lanyard stapled around it and a handhold you can grab onto. The buoy is fastened to a line on a spool in the escape chamber, and the line has knots tied in it every fathom—every six feet. Right above the escape hatch is an opening in the superstructure about three feet square. The buoy and line go up through this opening and you have

Author Flint Whitlock emerges topside from the escape hatch of *Pampanito*. (Whitlock photo)

to hang on to the line and count the number of knots as you go up so you know how far you have left to go. At 180 feet, there are thirty knots in the line. It's pitch-black out there, so you have no visual reference as to where you are. You can't tell up from down. The main thing is to never let go of the rope, or you'll get caught in the space between the pressure hull and the superstructure and never find your way out. You also don't want to come up too fast or else you'll get the bends."

After charging their Momsen Lungs from the air hose in the chamber, the four men opened the hatch and let out the buoy. Decker was the first one out, wrapping his legs around the line and climbing hand over hand, counting each knot and stopping to inhale and exhale at each one to prevent the bends.

After what seemed like an eternity in the icy water, Decker reached the surface just as the morning was turning light. The sea around him was chaotic with activity. Destroyers zipped here and there, at times coming dangerously close to him. All around was floating debris and the bobbing bodies of dead Japanese soldiers and sailors; ships burned fiercely on the horizon.

"When I got to the surface," Decker said, "I reached up to take off my nosepiece and noticed that my nose and cheeks were bleeding. I guess I came up faster than I should have and got a nosebleed and the small blood vessels in my cheeks broke. I was a little worried that the blood would attract sharks, because the waters off Foo Chow are shark-infested; we were wearing .45-caliber pistols and knives just in case." Decker's Momsen Lung had filled with water and turned useless as a life preserver, so he discarded it, along with the heavy knife and pistol.

Decker clung to the buoy and waited for Bill Ballinger and the other two men in his group to surface. Suddenly Ballinger popped up about a yard away from him, gasping and coughing and flailing his arms, his eyes filled with terror.

Decker said, "Ballinger is drowning. The man is screaming and vomiting and holding out his hand for me to grab him. Something told me, 'Don't you reach out and touch that man! *Absolutely don't do it!*' It's a well-known fact that a drowning man can pull a horse underwater. If he'd have gotten ahold of me, I'd have gone down with him. All I could do was watch the tide take him farther away from me, out to sea; I could hear him screaming off in the distance.

"Later on we figured what probably happened was that the relief valve on his Momsen Lung was folded and had a clip around it, like all the new ones did. Bill probably forgot to take the clip off and his lungs burst because there was no way for him to exhale on the way up to the surface."

More minutes went by and the other two men in his group failed to appear. Then the buoy bobbed and Lieutenant Hank Flanagan from the second group came up; he was the only one from his group of four to make it.[14]

Inside *Tang*, Jesse DaSilva was in the next group preparing to go up. He said, "I found myself at the foot of the ladder leading up into the escape trunk. I heard someone say, 'Let's have another man,' so I quickly climbed up into the trunk. I was the third man." A fourth man stepped to the ladder, climbed in, and the hatch was closed.

"Everything went just as we were taught at the escape tank back at Pearl Harbor. We flooded the trunk, filled our Momsen Lungs with oxygen, and tested them to see if they were working. As the water rose in the trunk, breathing became difficult as the pressure was building up. When the water level reached above the outer door, we opened it. Someone had already let out the buoy with a line attached from the previous escapes, so now it was my turn to follow the line to the surface."

DaSilva was the third man out. He slowly let himself up a fathom at a time, stopping and counting to ten at each knot. "About a third of the way up, breathing became difficult, but soon the problem went away and the water became lighter and suddenly I was on the surface. Nearby and holding onto the buoy were the men who had escaped before me."[15]

DaSilva joined Decker and Flanagan at the buoy and the three of them prayed that more of their shipmates would soon join them. But only three more sailors surfaced—Torpedoman's Mate Second Class Hayes O. Trukke, Torpedoman's Mate Third Class Pete Narowanski, and Chief Pharmacist's Mate Paul Larson; Larson had swallowed a lot of water and was in trouble.

A fourth man, one of the black mess stewards—either Ralph F. Adams or H. M. Walker—did surface, but far from the buoy. DaSilva tried saving him. "He came up some distance from us and acted like he couldn't swim. As I reached him he disappeared, so I turned to swim back to the others. I didn't realize I had drifted so far. It took a great effort to reach them. I realized that the tide was moving out to sea and there would be no chance to make the mainland of China that we could see off in the distance."[16]

Six men were all who would make it out from the escape chamber and cling to the buoy; something must have gone drastically wrong down below. Decker said, "All I can assume is that all the others let go of the line on the way up and their bodies got hung up in the space between the pressure hull and the superstructure."[17]

After several hours of clutching the buoy, the six Americans—Flanagan, Decker, DaSilva, Larson, Trukke, and Narowanski—were exhausted. Larson kept coughing, vomiting, crying. Finally, a Japanese destroyer escort that had been circling them approached.

DaSilva said, "It circled us several times and then stopped a short distance away, turning its guns towards us. I thought to myself, 'Well, this is it—they are going to shoot us.' But, instead, they lowered a small boat and came over and picked us up."[18]

A dinghy manned by angry Japanese sailors using their rifles as paddles rowed over to the group. The enemy sailors began grabbing the *Tang* crewmen and hauling them roughly into the boat like tuna.[19]

The Japanese sailors rowed back to the destroyer escort, the *P-34*,

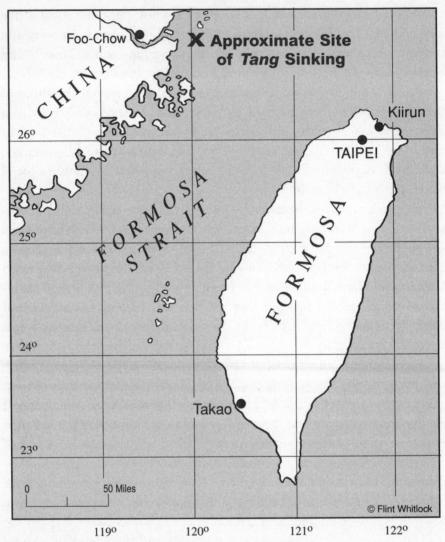

Foo-Chow

X Approximate Site
of *Tang* Sinking

CHINA

26°

Kiirun

TAIPEI

FORMOSA
STRAIT

25°

FORMOSA

24°

Takao

23°

0   50 Miles

© Flint Whitlock

119°   120°   121°   122°

Formosa and site of *Tang* sinking.

and the men climbed a rope ladder to the deck, where O'Kane and the
other three survivors from *Tang*'s bridge and conning tower sat huddled
together, their arms tied behind their backs. Decker was the last American up the ladder and looked back in time to see the Japanese sailors
throw Larson, the choking pharmacist's mate, overboard. He sank out
of sight. There were now a total of nine survivors from the *Tang*.

The destroyer escort had also picked up survivors from the ships that *Tang* had torpedoed and these men were on the deck, staring at the Americans with hate in their eyes. "These were guys who had been down in those engine rooms who had been scalded when the boilers exploded—they were as red as cooked lobsters," Decker related. "They're looking at us and you could almost hear them thinking: 'Those are the guys who did this to us.' Then we got the worst treatment that we received the whole time we were prisoners. Those Jap survivors would come over and grab us by the hair and stick lit cigarettes up our noses. Then they would slap and kick and beat the shit out of us."[20]

O'Kane noted with some compassion, "When we realized that our clubbings and kickings were being administered by the burned, mutilated survivors of our own handiwork, we found we could take it with less prejudice."[21]

DaSilva said, "One by one, the Japanese would take us aside and interrogate us. When it was my turn, they took me to another part of the ship and had me sit down between three of them. They offered me a ball of rice, but I could not eat it. One of them had an electrical device and he would jab me in the ribs with this and I would twitch and jump. They all thought this was very funny. The one that could speak English carried a large club about the size of a baseball bat. He would ask questions and if he didn't like the answers, he would hit me on the head with this bat. After some time, when they figured that I wasn't going to tell them anything, they took me back to the others.

"Later on, we were all taken to a small room and locked in there. It was so small that only two or three of us could lie down; the rest had to stand. It was very hot and there was only one small porthole for air which they would not let us open. Finally, we persuaded the guard to let us out, so they took us out and we were allowed to sit on the deck in the fresh air."[22]

This was a mixed blessing, for, as Decker recounted, "All we were wearing was our shorts. Some of us still had sandals on. Because we submariners never spent much time in the sun, we were fair-skinned; they kept us up on this hot steel deck under the blazing sun for five days, at the end of which time we were a mass of blisters. We got no water, no food. We thought, this is the end."[23]

CHAPTER 19

A LESSON IN CRUELTY

THE destroyer escort carrying the eight *Tang* survivors finally reached the port of Takao (today Kaohsiung) on the island of Formosa during the first week of November. The POWs were then taken by train to Taipei, the capital city, and with their hands tied behind their backs and blindfolds covering their eyes, were marched through the streets of Taipei. Clay Decker said, "They made us carry a sign that said something like, 'Here's an example of the superior race.' Little kids and old ladies came out and hit us with sticks."[1]

Jesse DaSilva noted that the small group was then loaded onto a truck and driven to some sort of civic building. "We stood before some officials and the blindfolds were removed. There were a few words said, then the blindfolds were put back on and we were taken back to the truck and taken to some old buildings. We were separated and I was put in a small room with no floors, just dirt and gravel. I was told to stay there and say nothing. They brought me something to eat but I couldn't eat whatever it was."

DaSilva recalled that sleep was hard to come by. "Several times during the night, two or three Japanese would come and shine a flashlight in my face and start asking me questions. When they did not get the answers they wanted, they would slap me. When morning came, they lined all of us up again and put the blindfolds back on and put us on a truck and took us to the train station. Once on the train the blindfolds were removed. We were in a regular passenger-type car and all the shades were drawn. When we left the station, the shades were allowed to be raised. It was like going back a hundred years. The only thing I saw were people working in the fields with hand plows pulled by oxen. It was an all-day trip and we finally arrived at our destination at the other end of the island."[2]

According to Decker the group was taken to an army camp outside Taipei. "They threw us in a potato cellar overnight. We ate raw, dirty potatoes—didn't wash them or anything." While the *Tang*'s crewmen hungrily devoured the uncooked spuds, bloodthirsty mosquitoes feasted on the men.[3]

The following day the prisoners were moved to the port city of Kii-run, where they were locked into a medieval-style prison for the night. The captives were fed a meal of hot rice and fish wrapped in cane husks, given blankets, and allowed a full night's sleep for the first time since the sinking.

The next morning the prisoners were rousted out of bed early and taken down to the port, where they were marched to a destroyer bound for Japan. O'Kane, as befitting an officer of his rank, was afforded proper protocol and even given use of the destroyer captain's cabin. From one of the portholes he could observe the ship's drills and activities, for which he had a professional's admiration. "The gun crews were exceptional," he noted, "their speed telling why we had suffered setbacks earlier in the war."

The destroyer's captain was a literate man with a fine command of English. At one point during a conversation, the captain asked O'Kane, "How is it that you speak no Japanese but seem to understand my English? How could we expect to understand each other's problems when you made no attempt to learn even a word of our language?"

From a bookshelf the captain pulled down a copy of Margaret Mitchell's Civil War classic, *Gone With the Wind,* and held it before the *Tang*'s skipper. O'Kane said, "He expressed the opinion that if most influential adults had read this book, our nations might have found a solution to the problems and avoided this war. I could not disagree."

The destroyer sailed into Osaka Bay and docked at Kobe, where the POWs were marched through a cold sleet to the naval training base there. Loaded onto another train, the Americans headed inland to Yokohama. O'Kane was depressed to see, from the train's windows, Japan's war factories going full blast; years of bombing had hardly touched them. "Here I knew that Japan, with her routes to China quite defensible, could be defeated only by invasion," he concluded.[4]

At Yokohama, the POWs detrained and were loaded onto a bus that took them up a winding mountain road, finally depositing them at a small, secret naval intelligence prison at Ofuna, whose official name was

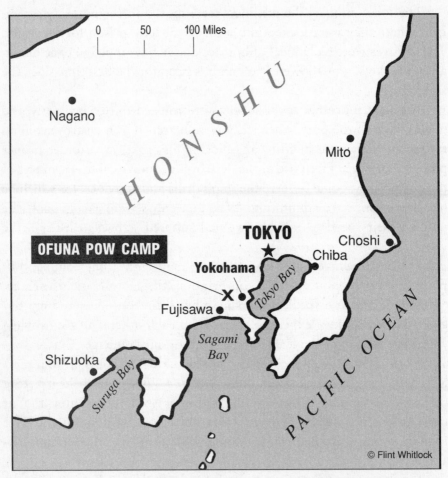

Yokohama-Tokyo area, showing location of Ofuna Naval Intelligence Prisoner Camp.

"Navy Yokosuka Guard Unit Ueki Detachment," located south of the city.[5] Its unofficial name was the "Torture Farm."[6]

Jesse DaSilva remembered, "It was raining when we reached the interrogation camp of Ofuna. When I had made my escape from *Tang*, the only piece of clothing I had on was a pair of pants, so all the time we were walking I was very wet and cold. When we reached the camp, my feet were very sore and numb from the cold."[7]

At Ofuna, O'Kane and the pitiful remnants of his surviving crew— Clay Decker, Jesse DaSilva, Hank Flanagan, Larry Savadkin, Bill Leibold, Floyd Caverly, Pete Narowanski, and Hayes Trukke—received food, bedding, and clothing.

In the coming months they would also receive lessons in the Japanese language—and a lesson in Japanese cruelty.[8]

ALLIED servicemen who were captured by the Germans in World War II, for the most part, considered themselves lucky. The Germans, with a few notable exceptions, treated their POWs, if not honorably, at least according to the rules laid down by the Geneva Convention. (The Russians, of course, were never well treated by their German captors.) Many of the American and British POW camps in Germany were well run, had adequate (although not abundant) quantities of food and medicine, and the POWs were even allowed such luxuries as camp libraries, movies, theatrical productions, and athletic activities.

Those incarcerated in Japanese prisoner-of-war camps, however, enjoyed no such niceties. Virtually every one of the hundreds of Japanese prisoner-of-war camps was a place of sadistic and inhuman physical and mental treatment. Prisoners were regularly abused, beaten, starved, tortured, and set to work performing hard labor despite their wounds, illnesses, or other physical infirmities. Prisoners who could not keep up, whether on the march to the work site or at the work site itself, were summarily executed.

The ill treatment can be attributed to the perversion of the warriors' code of *bushido*. The vast majority of Japanese soldiers, sailors, and airmen believed deeply that a true warrior never surrenders or allows himself to be captured. As long as he still possesses a breath in his body and the strength to fight back, he must do so. To surrender is dishonor of the worst kind. Therefore, many Japanese felt that they were justified in mistreating or killing any Allied serviceman (and woman, too, for that matter) who willingly gave up or was captured, for their prisoners were nothing more than despicable cowards who did not deserve to live.[9]

THE nine *Tang* survivors now joined hundreds of others at the Ofuna POW Camp, a place of unremitting misery enclosed by a wooden stockade wall.

Jesse DaSilva recalled, "The whole camp was built in a U-shape, with the Japanese quarters in the middle and the prisoner barracks on each side. These were divided by a fence down the middle. The newer prisoners like myself were kept on one side and the older ones on the other. At first we were not even allowed to talk to each other, but later on we could talk to each other but not the older prisoners."

He also remembered that the Japanese "took us into a room where they gave each of us a dry shirt and pants and a pair of tennis shoes that were three sizes too small. This was all the clothing I ever received the whole time I was a POW. They also gave us three blankets, a bowl of rice, and some soup. They took us to the barracks which consisted of individual cells approximately six feet long and ten feet wide, with a barred window at the end. The floor was raised, with a grass mat three by six feet at one end. With the three blankets and the grass mat, this was to be my bed for the next six months.

"It was winter and they would allow us to go out into the compound for exercise. The only clothing we had was what we had on our backs, so they let us take a blanket with us. There we were all walking around in a circle with blankets over our heads, looking like a bunch of old Mother Hubbards. During this winter we experienced at least two feet of snow on the ground. There was no heat in the cells and, in fact, you could see right through the cracks in the walls. So we talked the guards into letting several of us get together in one cell. This way the body heat would at least make it a little warmer. We sat around in a circle and talked about food, food, and more food, as our rations were getting smaller and smaller."

The *Tang* survivors had been at Ofuna for just a couple of days when the Japanese gave the Americans a lesson designed to make a lasting impression. DaSilva said, "The Japanese opened the gates that separated the two compounds and had the older prisoners lined up facing the guards. Some prisoners were singled out for certain offenses and were beaten with a club across the buttocks until they collapsed. After watching this, I knew what could be expected if we didn't do what we were told."[10]

O'Kane expanded on this, noting that the guards "were misfits from the navy. Following morning quarters on our second day at Ofuna, the nine of us, who were the only prisoners on the west side of the divided compound, were marched through the gate to the other side. There, Lieutenant Commander J. A. Fitzgerald, skipper of our lost submarine *Grenadier*, and two others, all three walking skeletons, were called from the other prisoners' ranks. We watched the largest guards, three at a time in rotation, club these men into unconsciousness while other guards held them up so the beatings could continue. Caverly was as tough as they come and had even been a professional boxer, but this sight made him vomit."

O'Kane also noted that, during the night, "gangs of guards would roam the corridors to beat prisoners who had been singled out for 'special' treatment and others whom they apparently simply disliked."[11]

Shortly after arriving at Ofuna, the *Tang* survivors were taken aside and interrogated individually. When it was DaSilva's turn, he was marched into a small room sparsely furnished with a table and two chairs. "A Japanese officer sat opposite me," he said. "He was very polite and spoke very good English. He offered me a cigarette and asked how everything was. He told me he had been educated in the U.S. He then asked me the same questions over and over, and I would give him the same answers. Then he let me leave. This only happened a few times; I guess he figured I didn't know anything."

As 1944 was coming to an end, a young B-29 flier who had been shot down was brought to Ofuna. "He was badly wounded and soon he died as our medical facilities were like nothing," said DaSilva, who volunteered to be on the burial detail, knowing that by doing so he would receive a boiled potato as payment. "We had to carry him some distance from the camp in deep snow to a hilly wooded area and then dig a hole and bury him.

"Because of the snow and the cold I don't think I had any feeling in my feet for about four months. We would stamp our feet and walk as much as possible to keep the circulation going. In the beginning, we were given a bath once a week. We would wash up first with a small pan of water and soap, then climb into this large tub of real hot water and soak. Boy, did that bath feel good. This was the only time I could get feeling back into my feet. But then they stopped letting us take baths."[12]

Perhaps thinking that hungry, desperate men would be more inclined to divulge military information under interrogation, the Japanese put the prisoners on a starvation diet—a small bowl of barley for breakfast and dinner, with a thin soup for lunch—totaling approximately 300 calories per day. "Fortunately, we knew nothing about our forces' war plans," O'Kane said.[13]

WHILE the prisoners were sweating out the war at Ofuna, the war at sea raged on. And, despite a drastic reduction in the number of enemy vessels plying the waters, legends of the Submarine Service were still being born.

The submarine *Redfish* had taken a pounding during her initial war patrol in July 1944; in October, after several months of repair work, she was ready for her second patrol. Electrician Bill Trimmer said it was a patrol "which I will never forget, and neither will the Japanese."

It was not until 20 November that *Redfish*'s skipper, Lieutenant Commander Louis D. "Sandy" MacGregor Jr., spotted his first target on his second patrol—a small patrol boat off the northeast coast of Formosa. It was not worth a torpedo, so *Redfish* went in for the attack on the surface. Trimmer said, "We sank it with our five-inch deck gun. The next day we did the same thing to another patrol boat. We had a man wounded, one of my third-class electricians; a bullet just grazed the top of his head. The captain took him off watch, and after three days I found him in the crew's mess, playing cards. I put him back on watch. He protested to the captain to no avail."

A few days later, *Redfish* joined a wolfpack that included the *Bang* and another sub, and soon spotted a seven-ship convoy. During the attack, the other sub had a torpedo jam in one of her forward tubes and was forced to turn back for Saipan with the armed fish protruding from her bow like a tusk. A destroyer went after the two-boat wolfpack and forced *Redfish* into a 580-foot dive, but she soon came up to resume the attack. Trimmer said, "That night, we sank two freighters and an unidentified ship. The *Bang* did most of the damage that night, and that convoy never reached its destination."

Running low on supplies, *Redfish* headed to Saipan for refitting, then resumed patrolling in the North China Sea. "We had to get from the Pacific to the North China Sea through the Cornett Straits," said Trimmer. "Every other way was heavily mined. The North China Sea is very shallow, averaging about 300 feet. That may sound good to most ships, but not for submarines. We went all the way to the China coast and could see the lights of Shanghai, but we couldn't find any targets in this sea. On December 8, we received a message from another sub operating in our area saying that there was a task force consisting of a large aircraft carrier—the *Junyo*—a battleship, and three destroyers."

At about 0200 hours on 9 December, *Redfish* discovered the convoy headed straight for her. "The destroyer escort didn't see us and we ran behind them and hit the carrier," said Trimmer, "which had already been hit by another sub. The carrier slowed to two knots and we made a circle running at full speed, only slowing long enough to fire torpedoes. We got another hit on her, but she was a tough old lady and kept going."[14]

Ten days later *Redfish* encountered another flattop. The recently commissioned, 17,300-ton light carrier *Unryu*, escorted by three destroyers, had departed Kure for Manila on 17 December with a load of kamikaze planes and pilots, torpedoes, suicide boats, and thirty flying rocket bombs. During the voyage, a typhoon struck the China Sea, tossing the small task force around like toy boats.* In spite of the heavy seas, Skipper MacGregor got a bead on the carrier, announced, "This is a big

---

* The December 1944 typhoon was one of the fiercest Pacific storms on record. Halsey's Third Fleet was especially hard hit. Three destroyers capsized with a loss of all hands, and a light cruiser, three light carriers, two escort carriers, and three destroyers were all badly damaged; dozens of other warships suffered light to moderate damage. Seven hundred and ninety Americans died in the storm and 146 warplanes were swept from the carriers' decks. (Tuohy, 96–97)

baby," and launched a spread of six fish at it from a range of 1,470 yards.

The carrier's captain spotted the torpedoes' wakes spearing toward for him and attempted an emergency maneuver, but it was too late; one of the six torpedoes slammed into the hull just below the bridge, causing massive damage. With its steam and electrical systems knocked out, *Unryu* came to a dead stop—becoming the proverbial sitting duck. Remaining at periscope depth, and disregarding the danger posed by the destroyers in full search mode, MacGregor fired another salvo. One of the torpedoes detonated the flying bombs and aviation gas stored belowdecks, blew off the carrier's bow, and ripped *Unryu* apart as though it was made of cardboard. The ship listed heavily to starboard and started burning like a huge gray torch.

Within twelve minutes of the massive explosion, *Unryu* began its death dive, and although the captain ordered abandon ship, hundreds of sailors refused to leave the stricken vessel, preferring with their last remaining seconds of life to fire their antiaircraft guns at *Redfish*'s periscope. Almost instantly the carrier keeled farther to starboard and plunged headfirst, leaving a great void where she had been, and taking to the bottom over 1,200 officers and men, including the captain. Escort vessels picked up only 146 survivors.[15]

The furious destroyers redoubled their efforts to find and kill *Redfish*, and they nearly succeeded. Bill Trimmer recalled that the sub submerged as fast as she could. "It was 1710 [5:10 P.M.]. We were passing 150 feet when several well-placed depth charges went off right under our starboard bow. We hit the bottom at 250 feet and just laid there."

Before long, the situation became desperate. Trimmer, in the maneuvering room, recalled, "All the lights went out and we were searching for the battle lanterns. With them we found our emergency lighting switches that operated two 25-watt, watertight lights in each compartment; only half of the emergency lights were working. All running equipment in the boat was knocked off-line, so we had no power. We did have our sound power phones, because they generated their own power when you talked into them. Every compartment had their phones on and that was all the communication we had.

"The phone talker was giving us reports, which were not good. Damage included the loss of all hydraulic power; steering rudder jammed hard port; bow and stern planes jammed on hard rise; and there was a rumor that there was chlorine gas in the forward battery. We shifted all power to after battery."

Compounding the problems were fires and flooding in the forward torpedo room. In the after torpedo room, one fish had armed itself in the number eight tube. The gyrocompass had been knocked out. And the enemy destroyers were crisscrossing above the sub's location, doing their best to live up to their name.

MacGregor told Trimmer to report to the control room and repair the gyrocompass—a delicate job that took two hours—while the sub was being battered and buffeted by the destroyers. "I was lucky and had something to do, and not just sit and wait," said the electrician. He was then detailed to try to repair the lighting system. Crawling into the forward battery well, Trimmer held his breath to keep from inhaling toxic battery-acid fumes, found the problem, and quickly corrected it. The other half of the emergency lights came on. Returning to the maneuvering room, he came across a man getting stitched up by the pharmacist's mate; the concussion from the depth charges had slammed one of the heavy, watertight doors on the man's head, nearly severing an ear.

At nearly 1900 hours, *Redfish*, after having had emergency repairs done, prepared to surface. "Blow the ballast tanks" came the order. Trimmer was watching a sea-pressure gauge and it didn't move. "We had created a vacuum in the mud," he said, "and were stuck to the bottom of the North China Sea. There was nobody within 1,500 miles to help us. I heard, 'Blow safety tank,' and again there was no change in sea pressure."

After a few minutes of rocking the boat, the sub finally broke the suction and began slowly rising. *Redfish* reached periscope depth and MacGregor looked around; it was dark and the only destroyer he could see was 900 yards away, playing its searchlight across the water in a hunt for survivors of the *Unryu*. Trimmer said, "We surfaced. It was a beautiful sound to hear those big 1,600-horsepower Fairbanks-Morse engines start up. At 1940 hours, we were running at flank speed away from them, opening the range very rapidly. A submarine at night on the surface is very hard to see."

The next day the crew repaired as much of the damage as they could and struggled back toward Midway, dodging enemy aircraft and patrol boats by day. It took ten days of anxious sailing before *Redfish* reached Midway, where a military band and sacks of mail were waiting for her. After a brief inspection and a refit of food and fuel, she took off for Pearl Harbor, three days away. The damage was too great for Pearl's facilities, so *Redfish* and crew continued on to Hunters Point, California. Even Hunters Point could not make her battle worthy again, and *Redfish* was ordered all the way back to Portsmouth, New Hampshire, for a major rebuild. It took until 23 July 1945 before all the repairs were made. By then the war was nearly over.[16]

But, in December 1944, there was still a lot of war left.

ABOUT the time *Redfish* was beginning her nearly fatal patrol, another American sub, Eli Reich's *Sealion II*, as if in an act of penance for her earlier sinking of the POW ship, became the first and only American submarine to sink a Japanese battleship.

Sealion II had departed Pearl Harbor for her third war patrol, this time to the waters between Japan and the Philippines, north of Formosa. Discovering a task force consisting of a large cruiser and three battleships—*Yamato*, *Kongo*, and *Nagato*—all of which had been damaged during the Battle of Leyte Gulf, plus numerous other escorts and support vessels, *Sealion II* tracked the enemy at a safe distance, waiting for just the right moment to strike. Early on Tuesday, 21 November 1944, as a storm began to roil the waters, *Sealion II* made her move. Lying off *Kongo*'s port side, Reich fired a spread of tin fish at the massed targets and heard several explosions. *Kongo* was damaged and the destroyer *Urakaze* was sunk with a loss of fourteen officers and 293 men; the convoy kept going with *Sealion II* in hot pursuit.

Reich's patrol report at 0330 hours reads, "Chagrined at this point to find subsequent tracking enemy group still making 16 knots, still on course 060T. I feel that in setting depth at 8 feet, in order to hit a destroyer if overlapping our main target, I've made a bust—looks like we only dented the armor belt on the battleships."

But Reich stayed with the convoy despite the attempts of the escorts to seek out and destroy the sub. At 0520 hours, Reich's radar operator reported that *Kongo* seemed to have stopped completely. Four minutes later, Reich noted, "Tremendous explosion dead ahead—sky brilliantly illuminated, it looked like a sunset at midnight, radar reports battleship pip getting smaller—that it has disappeared—leaving only two smaller pips of the destroyers. Destroyers seem to be milling around vicinity of target. Battleship sunk—the sun set."[17]

For years, the cause of *Kongo*'s explosion and sinking remained a mystery, but author/researcher Anthony Tulley seems to have hit on the answer. Reich's first torpedo had damaged *Kongo*'s bow to such an extent that the ship's captain was forced to stop in order for divers to go over the side in the pitching swells in an effort to seal the gash in the hull. Damage control could not stop the tremendous amount of water pouring into *Kongo*, however, and the ship was listing to port, a list that was growing worse with each passing minute.

At about 0522 hours, with *Kongo* leaning about sixty degrees, the captain gave the order to abandon ship, and men began jumping into the chilly waters. Two minutes later the battleship's forward magazines unexpectedly exploded, tearing the guts out of *Kongo* and sending the dreadnought to the bottom. Tulley writes, "All that was left was one of *Kongo*'s float planes . . . burning on the water . . . Only a total of thirteen officers and 224 petty officers and men survived *Kongo*'s catastrophic sinking. Some 1,250 perished." The cause of the explosion is not certain, but was possibly the result of falling shells or sparks.[18]

For his actions in bringing about the demise of one of Japan's major warships, Reich was awarded his third Navy Cross.[19]

STILL trying to survive prison life, Jesse DaSilva recalled that, just before Christmas 1944, the POWs received some Red Cross parcels. He said, "This sure was a pleasant surprise. The boxes contained all sorts of things, like soap, cigarettes, gum, a chocolate bar, powdered milk, dried prunes or raisins, canned fish and meat, a small block of cheese, canned butter, and a can opener. The bartering would begin. Some prisoners wanted the chocolate bars while others wanted cigarettes. Me, I kept just what I had and rationed it to myself accordingly. We received three boxes in all over a period of time. The Japanese had more boxes but they would not give them to us. We figured that they wanted them for themselves."[20]

After a few months, the "new" prisoners became the "old" prisoners and were transferred to the other side of the wire. One of those inside the "old" compound was an already legendary figure: the maverick Marine Major Greg "Pappy" Boyington, who had commanded Flying Squadron VMF-214, better known as the "Black Sheep Squadron," before being shot down over Rabaul and captured on 3 January 1944. Boyington had personally destroyed twenty-eight enemy aircraft and, after being reported shot down and presumed dead, was awarded the Medal of Honor, posthumously.

Pappy Boyington, however, was very much alive, but recovering from injuries he sustained when he parachuted to safety. In his autobiography, Boyington said that Ofuna was a secret camp where the Japanese navy kept some seventy to ninety "special" prisoners—submarine survivors, pilots, and various types of technicians. Living conditions at the camp were so miserable that the Japanese felt the prisoners' spirits would be broken and that they would be more likely to divulge privileged information. The Japanese also did not inform the Red Cross or anyone else what prisoners were being held there, so their relatives back home had no idea if they were dead or alive.[21]

Boyington did what he could to buoy the spirits of his fellow prisoners. DaSilva recalled, "Boyington was assigned to the kitchen detail; therefore, he was able to obtain certain privileges and would help us in every way he could."[22]

For example, Boyington said that, whenever possible, he would steal food from the guards' larder and slip it into the prisoners' rations. Once he went overboard. He stole so much of the guards' high-protein bean paste and slipped it into the prisoners' thin soup that everyone got diarrhea. "I naturally assumed that it went unnoticed, as nobody accused me, but there was one hell of a to-do around the camp because they couldn't track down the cause," he said.[23]

The war was coming dangerously close to the POWs. Dick O'Kane recalled that in February 1945, "We witnessed the grandest show yet, a great carrier strike [on Yokohama], which signified to us that the Philip-

Marine flying ace Greg "Pappy" Boyington.
(Courtesy National Air and Space Museum, Smithsonian Institution [SI 76-2766])

pines were secure, for otherwise our carriers could not be this far north. As before, a glance to the skies meant a beating from the guards, but the sight of torpedo bombers just yards away was worth it."[24]

While at Ofuna, the POWs had an obscured, distant view of the huge 9 March 1945 firebomb raid on Tokyo. A massed formation of 334 B-29s overflew the city and rained incendiary bombs on the capital, destroying a million buildings within a sixteen-square-mile area, killing nearly 84,000 people, and leaving a million and a half homeless. It was one of the deadliest air raids of the entire war.[25]

DURING *Aspro*'s sixth patrol in December 1944, Dick Mohl, a cook and baker, recalled that the trip nearly ended in self-made disaster. He said, "One night we picked up radar contact—three vessels and an escort— and we plotted their course for a few hours. We ran up ahead and dove and waited for them to cross our bow. The skipper—Bill Stevenson—was going to fire six fish, two for each ship. We fired six; one left the tube, the other five ran inside the tubes—got stuck.*

"I'm up in the forward room on the sound head and you want to talk about a scared young kid. After they told the captain about the stuck torpedo, we turned and went the other way. The captain came up and sat on the bunk next to me and said, 'Mohl, tell Conn I'm in the forward room and find out what happened.' I figured that if he could come up here and

---

* When a torpedo was fired, a wire umbilical snapped at launch, which allowed the arming vane in the torpedo's nose section to begin spinning. A torpedo was not armed until it had traveled approximately 350 feet. (Keith, 186)

sit down next to me, I've got to be pretty brave, too. They found the reason. So they got rid of all but one torpedo, but on that one they couldn't close the outer door. That meant part of the torpedo was sticking out. My knowledge of torpedoes is that once that little wheel in there makes so many revolutions, it can go off. We were submerged all day and moving forward at three knots; I hung out in the after torpedo room as much as possible, as far away from those torpedoes as I could get.

"When we surfaced at night, the captain decided to come up stern first—and the torpedo rolled out of the bow tube! When it hit the bottom there was a big bang—it was armed! Never a dull moment in the submarine force!"[26]

CHAPTER 20

A WRITHING, TWISTING MAELSTROM

"By January 1945," writes Samuel Morison, "Japanese shipping in the South China Sea had thinned out to a mere trickle."

One reason for the trickle of ship traffic was that American submariners—and their torpedoes—were much more effective and efficient than they had been during the first half of the war. The other reason was that, thanks to the unbroken string of American victories in the Pacific, Japan had fewer outposts to resupply and reinforce.

Dai Nippon could no longer ignore the tsunami of defeat and destruction roaring her way during first three months of 1945, but still she held on, like a drowning man clinging to a piece of flotsam, evidently hoping for a miracle that would somehow reverse the tidal wave. All of her hopes seem to have been pinned on her air armada of suicide pilots.

For a week in January, Admiral Halsey's Third Fleet and Task Force 38 pounded targets on Formosa, softening it up for a planned invasion, Operation Causeway. The Japanese fought back with ferocious kamikaze attacks, causing serious damage to, and heavy casualties aboard, the carriers *Langley* and *Ticonderoga*, and the destroyer *Maddox*.

The kamikaze, however, could not stop the tank and infantry divisions of Lieutenant General Walter Krueger's U.S. Sixth Army, which had landed at the end of January on the beaches rimming Lingayen Gulf on the main Philippine island of Luzon. The capital was entered on 3 February but would not be declared secure for another month.

Now the mop-up could begin. Japanese gun positions on Corregidor were silenced by intense bombing, and enemy units occupying the Bataan Peninsula were pushed into the mountains, where they would pose no threat. It would take until the end of June before the entire island of Luzon could be considered "secure."[1]

ALTHOUGH floating targets were growing scarce, the American submarine force remained busy throughout the months of January and February 1945. On 6 January, Thomas L. Wogan's *Besugo* (SS-321) and *Hardhead* (SS-365), commanded by Frank Greenup, formerly the executive officer on *Seal*, were patrolling along the Malayan coast near Singapore when they came across a large tanker escorted by three ships. *Besugo* got off a perfect shot and sent the tanker under; both submarines slipped out of the area before the escorts even knew what had hit them.[2]

On 24 January, *Blackfin* (SS-322), captained by William L. Kitch, encountered another convoy escorting a tanker. After firing a spread of torpedoes, *Blackfin* claimed one destroyer sunk and the tanker damaged. On the thirty-first, another submarine, Royce L. Gross's *Boarfish* (SS-327) sank one freighter off Indochina and crippled another, which was finished off the next day by aerial bombers. On 6 February, Paul E. Summers's *Pampanito* (SS-383) sank a 7,000-ton freighter off the coast of Malaya; on the eighth *Pampanito* added a 3,520-ton cargo-passenger ship to her battle flag.[3]

Batfish (SS-310), under John K. Fyfe, racked up one of the most remarkable sub-vs.-sub records of the war. On 9 February, *Batfish* was in Luzon Strait on her sixth war patrol when she encountered the Japanese submarine *RO-55*. Three torpedoes were fired at close range, one struck home, and the *RO-55* ceased to exist; the next night another sub, the *RO-112*, came into range and was blasted into oblivion, but *Batfish* was not yet finished. On 12 February, the *RO-115* was heading through the Luzon Strait when it was introduced to one of *Batfish*'s torpedoes. Scratch a third enemy sub.[4]

February 19 saw a large destroyer, the *Nokaze,* erupt in spectacular fashion off the coast of Indochina, thanks to the superb gunnery of Lieutenant Commander David B. Bell and his crew aboard *Pargo* (SS-264). Bell noted, "The nearest thing that can describe it are the pictures of U.S.S. *Shaw* blowing up at Pearl Harbor on December 7th; so we have unofficially chalked this one up as 'Revenge of the *Shaw*!'"[5]

Another successful patrol—this one by Frank M. Smith's *Hammerhead* (SS-364) on 23 February—resulted in the destruction of the 900-ton destroyer escort *Yaku* near Cam Ranh Bay, Indochina. On 26 February, *Blenny,* piloted by Bill Hazzard, sank the 10,000-ton tanker *Amato Maru,* beyond the mouth of the Saigon River. January and February were very good months for the American submarine force.[6]

Not all the news was good, however. On 4 February, Conde L. Raguet, in command of *Barbel* (SS-316), reported that his boat was being attacked by a Japanese aircraft. Communication was lost, and so was *Barbel,* in the waters near the Palawan Passage; eighty-one men went down with her.

A less tragic incident occurred on 13 February, when *Hoe* (SS-258), captained by Miles P. Refo, collided with James E. Stevens's *Flounder* (SS-251) off the coast of Indochina. "They bounced off each other like a couple of slow-rolling billiard balls, and sustained but slight damage," notes Samuel Morison. *Hoe* continued on her patrol, sighting a tanker and two escorts, and sinking one of the escorts on 25 February.[7]

FARTHER to the east, in mid-February, a huge armada of Admiral Spruance's warships assembled to pummel the stinking sulfuric island of Iwo Jima—"an ugly, smelly glob of cold lava squatting in a surly ocean," to borrow William Manchester's description. The island was needed as an air base for B-29s. Although the Marines had asked for nine days of preliminary naval bombardment, the Navy gave their infantrymen only three.[8]

On the morning of 19 February, American landing craft deposited more than 30,000 young men of the 3rd, 4th, and 5th Marine Divisions onto the black volcanic sand beneath Mount Suribachi's brooding brow, where they were met by 14,000 of General Tadamichi Kuribayashi's

Marines grapple with the soft volcanic soil and heavy enemy fire on Iwo Jima.
Mount Suribachi looms in the background. Photo taken 19 February 1945.
(Courtesy National Archives)

well-entrenched soldiers and 7,000 of Rear Admiral Toshinosuke Ichi-
maru's fanatic Marines. For nearly three months the Marines and Japanese battled each other in some of the bloodiest, most gut-wrenching,
hand-to-hand combat ever seen.

Sailors aboard American ships were not immune from death and
destruction during the Iwo Jima operation, either. Kamikaze suicide pilots brought death from the air, slamming their gasoline-and-bomb-
laden machines into the fleet; the aircraft carrier *Bismarck Sea* was sunk
in this manner and 218 men aboard her were killed. Other ships also felt
the sharp sting of the kamikaze—men who preferred death to living. As
a consequence, they and hundreds more Americans died.

When the last Japanese strongpoint on Iwo Jima had finally been
wiped out, the enemy body count stood at 20,000. A staggering total of
26,038 Marines had also become casualties during the fighting; includ-

ing 6,821 who lost their lives taking the barren, eight-square-mile island away from the enemy. It was the highest casualty rate sustained in any battle in the long history of the Marine Corps.[9]

IT was decided in the fall of 1944, after Iwo Jima had been neutralized, to abandon the plans for Operation Causeway—the invasion of Formosa—and concentrate instead on hitting Okinawa, the largest and most central island of the Ryuku chain, a loose semicircle of islands that connect Formosa with Kyushu. Because Okinawa had belonged to Japan since 1879, American planners assumed that the Japanese would defend it and its neighboring islands to the death. The assumptions would prove to be correct.

The carrier U.S.S. *Bunker Hill* on fire after taking two kamikaze hits in thirty seconds; 345 crewmen were killed, 264 wounded, and 43 missing. Photo taken 11 May 1945.
(Courtesy National Archives)

On 1 April 1945—a day that was both Easter Sunday and April Fools' Day—seven Marine and Army divisions, some 154,000 men, nearly the equivalent of the force that had stormed ashore at Normandy, began landing on the west-central coast of Okinawa in Operation Iceberg—destined to be the greatest land battle of the Pacific war. Waiting for them were more than 150,000 Japanese defenders under General Mitsura Ushijima, each man sworn to fight to his last breath.[10]

Okinawa was a battle that would last for three months and result in 110,000 Japanese and 12,520 American deaths; another 36,631 U.S. troops would be wounded.[11] Okinawa so resembled a charnel house that William Machester was prompted to write, "There was so much death around that life seemed almost indecent."[12]

Thirty-six American ships would be sunk during the siege, most of them by kamikaze, and another 368 damaged. But when the smoke at last cleared, the island was in American hands, and the airfields there would be used as launching pads by American bombers to pound targets in mainland Japan.

The battle for Okinawa also provided a grim preview of what an American invasion force could expect to encounter if it tried to land on the Home Islands of Japan.[13]

As with the previous island campaigns, the role of the American submarine force at Okinawa would primarily consist of interdicting any enemy convoys that attempted to come to the aid of the defenders.

BESIDES growing exceedingly scarce, targets were also becoming exceedingly small, for American submarines and surface ships had decimated Japan's fleets. About the only thing that *Aspro* found worth shooting at on her seventh war patrol in June 1945 were junks, sampans, fishing boats, and patrol boats. "On the previous run of the *Aspro* in April," said Dick Mohl, the baker on *Aspro*, "the captain, 'Jungle Jim' Ashley—we called him that because he always wore a jungle hat—sank a small vessel with one torpedo. People told me the target was about the size of a seagoing tug. It just folded in half and went down.

"Well, it's customary in the submarine force for the baker to make a victory cake for the skipper. Because this boat was so small, I decided to

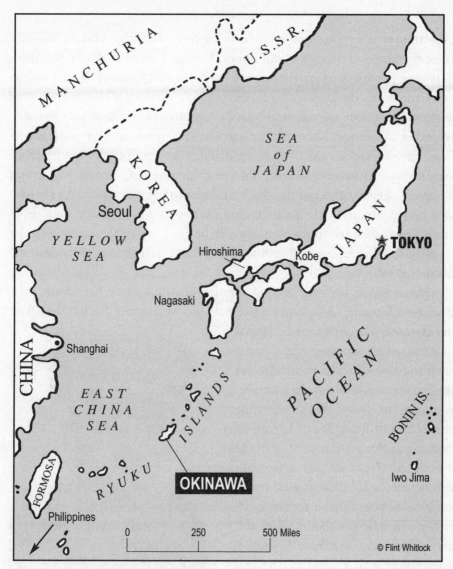

Okinawa and the Ryuku Island chain.

put some fun in the game, so in addition to the regular cake, I made the captain a *cupcake*! I carried it out and presented it to him and said, 'Captain, you have to admit it was a small ship.' He looked at that cupcake and looked at me and said, 'Okay, Mohl—you've had your fun. Now give me the *big* cake,' so I did."[14]

* * *

HEROISM was in abundance aboard *Tirante* (SS-420). Having already sunk five ships, *Tirante*'s commander, George L. Street III, on the sub's first war patrol, was in the harbor of Korea's Quelpart Island in the early morning darkness of 14 April 1945. Although the harbor was shallow, profusely mined, and heavily guarded, Street and his crew disregarded all dangers and penetrated the enemy anchorage on the surface, determined to cause as much trouble as possible. Two torpedoes sent into an ammunition ship did the trick; the ship erupted in grand Vesuvian style, wrecking the dock and several nearby craft. As the sub was being pursued out of the harbor by two enemy frigates, two shots from *Tirante*'s stern tubes blew the sub hunters out of the water and she made good her escape. For his daring run, Street was awarded the Medal of Honor.[15]

Street wasn't the only daring submarine commander late in the war. Back on 8 January 1945, Eugene B. Fluckey, commanding *Barb* (SS-220) on her eleventh war patrol, had engaged in a two-hour running night battle with convoy escorts as he tried to get into position to sink a large ammunition ship, the *Shinyo Maru,* along the east coast of China. At last he saw an opening and made the most of it; the ammo ship went up like a Roman-candle factory. Fluckey said, "The target now resembled a fantastic, gigantic phosphorous bomb. The volcanic spectacle was awe inspiring. Shrapnel flew all around us." Several other ships were damaged.

Many commanders might have been satisfied by such a show of pyrotechnics and headed for home, but not Fluckey; he still had several more torpedoes on board and he planned to expend them all.

George L. Street III, commander of *Tirante* and recipient of the Medal of Honor.
(Courtesy Naval Historical Center)

Fluckey and *Barb* had been patrolling the waters off Foo Chow, close to where *Tang* was lost, when he learned that a flotilla of eleven transports was sheltered in the anchorage of Namkwan Bay. What better place to find multiple, unsuspecting targets than inside an enemy-controlled harbor? It was like going hunting in a zoo.

As he steered *Barb* into Namkwan Bay on 22 January, Fluckey's periscope sweep was greeted by the sight of thirty Japanese ships of various descriptions—a two-mile-long chain of vessels—"the most beautiful target of the war," as Fluckey put it. But an attack in these shallow, uncharted waters was rife with peril. Not only did rocks and mines hinder his planned attack and escape routes, but the ships themselves were heavily armed.

Disregarding the danger, Fluckey ordered, "Battle Stations Submerged," and waded into the flotilla. Penetrating a screen of frigates, he fired four torpedoes from his forward tubes, spun around, and fired four more from the aft. All eight fish struck home and six targets, including another ammunition ship, erupted in spectacular, Technicolor fashion. With enemy destroyers hot on her tail, *Barb* left the scene on the surface, spewing diesel exhaust and dodging shells for over an hour as she headed for deep water. Clay Blair called the raid "the most daring patrol of the entire war."[16]

At last eluding her pursuers, *Barb* made it safely back to Pearl, but not before sinking another Japanese ship on her way out of Chinese waters. It was not for nothing that the skipper was known as "Lucky Fluckey."[17]

Good news travels fast, and as *Barb* pulled into her berth at Pearl Harbor on 15 February 1945, Fluckey and his crew were greeted by a most distinguished group: Admiral Nimitz, General Douglas MacArthur, and President Franklin D. Roosevelt. One month later, for his "conspicuous gallantry and intrepidity at the risk of his life above and beyond the call of duty," Fluckey was awarded the Medal of Honor by Secretary of the Navy James Forrestal.

Following an overhaul at Mare Island, Fluckey and *Barb* set out again on their twelfth patrol. Was it tempting fate to return to combat after eleven patrols, or was Fluckey really lucky?

On 3 July 1945, off the coast of Hokkaidō, Japan, *Barb* surfaced and launched a dozen rockets at the coastal town of Shikuka on Patience Bay—the first time a submarine had been used as a firing platform for

aerial missiles. Two days later, *Barb* sank the freighter *Sapporo Maru* off
Hokkaidō. Someone then had the bright idea of landing a raiding party
on the mainland of Japan and blow up a train! A suitable rail line was
found running along the coast of Patience Bay.

Constructing a charge made from fifty-five pounds of torpex with a
detonator set to be triggered by the weight of a passing train, the eight-
man volunteer group of saboteurs from *Barb* crawled from the hatch on
the night of 22–23 July, paddled ashore in rubber rafts, and planted the
bomb beneath the track. "Fluckey's Commandoes" paddled back to the
Barb just as a blacked-out train approached. At 0147 hours on 23 July,
the train went sky-high.

"Boom! Wham! What a thrill," wrote Fluckey, who had been watching from *Barb*'s half-submerged bridge. "The flash of the charge exploding changed into a spreading ball of sparkling flame. The boilers of the
engine blew. Engine wreckage flying, flying, flying up some 200 feet, racing ahead of a mushroom of smoke, now white, now black. Cars piling
up, into, and over the wall of wreckage in front, rolling off the track in a
writhing, twisting maelstrom of Gordian knots."

It was later reported that *Barb* had "sunk" a sixteen-car troop train
full of Japanese soldiers, and the silhouette of a locomotive was added to
her battle flag. It was the only time American troops conducted ground-
combat operations on Japan proper during the entire war.

Admiral Lockwood wrote a letter of praise to Fluckey, noting, "Your
gun attacks and frigate attacks were daring in the extreme and your
saboteur expedition was considerably too risky. However, fortune favors
the bold and you made a splendid success of it."[18]

BUT all that was still in the future. One drizzly morning after breakfast
in April 1945, the American POWs at Ofuna were lined up in front of
their barracks and angrily accused by the commandant of stealing some
of the Red Cross food parcels that were locked up in one of the barracks.
Their captors demanded that the person responsible step forward and
confess to his thievery.

Decker said, "Naturally, nobody took the blame, so the Japanese
made us stand at attention outside in the rain until the guilty party ad-

Eugene Fluckey, commander of *Barb* and recipient of the Medal of Honor.
(Courtesy Naval Historical Center)

mitted his crime. We knew that if anyone *did* confess, he would probably be taken away and beaten or shot. Our only hope was to stick together and say nothing."[19]

DaSilva recalled that the group remained at attention in front of the barracks all day without lunch. "Come dinner time, still nothing, so they made us get into a pushup position and if anyone moved, a guard would hit us with a club across the buttocks. This didn't seem to work, either, so they took us back inside the barracks and lined us up in the center and asked again who was responsible. Still no answer. Then the guards took turns whacking us across the buttocks several times each. Still no answer. Finally they quit and gave us our dinner."[20]

The next day fifteen of the prisoners—six of the nine *Tang* survivors, plus Boyington and eight other aviators—were transferred to a different camp. Richard O'Kane, Larry Savadkin, and Hank Flanagan were not among this group, but would follow in June. The group, under heavy guard, was placed on a streetcar and driven, according to Boyington's estimate, about twenty-five miles in the direction of Tokyo, then marched another five miles.

The new camp, Omori, was on a man-made island on the western shore of Tokyo Bay and connected to the mainland by a narrow causeway. Boyington noted that he and the other POWs were locked up in a small room "that remained our sleeping cell until the end of the war."[21]

As the ranking officer and only American in the group who could speak Japanese (he had learned it before the war while stationed in the Orient), Boyington was elected by the prisoners to be in command of the little group. Said DaSilva, "We were all put together in one building and still not allowed to see or talk with the other prisoners in the camp. We were kept like this as 'special prisoners' all the time we were there."[22]

Clay Decker expanded on DaSilva's recollection. "We weren't officially classified as prisoners-of-war; we were 'Special Prisoners of the Empire of Japan.' They claimed that when we sank Japanese ships, 90 percent of the persons on board were civilians. So we were accused of making war on civilians and weren't entitled to prisoner-of-war status. As a consequence, we only got half the normal food ration, and we weren't able to mingle or associate with any other prisoners in any of the camps we were in."[23]

As at Ofuna, the building in which the Americans were confined consisted of a dirt floor in the center and raised wooden platforms on each side where the prisoners slept. "We all had diarrhea," said DaSilva, "and I had developed beriberi so, between the two, I wasn't in too good of shape. Our food by now consisted of a bucket of rice that was divided equally among us, and that turned out to be half a cup each, along with a small bowl of soup three times a day. When I say rice, I mean it was a combination of barley, milamaze, and rice." On rare occasions, their captors would supplement the thin soup with a few pieces of dried fish. The prisoners never received any chicken, beef, or other types of meat. Already thin, they began to lose weight at an alarming rate.

The Americans were given permission to plant their own vegetable garden to supplement their meager rations. "I did everything possible to obtain extra food," DaSilva confessed, "so, as vegetables in the garden became ripe, I would pick them and eat them raw when the guard wasn't looking. When you're starving, anything besides your normal ration of soup and rice tastes good."[24]

After the Americans had idled at Omori for about a month, they decided they wanted to do something other than just rot away in a cell, so Boyington talked the camp commandant into sending the group out on work details.

The work involved going out early each morning to the outskirts of Tokyo and Yokohama and picking up the debris left after the daily American bombing raids. The POWs were required to pick up heavy

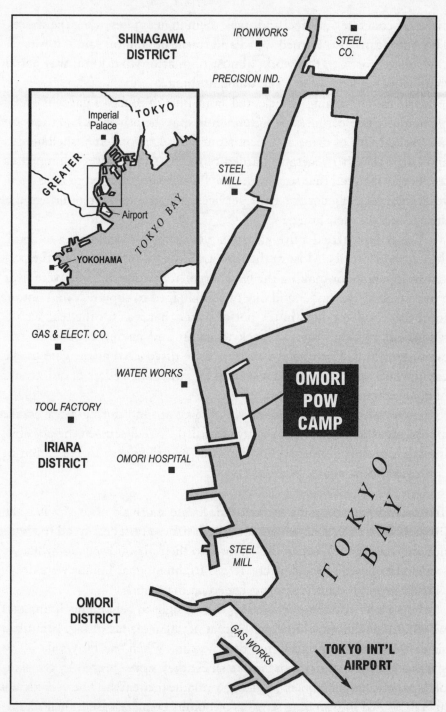

Tokyo and environs, showing Omori POW Camp.

pieces of concrete and steel and stack them in neat piles along the streets. The Americans also burned wood and trash. Boyington said, "It was really rough work . . . But work, almost no matter what kind, was better than being made to sit in a cell doing nothing."

One task—turning the cleared land into productive gardens—was particularly unpleasant. Boyington noted that the prisoners had to scoop out bucketloads of urine and feces from the toilets of demolished houses and carry them to vegetable-garden plots, where they were dumped as fertilizer. He noted that sometimes the POWs were allowed to take a few vegetables as payment for their services, but the meager offerings did little to satisfy their hunger.[25]

The group carried a five-gallon can of water for making tea to drink during their breaks. Most of the time DaSilva volunteered to be the person responsible for making the tea. "I remember one time we were near a fish market," he said, "and one of us managed to slip away and obtain some fish. I boiled them in the pot of water that was for the tea. We intended on bringing the fish back to camp and having them with our evening meal. Unfortunately, the fish were discovered at the gate to the camp when we returned and it was taken away; the leaders of our group, of course, were punished."

Once, when the work party was sitting around during a tea break, an old, stray dog appeared. DaSilva recalled, "We discussed the possibility of eating this animal if only someone had the nerve to kill it. But of course, nobody would."[26]

Tokyo was becoming the target of more and more air raids. "When the fireworks started," DaSilva noted, "the Japanese boarded up all the windows in the barracks, then they went into their air-raid shelters while we were left exposed to the dangers. It was frightening, as bombs were dropping all around; some fragments ended up in camp."[27]

Boyington said that the air raids were a sight to behold, terrifying and wonderful at the same time, with great aerial armadas of big, beautiful, silver B-29s that nearly blotted out the sun. When the POWs dared to sneak a glance at the combat in the skies, they were cheered by the sight of Japanese fighter planes plunging in flames to earth. The Americans also delighted in watching streams of bombs being released, their explosions shaking the earth and rattling the camp's windows, even when the bombs crashed close to Omori.[28]

Clay Decker added, "It looked to us like the world was coming to an end. The fires burned for days and days, with flames and an eerie orange glow night after night. Ashes from the burning buildings fell on our camp like black snow. The guards were not too pleased with what our fliers had done, so they were especially cruel to us over the next couple of weeks. I guess I don't blame them. I assume a lot of them had relatives in Tokyo who perished in the fires."[29]

The prisoners tried hard to contain their joy at seeing the enemy's capital city being systematically reduced to cinders because the Japanese guards were quick to lash out at anyone showing too much emotion. Boyington said that whenever a prisoner was seen to be smiling during an air raid, the guards hit him with a rifle butt or slapped him in the face. "And sometimes we were just slugged because feelings were running a bit high," he said.[30]

The systematic incineration of Tokyo signaled the beginning of the end for Japan—a sign that the day was fast approaching when millions of American infantrymen were expected to hit the beaches and begin the final reckoning. Martin Gilbert writes, "In the next three months, the cities of Nagoya, Osaka, Kobe, Yokohama, and Kawasaki were likewise attacked and pulverized, and more than a quarter of a million Japanese civilians killed, for the loss of only 243 American airmen."[31]

The prisoners at Omori—filthy, covered with lice and sores, racked by dysentery, malaria, beriberi, scurvy, and a host of other diseases, and growing weaker and scrawnier by the day—wondered if they would live to see the hour of their liberation.

CHAPTER 21

BEAR THE UNBEARABLE

ON 30 April 1945, while American forces were closing in like buzzards around Japan, and American, British, and Soviet troops were squeezing the Third Reich to death, Adolf Hitler, deep in his Berlin bunker, bit down on a cyanide capsule at the same moment he blew his brains out with a pistol.

With Hitler dead, Nazi Germany's days were numbered. Pounded without pause from the air and penetrated from two sides on the ground, Germany became a diminishing perimeter, a cancerous tumor being slowly starved and shrunken. The Soviets had driven deeply into what was left of the burning, rubble-strewn capital and were closing in on Hitler's final hiding place, the *Führerbunker* beneath the battered Reich chancellery. Except for a few hard-line units that refused to give up when they got the word of their Führer's suicide, the Third Reich was no more. The war in Europe was finally over; the war in the Pacific, however, went on.[1]

RON Smith's war, however, was finished. The Smith's son, Ronal Lynn, was born on May 17, 1945, in Marilynn's hometown of Salida, Colorado. During that time, Smitty was transferred from Great Lakes to the Crane Naval Ammunitions Depot, near Burns City, Indiana, about thirty-five miles southwest of Bloomington, where he received a stunning letter.

"Marilynn and the baby were supposed to come join me," Smitty said, "but I received a 'Dear John' letter from her while I was at Crane. I guess she didn't want to be married to me anymore. The letter was kind of a shock, but it didn't really affect me all that much. I was young and could not separate sex from love at that time. I had more than enough 'girlfriends,' so I didn't lose a lot of sleep over it. In a way, I was relieved—I wouldn't have the responsibility of a family."[2]

FRANK Toon was still in the Pacific, and was still in combat. On 25 May 1945, his Fremantle-based boat, *Blenny,* was on its third war patrol in the South China Sea. Toon recalled, "The whole patrol was a merry-go-round for the gun crews. I was the 'trainer' on the forward five-inch gun, and we had lots of opportunity to shoot. As I recall, we sank sixty-three small targets in thirty days. A lot of these small targets would be sunk with just one five-inch shot. Of course, we kept running out of ammo and were always looking for a submarine that had extra ammo left over when heading home. We would then transfer it aboard *Blenny* by breeches buoy. It was always amusing to hear Captain Hazzard call below to 'send up one five-inch bullet.' Darn *big* bullets!"

Toon remembered an incident that was humorous only in hindsight— the time his commanding officer was blown through the hatch. "We had spent all day lying on the bottom to repair problems with the port shaft," he said. "I was the 'watch quartermaster' when we surfaced, and there was a lot of air pressure that had built up inside the boat. I opened the hatch and jumped back to allow the captain to be first up. Just as he started up, the lower hatch blew open and the captain was 'launched' up through the hatch, banging his head. 'Doc' Taylor had a chance to practice his sewing! If that lower hatch had blown open a second or two earlier, it would have been *me* that went out the hatch!"[3]

ON Monday, 16 July 1945, the predawn skies around Alamogordo, New Mexico—110 miles south of Albuquerque—suddenly were illuminated with the brilliance of a thousand suns.

The first atomic bomb—the product of the top secret Manhattan Project—had just been successfully tested. The multibillion-dollar project, under the command of Major General Leslie R. Groves and a team of scientists headed by University of California at Berkeley professor of theoretical physics Dr. J. Robert Oppenheimer, had been progressing to this point for nearly four years.

Following the discovery of the neutron in 1932, it was determined that it was possible—given enough money and scientific brainpower and fissionable material—to build a superweapon. The only question had been, who would build it first—the Germans, the Japanese, or the Americans? The fear at the highest echelons of the American and British governments in the early 1940s was that the Germans and Japanese were both working on similar projects, and that either—or both—would use such a weapon against the Allies as soon as they had the chance. The Americans and British were determined to beat the Germans and Japanese to the atomic punch; the collapse of Germany in May 1945 meant that all of the work could be directed at knocking the sole combatant enemy nation—Japan—out of the war.

So secret was the Manhattan Project that Vice President Harry S. Truman, who had inherited the presidency of the United States when Roosevelt died suddenly of a massive cerebral hemorrhage on 12 April 1945, had not even known of its existence. He was quickly brought up to speed.

A debate went on behind closed doors. While some felt that an atomic bomb—if it actually worked—was morally reprehensible because it could indiscriminately kill hundreds of thousands of innocent civilians, the majority argued that such a result was far more moral than allowing the war that had been raging for six years—a war in which 50 million people had already perished—to drag on for months, or even years, and cause even greater casualties, sorrow, and devastation.

The invasion of Japan was even now in the final stages of planning, and scores of combat-weary divisions in Europe were alerted for deployment to the Far East. On 18 June 1945, President Truman met at the White House with General Dwight D. Eisenhower; General George C. Marshall, chairman of the Joint Chiefs of Staff; Secretary of War Henry Stimson; Secretary of the Navy James Forrestal; and a handful of other high-ranking advisers to discuss the matter and come to a resolution.[4]

Everyone was painfully aware of the hard truth: Japanese fighting men, even when trapped on cut-off Pacific islands with absolutely no hope of reinforcement or victory, clung tenaciously to their *bushido* code and never surrendered. They almost always fought to the death—and sometimes beyond; the bodies of dead comrades were frequently booby-trapped to blow up when moved by American soldiers and Marines checking for life or war souvenirs.

If the invasion of Japan took place, it was assumed—and with good reason—that every Japanese man, woman, and child would fight as guerrillas to inflict maximum casualties on the invaders. It was also estimated that Japanese casualties in such an invasion would approach or exceed one million, with American casualties running about the same. Admiral Shibasaki's assertion that "a million men could not take this island in a hundred years" would be better applied to Japan itself than to Tarawa. William Manchester writes, "We assumed we would have to invade [the Japanese Home Islands of] Kyushu and Honshu, and we would have been unsurprised to learn that MacArthur, whose forecasts of losses were uncannily accurate, had told Washington that he expected the first stage of that final campaign to 'cost one million casualties [dead and wounded] to American forces alone.' "[5]

Thus came the ultimate question: Would it not be preferable—even merciful—to use a weapon that could snuff out this horrible war in an instant, the way one blows out a candle?

At the time the choice seemed simple. What if a superweapon with power beyond imagining could call a sudden halt to all the suffering and bloodshed that the Second World War had brought about? It was Japan that had thrust America into the global conflict on 7 December 1941, and it was Japan that must pay the ultimate price for her perfidy—even if it meant the unfortunate and tragic sacrifice of one or two Japanese cities full of innocent civilians.

Someone at the meeting advanced the idea of telling the Japanese government that the United States possessed a weapon of such unimaginable power that it could totally destroy the entire nation of Japan. Someone else suggested dropping warning leaflets or holding a demonstration and exploding one of the bombs—there had been only enough fissionable material to build three of them—on some sparsely populated island near Japan and inviting Nippon's leaders to witness it. This was countered by someone pointing out that the Alamogordo bomb had worked because it was mounted on a stationary tower and had been detonated under controlled scientific conditions; what if one of these complex, delicate instruments, when dropped by an aircraft, turned out to be a dud? Wouldn't that just convince the Japanese that the United States was bluffing and merely serve to strengthen Japanese resolve? Good point, the group agreed.[6]

Statistics vary widely, but already over 400,000 American servicemen and women had been killed in the war (with over 600,000 wounded), along with more than 360,000 British troops (including colonials), 200,000 French, 1.4 million Chinese, 10 million Soviets, over two million Germans, 200,000 Italians, and over two million Japanese troops, to name but a few. This list does not include the approximately 55.3 million civilians worldwide who had died as a result of the war.[7]

The time, everyone finally agreed, had come to end the war—and the world's agony—with one tremendous blow.[8]

If Truman hesitated to consider the moral dilemma posed by the use of such a tremendous and horrible weapon, or agonized over his decision, such a hesitation was only momentary. He gave the order.

On 24 July 1945, General Thomas T. Hardy, acting chief of staff of the Army, sent a communiqué to General Carl Spaatz, commander of the United States Army Strategic Air Force:

> The 508 Composite Group, 20th Air Force, will deliver the first special bomb as soon as weather will permit visual bombing after about 3 August 1945 on one of the targets: Hiroshima, Kokura, Niigata and Nagasaki . . .[9]

The order was relayed to the island of Tinian, where Colonel Paul Tibbetts and his aircraft, a B-29 Superfortress bomber with the name of his mother, Enola Gay, painted on the nose, waited.

It was decided to give Japan one last chance to surrender—or suffer the unstated consequences. On 26 July, Japan was sent an ultimatum known as the Potsdam Declaration, signed by representatives of China, Britain, and the United States, which demanded that she surrender immediately or be annihilated; the Japanese prime minister, wrongly assuming the document's war-weary signers were bluffing, flatly rejected the demand.

At 0815 hours, Japan time, 6 August 1945, much of the city of Hiroshima suddenly ceased to exist. A single uranium bomb dropped by Tibbetts and the crew of *Enola Gay* detonated in the clear sky above the heart of the city. In a flash, 78,000 people were dead, 37,000 were injured, and another 13,000 were missing. Sixty percent of the city had been flattened and turned into a charred, nearly unrecognizable landscape.[10]

Still, the Japanese government did not concede. Perhaps they thought the Americans had but one atomic bomb. Perhaps they were still confused and reeling and unclear about what had happened to Hiroshima. In either case, a second demand for surrender was also rejected.

On 8 August, the Soviet Union, in the diplomatic equivalent of beating up a corpse, declared war on Japan.

The following day a B-29 with the name *Bock's Car* painted on its nose, and piloted by Major Charles W. Sweeney, flew at 29,000 feet above the city of Nagasaki and released another atomic bomb, this one with a plutonium core. Nearly 100,000 people died or were wounded in the searing blast and the firestorm that followed. As Lansing Lamont writes in *Day of Trinity*, "Nagasaki in all its horror told the Japanese that Hiroshima had been no fluke or lone experiment. It said in effect: Here is a second example of what the bomb can do, and there are more."[11]

Even the destruction of Nagasaki did not bring about an immediate cessation of fighting. In China, on 10 August, the Communists mounted a final offensive against their occupiers; the next day Soviet warships bombarded Japanese installations on southern Sakhalin Island. On 12 August, Soviet infantry and armor launched an annihilating attack against Japanese defenders holed up in a Manchurian fortress. On the fourteenth, over 800 American B-29s clobbered enemy installations throughout Honshu with conventional high-explosive munitions.

The horror—and the fear of further atomic and conventional bombings against which Japan had no defense—finally sank in. With her cities flattened, her army and navy crushed, and enemies encircling her like vultures, Japan had no alternative but to give up. During a meeting with his Supreme War Council and the entire cabinet on 14 August, Emperor Hirohito declared that his country must accept the Potsdam Declaration and "bear the unbearable."

Hearing rumors that the emperor might order Japan's capitulation, a thousand hard-line troops stormed the Imperial Palace grounds in hopes of preventing the surrender; they were beaten back by the Imperial Guards in a bloody confrontation.

The next day, a prerecorded message from the emperor was broadcast on nationwide radio in which he informed his people of his painful decision. On the sixteenth, the confirmation that the emperor had directed the armed forces of Japan to cease fire immediately was transmitted by radio to General MacArthur's headquarters. Japan surrendered unconditionally. The Second World War was, at long last, finished.[12]

FRANK Toon, aboard the submarine *Blenny,* recalled, "We had just received a message by light from the tender: The war was over! We were making a sound run in Subic Bay in the Philippines when all the fireworks started. I still remember shooting off all our Very shells and flares to join in the celebration. We put on the smoke generators before making a run around the bay on our way back to the tender. That smoke screen surely clouded things up! Everyone was happy! *THE WAR WAS FINALLY OVER!*"[13]

"WE didn't have a radio at the hospital and no one got a newspaper—I got the news about the A-bomb from the other men," said Ron Smith, who was back in the hospital at Great Lakes for further testing and evaluation. He was astounded when word of the secret weapon that had brought about the end of the war raced through the hospital.

Smitty said, "I didn't understand what the atomic bomb was at that time, but I was overjoyed that we had a new 'superweapon.' I felt *no* pity whatsoever for the Japs; we could have exterminated the whole race and it wouldn't have bothered me one bit. When they surrendered, I was thankful that the war was finally over. There was no big celebration at the hospital, just relief—a great sense of relief from the nagging anxiety that had been with me for several years. I just wanted to go somewhere and sleep in peace.

"Ironically, they had all of us patients restricted to the hospital, but they let all the men from boot camp out to celebrate in Chicago while they kept the combat veterans 'chained down.' Since I only had about six months left on my enlistment when the war ended, I was offered a discharge. I took it."[14]

AT Omori, the American prisoners had heard rumors about the atomic bombs and were very hopeful that the rumors were true and that such awesome weapons might soon lead to their liberation.

Jesse DaSilva said, "We knew that the war was getting closer to the end. We knew what was happening all the time as bits of information would filter through the camp. We knew when the atomic bomb had been dropped and we couldn't believe the results."[15]

Clay Decker noted, however, that the prisoners had one big worry. "In August many of the guards were crying, almost hysterical, probably because they had friends and relatives in Hiroshima and Nagasaki. We were afraid that they might take revenge against us and kill us all. After all, they had lost the war, so what else did they have to lose? We figured they would kill us and then commit suicide."[16]

Jesse DaSilva said, "One morning we woke up and it was very quiet. We discovered there was only one guard in the whole camp. He told us the war was over, so we just took over the camp."[17]

Some of the prisoners found brushes and white paint in a camp storehouse, crawled onto the roofs of the buildings, and painted giant signs reading P.W. and PAPPY BOYINGTON HERE, in hopes that American airmen, flying over Tokyo Bay, would see them and come to their rescue.[18]

It worked. DaSilva recalled that aircraft flew over the camp and dropped tons of food and clothing. "It got so bad that this stuff was crashing through the buildings, so we had to put a sign on the compound telling them to drop it outside of camp," he said.[19]

Clay Decker said, "They airdropped a lot of food and medicines to

Roof signs at Omori POW Camp.
(Courtesy National Archives)

us. Some of our lads got sick gorging themselves on all the food, so we needed to be careful about how much we ate and not overdo it."[20]

THE atomic bombs weren't the only weapons that brought Japan to her knees. The American submarine force had much to do with it. A 1999 study by Michel Poirier points out that the Japanese Merchant Marine fleet lost 8.1 million tons of vessels during the war; American submarines accounted for 4.9 million of those tons, or 60 percent of the total.

The submarines were also instrumental in preventing the raw materials that Japan's war industries desperately needed from reaching the factories that would turn them into tanks, ships, airplanes, guns, bombs, bullets, uniforms, and the other necessities of war. Japan's imports of sixteen key materials fell from 20 million tons in 1941 to 10 million tons in 1944, and to a meager 2.7 million tons during the first half of 1945. Imports of bauxite, essential for the production of aluminum, plunged 88 percent between the summer and fall of 1944. The next year, pig-iron imports fell 89 percent, raw cotton and wool were down over 90 percent, lumber down 98 percent, and so on. Not one ounce of sugar or raw rubber reached Japan during the first six months of 1945.

Because of the submarines, millions of Japanese bullets and tens of thousands of bombs and artillery shells never arrived at the battlefronts to kill Americans. Millions of gallons of oil and gasoline bound for Japanese tanks, trucks, ships, and aircraft also never reached their destinations. From August 1943 to July 1944, oil imports dropped from 1.75 million barrels of oil a month to just 360,000 barrels per month. As Poirier says, "After September 1943, the ratio of petroleum successfully shipped that reached Japan never exceeded twenty-eight percent, and during the last 15 months of the war the ratio averaged nine percent. The losses are especially impressive when one considers that the Japanese Navy alone required 1.6 million [barrels] monthly to operate."

By the last year of the war, the Japanese tried to cope with the shortages through desperate measures. Because of the lack of fuel, flight schools sent new pilots off to their units—and their doom—with only a fraction of the number of hours needed to attain proficiency in the sky. Because of the severe lack of petroleum products, the number of hours a new airplane engine could be tested was drastically reduced. And, due to the shortage of high-quality aluminum, planes were built with an increasing number of wooden parts. Likewise, thousands of Japanese troops being shuttled to island battlefields never made it. Food and medicine needed to keep isolated Japanese garrisons alive and healthy similarly failed to arrive.

Shipbuilding in Japan was reduced to a mere trickle of what it had been early in the war. With the nearly total cutoff of iron ore, the ability of the Japanese shipbuilding industry to replace the country's massive losses after the autumn of 1944 was severely crippled. Poirier writes, "The requirement to build escort ships and naval transports (also to replace merchant losses) reduced the potential to build more powerful combatants.

"As a result, while the IJN used fourteen percent of its construction budget for escorts and transports in 1941, the percentage shot up to 54.3 percent in 1944. More astonishing, the need for escorts and merchants was so grave that, after 1943, the Japanese Navy started construction on no ship bigger than a destroyer!"

Transports, merchantmen, and oilers weren't the only vessels decimated. During the course of the war, American submarines sank 700,000 tons of Japanese warships, including one battleship, eleven cruisers, eight aircraft carriers, and scores of smaller ships.

Food, too, was in short supply in the Home Islands, with the average caloric intake of urban dwellers plunging 12 percent *below* the minimum daily requirement.[21]

Without a doubt, then, American submarines had a huge impact on Japan's ability to wage war. The American submarines were the noose that slowly strangled Japan to death.

The price of victory, however, was high. Of the approximately 15,000 men who served in the 288 American submarines from 1941 to 1945, 374 officers, 3,131 enlisted men, and fifty-two submarines—22 percent of the total—were lost.[22]

THE American fleet, with Admiral Halsey in command, sailed into Tokyo Bay on 29 August 1945 aboard the battleships *Missouri*, *Iowa*, and *South Dakota*, light cruiser *San Juan*, and hospital ship *Benevolence* to prepare to occupy what was left of the burned-out capital. On that same day, the *San Juan*, *Benevolence*, and two high-speed transports, U.S.S. *Reeves* and *Gosselin*, approached Omori. Three naval officers—Roger Simpson, Joel Boone, and Harold Stassen—the latter the former governor of Minnesota who had resigned the office to join the Navy in 1943—debarked and approached the camp's gates to investigate conditions inside.

Another officer who accompanied them into the camp wrote, "When the prisoners realized what was happening, indescribable and pitiful scenes of enthusiasm and excitement took place—men even jumped into the water and started swimming out to the boats . . . They found the camp conditions unspeakable with every evidence of brutality and wretched treatment. What our people found there will contrast the Nips' present ingratiating attitude.

"Simpson, Stassen, and Boone did a magnificent job—without regard to their own safety they waded into the situation, bluffed the Japanese camp guards, and gave them a complete brushoff. Joel Boone made his way to a Japanese hospital three miles away, and singlehandedly took over the situation, telling the Nips that he didn't give a goddamn what their orders were . . .

"The work went on all night and some seven hundred prisoners were processed through the *Benevolence*, the desperately sick being hospitalized, and the ambulatory cases moved to the APDs [*Reeves* and *Gosselin*]. On the following day the work continued and by the evening of the 30th about one thousand POWs had been freed."[23]

Happy liberated American, Dutch, and British POWs at Omori. Clay Decker is in foreground (circled).
(Courtesy Clay Decker)

Jesse DaSilva said, "I was taken aboard the hospital ship *Benevolence* and was put to bed and given blood and other medication. I was also given a meal of bacon and eggs. When I was captured I weighed 170 pounds. Now I was down to about 100 pounds and was in no condition to be flown home. Later I was transferred to the hospital ship *Rescue*, which was returning to the States. It took twenty-one days, but I didn't care—I knew I was going home! I arrived back in the States exactly two years since had I left on October 25, 1943, and one year to the day that our submarine was sunk—on October 25, 1944."[24]

Clay Decker, naturally, was overjoyed at being liberated. "The first thing I thought about was that, at last, I would get to go home and see Lucille and little Harry.

"Pappy Boyington and nineteen other officers were the first to be returned to the States by transport plane. Somehow I got to be a part of that group. Twenty officers and one enlisted man. I asked Pappy, 'Did you get me on this flight?' And he said, 'Aww, Deck, I didn't have anything to do with it.' But he said it with a smile, so I know damn good and well he did."

After a couple of days flying over nothing but ocean, and stopping briefly at Wake, Midway, and Hawaii to refuel, the transport at last approached the California coast. Everyone on board had their faces pressed against the small windows. Decker said, "There was the Golden Gate Bridge down below us. What a sight! And the hills around San Francisco Bay, with all their little houses and buildings and roads. It looked like the world's most beautiful model-train layout; I couldn't believe it was actually real, that I was actually home."[25]

It was not the happy homecoming Decker had expected it to be, for he was in for one final shock.

ONE might think that the end of the war would have brought an outpouring of jubilant gloating among the victors at the highest echelons of government, but just the opposite was the case. The war had been too long, too bloody, too expensive for either jubilation or gloating. The awesome destruction and death toll wrought by the two atomic bombs, and by the carpet bombing of Japan's cities and the Third Reich, were too terrible to celebrate in any grand fashion. There was no time to rest on the laurels of victory, either, for a new world needed to be built atop the ashes of the old, destroyed one.

Immediately after the war Secretary of War Henry L. Stimson said with extreme gravity, "In this last great action of the Second World War, we were given final proof that war is death. War in the twentieth century has grown steadily more barbarous, more destructive, more debased in all its aspects. Now, with the release of atomic energy, man's ability to destroy himself is very nearly complete. The bombs dropped on Hiroshima and Nagasaki ended a war. They also made it wholly clear that we must never have another war. This is the lesson men and leaders everywhere must learn, and I believe that when they learn it they will find a way to lasting peace. There is no other choice."[26]

More than sixty years later, the world is still waiting for the lesson to be learned.

EPILOGUE: THE VELOCITY
OF POSTWAR HISTORY

ON 2 September 1945, the official surrender ceremony took place aboard Halsey's flagship, the battleship *Missouri,* anchored in Tokyo Bay. A contingent of fifteen somber-faced Japanese diplomats in top hats and tails, led by Prince Higashikuni Naruhiko (who had been prime minister only since 17 August 1945) and Foreign Minister Mamoru Shigemitsu, arrived at the ship and were escorted aboard. Awaiting them were the equally somber-faced General MacArthur, Admirals Nimitz, Halsey, and Lockwood, the emaciated, recently freed General Jonathan Wainwright (held in Japanese POW camps since the fall of the Philippines), and hundreds of other American officers and enlisted men.[1]

In the waters of Tokyo Bay were twelve American submarines: *Archerfish, Cavalla, Gato, Haddo, Hake, Muskallunge, Pilotfish, Razorback, Runner II, Sea Cat, Segundo,* and *Tigrone*. It was only fitting that representatives of the force that struck the first blows against the Japanese were present as "honored guests" at the surrender.[2]

In a very brief ceremony at which no smiles or handshakes were exchanged, the Japanese representatives dutifully signed the instruments of surrender, followed by the American witnesses, and then MacArthur said, "I now declare these proceedings closed."[3]

Seaman Bernard Schwartz, who had been in a submarine relief crew and would soon be known as the actor Tony Curtis, recalled viewing the ceremonies through binoculars from the nearby submariner tender U.S.S. *Proteus*. "That was one of the greatest moments in my life," Curtis said, "to be eighteen, almost nineteen, standing on the signal bridge and watching the signing of that document. I felt so proud to be part of the service at that time."[4]

The United States and other Western nations began a rapid demobilization. The tools of war were thought to be of no further use; the First World War had been billed as being "the war to end all wars," but it became the seed that sprouted into the next one. This time, as many were convinced, the deaths and devastation were so awful and widespread that surely the Second World War was "the war to end all wars," or at least "the war to end all *world* wars."

Therefore, millions of rifles, guns, planes, ships, and massive stockpiles of bombs and ammunition were dumped, discarded, dismantled,

Aboard the U.S.S. *Missouri*, Admiral Chester Nimitz signs the Declaration of Surrender as a witness as General Douglas MacArthur (left) and Admiral William Halsey (second from left) look on, 2 September 1945.
(Courtesy National Archives)

destroyed. Most of the submarines the United States had built before and during the war became obsolete with the coming of the first nuclear submarine, U.S.S. *Nautilus* (SSN-571, commissioned in 1954). The subs that survived the war met a variety of fates: some were "mothballed," i.e., put into storage in case of possible future need, while the remainder were scrapped, used as targets, sunk to provide underwater habitats for sea life, or sold to other nations.

Millions of men, too, suddenly found themselves "war surplus" upon the outbreak of peace and of no further military value. They were discharged, given a small sum of "mustering-out" pay, awarded medals for their service, and sent home, where they hoped to pick up the unraveled threads of their previous lives. Many of the officers who played key roles in the Allied victory continued their distinguished military careers, served in the public sector, or entered private enterprise.

General **Douglas MacArthur** was instrumental in helping America's bitter enemy recover after the war. He remained in Japan as commander of the Allied occupation forces and, during his tenure, oversaw the rebuilding and revitalization of the nation. He introduced major reforms in Japan's social, political, and economic systems, and was the architect of her democratic constitution. Never was a conquerer more benevolent.

But hardly had the fires of war been extinguished than the West had a falling-out with Josef Stalin and the Soviet Union. To further inflame fears, Red China's Mao Tse-tung defeated Chiang Kai-shek's Nationalists, who fled to Formosa, where they set up an independent, non-Communist government. Communism became the new enemy—an alarming, growing menace that was even more widespread than Fascism. Furthermore, spies in Oppenheimer's atomic-bomb research facility had given the Soviets the top secret plans to the weapon, and Stalin began building his own nuclear arsenal. China would not be far behind.

An "iron curtain," to use Churchill's term, had split Berlin down the middle and descended over Europe, and it appeared as if the Communist and free worlds would go to war. They did, but on a small scale in Korea, following the June 1950 invasion of the south by the Communist north. President Truman appointed MacArthur to lead the United Nations' military effort to throw back the Reds; he succeeded, and an uneasy truce has held there ever since July 1953.[5]

AFTER serving as Commander in Chief, Pacific, **Chester W. Nimitz** was named commander of the United States Fleet in December 1945—a position he held for two years. He then retired from the Navy and became a regent of the University of California, as well as a roving ambassador for the United Nations. He also served as chairman of the Presidential Commission on Internal Security and Individual Rights under President Truman.[6]

After the war, Nimitz wrote, "During the dark, early months of World War II, it was only the tiny American submarine force that held off the Japanese Empire and enabled our fleets to replace their losses and repair their wounds. The spirit and courage of the Submarine Force shall never be forgotten."[7]

The beloved admiral passed away in February 1966 and is buried in Golden Gate National Cemetery, San Bruno, California. In 1968, the keel of the nuclear-powered aircraft carrier U.S.S. *Nimitz* (CVN-68) was laid; the ship was commissioned in May 1975.[8]

THREE months after the Japanese surrender, **William F. "Bull" Halsey** was promoted to Admiral of the Fleet. He retired from the Navy in March 1947 and went into private industry, serving on the board of directors of two subsidiaries of ITT (International Telephone and Telegraph Company). He died in Pasadena, California, in August 1959 and is buried in Arlington National Cemetery. Two ships were named in his honor: the guided-missile frigate (later cruiser) U.S.S. *Halsey* (CG-23) and a modern destroyer (DDG 97).[9]

ON 18 December 1945, Rear Admiral **Charles A. Lockwood Jr.,** head of the Pacific Submarine Force, was ordered back to Washington, D.C., to assume the duties of Naval Inspector general within the Navy Department. He retired in September 1947 as a vice admiral and returned home to Los Gatos, California, to write his memoirs, *Sink 'Em All* and

Down to the Sea in Subs. He also coauthored several submarine and war histories, including *Battles of the Philippine Sea*, *Hell Cats of the Sea*, and *Hell at 50 Fathoms*. The 1957 Ronald Reagan/Nancy Davis Hollywood film, *Hellcats of the Navy*, was based on one of Lockwood's books.

No one knew or loved submariners better than their commander, "Uncle Charlie" Lockwood. Of them he wrote that they were no supermen or extraordinary heroes—just well-trained Americans who had been provided with the finest tools of war.

"May God grant there will be no World War III", he said, "but, if there is, whether it be fought with the weapons we know or with weapons at whose type we can only guess, submarines and submariners will be in the thick of the combat, fighting with skill, determination and matchless daring for all of us and for our United States of America."

Lockwood died on 6 June 1967 and, like Nimitz, was buried at the Golden Gate National Cemetery, San Bruno, California.[10]

MAJOR **Greg "Pappy" Boyington** was promoted to lieutenant colonel shortly after his release from Omori prison. On 5 October 1945, he was presented with the Medal of Honor from President Truman in a special ceremony at the White House. The medal had been granted by President Roosevelt in March 1944 and held by Congress in the event that Boyington was found alive. Following the presentation of the award, Colonel Boyington made a Victory Bond tour of the United States; he retired from the Marine Corps in August 1947, then hit a rough patch from which he never fully recovered. His postwar career was marked by a serious drinking problem, which led to a string of broken marriages and failed jobs. He found work selling beer, stocks, and jewelry, and also as a pro wrestling referee, but his favorite activity, even after his health deteriorated, was meeting the public and signing autographs at air shows.

In 1958, he published his autobiography, *Baa Baa Black Sheep;* in 1976, Universal Studios turned his life into a television series, *Black Sheep Squadron,* starring Robert Conrad—a series that ran for two years and is still in syndication.

Boyington died of lung cancer in January 1988, and was buried in Arlington National Cemetery.[11]

Tang's skipper, Lieutenant Commander **Richard O'Kane,** was suffering from numerous diseases and weighed only eighty-eight pounds when he was released from Omori prison. He recovered from his ordeal and went on to build a fine Navy career, retiring in 1957 as a rear admiral. He passed away on 16 February 1994, but did not pass into obscurity. American destroyers are traditionally named after outstanding sailors. In keeping with this tradition, the 505-foot-long *Aegis*-class U.S.S. *O'Kane* (DDG-77) was launched on the Kennebec River on 30 March 1998, at the Bath Iron Works in Bath, Maine. U.S. Representative Tom Allen, who spoke at the launching ceremony, said, "The destroyer we launch today honors Richard O'Kane, a genuine hero from an age when heroism truly meant something."

While others also spoke of the virtues of heroism, fortitude, and self-sacrifice required for the United States to defeat a brutal and determined enemy, outside the gates a group of some forty people demonstrated against America's military. They beat drums and held banners, including one that said "USA—NO. 1 MAKER OF WEAPONS OF MASS DESTRUCTION."[12]

LIKE many veterans, **Bill Trimmer** was dismayed to see a wave of antimilitary sentiment sweep over the country during and after the Vietnam War. "I am a forgiving person," he said, "but I have trouble forgiving anyone that tears up a draft card, burns a flag, or refuses to fight for our country. I fought once and I would do it again if necessary."[13]

FRANK Toon said, "I get together not only with my *Blenny* shipmates, but with sailors from other boats as well. In fact, it seems like *all* submariners are part of a 'brotherhood,' regardless of when or where they served. We had something in common not normally shared by others.

"When I think back on the war, mainly what I think of are *all* the young men who were lost and never had the opportunity to go on with their lives and raise families like the rest of us did. As for a specific boat,

I always seem to think of *Bullhead* [SS-332], the last American submarine sunk in World War II. It was lost on 6 August 1945—just about a week before the war was over."*[14]

THE first thing **Clay Decker** did after he landed at the Naval Air Station in Oakland, California, was to find a phone booth and call Lucille to let her know he was alive, that he was home.

But the ex-POW got the biggest jolt of his life, even bigger than the one that struck *Tang* on her last voyage. "To say she was shocked to hear from me would be an understatement," he said. "After the *Tang* went down, the Navy told her that I was missing in action and presumed dead. The Japs never contacted the Red Cross or anybody else to let them know that we were alive and in the prison camps, so she just naturally assumed I was dead and got remarried. I guess I can't really blame her for that, but I can tell you, it was pretty devastating at the time. Incredibly devastating."

He tried not to dwell on his situation. He moved to Denver, met Ann Reinecker and remarried in 1947, and thought about what he should do with the rest of his life. The oil business seemed promising, and for fifteen years he was district supervisor for Skelly Oil before starting Decker Disposal, his own trash-hauling company. He sold the business and retired in 1986, but stayed active in veterans affairs, especially submarine veterans' groups. In later years he suffered from health problems and died on Memorial Day weekend, 2003, at age eighty-two.[15]

AFTER his discharge and divorce, **Ron Smith** returned to Hammond, met Georgianna Trembczynski of Calumet City, Illinois, and married her in November 1946. As of 2007, they had been married for sixty-one years.

"From 1946 to 1948, I held a lot of jobs," he said. "Taxi driver, school supply salesman, delivery truck driver, office equipment and supply salesman, to name just a few."

---

* Fremantle-based *Bullhead*, commanded by Edward R. Holt Jr., was lost north of Bali while on her third war patrol. (Blair, 949; www.history.navy.mil/faqs/faq82-1)

Clay Decker in 2003.
(Whitlock photo)

In 1948, Smitty began a long career in the automotive business. Although he, like many of the men who fought in the Pacific, swore he would never buy any Japanese products, in 1969 he went to work for Toyota and was named Toyota's "District Manager of the Year" in 1970. He bought into a dealership in Austin and later sold it to a partner. He then bought a Ford dealership in Elgin, near Austin, which he held for four years, leaving there to manage a leasing company for a dealership conglomerate. He retired in 1984 and today lives in Austin, where he spends much of his free time in matters dealing with submarine veterans.

Not a day goes by that he doesn't think about his service in the Navy. "I often think of the men I knew who were killed in the Submarine Service. To me, they are not names on a marble slab memorial; they are living, laughing, dedicated men that I worked with and played with and loved like brothers. Whenever I ponder a political or philosophical thought, I wonder, 'What would *they* think?'

"I look at all the technical advances we have made since the war—the cure for polio and other diseases, submarines that can stay submerged for months, television, superhighways, space travel, telephones without wires, computers, and, of course, the Internet. They would certainly be surprised and thankful. While I appreciate the technical progress we have made, I don't like the social and political changes that have occurred in our society, and I can assure you that my friends who died in their youth for this great country would not approve of them either."[16]

SMITTY'S submarine *Seal* survived the war, making two more war patrols and sinking four freighters, damaging three, and sinking a destroyer with a "down the throat" shot. Worn out, the gallant old boat terminated her

Ron, Rex, and Bob Smith (who served aboard the
submarine *Bluefin*), shown at home in Hammond,
Indiana, after the war.
(Courtesy Ron Smith)

combat service at Pearl Harbor on 29 November 1944. From then until 1
June 1945, she served as a training boat in Hawaii, then became a float-
ing classroom at the Submarine School in New London until war's end.
On 14 November 1945, *Seal* was decommissioned and dropped from the
Navy's rolls of active vessels. On 6 May 1957, she was deleted from all
records, then sold for scrap and cut into pieces.[17]

THE name Pacific once again seems apropos for the body of water sepa-
rating Japan and the United States. The immense fleets that once fought

above and below the waves are long gone; the men who survived the savage conflicts for the islands and atolls are now a fading breed. All but a handful of proud, battle-weary submarines are also gone. The memorials to those who gave their lives on faraway shores, on the waves and below, are crumbling, obscured by time, vegetation, and graffiti. Worse, the "deathless deeds" are slowly being consigned to the scrap heap of history.

The old animosities and hatreds between the two nations, fortunately, have melted over the course of six decades. Young Americans today—eating sushi, driving their Japanese cars, watching their Japanese televisions, and taking photos with their Japanese cameras—wonder what the fuss was all about.

The fuss, of course, was about nothing less than the fate of the world—a fact sadly forgotten during the past half century and ignored in the schools of Japan and the United States. Students on both sides of the ocean are not learning the important lessons of history. Immense battles so famous in their time—the battles of Guadalcanal, Coral Sea, Midway, Iwo Jima, Guam, Okinawa, and Leyte Gulf, to name but a few—are virtually unknown today to the public at large. And some believe that the virtues that brought about a hard-won Allied victory are also in danger of extinction: hard work, physical and mental toughness, and the willingness to sacrifice one's self for a greater good.

In a world of relativism, history has been perverted and the old values subverted. The atomic bombing of Hiroshima and Nagasaki, necessary to bring an end to the most awful war the world had ever known, is viewed by some as an American war crime, while Japan's rape of Nanking and the many other atrocities committed by the soldiers of Nippon are conveniently dismissed. America, long hailed as the bulwark of freedom and democracy, is vilified by some as it stands nearly alone in the worldwide struggle to stop the spread of militant Islam and its bloody by-product: terrorism.

THE author William Manchester summed up the situation neatly, if bitterly: "Those of us who fought in the Pacific believed we would be remembered, that schoolchildren would be told of our sacrifices and taught the names of our greatest battles. But we didn't anticipate the velocity of postwar history; didn't realize that events would succeed one another more and more rapidly, in a kind of geometric progression, swamping the recent past in an endless flood of sensationalism."[18]

ACKNOWLEDGMENTS

MANY people deserve credit for making this book reality. First and foremost are the submariners, both living and dead, who allowed us to tell their stories. Without them and their brave sacrifices, there would be no story to tell.

A number of historians and authors also deserve to step forward and be thanked for their mighty contributions to this endeavor. These fine men include Clay Blair Jr.; Theodore Roscoe; Richard H. O'Kane; Charles Lockwood; William Manchester; Norman Polmar; Edward C. Whitman; and all those anonymous authors whose websites represent a heartfelt salute to the courage of the men of the United States Navy.

Thanks, too, must go to the U.S. Submarine Veterans of World War II, Inc.; Pete Sutherland, historian of the U.S.S. *Pampanito* at the National Maritime Museum in San Francisco; Robert "Dex" Armstrong in Washington, D.C., for help with research; the staffs at the Naval Historical Center at the Washington Navy Yard and National Archives in College Park, Maryland; and Dr. Dirk Ballendorf, Professor of History and Micronesian Studies, University of Guam, Mangilao, Guam.

We also wish to acknowledge the contributions of our agent, Jody Rein, and our editor at Berkley/Caliber, Natalee Rosenstein, and her assistant, Michelle Vega. And to our wives, we offer our deepest gratitude for standing by their men.

NOTES

Chapter 1

1. Gordon W. Prange, *At Dawn We Slept: The Untold Story of Pearl Harbor* (New York: Penguin, 1981), 539–540.
2. William Trimmer, "Bill Trimmer's Story" (undated, unpublished memoir)
3. Prange, 539–540.
4. Doris Kearns Goodwin, *No Ordinary Time. Franklin & Eleanor Roosevelt: The Home Front in World War II* (New York: Touchstone/Simon & Schuster, 1994), 288–289.
5. William L. O'Neill, *A Democracy at War: America's Fight at Home and Abroad in World War II* (New York: Free Press/Macmillan, 1993), 106.
6. Clay Blair, Jr., *Silent Victory: The U.S. Submarine War Against Japan* (New York: Lippincott, 1975), 77–80.
7. Trimmer memoir.
8. Blair, 77–80.
9. Blair, 104.
10. Blair, 84.
11. Ron Smith interview by Flint Whitlock, 1 February 2005.
12. Martin, Gilbert, *The Second World War: A Complete History* (New York: Henry Holt, 1989), 275–276; John F. Wukovits, *Pacific Alamo, The Battle for Wake Island* (New York: New American Library, 2003), 55–56; O'Neill, 111; www.answerscom.
13. Blair, 104–112.
14. Louis Morton, *United States Army in World War II: The War in the Pacific—The Fall of the Philippines* (Washington, D.C.: United States Army Center of Military

History, 1995 [reprint]), 125–138; William Manchester, *Goodbye Darkness: A Memoir of the Pacific War* (New York: Bantam, 1980), 71.

15. Gilbert, 282–283.
16. Manchester, 328–329.
17. Gilbert, 280–293.
18. Blair, 33–34, 47.
19. Theodore Roscoe, *United States Submarines Operations in World War II* (Annapolis, MD: Naval Institute Press, 1976), 252.
20. Roscoe, p. 4, 12–13; Michael E. Haskew, ed., *The World War II Desk Reference* (New York: HarperCollins/Grand Central Press, 2004), 28.
21. O'Neill, 9.
22. Prange, 344.
23. Irvine E. Eastman, ed., *World Almanac and Book of Facts for 1940* (New York: New York World-Telegram, 1940), 849.

Chapter 2

1. Manchester, 94–95.
2. Roscoe, 875–877.
3. Blair, 113.
4. *Skipjack* and *Tarpon* war patrol reports, Operational Archives Branch, Naval Historical Center, Washington, D.C.
5. Roscoe, 71; Blair, 148.
6. *Grayback* and *Sturgeon* war patrol reports; Gilbert, 294; Blair, 144; Charles A. Lockwood, *Sink 'Em All: Submarine Warfare in the Pacific* (New York: E. P. Dutton, 1951), 61.
7. *Sargo* war patrol report; Blair, 116–118.
8. *Pollack, Plunger, Gudgeon* war patrol reports; Roscoe, 34, 51; Blair, 89–91.
9. Blair, 878, 881.
10. Blair, 98.
11. Blair, 89.
12. www.navweaps.com/Weapons/WTUS_Notes; www.keyportmuseum.cnrnw.navy.mil/html/part1; www.geocities.com/Pentagon/1592/ustorp2.htm.
13. Duane Whitlock interview by Flint Whitlock, 23 January 2007.
14. *Seadragon* patrol report.
15. Whitlock interview.
16. Blair, 183.
17. Trout war patrol report; Roscoe, 79–80; www.corregidor.org/chs/trident/uss trout; www.csp.navy.mil/centennial/ troutgld.
18. Blair, 152.

19. *S-37* war patrol report; Roscoe, 73–74.

20. Gilbert, 300.

21. www.mhric.org/fdr/chat20.

22. Gilbert, 303.

23. *Perch* war patrol report; www.csp.navy.mil/ww2boats/perch.

24. *Sargo* war patrol report; Blair 162–163. www.submarinesailor.com/Boats/
    SS188Sargo/history; home.st.net.au/~dunn/friendlyfire/ussubO1;

25. Gilbert, 307.

26. Gilbert, 302–307, 312, 316–318.

27. Blair, 191–192.

28. Blair, 881.

29. Roscoe, 134–143.

30. Smith interview, 1 February 2005.

Chapter 3

1. www.militarymuseum. org/Lockwood.

2. Blair, 249–250.

3. Lockwood, 75.

4. *Skipjack* war patrol report.

5. Blair, 249–251.

6. *Tautog* war patrol report.

7. *Greenling, Drum, Silversides* war patrol reports; Blair, 204–206.

8. Blair, 195–199; Robert D. Ballard and Michael H. Morgan, *Graveyards of the
   Pacific* (Washington, D.C.: National Geographic/Madison Press, 2001), 73–89.

9. Blair, 197–198.

10. Blair, 207–210.

11. Roscoe, 121–123; www.history.acusd.edu.

12. Blair, 244–246.

13. Blair, 70; Roscoe, 123–126.

14. Russell Spurr, *A Glorious Way to Die: The Kamikaze Mission of the Battleship
    Yamato* (New York: Bantam, 1981), 22–26.

15. Roscoe, 121–127.

16. Blair, 214.

17. Blair, 214–215; Roscoe, 123–127.

18. *Nautilus* war patrol report; Blair, 220–221; Jonathan Parshall and Anthony Tully,
    Shattered Sword: The Untold Story of the Battle of Midway (Washington:
    Potomac Books, 2005), 184–185.

19. *Nautilus, Tambor, Trigger* war patrol reports; Blair, 221–223.

20. Blair, 225.

21. Blair, 216.
22. *Growler, Triton* war patrol reports; Blair, 246–248.

Chapter 4

1. Samuel E. Morison, *History of United States Naval Operations in World War II: Breaking the Bismarcks Barrier, 22 July 1942 – 1 May 1944* (Vol. VI), (Boston: Little, Brown, 1949), ix–x.
2. Blair, 282–292.
3. James C. Fahey, *The Ships and Aircraft of the United States Fleet*, Second War Edition (New York: Gemsco, 1944), 30; Blair, 43n, 55n, 61n, 112–118, 142, 147, 154, 167, 249, 250–257; Roscoe, 34–35, 144–145, 250–252.
4. Blair, 297–299.
5. Morison, *Breaking the Bismarcks Barrier*, ix.
6. Gilbert, 350.
7. Gilbert, 353.
8. *Drum, Grayling, Greenling, Grenadier, and Gudgeon* war patrol reports; Roscoe, 154.
9. Blair, 269–271; www.ww2pacific.com/savo.
10. William J. Ruhe, *War in the Boats: My WWII Submarine Battles* (Washington, D.C.: Brassey's/Potomac Books, 1996), 5.
11. *S-38* war patrol report; Blair, 273–274; James F. DeRose, *Unrestricted Warfare* (New York: John Wiley & Sons, 2000), 273; www.thesaltysailor.com/s-boats/s38.
12. *S-44* war patrol report; www.subnet.com/fleet/ss155; www.navy.history/mil.
13. *S-39* war patrol report; Blair, 272–275; Roscoe, 153–154.
14. Blair, 283, 291.
15. Roscoe, 157–158.
16. Blair, 282, 291–293.
17. Roscoe, 159.
18. Blair, 277–281.
19. Blair, 269, 276.
20. Manchester, 191–207.
21. Miller, John, Jr. *United States Army in World War II: The War in the Pacific— Guadalcanal: The First Offensive* (Washington, D.C.: United States Army Center of Military History, 1989 [reprint]), 1–30, 350.
22. Blair, 276–277

Chapter 5

1. Smith interview, 12 February 2005.
2. Roscoe, 252–253.
3. Lockwood, 75.

4. Smith interview, 15 February 2005.
5. Reynold Dittrich, interview by Thomas Saylor, Ph.D., Director, Oral History Project, Concordia University, St. Paul, MN, 5 March 2002.
6. Smith interview, 15 February 2005.
7. Blair, 93, 120, 167.
8. Smith interview, 15 February 2005.

Chapter 6
1. Smith interview, 15 February 2005.
2. Michael C. Geletka, interview by Flint Whitlock, 3 September 2005.
3. U.S.S. *Pampanito* pamphlet, n.d.
4. Smith interview, 15 February 2005.
5. Plaque in U.S.S. *Cobia*, Manitowoc, WI.
6. Frank Toon, interview by Flint Whitlock, 3 September 2005.
7. www.pbs.org/wgbh/nova/lostsub/hist1918.html.
8. www.fleetsubmarine.com.
9. Norman Polmar, *The American Submarine* (Annapolis, MD: Nautical and Aviation Publishing Co., 1981), 51.
10. Carl W. Vozniak, interview by Flint Whitlock, 3 September 2005.

Chapter 7
1. *Steep Angles and Deep Dives* (Bangor, WA: Submarine Research Center [n.d.]), 49–50.
2. Smith interview.
3. Polmar, 53; James F. Calvert, *Silent Running: My Years on a World War II Attack Submarine* (New York: John Wiley & Sons, 1995), 7.
4. Smith interview, 22 February 2005.
5. Gilbert, 355, 361, 367, 369, 370, 398.
6. *Grouper* war patrol report; Gilbert, 366; www.hamstat.demon.co.uk/HongKong/Lisbon_Maru; www.nesa.org.uk/lisbon_maru; www.cofepow.org.uk/pages/ships_lisbon_maru; bbs.chinadaily.com.cn/forumpost1.
7. *Haddock* war patrol report.
8. Blair, 300–301.
9. Blair, 303–304; Roscoe, 162.
10. Blair, 304.
11. DeRose, 36–65.
12. *Trout* war patrol report; Morison, *History of United States Naval Operations in World War II: The Struggle for Guadalcanal, August 1942–February 1943* (Vol. V). (Boston: Little, Brown, 1960), 225–287; www.angelfire.com; www.history.navy.mil; www.corregidor.org/chs/trident/uss-trout.

13. Morison, *The Struggle for Guadalcanal,* 288–315.

14. *Albacore, Greenling, Guardfish, Nautilus, Triton* war patrol reports; Blair, 308.

15. *Gudgeon* war patrol report; www.chinfo.navy.mil/navpalib/cno/n87/usw/issue _23/saviors2.htm.

Chapter 8

1. Smith interview, 22 February 2005.

2. *Los Angeles Times,* 24 February 1942; www.csus.edu/indiv/s/scottjc/marsh; www.members.tripod.com/~earthdude1/fugo.

3. Harlan Lebo, *Casablanca: Behind the Scenes* (New York: Simon & Schuster/ Fireside, 1992), 128.

4. Smith interview, 22 February 2005.

5. Smith interview, 1 March 2005.

6. Lockwood, 61.

7. Trimmer memoir.

8. *Greenling, Growler, Guardfish, Nautilus, Swordfish* war patrol reports.

9. *Growler* war patrol report; Blair, 347–348; home.st.netau/dunn/usnavy/fre- mantlesubmarinebase.

10. Smith interview, 1 March 2005.

11. Blair, 339–340.

Chapter 9

1. Blair, 355–356.

2. George Grider (as told to Lydel Sims), *War Fish* (Boston: Little, Brown, 1958), 68–69.

3. Grider, 100–101; Blair, 357–358.

4. William Tuohy, *The Bravest Man: The Story of Richard O'Kane and U.S. Subma- riners in the Pacific War* (Sparkford, England: Sutton, 2001), 33–34.

5. Blair, 358–360.

6. Smith interview, 1 March 2005, Fahey, 30; Blair, 43n, 55n, 61n, 142, 154, 167, 249, 250–257.

7. Edward L. Beach, *Submarine!* (New York: Henry Holt, 1952), 121–122.

8. Smith interview, 1 March 2005.

9. Roscoe, 38.

10. Seal war patrol report; Roscoe, 118, 165–166.

11. Smith interview, 3 March 2005.

12. Smith interview, 3 March 2005.

13. www.salute.co.uk/salutegames/yamamoto.

14. Blair, 349–350.

15. Smith interview, 3 March 2005.

16. Lockwood, 78.

17. Smith interview, 3 March 2005.

18. Robert J. Casey, *Battle Below: The War of the Submarines* (New York: Bobbs-Merrill, 1945), 358–365.

19. Roscoe, 167–168.

20. Smith interview.

21. Lockwood, 79.

22. Smith interview, 3 March 2005.

Chapter 10

1. Smith interview, 8 March 2005.

2. Lockwood, 85.

3. Smith interview, 8 March 2005.

4. Lockwood, 96.

5. Smith interview, 8 March 2005.

6. Blair, 367–369.

7. www.ussvi.org/mem/210cnvnt.

8. Blair, 381.

9. Smith interview.

Chapter 11

1. Gilbert, 398, 419, 439.

2. Blair, 397.

3. Tuohy, 245.

4. O'Neill, passim.

5. Smith interview, 21 March 2005.

Chapter 12

1. Smith interview, 21 March 2005; Lockwood, 118–119.

2. Smith interview, 4 April 2005.

3. Robert P. Beynon, *U.S.S.* Bowfin: *The Pearl Harbor Avenger* (Deland, FL: Just Books 1, 2005), 95.

4. Lockwood, 132.

5. Smith interview, 4 April 2005.

Chapter 13

1. Smith interview, 4 April 2005.

2. www.chinfo.navy.mil/navpalib/cno/n87/usw/issue_8/submarine_hero.

3. Ibid.

4. Lockwood, 134–136; Bla ir, 490–497; www.chinfo.navy.mil/navpalib/cno/n87/usw/issue_8/submarine_hero.

5. Smith interview, 14 April 2005; *Seal* war patrol report.
6. Gilbert, 476.
7. Manchester, 258–270, 282.
8. Gilbert, 476.
9. Manchester, 271–294.
10. Lockwood, 140–141.
11. Smith interview, 14 April 2005; *Seal* war patrol report.
12. Morison, *Breaking the Bismarcks Barrier,* 389–391, 410.
13. *Albacore* war patrol report.
14. Gilbert, 488–489, 491, 495.
15. *Bowfin, Skipjack,* and *Tinosa* war patrol reports.
16. Eric Hammel, *Pacific Warriors: The U.S. Marines in World War II* (St. Paul, MN: Zenith Press, 2005), 163–170; Philip A. Crowl, *United States Army in World War II: The War in the Pacific—Campaign in the Marianas* (Washington, D.C.: United States Army Center of Military History, 1993 [reprint]), 206–301.
17. Smith interview, 14 April 2005.
18. www.history.navy.mil.
19. Smith interview, 14 April 2005.
20. www.history.navy.mil.
21. Smith interview, 14 April 2005.
22. Blair, 648–650.
23. *Guardfish, Parche, Seahorse, Steelhead* war patrol reports; Blair, 654.

Chapter 14

1. Decker interview, 15 February 2003.
2. DeRose, 144.
3. Decker interview.
4. DeRose, 144.
5. Decker interview.
6. Richard H. O'Kane, *Clear The Bridge! The War Patrols of the U.S.S.* Tang (New York: Rand McNally, 1977), 39–40; DeRose, 144–145.
7. Decker interview.
8. Beach, 65.
9. O'Kane, *Clear the Bridge,* 50; Beach, 152.
10. O'Kane, *Clear the Bridge,* 25–34.
11. Decker interview.
12. O'Kane, *Clear the Bridge,* 55–126.
13. Decker interview.

14. Ibid.

15. *Tunny* war patrol report; Akira Yoshimura (Translated by Vincent Murphy), *Battleship Musashi: The Making and Sinking of the World's Biggest Battleship* (Tokyo: Kodansha, 1999), 146–147; www.history.navy.mil/photos/sh-fornv/japan/japsh-m/musashi.

16. Smith interview, 19 May 2005.

17. Morison, *History of U.S. Naval Operations in World War II:* Leyte, Vol. XII (Boston: Little Brown, 1960), 86–87.

18. O'Kane, *Clear the Bridge*, 140.

19. Smith interview, 19 May 2005.

20. Decker interview.

21. O'Kane, *Clear the Bridge*, 169–192.

22. Decker interview.

23. Blair, 548; www.csp.navy.mil/ww2boats/tullibee.

24. Decker interview.

25. Smith interview, 19 May 2005.

26. Geletka interview.

27. Beynon, 219–220.

28. Beach, 97–98.

29. Geletka interview.

30. Flint Whitlock, *The Fighting First: The Untold Story of the Big Red One on D-Day* (Boulder, CO: Westview, 2004), 236.

31. Smith interview, 19 May 2005.

32. Decker interview.

33. O'Kane, *Clear the Bridge,* 202.

Chapter 15

1. *Harder* war patrol report; Beach 102–103.

2. Harry "Bud" Dunn, interview by Flint Whitlock, 3 September 2005.

3. Dunn interview; uboat.net/allies/warships/ship/3003.

4. Geletka interview.

5. Dunn interview.

6. Geletka interview.

7. *Harder* war patrol report.

8. Geletka interview.

9. Beach, 97–114.

10. Geletka interview.

11. Smith interview, 19 May 2005.

12. *Cavalla* war patrol report; Paul S. Dull, *A Battle History of the Imperial Japanese*

Navy (1941–1945) (Annapolis: Naval Institute Press, 1978), 308; en.wikipedia .org/wiki/Japanese_aircraft_carrier_Shokaku.

13. *Albacore* war patrol report; Dull, 307–308; www.uboat.net/allies/warships/ship/ 2964.
14. Ballard, 197–207.
15. O'Kane, *Clear the Bridge*, 207–231.
16. Decker interview.
17. O'Kane, *Clear the Bridge*, 231–266.
18. Decker interview.
19. O'Kane, *Clear the Bridge*, 268.
20. O'Kane, *Clear the Bridge*, 441.
21. Gilbert, 557–559.
22. Gilbert, 559.
23. Gilbert, 563–564.
24. www.onwar.com/articles/f0102.
25. O'Kane, *Clear the Bridge*, 269–303.

Chapter 16

1. Flint Whitlock, *The Rock of Anzio: From Sicily to Dachau - A History of the 45th Infantry Division* (Boulder: Westview, 1998), 314–318.
2. Carl W. Vozniak, interview by Flint Whitlock, 3 September 2005.
3. F. Willard Robinson, *Navy Wings of Gold* (Eugene, OR: River Park Press, 2001), 296–301.
4. Vozniak interview.
5. *Finback* war patrol report; www.uboat.net/allies/warships/ship/2976.
6. www.bushlibrary.tamu.edu/tour/finback.
7. Robinson, 301.
8. Smith interview, 19 May 2005.
9. www.csp.navy.mil/centennial/harder.
10. Geletka interview.
11. *Hake* war patrol report; Beach, 114; www.csp.navy.mil/centennial/harder.
12. Robert B. Smith, "Tragic Voyage of *Junyo Maru*." *World War II* magazine, March 2002.
13. www.anzacday.org.au/history/www2/anecdotes/survivors.
14. R. B. Smith.
15. Richard L. Himmell, Robert S. LaPorte, and Ronald E. Marcello, eds. *With Only the Will to Live: Accounts of Americans in Japanese Prison Camps, 1941–1945* (Wilmington, DE: Scholarly Resources, 1994), 41–43.
16. Blair, 744–745.

Chapter 17

1. Robinson, 297; Gilbert, 592.

2. Gilbert, 594, 601.

3. Wukovits, "Clash in the Sibuyan Sea," *WWII History* magazine, November 2004.

4. Gilbert, 601.

5. *Dace* and *Darter* war patrol reports; Blair, 726–733; Wukovits, "Clash in the Sibuyan Sea"; www.subnet.com/fleet/ss227.

6. Jim Clepper correspondence with Ron Smith (n.d.).

7. *Dace* war patrol report; www.subnet.com/fleet/ss227.

8. Yoshimura, 166–171.

9. Yoshimura, 176; Gerald Astor, *Wings of Gold: The U.S. Naval Air Campaign in World War II* (New York: Presidio, 2005), 365; www.history.navy.mil/photos/sh-fornv/japan/japsh-m/musashi.

10. Harry Popham, "Eyewitness to Tragedy: Death of U.S.S. *Princeton*," *World War II* magazine, May 1997.

11. www.anglefire.com/fm/odyssey/halsey.

12. Wukovits, "Clash in the Sibuyan Sea."

13. Astor, 359–375.

14. navysite.de/cve/cve73.

15. Gilbert, 606; en.wikipedia.org/wiki/Kamikaze; navysite.de/cve/cve73.

16. navysite.de/cve/cve73.

17. Manchester, 407.

18. www.naval-history.net/WW2194406-2.

19. Blair, 931–936.

20. Smith interview, 19 May 2005.

Chapter 18

1. Decker interview.

2. O'Kane, *Clear the Bridge*, 454–455.

3. Decker interview.

4. O'Kane, *Clear the Bridge*, 455 .

5. Decker interview.

6. Cindy Adams, "USS *Tang* Survivors," *Polaris*, February 1981.

7. O'Kane, *Clear the Bridge*, 456.

8. Adams.

9. Decker interview.

10. O'Kane, *Clear the Bridge,* 459.

11. O'Kane, *Clear the Bridge,* 456.

12. Decker interview.

13. Adams.

14. Decker interview.
15. Adams.
16. Ibid.
17. Decker interview.
18. Adams.
19. Decker interview.
20. Decker interview.
21. O'Kane, *Clear the Bridge,* 459.
22. Adams.
23. Decker interview.

Chapter 19

1. Decker interview.
2. Adams.
3. Decker interview.
4. O'Kane, *Clear the Bridge,* 460–461.
5. Mansell.com/pow_resources/camplists/tokyo/ofuna.
6. Tuohy, 356.
7. Adams.
8. O'Kane, *Clear the Bridge,* 459–460; Decker interview.
9. mcel.pacificu.edu/as/students/bushido.
10. Adams.
11. O'Kane, *Clear the Bridge,* 463.
12. Adams.
13. O'Kane, *Clear the Bridge,* 463–464.
14. Trimmer memoir.
15. *Redfish* war report; Blair, 777–778; www.combinedfleet.com/Unryu.
16. Trimmer memoir.
17. *Sealion II* war patrol report.
18. www.combinedfleet.com/Kongo.
19. Lockwood, 175.
20. Adams.
21. Gregory Boyington, *Baa Baa Black Sheep* (New York: Putnam's, 1958), 272, 275.
22. Adams; www.subvetpaul.com/SAGA_2_81.
23. Boyington, 320.
24. O'Kane, *Clear the Bridge,* 465.
25. Gilbert, 649.
26. Richard "Dick" Mohl interview by Flint Whitlock, 4 September 2005.

Chapter 20

1. Morison, *History of United States Naval Operations in World War II: The Liberation of the Philippines—Luzon, Mindanao, the Visayas, 1944–1945,* Vol. XIII (Boston: Little, Brown, 1959), 179, 184–210, 280.

2. *Besugo* and *Hardhead* war patrol reports.

3. *Blackfin, Boarfish,* and *Pampanito* war patrol reports.

4. *Batfish* war patrol report.

5. *Pargo* war patrol reports.

6. *Blenny* and *Hammerhead* war patrol reports.

7. *Flounder* and *Hoe* war patrol reports; Keith, 165–193; Morison, *The Liberation of the Philippines,* 178–185.

8. Manchester, 388–390.

9. Manchester, 395; Gilbert, 642–643; Keith Wheeler, *The Road to Tokyo* (Alexandria, VA: Time-Life Books, 1979), 57.

10. Roy E. Appleman, James M. Burns, Russell A. Gugeler, and John Stevens, *United States Army in World War II: The War in the Pacific—Okinawa: The Last Battle* (Washington, D.C.: United States Army Center of Military History, 1993 [reprint]), 1–9.

11. Ibid., 473–474.

12. Manchester, 437.

13. Appleman, et al, 473–474.

14. Mohl interview.

15. *Tirante* war partrol report; Blair, 816–819.

16. Blair, 783–786.

17. Eugene B. Fluckey, *Thunder Below! The USS* Barb *Revolutionizes Submarine Warfare in World War II* (Urbana: University of Illinois Press, 1992), 421; Morison, *The Liberation of the Philippines,* 298.

18. Fluckey, 219–220, 257–277, 367–385, 409; Peter Collier, *Medal of Honor: Portraits of Valor Beyond the Call of Duty* (New York: Artisan/Workman, 2003), 83; www.ussnautilus.org/fluckey.

19. Decker interview.

20. Adams.

21. Boyington, 321–323.

22. Adams.

23. Decker interview.

24. Adams.

25. Boyington, 325–326.

26. Adams.

27. Ibid.

28. Boyington, 330.
29. Decker interview.
30. Boyington, 327.
31. Gilbert, 649.

Chapter 21

1. Gilbert, 662–695.
2. Smith interview, 2 September 2005.
3. Toon memoir.
4. Lansing Lamont, *Day of Trinity* (New York: Atheneum/ Signet, 1965), 108–109.
5. Manchester, 404.
6. Lamont, 230.
7. J. Lee Ready, *World War Two Nation by Nation* (London: Arms and Armour Press, 1995), 65, 93, 118, 167, 181; Hans Dollinger, *The Decline and Fall of Nazi Germany and Imperial Japan* (New York: Bonanza, 1967), 422.
8. Lamont, 230.
9. Dollinger, 385.
10. Lamont, 200, 202.
11. Lamont, 203.
12. Dollinger, 397; Gilbert, 716–717.
13. Toon memoir.
14. Smith interview, 2 September 2005.
15. Adams; www.subvetpaul.com/SAGA_2_81.
16. Decker interview.
17. Adams.
18. Decker interview.
19. Adams.
20. Decker interview.
21. Michel T. Poirier, "Results of the German and American Submarine Campaigns of World War II" (unpublished monograph), 1999.
22. Roscoe, 493.
23. www.warbirdforum.com/navy.
24. Adams.
25. Decker interview.
26. Dollinger, 392.

Epilogue

1. Blair, 847–848.
2. Blair, 957.
3. Blair, 848.

4. www.oralhistoryproject.com/tcurtis_nav.

5. Stanley Weintraub, *MacArthur's War: Korea and the Undoing of an American Hero* (New York: Free Press, 2000), passim.

6. www.famoustexans.com/chesternimitz.

7. en.wikiquote.org/wiki/Chester_Nimitz.

8. www.famoustexans.com/chesternimitz.

9. en.wikipedia.org/wiki/William_F._Halsey,_Jr..

10. www.militarymuseum.org/Lockwood.

11. www.medalofhonor.com/PappyBoyington.

12. "U.S.S. *O'Kane* Launched," Press Report: March 30, 1998; www.arlington cemetery.net/rokane.htm.

13. Trimmer memoir.

14. Toon memoir.

15. Decker interview.

16. Smith interview, 25 March 2006.

17. Smith interview, 25 March 2006; www.geocities.com/ Athens/Acropolis/7612/ seal.

18. Manchester, 141.

BIBLIOGRAPHY

Oral Histories

Alvey, Harry (U.S.S. *Pargo* and *Paddle*). Interview by Flint Whitlock, 3 September 2005.

Benites, Robert "Ben" (*S-42* and *Springer*). Interview by Flint Whitlock, 4 September 2005.

Decker, Clayton O. "Deck" (*Tang*). Interview by Flint Whitlock, 15 February 2003.

Decker, Harry. Interview by Flint Whitlock, 19 January 2005.

Dittrich, Reynold (*Aspro*). Interview by Thomas Saylor, Ph.D., Director, Oral History Project, Concordia University, St. Paul, MN, 5 March 2002. Used by permission.

Dunn, Harry "Bud" (*Hoe* and *Harder*). Interview by Flint Whitlock, 3 September 2005.

Gantnier, John B. (*Porpoise* and *Moray*). Interview by Flint Whitlock, 4 September 2005.

Geletka, Michael C. (*Harder*). Interview by Flint Whitlock, 3 September 2005.

Keeton, Afton (*Seadragon*). Interview by Flint Whitlock, 3 September 2005.

Mohl, Richard "Dick" (*Aspro*). Interview by Flint Whitlock, 4 September 2005.

Rothenburg, Irving M. "Doc" (*Cabrilla* and *Halibut*). Interview by Flint Whitlock, 3 September 2005.

Shaw, John F. (*Bashaw*). Interview by Flint Whitlock, 4 September 2005.

Smith, Ron (*Seal*). Interview by Flint Whitlock, 1, 12, 15, 22 February 1; 3, 8, 21 March; 4, 14 April; 19, 24 May; 2 September 2005; 25 March 2006.

Sutherland, Pete. Interview by Flint Whitlock, 15 January 2005.

Toon, Frank (*Blenny*). Interview by Flint Whitlock, 3 September 2005.

Turner, Marion "Turk" (*Perch*). Interview by Flint Whitlock, 3 September 2005.

Vozniak, Carl W. (*Finback* and *Parche*). Interview by Flint Whitlock, 3 September 2005.

Whitlock, Duane (*Permit*). Interview by Flint Whitlock, 23 January 2007.

Unpublished Memoirs

Trimmer, William. "Bill Trimmer's Story." (Undated)

Published Books

Appleman, Roy E., James M. Burns, Russell A. Gugeler, and John Stevens. *United States Army in World War II: The War in the Pacific—Okinawa: The Last Battle.* Washington, D.C.: United States Army Center of Military History, 1993 (reprint).

Astor, Gerald. *Wings of Gold: The U.S. Naval Air Campaign in World War II.* New York: Presidio, 2005.

Ballard, Robert D., and Michael H. Morgan. *Graveyards of the Pacific.* Washington, D.C.: National Geographic/Madison Press, 2001.

Ballard, Robert D., and Rick Archbold. *Return to Midway.* Washington, D.C.: National Geographic/Madison Press, 1999.

Beach, Edward L. *Submarine!* New York: Henry Holt, 1952.

Beynon, Robert P. *U.S.S. Bowfin: The Pearl Harbor Avenger.* Deland, FL: Just Books 1, 2005.

Blair, Clay, Jr. *Silent Victory: The U.S. Submarine War Against Japan.* New York: Lippincott, 1975.

Boyington, Gregory. *Baa Baa Black Sheep.* New York: Putnam's, 1958.

Calvert, James F. *Silent Running: My Years on a World War II Attack Submarine.* New York: John Wiley & Sons, 1995.

Camp, Dick. *Battleship Arizona's Marines at War: Making the Ultimate Sacrifice, December 7, 1941.* St. Paul, MN, Zenith Press, 2006.

Cannon, M. Hamlin. *United States Army in World War II: The War in the Pacific—Leyte: The Return to the Philippines.* Washington, D.C.: United States Army Center of Military History, 1993 (reprint).

Casey, Robert J. *Battle Below: The War of the Submarines.* New York: Bobbs-Merrill, 1945.

Collier, Peter. *Medal of Honor: Portraits of Valor Beyond the Call of Duty.* New York: Artisan/Workman, 2003.

Crowl, Philip A. *United States Army in World War II: The War in the Pacific—Campaign in the Marianas.* Washington, D.C.: United States Army Center of Military History, 1993 (reprint).

—— and Edmund G. Love. *United States Army in World War II: The War in the Pacific—Seizure of the Gilberts and Marshalls.* Washington, D.C.: United States Army Center of Military History, 1993 (reprint).

DeRose James F. *Unrestricted Warfare*. New York: John Wiley & Sons, 2000.

Dollinger, Hans. *The Decline and Fall of Nazi Germany and Imperial Japan*. New York, Bonanza, 1967.

Dull, Paul S. *A Battle History of the Imperial Japanese Navy (1941–1945)*. Annapolis: Naval Institute Press, 1978.

Enright, Joseph. *Shinano!* New York: St. Martin's Press, 1987.

Fahey, James C. *The Ships and Aircraft of the United States Fleet*. Second War Edition. New York: Gemsco, 1944.

Fisher, Harry, Robert Link, and Hughston Lowder, eds. *United States Submarine Veterans of World War II,* Vol. II. Dallas: Taylor Publishing, 1987.

Fluckey, Eugene B. *Thunder Below! The USS* Barb *Revolutionizes Submarine Warfare in World War II*. Urbana: University of Illinois Press, 1992.

Gailey, Harry A. *Peleliu 1944*. Annapolis: Nautical and Aviation Publishing Co., 1983.

Galantin, I. J. *Take Her Deep! A Submarine Against Japan in World War II*. Chapel Hill, NC: Algonquin, 1987.

Gallery, Daniel V. *Twenty Million Tons Under the Sea*. Chicago: Henry Regnery, 1956.

Gilbert, Martin. *The Second World War: A Complete History*. New York: Henry Holt, 1989.

Goodwin, Doris Kearns. *No Ordinary Time. Franklin and Eleanor Roosevelt: The Home Front in World War II*. New York: Touchstone/Simon & Schuster, 1994.

Gow, Ian. *Okinawa 1945: Gateway to Japan*. Garden City, NY: Doubleday, 1985.

Grider, George (as told to Lydel Sims). *War Fish*. Boston: Little, Brown, 1958.

Hammel, Eric. *Pacific Warriors: The U.S. Marines in World War II*. St. Paul, MN: Zenith Press, 2005.

Haskew, Michael E., ed. *The World War II Desk Reference*. New York: HarperCollins/Grand Central Press, 2004.

Himmell, Richard L., Robert S. LaPorte, and Ronald E. Marcello, eds. *With Only the Will to Live: Accounts of Americans in Japanese Prison Camps, 1941–1945*. Wilmington, DE: Scholarly Resources, 1994.

Hoyt, Edwin P. *Bowfin*. New York: Van Nostrand Reinhold, 1983.

———. *Guadalcanal*. New York: Stein & Day, 1981.

———. *The Destroyer Killer*. New York: Pocket Books, 1989.

Keith, Don. *In the Course of Duty: The Heroic Mission of the USS* Batfish. New York: Penguin/New American Library, 2005.

Kernan, Alvin. *The Unknown Battle of Midway: The Destruction of the American Torpedo Squadrons*. New Haven: Yale University Press, 2005.

Lamont, Lansing. *Day of Trinity*. New York: Atheneum/Signet, 1965.

Lebo, Harlan. *Casablanca: Behind the Scenes*. New York: Simon & Schuster/Fireside, 1992.

Lockwood, Charles A. *Sink 'Em All: Submarine Warfare in the Pacific*. New York: E. P. Dutton, 1951.

Lowder, Hughston E. *Batfish: The Champion "Submarine-Killer" Submarine of World War II*. New York: Prenctice Hall, 1980.

Manchester, William. *Goodbye Darkness: A Memoir of the Pacific War*. New York: Bantam, 1980.

Miller, John, Jr. *United States Army in World War II: The War in the Pacific—Guadalcanal: The First Offensive*. Washington, D.C.: United States Army Center of Military History, 1989 (reprint).

Morison, Samuel E. *History of United States Naval Operations in World War II: Coral Sea, Midway, and Submarine Actions, May 1942–August 1942*, Vol. IV. Boston: Little, Brown, 1949.

———. *History of United States Naval Operations in World War II: The Struggle for Guadalcanal, August 1942–February 1943*, Vol. V. Boston: Little, Brown, 1960.

———. *History of United States Naval Operations in World War II: Breaking the Bismarcks Barrier, 22 July 1942–1 May 1944*, Vol. VI. Boston: Little, Brown, 1950.

———. *History of United States Naval Operations in World War II: Aleutians, Gilberts and Marshalls, June 1942–April 1944*, Vol. VII. Boston: Little, Brown, 1960.

———. *History of United States Naval Operations in World War II: New Guinea and the Marianas, March 1944–August 1944*, Vol. VIII. Boston: Little, Brown, 1960.

———. *History of United States Naval Operations in World War II: The Liberation of the Philippines—Luzon, Mindanao, the Visayas, 1944–1945*, Vol. XIII. Boston: Little, Brown, 1959.

Morton, Louis. *United States Army in World War II: The War in the Pacific—The Fall of the Philippines*. Washington, D.C.: United States Army Center of Military History, 1995 (reprint).

O'Kane, Richard H. *Clear the Bridge! The War Patrols of the U.S.S. Tang*. New York: Rand McNally, 1977.

———. *Wahoo*. New York: Bantam, 1987.

O'Neill, William L. *A Democracy at War: America's Fight at Home and Abroad in World War II*. New York: Free Press/Macmillan, 1993.

Parshall, Jonathan, and Anthony Tully. *Shattered Sword: The Untold Story of the Battle of Midway*. Washington: Potomac Books, 2005.

Polmar, Norman. *The American Submarine*. Annapolis: Nautical and Aviation Publishing Co., 1981.

Prange, Gordon W. *At Dawn We Slept: The Untold Story of Pearl Harbor.* New York: Penguin, 1981.

Ready, J. Lee. *World War Two Nation by Nation.* London: Arms and Armour Press, 1995.

Reynolds, Clark G. *The Carrier War (Epic of Flight* series). Alexandria, VA: Time-Life Books, 1982.

Robinson, F. Willard. *Navy Wings of Gold.* Eugene, OR: River Park Press, 2001.

Roscoe, Theodore. *United States Submarines Operations in World War II.* Annapolis: Naval Institute Press, 1976.

Ruhe, William J. *War in the Boats: My WWII Submarine Battles.* Washington, D.C.: Brassey's/Potomac Books, 1996.

Smith, Ron. *Torpedoman.* Privately published, 1993.

Spurr, Russell. *A Glorious Way to Die: The Kamikaze Mission of the Battleship Yamato.* New York: Bantam, 1981.

Steep Angles and Deep Dives. Bangor, WA: Submarine Research Center (date unknown).

Tillman, Barrett. *Clash of the Carriers: The True Story of the Marianas Turkey Shoot of World War II.* New York: NAL Caliber, 2005.

Trumbull, Robert. *Silversides.* New York: Henry Holt, 1945.

Tulley, Anthony P. *Total Eclipse: The Last Battles of the Imperial Japanese Navy— Leyte to Kure, 1944 to 1945.* (Unpublished manuscript)

Tuohy, William. *The Bravest Man: The Story of Richard O'Kane and U.S. Submariners in the Pacific War.* Sparkford, England: Sutton, 2001.

Underwood, Lamar, ed. *The Greatest Submarine Stories Ever Told.* Guilford, CT: Lyons Press, 2005.

Van der Vat, Dan. *Pacific Campaign: The U.S.-Japanese Naval War, 1941–1945.* New York: Simon & Schuster, 1991.

Weedon, Martin. *Guest of the Emperor.* London: Arthur Barker, 1948.

Weintraub, Stanley. *MacArthur's War: Korea and the Undoing of an American Hero.* New York: Free Press, 2000.

Wheeler, Keith. *The Road to Tokyo.* Alexandria, VA: Time-Life Books, 1979.

———. *War Under the Pacific.* Alexandria, VA: Time-Life Books, 1981.

Whitlock, Flint. *The Fighting First: The Untold Story of the Big Red One on D-Day.* Boulder, CO: Westview, 2004.

———. *The Rock of Anzio: From Sicily to Dachau—A History of the 45th Infantry Division.* Boulder, CO: Westview, 1998.

Wolfert, Ira. *Battle for the Solomons.* Boston: Houghton Mifflin, 1943.

World Almanac and Book of Facts for 1940. Irvine, E. Eastman, ed. New York: New York World-Telegram, 1940.

Wukovits, John. *Pacific Alamo: The Battle for Wake Island.* New York: New American Library, 2003.

Yoshimura, Akira. (Translated by Vincent Murphy.) *Battleship Musashi: The Making and Sinking of the World's Biggest Battleship.* Tokyo: Kodansha, 1999.

Periodicals
Adams, Cindy. "USS *Tang* Survivors." *Polaris,* February 1981.
Guttman, John. "Invasion Fleet Challenged." *World War II* magazine, January 1992.
"Knock at the Door." *Time,* 18 October 1943.
Lippman, David H. "Decision Unattained." *World War II* magazine, March 1993.
———. "First Naval Battle of Guadalcanal." *World War II* magazine, January 1997.
———. "Turning Point in the Pacific." *World War II* magazine, November 1997.
Popham, Harry. "Eyewitness to Tragedy: Death of U.S.S. *Princeton.*" *World War II* magazine, May 1997.
Smith, Robert B. "Tragic Voyage of *Junyo Maru.*" *World War II* magazine, March 2002.
Thoreson, L.L. "Mare Island—Where the Pacific Fleet is Maintained." *California— Magazine of the Pacific,* June 1939.
Wukovits, John F. "Scratch One Flattop." *World War II* magazine, September 1988.
———. "Clash in the Sibuyan Sea." *WWII History* magazine, November 2004.

Newspapers
Denver Post. "Rector obituary." April 20, 2005.
Fong, Tillie. "Submariner's Close Brush With Death." *Rocky Mountain News,* August 17, 2000.
Los Angeles Times. "Submarine Shells Southland Oil Field." February 24, 1942.
New York Times. "Rector obituary," April 19, 2005.

Web Sites
amh.freehosting.net/tang
bbs.chinadaily.com.cn/forumpost1
corregidor.org/chs_crypto1/purple
en.wikiquote.org/wiki/Chester_Nimitz)
en.wikipedia.org/wiki/Japanese_aircraft_carrier_Shokaku
en.wikipedia.org/wiki/Kamikaze
en.wikipedia.org/wiki/USS_Thresher
en.wikipedia.org/wiki/William_F._Halsey,_Jr.
home.earthlink.net/~nbrass1/3enigma
home.st.net.au/~dunn/friendlyfire/ussubO1
home.st.net.au/~dunn/usnavy/fremantlesubmarinebase
jearnshaw.me.uk
Mansell.com/pow_resources/camplists/tokyo/ofuna

mcel.pacificu.edu/as/students/bushido
navysite.de/cve/cve63
navysite.de/cve/cve73
people.csp.edu/saylor/OHP/DittrichR
www.ahoy.tk-jk.net/Solomons/BattleofGuadalcanal
www.angelfire.com
www.anglefire.com/fm/odyssey/halsey
www.answers.com/asiaticfleet
www.anzacday.org.au/history/ww2/anecdotes/survivors
www.arlingtoncemetery.net
www.bushlibrary.tamu.edu/tour/finback
www.chinfo.navy.mil/navpalib/cno/n87/usw/issue_8/submarine_hero
www.chinfo.navy.mil/navpalib/cno/n87/usw/issue_11/rising_victory
www.chinfo.navy.mil/navpalib/cno/n87/usw/issue_23/saviors2
www.chinfo.navy.mil/navpalib/ships/submarines
www.cofepow.org.uk/pages/ships_lisbon_maru
www.combinedfleet.com
www.combinedfleet.com/Kongo
www.combinedfleet.com/Unryu
www.corregidor.org/chs/trident/uss/trout
www.csp.navy.mil/centennial/harder
www.csp.navy.mil/ww2boats/albacore
www.csp.navy.mil/ww2boats/cisco
www.csp.navy.mil/ww2boats/perch
www.csp.navy.mil/ww2boats/runner
www.csp.navy.mil/ww2boats/tullibee
www.csus.edu/indiv/s/scottjc/marsh
www.cr.nps.gov
www.cv6/1942
www.famoustexans.com/chesternimitz
www.fleetsubmarine.com
www.fleetsubmarine.com/ss-197
www.fortunecity.com
www.freewebs.com
www.geocities.com/Pentagon/1592/ustorp2
www.geocities.com/seal
www.hamstat.demon.co.uk/HongKong/Lisbon_Maru
www.history.acusd.edu
www.history.navy.mil
www.history.navy.mil/faqs/faq82-1

www.history1900s.about.com
www.ibiblio.org/hyperwar/USN/ships
www.infoplease.com/askeds
www.keyportmuseum.cnrnw.navy.mil
www.leisuregalleries.com/gagemillerdiary
www.lostsubs.com/SSN-589
www.mansell.com/pow
www.maritime.org/pamphome
www.medalofhonor.com/PappyBoyington
www.members.tripod.com/~earthdude1/fugo
www.members.tripod.com/obrien
www.mhric.org/fdr/chat20
www.militarymuseum.org/Lockwood
www.milnet.com/pentagon/navy/sub-chrono
www.napalm.net
www.naval-history.net/WW2194406-2
www.navweaps.com/Weapons/WTUS_Notes
www.navy.history/mil
www.nesa.org.uk/html/lisbon_maru
www.onr.navy.mil/blowballast/momsen
www.onwar.com/articles/f0102
www.oralhistoryproject.com/tcurtis_nav
www.pbs.org/wgbh/nova/lostsub/hist1918
www.rontini.com
www.rtcol.com
www.salute.co.uk/salutegames/yamamoto
www.submarinesailor.com/Boats/SS188Sargo/history
www.subnet.com/fleet/ss155
www.subnet.com/fleet/ss179
www.subnet.com/fleet/ss211
www.subnet.com/fleet/ss227
www.subvetpaul.com/SAGA_2_81
www.subvets.com/subleague/articles/tang
www.sun-inet.or.jp
www.thesaltysailor.com/s<->boats/s38
www.txoilgas.com
www.20thaaf.com/500thBG/881stSq/RosaliaRocket/king
www.uboat.net/allies/warships/ship/2964
www.uboat.net/allies/warships/ship/2976
www.uboat.net/allies/warships/ship/3003

www.ussnautilus.org/fluckey
www.ussvi.org
www.ussvi.org/mem/210cnvnt
www.wa.essortment.com
www.warbirdforum.com/navy
www.warsailors.com
www.ww2pacific.com/savo
www.xmission.com

Miscellaneous

Smith correspondence with Jim Clepper, August 1, 2005.

Whitlock correspondence with Dr. Dirk Ballendorf, Professor of History and Micronesian Studies, University of Guam, Mangilao, Guam, 2005.

"Guadalcanal." Episode from the television documentary *Victory at Sea*. National Broadcasting Company, 1952.

Poirier, Michel T. "Results of the German and American Submarine Campaigns of World War II." (Unpublished monograph), 1999.

"U.S.S. *O'Kane* Launched," Press Report: March 30, 1998.

Submarine War Patrol Reports, Classified Operational Archives, Navy Yard, Washington, D.C.; and Submarine Force Library, U.S. Submarine Base, New London, CT.

U.S.S. *Pampanito* (pamphlet). San Francisco: San Francisco Maritime National Park Association, 2003.

CREDITS AND PERMISSIONS

The authors gratefully acknowledge permission to quote from the following:

Clear the Bridge! The War Patrols of the U.S.S. Tang by Richard H. O'Kane © 1977 by Richard H. O'Kane. Used by permission.

Goodbye, Darkness by William Manchester © 1979, 1980 by William Manchester. Reprinted by permission of Don Congdon Associates, Inc..

History of United States Naval Operations in World War II, 15 volume set by Samuel Eliot Morison. Reprinted by permission of Little, Brown & Company.

Silent Victory: The U.S. Submarine War Against Japan by Clay Blair, Jr. © 1975. Reprinted by permission of the author and the author's agents, Scovil Chichak Galen Literary Agency, Inc.

The unpublished memoirs of William Trimmer of his Navy service in World War II.

U.S. Submarine Operations in World War II by Theodore Roscoe © 1976. Reprinted by permission of Naval Institute Press.

With Only the Will to Live, edited by Robert LaForte, Ronald Marcello and Richard Himmel. Reprinted by permission of SR Books, an imprint of Rowman & Littlefield Publishers, Inc.

INDEX

(*Italics* denote photograph)